Trade, Land, Power

TRADE, LAND, POWER

THE STRUGGLE FOR EASTERN NORTH AMERICA

DANIEL K. RICHTER

PENN

UNIVERSITY OF PENNSYLVANIA PRESS

PHILADELPHIA

Published by
University of Pennsylvania Press
Philadelphia, Pennsylvania 19104-4112
www.upenn.edu/pennpress

Printed in the United States of America on acid-free paper
10 9 8 7 6 5 4 3 2 1

Library of Congress Cataloging-in-Publication Data

Richter, Daniel K.
Trade, land, power : the struggle for eastern North America /
Daniel K. Richter. — 1st ed.
p. cm.
Includes bibliographical references and index.
ISBN 978-0-8122-4500-4 (hardcover : alk. paper)
1. Indians of North America—First contact with Europeans.
2. Indians of North America—History—Colonial period, ca.
1600–1775. 3. Indians, Treatment of—North America—History.
4. Indians of North America—Government relations. 5. North
America—History—Colonial period, ca. 1600–1775. I. Title.
E98.F39R54 2013
973.2—dc23
2012049810

To Sharon,
still

CONTENTS

Introduction   1

PART I. NATIVE POWER AND EUROPEAN TRADE

Chapter 1. Tsenacomoco and the Atlantic World:
Stories of Goods and Power   13

Chapter 2. Brothers, Scoundrels, Metal-Makers: Dutch Constructions
of Native American Constructions of the Dutch   42

Chapter 3. "That Europe be not Proud, nor America Discouraged":
Native People and the Enduring Politics of Trade   53

Chapter 4. War and Culture: The Iroquois Experience   69

Chapter 5. Dutch Dominos: The Fall of New Netherland
and the Reshaping of Eastern North America   97

Chapter 6. Brokers and Politics: Iroquois and New Yorkers   113

PART II. EUROPEAN POWER AND NATIVE LAND

Chapter 7. Land and Words: William Penn's Letter
to the Kings of the Indians   135

Chapter 8. "No Savage Should Inherit": Native Peoples, Pennsylvanians,
and the Origins and Legacies of the Seven Years War   155

Chapter 9. The Plan of 1764: Native Americans and a British Empire
That Never Was   177

Chapter 10. Onas, the Long Knife: Pennsylvanians and Indians
After Independence   202

Chapter 11. "Believing that Many of the Red People Suffer Much for the
Want of Food": A Quaker View of Indians in the Early U.S. Republic   227

Notes   251

Index   307

Acknowledgments   315

Introduction

I have long suspected, despite some fine examples to the contrary, that anyone who compiles a volume of his or her own essays is either afflicted by egotism, cursed with hubris, or excused by scholarly venerability.[1] I prefer to believe that none of these conditions apply to me. With respect to the last, however, I must confess to having been at this business for three decades and to turning, at least temporarily, toward new fields of inquiry. So the essays compiled here sum up a phase in my scholarly career. The pieces were written at various times, for various purposes, since 1983. As I composed them, I did not set out to explore any single interpretation but only to pursue my general interest in the interactions of Native people and Europeans in early America in general and in the mid-Atlantic region in particular. As I looked back on them, however, and as I thought about them roughly in the chronological order of the topics they explored, I discovered that three themes forcefully emerged, themes I call *trade, land,* and *power*. It seemed useful, then, to gather the essays in one place.[2]

* * *

To begin to understand how trade, land, and power entwined, we could do worse than to listen to a man who, in his own eighteenth-century lifetime, stood accused of no small measure of egotism, hubris, and premature old age: Teedyuscung, "King of the Delawares." It was late July 1756, and Teedyuscung, along with a handful of other Indians and Euro-Americans, was desperately seeking a way out of the bloody violence of what we now call the Seven Years War, violence that he himself, in his frustration with Pennsylvanians, had helped to initiate. At a treaty conference in Easton, Pennsylvania—where the Delaware leader lived up to his reputation for eloquence as well as for bluster, bravado, and, tragically, excessive drinking—he made a rambling speech outlining his credentials and purposes. Asked if he had finished talking, he said "he had for the present," depending on what the English had to say in return.

But "'the main Thing,' he added 'is yet in my Breast.'" Hand over heart, "he repeated the *Delaware* Word, *Whish-shicksy* . . . , with great Earnestness."[3]

At that point in the proceedings, Pennsylvania's longtime go-between with Native peoples, Conrad Weiser, "who knew the Word to have a very extensive and forcible Sense" but had not previously met Teedyuscung, "desired the Interpreter to ask him what he meant by *Whish-shicksy* on this particular Occasion." Through that interpreter, the Delaware orator responded with an example:

> Suppose you want to remove a large Log of Wood, that requires many Hands, you must take Pains to get as many together as will do the Business; if you fall short but one, though never so weak an one, all the rest are to no Purpose. Though this be in itself nothing, yet, if you cannot move the Log without it, you must spare no Pains to get it. *Whish-shicksy*; be strong; look round you; enable us to engage every *Indian* Nation we can; put the Means into our Hands; be sure [to] perform every Promise you have made to us; in particular do not pinch Matters neither with us or other *Indians*; we will help you but we are poor, and you are rich; make us strong, and we will use our Strength for you and, besides this, what you do, do quickly; the Times are dangerous; they will not admit of Delay. *Whish-shicksy*; do it effectually, and do it with all possible Dispatch.[4]

In the margin of one of several transcripts of Teedyuscung's speech, someone later inserted a reference to Moravian missionary David Zeisberger. According to the unidentified annotator, Zeisberger said *Whish-shicksy* or "Wischixi" means "be active, nimble." Fellow Moravian John Heckewelder defined *Wischiksik* as "*be ye vigilant, in earnest, quick!* (about it)." Heckewelder further explained that "the word wischiksi or wischixi is by the white people interpreted as signifying '*be strong,*' which does not convey the true meaning of this word: it comprehends more; it asks for *exertions to be made, to fulfil the object.*" Another Moravian dictionary—probably based on Zeisberger's—defines *wischiki* as "busily" and *wischixin* as "to be active, to be brisk, to be nimble; to exert one's self."[5]

Whatever the difficulties in translating Teedyuscung's utterance into English, the term conveyed more than a simple message of strength through unity, of the need for the weak to rely upon the strong. As Weiser said, it carried "a very extensive and forcible Sense." Teedyuscung's message was that real power came when the strong enabled the weak to bear a share of the burden: "We are poor, and you are rich; make us strong and we will use our Strength for you." Such a message was not just moral but material: "Put the Means into our Hands"; "do not pinch"; "make us strong." Teedyuscung's English hearers would have called the transfer of such material resources *trade,* or perhaps more bluntly *presents, subsidies,* or *bribes.* "You are sensible how averse I am, to purchasing the good behavior of Indians, by presents," British officer Sir Jeffrey Amherst blustered a few years later as he announced an ill-fated policy of ending the kinds of practices to which Teedyuscung alluded. But, as Amherst learned when his decisions helped to provoke the conflict known as "Pontiac's War," for Native people, "presents" went far deeper than the mercenary motives that Europeans saw in such exchanges. As markers of political facts, gifts sealed relationships and symbolized—perhaps even *were*—the source of power for the givers as much as for the receivers.[6] These, Teedyuscung seems to have meant, are what allowed people to "be strong" and "do it effectually."

So trade and power were nearly inextricable for Native people. For many centuries before Teedyuscung spoke, exchanges of items that anthropologists label "prestige goods" had embodied the connection.[7] In the Delaware leader's day, the shell beads called wampum, particularly when woven by the hundreds into elaborately patterned belts, continued that tradition, symbolizing relationships among people, serving as a record of important transactions and alliances, and conveying power through their very substance. "With this wompompeage they pay tribute, redeem captives, satisfy for murders and other wrongs, [and] purchase peace with their potent neighbors, as occasion requires," New Englander Daniel Gookin had said in the 1670s. "In a word, it answers all occasions with them, as gold and silver doth with us."[8]

Like nearly every other European, neither Gookin nor the Anglo-Pennsylvanians later gathered at the Easton treaty conference could quite wrap their minds around the idea that something deeper than monetary value was at work with wampum and other gifts. A letter to the conference participants from Moravian bishop August Gottlieb Spangenberg tried to convey a deeper understanding of the role wampum played for Teedyuscung and his compatriots. Spangenberg wrote that, according to a Moravian Delaware man named Augustus, "Teedyuskung is the Man who has occasioned the late war [when] he made an exceeding large Belt of Wampum and sent it to all the Indians living on the West Branch of Susquehanna [River], even to the Cherokee Nation with the following Words 'I am in exceeding great danger the English will kill

"The Indians giving a Talk to Colonel [Henry] Bouquet in a Conference at a Council Fire, Near His Camp on the Banks of Muskingum in North America, in October 1764." From [William Smith], *An Historical Account of the Expedition Against the Ohio Indians, in the Year MDCCLXIV* (London, 1766). Annenberg Rare Book and Manuscript Library, Van Pelt–Dietrich Library Center, University of Pennsylvania, Philadelphia. No portrait from life of the Delaware leader Teedyuscung is known to survive. This eighteenth-century illustration conveys some of the drama of a Native orator reading a wampum belt.

me, come and help me etc.'" Only Teedyuscung could call back the forces he had thus unleashed, claimed Augustus, but the Delaware chief is now "Poor and has no more Wampum to send Word to the Indians which he has brought in such a Spirit of War." He "must have a Belt of Wampum at least five or Six Feet long and Twelve Rows broad and besides the Belt he must have twelve Strings to send to the Several Chiefs to confirm the Words he sends." On the recommendation of Augustus and Weiser, Pennsylvania Governor Robert Hunter Morris rounded up every wampum bead he could find and set a group of Indian women to work to weave them into an appropriately grand belt to supply Teedyuscung's needs. The belt was only partly finished when the treaty conference ended, and the governor had to hand it over in that state, along with piles of unstrung beads and a suggestion that "the Women might finish it on rainy days or resting in their Journey home."[9]

Before witnessing that embarrassing demonstration of English impotence, Teedyuscung had revealed something else about the relationship between wampum and power. The Delaware leader presented the Pennsylvania governor with "a large Belt" that he said he had received from his "uncles," the chiefs of Haudenosaunee, or Six Nations of the Iroquois Confederacy. "This is a good Day," Teedyuscung declared, "whoever will make Peace, let him lay hold of this Belt, and the Nations around shall see and know it." Only after the governor had "take[n] hold of the Belt" and pronounced that "it is all very good" did Teedyuscung explain the imagery woven by its beads, imagery that centered land in its message about power. "You see," he explained, "a Square in the Middle, meaning the Lands of the *Indians*, and at one End the Figure of a Man, indicating the *English*; and at the other End another, meaning the *French*; our Uncles told us, that both these coveted our Lands; But let us Joyn together to defend our Lands against both."[10] A year later, Teedyuscung's interpreter would put things more bluntly at another conference with Anglo-Americans who again professed not to understand the Delaware leader's flowery language: "The Land is the cause of our Differences[,] that is our being unhappily turned out of the land is the cause, and thô the first settlers might purchase the lands fairly yet they did not act well nor do the Indians Justice for they ought to have reserved some place for the Indians."[11]

For Teedyuscung, then, as for countless other eighteenth-century Native leaders, a matrix of trade, land, and power defined relations with European colonizers. The colonizers' failure to understand the cultural significance of exchange and their single-minded focus on real estate lay at the heart of the struggle for control of eastern North America.

*   *   *

Exchange is thus the unifying theme of my first group of chapters, which explore meanings inadequately captured by the English word *trade* and inadequately translated from the Delaware word *Whish-shicksy*. The exploration begins in the late sixteenth- and early seventeenth-century Chesapeake Bay region, where indigenous people who called their territory "the densely inhabited land," or *Tsenacomoco*, attempted to fit Europeans and their goods into Native systems of power.[12] Subsequent essays trace similar processes through the tangled economic, military, and political webs that Indians created with Dutch, French, and English colonists during the seventeenth century. The Dutch—who, more than any other seventeenth-century Europeans, built their imperial enterprises on global trade—loom particularly large in these stories. Through it all, power flowed not merely through transfers of material goods but through the personal relationships and networks of kin and community that those transfers represented.

For eastern Native Americans, what Europeans called *trade* was nearly always embedded in efforts to strengthen human connections, socially as well as materially. Two essays on seventeenth-century experiences of Haudenosaunee Iroquois peoples provide glimpses of these processes. Warfare that might appear to be (and was) about acquiring trade routes and hunting territories was also (and more fundamentally) about acquiring human captives to restrengthen disease-ravaged, mourning families. And diplomacy that might appear to be (and was) about grand geopolitical strategy was also (and more fundamentally) dependent on individual brokers who mediated among kin groups and factions and sealed relationships with exchanges of wampum and other prestige goods.

Few Europeans dominate memories of such exchange-based power relations more than the founder of Pennsylvania, the Quaker William Penn. Our most iconic image of him, after all, portrays him "dispensing peace and yard goods to the Indians."[13] Teedyuscung, along with many other eighteenth-century Native orators, recalled Penn as "the good old man, . . . who was a friend to the Indian." He was, the Delaware said, a man who should "Inspire the people of this Province at this time."[14]

Or so Teedyuscung and his Native contemporaries hoped, but he surely knew that things were not that simple. An essay that reexamines Penn's policies opens the second half of this book and provides an initial foray into the theme of the remaining chapters: the ways in which eighteenth-century Euro-Americans rendered irrelevant—at least in their own minds—the Native

Benjamin West, *Penn's Treaty with the Indians*, 1771. Courtesy of the Pennsylvania Academy of the Fine Arts, Philadelphia. Gift of Mrs. Sarah Harrison (The Joseph Harrison, Jr., Collection). Full of anachronistic details and composed nearly a century after the 1682 event it portrays (an event for which there is no conclusive documentary record), West's painting demonstrates the mythic power of William Penn in memories of Pennsylvania's relations with Native Americans.

understandings of trade and power that had earlier prevailed. They did so by forcibly injecting land into the equation—not, certainly, for the first time in North American history, but on an unprecedented continental scale that came to dominate everything else. The turning point was the violent period from the Seven Years War through the U.S. War of Independence, events in which Penn's Pennsylvania successors played crucial roles. For them, as for so many eighteenth-century Euro-Americans, power grew from the individual pursuit of landed property rather than the collective exchange of material and cultural goods. As Teedyuscung tried to explain, land was the cause of the two peoples' differences. Indeed, it is not too much to say that struggles over land were what finally sorted many diverse Native and Euro-American peoples into the two categories called *white* and *red*.[15]

More than a century after that great sorting, Theodore Roosevelt observed in his triumphalist multivolume history, *The Winning of the West*, that the U.S. Revolution had a "twofold character." It was, he wrote, "a struggle for independence in the east, and in the west a war of conquest, or rather a war to establish on behalf of all our people, the right of entry into the fertile and vacant regions beyond the Alleghanies." For Roosevelt, "whether the whites won the land by treaty, by armed conquest, or, as was actually the case, by a mixture of both, mattered comparatively little so long as the land was won, . . . for the benefit of civilization and in the interests of mankind." Indeed, "all men of sane and wholesome thought must dismiss with impatient contempt the plea that these continents should be reserved for the use of scattered savage tribes, whose life was but a few degrees less meaningless, squalid, and ferocious than that of the wild beasts with whom they held joint ownership."[16]

My final two chapters suggest the laborious cultural as well as political work necessary for Euro-Americans to render those well-inhabited fertile regions vacant and their human stewards' claims to power contemptible. Leaders of the newly independent commonwealth of Pennsylvania wrapped themselves in William Penn's legacy while systematically expropriating Indian territory. A few years later, in what would become the U.S. state called, with little sense of irony, *Indiana*, even a Quaker missionary who devoutly believed he was acting in the best interest of Indians could not imagine a future in which indigenous people could derive any kind of power from their own traditions of trade and land use. By that time, when a Native leader used language similar to Teedyuscung's—"Listen to your children, here assembled; be strong, now, and take care of all your little ones"—the response was likely to be dismissive pity rather than engaged probing into the speaker's meaning.[17]

In the 1600s, Europeans had ignored Native understandings of the relationship between trade and power at their peril. By 1756, Anglo-Americans had to ask Teedyuscung to explain what he meant by *Whish-shicksy*, and in 1757 they had claimed not to understand what he meant when he said that "Land is the cause of our Differences." By 1800, they had stopped even listening to what Indian people had to say, for it seemed self-evident to them that Native American conceptions of power no longer mattered.[18]

*   *   *

To a degree I did not yet understand when I wrote many of these essays, they are attempts to start listening again. One of the formative books I read when I entered the historical profession was *Custer Died for Your Sins: An Indian Manifesto,* published in 1969 by Native American activist Vine Deloria, Jr. "It is time . . . to understand the ways of the white man," Deloria wrote in phrases Teedyuscung would have comprehended. "The white is after Indian lands and resources. He always has been and always will be." For me—a young white graduate student, newly transplanted in the year of the nation's bicentennial from Northern Kentucky to New York City and to a Columbia University campus still unrecovered from the upheavals of 1968—Deloria's tract was a powerful indictment. "There has not been a time since the founding of the republic when the motives of this country were innocent," Deloria concluded. "Is it any wonder that other nations are extremely skeptical about its real motives in the world today?"[19]

Such sentiments, of course, were far more popular in 1976 than they are in the early years of the twenty-first century. Perhaps it was too easy then for a young scholar to adopt them without fully internalizing them, to put them on like some now-dated polyester leisure suit. Even then, however, I knew the story had to be more complex, and more morally complicated than such sloganeering would allow us to understand. So I devoured the profoundly researched and deservedly angry works of historians such as Francis Jennings and weighed them against the profoundly learned and calmly reasonable advice of my dissertation adviser, Alden Vaughan. Meanwhile, influenced by my future wife, Sharon, I read deeply in anthropology, seeking insights into how human societies organized, made sense of, and differentiated themselves. As I tried to sort it all out, as I pursued my scholarly interests, something from Deloria remained that nagged the conscience. "There appears to be some secret osmosis about Indian people by which they can magically and instantaneously communicate complete knowledge about themselves to . . . interested whites," he jibed. "Anyone and everyone who knows an Indian who is *interested*, immediately and thoroughly understands them."[20]

After more than thirty years of scholarly study, I know more than ever that mere interest is insufficient, that understanding is elusive, and no easy judgments can be made about the wretched North American historical experience of Indians and Europeans, indigenous people and settler colonizers. I am less confident than I once was that any of us, whatever our degree of interest, can fully understand Teedyuscung and his contemporaries—much less fully comprehend some of the complicated issues that these essays touch upon. Who will ever be able to imagine, for instance, what was in the minds of people who experienced the awful stew of disease, death, mourning, warfare, captivity, and enslavement that washed through seventeenth-century Native America?[21] But nonetheless, I am more convinced than ever that we need to probe those mysteries, to trace the roles of trade, land, and power in the conquest of North America, to see Indians and Europeans equally as actors in the process, and, above all, to listen—as imperfectly as the sources permit—to what imperfect people like Teedyuscung tried to tell us about how our continent's historical wounds might find healing. *Whish-shicksy.*

PART I

Native Power and
European Trade

CHAPTER 1

Tsenacomoco and the Atlantic World: Stories of Goods and Power

In what might be the only surviving early seventeenth-century example of the genre, William Strachey, secretary of the Virginia Company of London, did his best to reduce to Roman letters a "scornefull song" that victorious Powhatan warriors chanted after they killed three or four Englishmen "and tooke one Symon Score a saylor and one Cob a boy prisoners" in 1611:

> 1. Mattanerew shashashewaw crawango pechecoma
> Whe Tassantassa inoshashaw yehockan pocosak
> Whe, whe, yah, ha, ha, ne, he wittowa, wittowa.
> 2. Mattanerew shashashewaw, erawango pechecoma
> Captain Newport inoshashaw neir in hoc nantion matassan
> Whe weh, yah, ha, ha, etc.
> 3. Mattanerew shashashewaw erowango pechecoma
> Thomas Newport inoshashaw neir in hoc nantion monocock
> Whe whe etc.
> 4. Mattanerew shushashewaw erowango pechecoma
> Pockin Simon moshasha mingon nantian Tamahuck
> Whe whe, etc.

Strachey explained that the refrain—which almost needs no translation—mocked the "lamentation our people made" for the deaths and captivities. But far more interesting is the gloss he provided for the verses. The Powhatans sang of "how they killed us for all our Poccasacks, that is our Guns, and for all Captain [Christopher] Newport brought them Copper and could hurt Thomas Newport (a boy whose name indeed is Thomas Savadge, whome

Captain Newport leaving with Powhatan to learne the Language, at what tyme he presented the said Powhatan with a copper Crowne and other guifts from his Majestie, sayd he was his soone) for all his *Monnacock* that is his bright Sword, and how they could take Symon . . . Prysoner for all his Tamahauke, that is his Hatchett."[1] In spite of all their material goods—their guns, their copper, their swords, their hatchets—and in spite of the fact that many of these same vaunted items had been given to the Powhatans by Virginia's leader Newport in the name of the mighty King James, the Englishmen had, at least on this occasion, been made subject to Native people's power.[2]

Like the song, this essay is a story about goods and power. Or, rather, it is three related stories about Chesapeake Algonquian men and what appear to have been their quests for goods and power from the emerging Atlantic world of the late sixteenth and early seventeenth centuries: Paquiquineo (Don Luis), who probably left the Chesapeake in 1561 and returned with a party of Spanish Jesuit missionaries nine years later; Namontack, who traveled to England with Christopher Newport in 1608 and again in 1609 (while the Thomas "Newport" Savage of the song took up residence in Powhatan country); and Uttamatomakkin (also known as Tomocomo or Tomakin), who made the oceanic voyage with Pocahontas in 1616–1617. We know very little about any of these men, their status, or their motives, and what we do know comes down to us in highly colored tales written by Europeans who were not exactly their friends. Nonetheless, for all the dangers of skimpy sources, of European chroniclers' distortions, and, possibly, of an overactive historian's imagination, the stories deserve serious attention. Traveling at particularly crucial moments in their people's early engagement with Europeans, the three voyagers allow us to glimpse something of what the emerging Atlantic world meant to the elite of the Powhatan paramount chiefdom—if not to the common people who gave their "densely inhabited land" its name, *Tsenacomoco*. In their travels, Paquiquineo and Namontack apparently attempted to exert control over the access to the goods the 1611 song would mock in order to build up the power of their people, their political superiors, and themselves. Uttamatomakkin's travels, by contrast, confirmed what the singers by then already knew: that power would have to be asserted in spite of, not by way of, "guifts from his Majestie."

*   *   *

Just as the arrival of Spaniards and English in the Chesapeake cannot be understood apart from the political and economic characteristics of competitive

Early Modern nation-states, the exploits of these three voyagers from Tsenacomoco—and the significance of material goods in the Powhatan song—
cannot be understood apart from the political and economic characteristics
of the social forms known as chiefdoms. In the classic definition of anthropologist Elman R. Service, "chiefdoms are *redistributional societies* with a
permanent central agency of coordination" and a "profoundly inegalitarian"
political order in which redistributive functions center on exalted hereditary
leaders.[3] For Service and his contemporary Morton Fried, the material un-
derpinnings of stratified chiefdoms lay in "differential rights of access to basic
resources . . . either directly (air, water, and food) or indirectly," through the
control of such basic productive resources as "land, raw materials for tools,
water for irrigation, and materials to build a shelter." More recent comparative archaeological work, however, moves beyond such straightforward mate-
rialist definitions to embrace a much more complex variety of cultural forms.[4]

Much of this work roots chiefdoms in what is known as a "prestige-goods
economy." As archaeologists Susan Frankenstein and Michael Rowlands explain, in such an economy, "political advantage [is] gained through exercising
control over access to resources that can only be obtained through external
trade." These resources are not the kind of basic utilitarian items described by
Service and Fried but instead "wealth objects needed in social transactions."[5]
They may be, as anthropologist Mary Helms explains, "crafted items acquired
ready-made from geographically distant places" or things "valued in their
natural, unworked form as inherently endowed with qualitative worth—
animal pelts, shells, feathers, and the like." In either case, they "constitute
a type of inalienable wealth, meaning they are goods that cannot be con-
ceptually separated from their place or condition of origin but always relate
whoever possesses them to that place or condition." The social power of such
goods thus comes from their association with their source, often described
as "primordial ancestral beings—creator deities, culture-heroes, primordial
powers—that are credited with having first created or crafted the world, its
creatures, its peoples, and their cultural skills." Indeed, inalienable goods
never fully belong to those to whom they have been given; they always remain in some sense the property of the giver. Those who control such prestige
goods wield power because of their connection to—and control over—power
at the goods' source.[6]

In eastern North America, the prestige goods that shaped the power of
chiefdoms were the crystals, minerals, copper, shells, and mysteriously crafted
ritual items that moved through the ancient trade routes of the continent.

Their potency came from their rarity and their association with distant sources of spiritual power. But those same characteristics made eastern North America's prestige-goods chiefdoms inherently unstable political forms. Lacking a monopoly of force to defend their privileges, chiefs depended for their status on a fragile ideological consensus at home and on equally fragile external sources of supply and trade routes they could not directly control. Chiefdoms thus perched on a fine line between slipping "back" into less hierarchical forms or moving "forward" toward the coercive apparatus of a state while "cycling" between periods of centralization and decentralization. As a result, as social forms, they were forever in flux.[7]

The basic political units of late sixteenth- and early seventeenth-century Tsenacomoco were just such unstable prestige-goods chiefdoms, headed by men and women called, respectively, *weroances* and *weroansquas*, whose titles descended, as John Smith explained, to "the first heyres of the Sisters, and so successively the weomens heires."[8] Most of these local chiefdoms were subordinate to a larger paramount chiefdom that Powhatan, or Wahunsonacock, presided over as *mamanatowick* in the early seventeenth century. The weroances and particularly the mamanatowick owed their status in part to kinship, through their own matrilineages and through marriage alliances with the multiple spouses to which apparently only the elite were entitled. (Wahunsonacock reputedly had a hundred wives strategically placed in subordinate towns.) In a way Service and Fried would recognize, weroances also to some extent controlled food surpluses, through tribute from subordinates and through corn, bean, and squash fields their people planted and harvested to be stored in their granaries. (These food stores may have taken on additional significance during the repeated droughts and crop failures of the late sixteenth and early seventeenth centuries.) But most importantly, weroances' power apparently rested on their control of such goods as copper from the continental interior and pearls from the Atlantic coast. As archaeologist Stephen R. Potter puts it, "chiefs handled worldly risks confronting their societies by serving as both a banker to their people and a culture broker to outsiders."[9]

To a significant degree, the power that derived from these functions came from a weroance's ability to distribute prestige goods to followers and thus create bonds of asymmetrical obligation. "He [who] perfourmes any remarkeable or valerous exployt in open act of Armes, or by Stratagem," observed Strachey, "the king taking notice of the same, doth . . . solemnely reward him with some Present of Copper, or Chayne of Perle and Beades."[10]

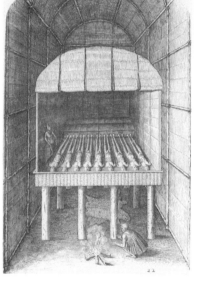

Illustrations from John Smith, *A Map
of Virginia . . .* (London, 1612); and
Thomas Hariot, *A Briefe and True Report
of the New Found Land of Virginia . . .*
(Frankfurt am Main, 1590). The fanciful
image of Powhatan that graced William
Hole's engraving of John Smith's 1612
map (left) is based on two engravings
of watercolors painted by John White at
Roanoke in 1585: an effigy of a spirit-being
(top right) and the structure in which the
bodies of deceased chiefs were preserved (bottom right). All of these images hint
at the status and power that chiefs derived from what modern scholars call "prestige goods." Reproduced by permission of The Huntington Library, San Marino,
California.

Lavish feasts from chiefly stores and perhaps the bestowal of sexual favors
from young women in the weroance's household served similar redistributive functions for diplomatic visitors.[11] Such actions merged into a broader
pattern that might best be described as the conspicuous display of chiefly
power. Wahunsonacock "hath a house in which he keepeth his kind of Trea-
sure, as skinnes, copper, pearle, and beades, which he storeth up against the
time of his death and buriall," wrote Smith. The structure was "50 or 60 yards

in length, frequented only by Priestes," and at each corner stood "Images as Sentinels, one of a Dragon, another a Beare, the 3rd like a Leopard and the fourth a giantlike man, all made evillfavordly according to their best workmanship." Smith—who, it should be recalled, appeared to be an emissary from a strangely female-less society—also went out of his way to note that the mamanatowick "hath as many women as he will, whereof when hee lieth on his bed, one sitteth at his head, and another at his feet, but when he sitteth, one sitteth on his right hand and another on his left."[12]

Such conspicuous display embodied the strength and wealth of the people and their connection to the sources of the power that prestige goods and marriage connections represented; indeed, the term *weroance* roughly translates as "he is wealthy."[13] Such goods visibly accumulated at the apex of the social and political order, in the person regarded "not only as a king but as halfe a God," the mamanatowick, a word incorporating the term *manitou,* or "spiritual power."[14] The material, the spiritual, and the political were inseparable in the person of the mamanatowick and the people for whom he acted. "The wealth of the chief and his distribution of it are alike means by which he confers life and prosperity on his people," anthropologist Margaret Holmes Williamson explains. "Indeed, he really has nothing of 'his own' as a private person. Rather, he is the steward of the group's wealth, deploying it on their behalf for their benefit." The mamanatowick "by being rich and generous and by living richly . . . makes bountiful the macrocosm that he represents."[15]

The material, the spiritual, and the political also came together in the fact that the vast majority of the powerful goods that chiefs accumulated were interred with them when they died. Weroances "bodies are first bowelled, then dryed upon hurdles till they bee verie dry, and so about the most of their jointes and necke they hang bracelets or chaines of copper, pearle, and such like, as they use to weare," Smith observed and archaeologists confirm. "Their inwards they stuffe[d] with copper beads and covered with a skin, hatchets and such," before wrapping the corpses "very carefully in white skins," and laying them on mats in a temple house with "what remaineth of this kinde of wealth . . . set at their feet in baskets."[16] In effect, then, because prestige goods died with the chief, weroances and would-be weroances always had to create for themselves anew the tribute networks, the trade connections, the diplomatic and marriage alliances, the masses of prestige goods that undergirded their power. This fact, more than some abstract historical force called "cycling," undergirded the inherent instability of these chiefdoms as political forms. And it brings us at last to our three travelers, who apparently sought just such connections, alliances, and goods, either as rising chiefs themselves or on behalf of the weroances who sent them.[17]

*   *   *

We cannot be absolutely certain that the man usually known by the Spanish name Don Luis or Don Luis de Velasco was originally from Tsenacomoco or even that Tsenacomoco was the same place that he and the Spanish called *Ajacán*. Yet through careful detective work, scholars Clifford M. Lewis and Albert J. Loomie reasonably concluded decades ago that "there are enough indications available to link Don Luis with the ruling Powhatan clique" and that Ajacán included territories between the James and York Rivers that were later known to be part of the Powhatan paramount chiefdom.[18] Spanish sources variously describe Paquiquineo as "a young *cacique*," as "a person of note" who "said he was a chief," as "the Indian son of a petty chief of Florida" who "gave out that he was the son of a great chief," as a chief's son "who for an Indian was of fine presence and bearing," or as "the brother of a principal chief of that region."[19] Unhelpfully, the same sources say that in 1570, he was either "more than twenty years of age" or "a man of fifty years."[20] It is quite possible that, as Lewis and Loomie suggest, Paquiquineo was either the brother or father of Wahunsonacock and his successors Opitchapam and Opechancanough. Given the matrilineal descent of chief's titles and European chroniclers' unfamiliarity with the intricacies of Algonquian kinship terms, Paquiquineo might also have been the uncle of these later paramount chiefs. There is less reason to believe that, as historian Carl Bridenbaugh suggested, Paquiquineo actually *was* Opechancanough, although nearly anything is possible. Whatever the case, he was almost certainly a member of a chiefly lineage, if not that of the paramount mamanatowick, then of a subsidiary weroance.[21] The one surviving Spanish document that uses his Algonquian name suggests his high status by referring to his traveling companions as his Indian servants ("*su criado indios*").[22]

And, whatever the case, Paquiquineo seems to have gone into the Atlantic world because of his chiefly lineage, either on his own initiative, or at the behest of his weroance, or because the Spanish perceived him as a high-value captive. We do not know exactly how he found his way onto what was probably Antonio Velázquez's ship *Santa Catalina* in 1561. Accounts written more than a generation later give three different versions of the story. Francisco Sacchini wrote that "the brother of a principal chief of that region gave himself up to some Spaniards sailing near Ajacán," although "none of his family knew of this." In much more detail, Luis Gerónimo de Oré explained that "while the *Adelantado*, Pedro Menéndez, was governing the *presidios* of Florida, a ship from the port of Santa Elena lost its course towards the north, at a latitude of 37½° and put into a large bay which the sailors called the Bahía de Madre de Dios" and that "from among some Indians who came aboard they retained a young *cacique*." Bartolomé Martínez improbably had Menéndez himself sailing into the Chesapeake. Native people "came alongside in canoes and boarded the flagship," where "His Excellency, as was his custom, like another Alexander, regaled them with food and clothing." The boarding party included "a chief who brought his son." The *adelantado* "asked the chief for permission to take [Paquiquineo] . . . along that the King of Spain, his lord, might see him" and "gave his pledged word to return him with much wealth and many garments." According to Martínez, "This chief granted this and his Excellency took him to Castile, to the Court of King Philip II," who was "very pleased with him" and bestowed on "him many courtly favors and rich garments."[23]

The emphasis on clothing and material goods in these stories may capture something about how Paquiquineo understood his mission in an Atlantic world he would come to know too well. It is reasonable to assume that he planned to establish a relationship with Europeans who could provide him, his lineage, and his chiefdom with a source of the goods that brought political and economic power. Compared with other locations on the Atlantic coast, the Chesapeake had apparently experienced few European visitors, shipwrecks, and their associated influxes of material goods before Paquiquineo's departure. Verrazano missed the bay in 1524. An English ship apparently blew in on a storm in 1546 and found "over thirty canoes" full of Native people who already knew enough about Europeans to bring along "as many as a thousand marten skins in exchange for knives, fishhooks and shirts." But such episodes were rare on a coast much off course for Europeans plying routes to and from either the West Indies and the Spanish Main or Newfoundland. With enough knowledge of Europeans to understand their potential as a source of copper, beads, and other prestige goods, Paquiquineo would have set off to establish a personal alliance, and a personal exchange relationship, that would substantially reinforce the power of his lineage and chiefdom by bringing Europeans and their goods into the Chesapeake on a regular basis.[24]

Of course in 1561 he could not know that it would be nearly a decade before he could return home, or just how much of the Atlantic world he would see in the interim. Paquiquineo apparently spent most of his time in Mexico City, living with Dominican priests, learning Spanish, undergoing catechization, and acquiring his new name, in honor of his baptismal sponsor, the viceroy of New Spain. If he left home with any illusions that Spaniards were beneficent beings who would readily bestow their riches on Ajacán, those illusions must have been quickly dashed in the flesh-and-blood reality of the colonial capital that was rising on the ruins of Tenochtitlan—and on the backs of oppressed Native people.[25] Yet he must also have seen the ways in which *caciques* from outlying districts could extract favors from the imperial regime and in general how indigenous people with claims to elite heritage could carve out positions of relative power. Whatever he (and his Dominican teachers) did to attract the attention and favors of the viceroy must have encouraged Paquiquineo to believe he could turn his situation to advantage—if only he could get back home under the right conditions. "A clever talker," he touted "the grandeurs of his land," the willingness of his people to hear the gospel, and his eagerness to provide "the help which Timothy gave to Saint Paul."[26]

Such talk helped get him from Mexico to Havana, where in 1566 he set sail with a party of thirty soldiers and two Dominican friars to establish a mission in Ajacán. The expedition never reached its goal, however. Paquiquineo claimed to be unable to recognize the entrance to Chesapeake Bay (which could have been a ruse because he distrusted the soldiers or just the honest ignorance of a landlubber), and a storm finally blew the party so far out to sea that they gave up.[27]

But Paquiquineo did not. Menéndez had "chanced upon" him in Havana at some point during the 1565–1566 expedition that slaughtered the French Huguenot colony at Fort Caroline and planted Spanish garrisons at St. Augustín, Santa Elena (modern-day Parris Island, South Carolina), and elsewhere in *La Florida*. Perhaps Menéndez brought Paquiquineo with him to Spain in 1567. Certainly, at least according to Father Juan Rogel, who was stationed in Santa Elena at the time, the *adelantado* brought him back to Havana when he returned from Spain in 1569 or 1570.[28] According to Father Gerónimo de Oré, who visited Florida in 1614 and 1616 and drew upon interviews and manuscripts of those who remembered the events, when Paquiquineo learned in Spain that Jesuits were already at work in other parts of *La Florida*, he announced "that he would venture to take some priests to his country and that with the help of God and his own industry, the Indians of that land would be converted to the Faith." The Jesuits then "offered themselves to the King, and asked for his permission as well as for the necessary provisions to go to those parts, and to take with them the *cacique* Don Luis." Whatever may have happened in Spain, some such exchange took place in Havana, among Paqui-quineo, Menéndez, and the vice-provincial of the Jesuit mission to *La Florida*, Father Juan Baptista de Segura. The provincial had become increasingly disil-lusioned with the slow pace of conversions at Santa Elena and points adjacent and imagined in Ajacán a fresh mission field where, with Paquiquineo's help and without the corrupting influence of Spanish soldiers and laymen, the Je-suits could win souls, or martyrdom, or both.[29]

Thus, Paquiquineo, Segura, a freshly arrived priest named Luis de Quirós, three Jesuit brothers, three novices, and Alonso de Olmos, a boy whose father lived at Santa Elena, sailed for the Chesapeake late in the summer of 1570. When their ship stopped at Santa Elena, Father Juan de la Carrera, who was stationed there, tried to talk Segura out of his plan to establish a mission without an armed guard—a scheme he chalked up partly to the naiveté of Segura's "holy, sincere Christian heart" but mostly to the verbal wizardry of Paquiquineo, who had somehow sold Segura and Menéndez on the idea. "I pointed out the difficulty in the execution of the plan, saying that the In-dian did not satisfy me, and judging from what he had told me, I saw that he was a liar," Carrera wrote, thirty years after the fact, when he had long since been proved correct. Segura not only stood his ground but, said Carrera, sent Quirós to demand that the expedition be given "the best and the larger por-tion of everything I had in my charge, especially the church goods." Laden with "the best and richest articles . . . in the way of chalices, monstrances, and vestments and other articles besides church furnishings," the ship sailed for Ajacán. If Paquiquineo had set out a decade earlier in search of prestige goods, he had them now.[30]

Everyone arrived safely in the Chesapeake on 10 September 1570. A few days later, the ship that brought them departed with much of the meager food with which the expedition had been "ill-provisioned for the journey." Also on board was the only letter Quirós and Segura ever sent from the mission, which made clear that things were already going horribly wrong. The para-dise Paquiquineo had described had, unbeknownst to him, been suffering from "six years of famine and death." Many of those who had not perished had "moved to other regions to ease their hunger," and those who stayed be-hind said "that they wish[ed] to die where their fathers have died, although they have no maize, and have not found wild fruit, which they are accus-tomed to eat." No one on either side, Spanish or Indian, had enough food.[31]

Nonetheless, Paquiquineo had brought the Spanish and their goods. The people of Tsenacomoco "seemed to think that Don Luis had risen from the dead and come down from heaven, and since all who remained are his relatives, they are greatly consoled in him"—at least according to Quirós and Segura, who believed that those relatives had "recovered their courage and hope that God may seek to favor them, saying that they want to be like Don Luis, begging us to remain in this land with them." This may well have been true if the Jesuits were to provide the gifts of spiritual and material power for which Paquiquineo hoped. But two other things happened almost immediately, one spiritual, and one material, which may have determined the course of everything else that followed. "The chief has kept a brother of Don Luis, a boy of three years, who lies seriously ill, 6 or 8 leagues from here and now seems certain to die," Quirós and Segura reported. As the priests understood it, the chief "requested that someone go and baptize him, for which reason it seemed good to Father Vice-Provincial [Segura] to send last night one of Ours to baptize the boy so close to death."[32] There is no hint in the records of what happened on that sacramental journey. But there are many indications from elsewhere in North America of the conclusions that Native people drew when Jesuits wielded their water and spells and a child died anyway.[33]

The Jesuits may or may not have thus sealed a reputation as murderous sorcerers, but there is no question that they quickly dashed any hopes that they might be conduits for powerful prestige goods that Paquiquineo or other chiefs could control. "By a bit of blundering (I don't know who on the ship did it) someone made some sort of a poor trade in food," Quirós complained. Previously, "the Indians whom we met on the way would give to us from their poverty, [but] now they are reluctant when they see they receive no trinkets for their ears of corn." To nip such expectations of reciprocity—almost certainly the Native people did not see their provision of food to people who brought exotic goods in terms of barter—Segura "had forbidden that they be given something, so that they would not be accustomed to receiving it and then afterwards not want to bargain with us." Not surprisingly, "the Indians took the food away with them." For the moment, at least, Segura held firm in his conviction that the fathers "must live in this land mainly with what the Indians give" them. "Take care," Quirós warned his correspondent, "that whoever comes here in no wise barters with the Indians, if need be under threat of severe punishments, and if they should bring something to barter, orders will be given that Don Luis force them to give in return something equal to whatever was bartered, and that they may not deal with the Indians except in the way judged fitting here."[34]

Over the starving months of winter, the fathers apparently did break down and exchange some goods for food, but with local villagers, rather than with Paquiquineo, his chief, or his somewhat more distant town. Paquiquineo himself had almost immediately fled to that town, where he supposedly refused all communication with the fathers and settled down to what Jesuit chroniclers delighted in describing as the life of a "second Judas" who "allowed himself free rein in his sins, marrying many women in a pagan way."[35] The story as usually told then reached a gruesome end. Paquiquineo supposedly responded to a final desperate Jesuit plea for aid with a brutal attack, first on the messengers and then on the mission station, where Segura and the others died from blows with their own axes. As evidence of the murders—and, we might add, of the power of exotic goods—Spanish sailors sent the next summer to supply the mission claimed that Native men were wearing the slain priests' cassocks as they tried to lure them ashore.[36]

But everything the chroniclers and subsequent historians thought or think they know about what happened after September came from the lips of the only one of the Spaniards who survived the experience, the young boy Alonso—as embroidered by the rhetorical conventions of Catholic hagiography and by what may have been poorly translated boasts from Native people. Who knows what combination of survivor guilt and intimidation shaped the tales of a boy who, nearly two years after the crisis, found himself delivered up to a vengeful Menéndez? The governor had sailed up the river in "an armed *fragatilla* with 30 soldiers," had lured aboard Paquiquineo's uncle "with five of his leaders and eight other Indians," and had then forced Alonso to act as interpreter while Rogel hastily "catechized and baptized" eight or nine of the Tsenacomocans, "after which they were hanged from the rigging of the Governor's ship." To Rogel, it was "a marvelous thing in how short a time the Governor learned what was happening there from the mouth of the boy."[37] Marvelous indeed, particularly in light of the facts that Menéndez was in too much of a hurry to follow up on the boy's story about where the priests were buried and that Alonso admitted that he had not actually witnessed the murders he described. All we can know for certain is that the Jesuits died, that they utterly failed to live up to behavioral expectations of a prestige-goods economy, and that their deaths—whether by assassination or starvation—provoked a brutal retaliation by the Europeans.[38] The lessons Paquiquineo took away from his effort to master the Spaniards and their goods can only be imagined.

*   *   *

If we know little with certainty about Paquiquineo, we know even less about Namontack, the man who joined the English in the transaction that sent Thomas Savage to live with the Powhatans in 1608, as recalled in the song of 1611. But at least in his case, thanks to the work of scholars such as J. Frederick Fausz, Martin Quitt, and Frederic Gleach, we have a clearer sense of the broader historical narrative in which he fits, a narrative that begins shortly after the first arrival of the Jamestown colonists in 1607.[39]

As Wahunsonacock and his people apparently understood it, the weroance figure among the English was Christopher Newport, not John Smith, who consistently portrayed himself as Newport's subordinate. Newport's initial voyage of exploration up the James River in May 1607 thus assumed crucial significance for chiefs of Tsenacomoco seeking connections to goods and power. According to Gabriel Archer, Newport and his entourage "were entertayned with much Courtesye in every place." Two weroances subordinate to Wahunsonacock fairly tripped over themselves to arrange ceremonial welcomes that displayed their wealth and generosity. Escorted to the presence of the weroance of Arrohateck, Newport's entourage found the chief "satt upon a matt of Reedes, with his people about him" and another mat ready "layd for Captain Newport." After the visitors had feasted on roast deer, mulberries, corn and bean soup, and cornbread, the weroance presented Newport with "his Crowne which was of Deares hayre dyed redd." While everyone "satt merye banquetting with them, seeing their Daunces, and taking Tobacco, Newes came that the greate kyng Powatah was come: at whose presence they all rose of their mattes (save the kyng Arahatec), separated themselves aparte in fashion of a Guard, and with a long shout they saluted him." Assuming the newcomer was *the* Powhatan, rather than, as turned out to be the case, a subordinate weroance named Parahunt from the *town* called Powhatan, the English did their best to act like proper chiefs. "Him wee saluted with silence sitting still on our mattes, our Captaine in the myddest," reported Archer. Newport then "presented (as before . . . [he] dyd to kyng Arahatec) gyftes of dyvers sortes, as penny knyves, sheeres, belles, beades, glasse toyes etc. more amply then before."[40]

On the evening of the same day, ten miles farther upriver at a hilltop town Archer called "Pawatahs Towre," the two weroances jointly presided over another feast, at which the mats prepared for the guests were "layde right over against the kynges." As night came on, Newport "certifyed" to Parahunt that the English "were frendes with all his people and kyngdomes." In response, the weroance, according to Archer "very well understanding by the wordes and signes we made, the significatyon of our meaning," proposed "of his owne accord a leauge of fryndship with us, which our Captain kyndly imbraced." Newport, "for concluding therof gave him his gowne, put it on his back him-selfe, and laying his hand on his breast saying Wingapoh Chemuze (the most kynde wordes of salutayon that may be) he satt downe." The chiefly exchanges of gifts and food continued somewhat more awkwardly the next day when Newport invited Parahunt to a Sunday dinner of "two peeces of porke . . . sodd . . . with pease." Not surprisingly, the weroance and his party brought along some more appetizing food of their own—which may have been as much a political as a gastronomic statement—but everyone "fedd familiarly, without sitting in . . . state as before." Parahunt ate "very freshly of" the salt pork stew and washed it down with enough "beere, Aquavite, and Sack" to feel "very sick, and not able to sitt up long."[41]

As the competitive feasting continued, more than just a hangover trou-bled the ceremonial displays of chiefly harmony and asymmetrical redis-tribution.[42] A particularly tense moment occurred just before that informal Sunday meal, when "two bullet-bagges which had shot and Dyvers trucking toyes in them" turned up missing. On Newport's protest, the two weroances "instantly caused them all to be restored, not wanting any thing." That the re-covery was so easy suggests that the chiefs themselves had been the ones who redistributed "the shott and toyes to (at least) a dozen severall persons." This provided an opportunity for Newport, whether he fully understood his ac-tions or not, to assert his superiority to the two weroances by reenacting the redistribution of prestige goods and claiming the sole right to provide them. As Archer put it, he "rewarded the theeves with the same toyes they had stol-len, but kept the bulletes, yet he made knowne unto them the Custome of England to be Death for such offences."[43]

More troublesome for the future of Anglo-Powhatan relations was New-port's stubborn insistence that the weroances provide guides for an overland expedition beyond the falls of the James, Parahunt's more stubborn explana-tions of why that would be impossible, and Newport's defiant erection before he turned back of "a Crosse with this inscriptyon Jacobus Rex, 1607, and his owne name belowe." Parahunt did not see the cross go up at the base of the falls, or the Englishmen as they prayed for their monarch and their "owne prosperous succes in this his Actyon, and proclaymed him kyng, with a gre-ate showte." If Parahunt's family maintained any tradition of the travels of

Paquiquineo in the world of Europeans, however, they must have scoffed when the Tsenacomocans who witnessed the spectacle repeated Newport's disingenuous explanation "that the two Armes of the Crosse signifyed kyng Powatah and himselfe, the fastening of it in the myddest was their united Leaug, and the shoute the reverence he dyd to Pawatah."[44]

Against this uneasy backdrop, as the English returned downriver to Jamestown, they participated in feasts offered with progressively less enthusiasm, until, ominously, their guide (who was the brother-in-law of the weroance of Arrohateck) "tooke some Conceyt, and though he shewed no discontent, yet would he by no meanes goe any further." The reason soon became clear; the previous day, some two hundred Tsenacomocans had attacked the English fort.[45] As one colonist succinctly put it, "The people used our men well untill they found they begann to plant and fortefye, Then they fell to skyrmishing." The fighting continued for several weeks until the mamanatowick unilaterally declared a truce, while colonist after colonist succumbed to dysentery, salt poisoning, and malnutrition.[46] "Throughout the summer and autumn," Fausz concludes, "Wahunsonacock kept the depleted, disease-ridden colonists alive with gifts of food until he had restored their trust and earned a formal recognition of their grateful dependence"—a recognition driven home by the capture and ritual adoption of Smith at the end of the year.[47]

It is significant that, from a few days after the initial attack on Jamestown through the difficult period of skirmishing and truce, famine and disease, Newport was, as George Percy put it, "gone for England, leaving us (one hundred and foure persons) verie bare and scantie of victualls, furthermore in warres and in danger of the Savages."[48] Among the Powhatans, the reputation of the great man Newport, who knew something of how to behave at a feast and to distribute prestige goods, can only have risen in his absence, particularly in contrast to his underling Smith, who in his official capacity as "Cape Marchant" ran about the countryside dickering with and bullying weroances for the foodstuffs that, as Quitt has pointed out, could be given or received, but never appropriately bartered for, in a prestige goods economy.[49]

If we trust the Pocahontas-free version of Smith's captivity contained in his 1608 *True Relation*, the cape merchant reinforced Newport's reputation during his audience with Wahunsonacock. When the mamanatowick "asked mee the cause of our comming," Smith reported, "I tolde him, being in fight with the Spaniards our enemie, beeing over powred, neare put to retreat, and by extreame weather put to this shore, where . . . our Pinnsse being leake[y] wee were inforced to stay to mend her, till Captaine Newport my father came to conduct us away." And what a father Newport was:

> In describing to . . . [Wahunsonacock] the territories of Europe, which was subject to our great King whose subject I was, and the innumerable multitude of his ships, I gave him to understand the noyse of Trumpets, and terrible manner of fighting were under captain Newport my father, whom I intituled the Meworames which they call King of all the waters. At his greatnesse hee admired, and not a little feared: hee desired mee to forsake Paspahegh, and to live with him upon his River, a Countrie called Capahowasicke: hee promised to give me Corne, Venison, or what I wanted to feede us, Hatchets and Copper wee should make him, and none should disturbe us. This request I promised to performe: and thus having with all the kindnes hee could devise, sought to content me: hee sent me home with 4 men, one that usually carried my Gowne and Knapsacke after me, two other loded with bread, and one to accompanie me.[50]

In January 1608, shortly after Smith's return to Jamestown with no intention of demonstrating his subordination by relocating to the place Powhatan had assigned him, Newport—"father," "King of all the waters," font of "Hatchets and Copper," better known among his own people as what historian James Axtell has called "a one-armed, one-time pirate"—returned at last to Tsenacomoco with the "First Supply."[51] Copper flowed out of Jamestown, traded by Newport's seamen so liberally that Indian corn and furs "could not be had for a pound of copper, which before was sold for an ounce." Meantime, Wahunsonacock and his people "confirmed their opinion of Newport's greatnes . . . by the great presents Newport often sent him." In return, said Smith, "the Emperour Powhatan each weeke once or twice sent me many presents of Deare, bread, [and] *Raugroughcuns* [raccoons], halfe alwayes for my father, whom he much desired to see, and halfe for me: and so continually importuned by messengers and presents, that I would come to fetch the corne, and take the Countrie their King had given me, as at last Captaine Newport resolved to go see him." At about this point, Smith began to regret the whoppers he had told the Powhatans during his captivity: "The President, and the rest of the Councell, they knewe not, but Captaine Newport's greatnesse I had so described, as they conceyved him the chiefe, the rest his children, Officers, and servants."[52]

The chiefly progress of Newport and Smith to visit Wahunsonacock in

February 1608 had many rough moments, including some comical English efforts to cross fragile bridges or wade out to a barge marooned at low tide, several far less comical English refusals to lay down their arms during diplomatic ceremonies, and (on the way back to Jamestown) a tragic English episode of shooting first and asking questions later that left at least one Native man dead.[53] But as on his former embassies, Newport provided just enough evidence to confirm his reputation as a chief who might fulfill the Natives' economic and political expectations and take his subordinate place in Powhatan's domain. For his part, Wahunsonacock spared no effort to display his own power, wealth, and generosity. "Before his house stood fortie or fiftie great Platters of fine bread," said Smith, who entered to the sound of "loude tunes" and "signes of great joy" during a preparatory embassy while Newport waited for a future grand entry. Wahunsonacock, "having his finest women, and the principall of his chiefe men assembled, sate in rankes," presided "as upon a Throne at the upper end of the house, with such a Majestie as I cannot expresse, nor yet have often seene, either in Pagan or Christian; with a kinde countenance hee bad mee welcome, and caused a place to bee made by himselfe to sit." When Smith presented the mamanatowick "a sute of red cloath, a white Greyhound, and a Hatte; as jewels he esteemed them, and with a great Oration made by three of his Nobles . . . , kindly accepted them, with a publike confirmation of a perpetuall league and friendship."[54]

But, lest Smith get too comfortable over the turkey dinner that "the Queene of Appomattoc, a comely yong Salvage," then served him, Wahunsonacock reminded him of who the welcome had really been prepared for: "Your kinde visitation doth much content mee, but where is your father whom I much desire to see, is he not with you?" After Smith assured him that "the next day my Father would give him a child of his, in full assurance of our loves, and not only that, but when he should thinke it convenient, wee would deliver under his subjection the Country of Manacam and Pocoughtaonack his enemies," the mamanatowick put his visitor in his place in a different way. "With a lowd oration," Smith reported, "he proclaimed me a werowanes of Powhatan, and that all his subjects should so esteeme us, and no man account us strangers nor Paspaheghans, but Powhatans, and that the Corne, weomen and Country, should be to us as to his owne people." Smith, "for many reasons," made no objections to this declaration of dependence and, "with the best languages and signes of thankes" he could improvise, beat a hasty exit. But not before Wahunsonacock further displayed his power. "The King, rising from his seat," said Smith, "conducted me foorth, and caused each of my men to have as much more bread as hee could beare, giving me some in a basket, and as much he sent a board for a present to my Father."[55]

In Smith's account (and probably because it *is* Smith's account), Newport's subsequent audiences with Wahunsonacock seem almost anticlimactic. But in at least three ways beyond keeping the great man waiting, Newport acted his peaceful and generous chiefly part. When he arrived, he presented the mamanatowick with the thirteen-year-old Thomas Savage, "whom he gave him as his Sonne." When the issue of weapons at the council fire again came up, he commanded his "men to retire to the water side, which was some thirtie score [paces] from thence." And when, in response to Smith's efforts to start haggling over the price of provisions, Wahunsonacock announced to Newport that "it is not agreeable with my greatnes in this pedling manner to trade for trifles, and I asteeme you a great werowans," Newport bestowed on him "not . . . lesse then twelve great Coppers [to] try his kindnes." Although Smith carped that this gift of large kettles pried from the Powhatans no more grain than a single smaller one could have purchased elsewhere, Newport's display of asymmetrical generosity apparently had a great effect.[56] "Thanks to God, we are at peace with all the inhabitants of the surrounding country, trading for corn and supplies," colonist Francis Perkins wrote from Jamestown in March. Not only did Native people "value very highly indeed reddish copper," but "their great Emperor, or Werowance, which is the name of their kings, has sent some of his people to show us how to plant the native wheat, and to make some gear such as they use to go fishing."[57]

In April, Newport again sailed for England, taking with him Namontack, described as Wahunsonacock's "trusty servant, and one of a shrewd subtill capacity," who the mamanatowick "well affected to goe with him for England in steed of his Soone."[58] The thaw in Anglo-Powhatan relations after the mamanatowick declared the English his subordinates and presided over a ceremony in which the newcomers' weroance bestowed a massive gift of prestige goods suggests that Namontack went off into the Atlantic world with expectations similar to those Paquiquineo brought back to Tsenacomoco from Seville, Mexico City, and Havana. He would broker the connections that would bring his people a secure supply of the exotic goods that belonged to Europeans and thus master their power. But Namontack's people must also have realized something that those who initially welcomed Paquiquineo home did not. The powerful connections symbolized by prestige goods also opened the way to an array of more mundane, but economically vital, items: copper for tools and weapons as well as for display, iron axes and knives, cloth, perhaps

Copper items from Jamestown likely to have circulated in Tsenacomoco. James-towne Image 11, Courtesy of APVA Preservation Virginia.

even firearms. Solidifying the incorporation of the people who made these things into the polity of Tsenacomoco was important work indeed.[59]

And it was work that was not going well during Namontack's absence. Smith repeatedly reinforced the contrast between his own parsimony and Newport's chiefly generosity as well as his unwillingness to play the subordinate weroance role that the mamanatowick had assigned him. Wahunsonacock had, "to express his love to Newport, when he departed, presented him with 20 Turkies, conditionally to return him 20 Swords, which immediatly were sent him." Smith, however, refused to make a similar exchange, and the mamanatowick, "not finding his humor obaied in sending him weapons, . . . caused his people with 20 devises to obtain them, at last by ambuscadoes." The skirmishing ended only when Wahunsonacock "sent his messengers and his dearest Daughter Pocahuntas" to try to patch things up—and Smith had convinced himself that the Tsenacomocans were "in such feare and obedience, as his very name wold sufficiently affright them."[60] With Smith hardly able to conceal his contempt for the mamana-towick's authority, for the London Company's policies, and for what he considered Newport's coddling of Indians who should be ruled by force, the Powhatans may well have pinned much of their hopes on Namontack's successful return.

No doubt, as Smith suspected, Namontack had carried instructions "to know our strength and countries condition."[61] In England, Newport tried to show him some impressive sights, or at least to show him off to all the right people who could contribute to the expedition back to Jamestown that would be known the "Second Supply." According to Spanish ambassador Pedro de Zúñiga, "this Newport brought a lad who they say is the son of an emperor of those lands and they have coached him that when he sees the King he is not to take off his hat, and other things of this sort." Although Zúñiga was "amused by the way they honour[ed] him, for . . . he must be a very ordinary person," the royal treatment probably gave Namontack a simpler impression of the possibilities for mobilizing European material and political power than Paquiquineo had taken home from his longer and difficult travels. Whatever the case, the consensus among English on both sides of the Atlantic seemed to be that "they treated him well" and that "the Emperor, his father, and his people were very happy over what he told them about the good reception and entertainment he found in England."[62]

Whatever Namontack may have said when the English were not listening, his return to Tsenacomoco with Newport in the fall of 1608 brought the Powhatans' efforts to integrate English chiefs into a prestige-goods economy to their climax, in the remarkable episode of Wahunsonacock's coronation. Historians have almost universally agreed with Smith that the whole scheme was as cockamamie as the company's orders that Newport was not to return to England "without a lumpe of gold, a certainty of the south sea or one of the lost company of Sir Walter Rawley" or that he deliver to the Chesapeake a shipload of "Poles and Dutch to make pitch and tarre, glasse milles, and sope-ashes" with no plans for how they would be fed. "As for the coronation of Powhatan and his presents of bason, Ewer, Bed, Clothes, and such costly novelties, they had bin much better well spared, then so ill spent," Smith concluded. "We had his favour much better, onlie for a poore peece of Copper, till this stately kinde of soliciting made him so much overvalue himselfe, that he respected us as much as nothing at all."[63] Of course from Wahunsonacock's perspective, a "stately kinde of soliciting" and the prestige goods that Namontack's embassy had apparently acquired from the English king were exactly the point. Indeed, it is even possible that the only one of the English for whom the mamanatowick had any real respect was Newport, whose status as his subordinate weroance was about to be confirmed.

As at the previous ceremonial meeting between Newport and Wahunsonacock, Smith was in charge of the preliminaries and set off to deliver Namontack and an invitation that he "come to his Father Newport to accept
those presents, and conclude their revenge against the Monacans." A ceremonial welcoming dance that Smith utterly failed to understand—involving "30
young women [who] came naked out of the woods" carrying arrows, swords,
clubs, "a pot-stick" and other items as they "cast themselves in a ring about
the fire, singing, and dauncing with excellent ill varietie"—certainly gave no
hint of subordination to the English. A message from Wahunsonacock about
his power may also been conveyed when, having "solemnely invited Smith
to their lodging . . . all these Nimphes more tormented him then ever, with
crowding, and pressing, and hanging upon him, most tediously crying, love
you not mee?"[64]

In any event, there was no question who was in charge the next day when
Wahunsonacock gave Smith an audience: "If your king have sent me presents,
I also am a king, and this my land; 8 daies I will stay to receave them. Your
father is to come to me, not I to him, nor yet to your fort, neither will I bite
at such a baite: as for the Monacans, I can revenge my owne injuries. . . . But
for any salt water beyond the mountaines, the relations you have had from
my people are false." So much for the south sea; so much for English military
might; so much for Smith, who then watched politely as Wahunsonacock literally drew him a map to show him the facts.[65]

Perhaps Paquiquineo had hoped for a scene like the one that played out
next: Newport and fifty of his men processing overland to the capital while
three barges brought prestige goods up the river. Like Smith, most historians
play the scene for a laugh:[66]

All things being fit for the day of his coronation, the presents were
brought, his bason, ewer, bed and furniture set up, his scarlet cloake
and apparel (with much adoe) put on him (being perswaded by Namontacke they would doe him no hurt.) But a fowle trouble there
was to make him kneele to receave his crowne, he neither knowing
the majestie, nor meaning of a Crowne, nor bending of the knee,
indured so many perswasions, examples, and instructions, as tired
them all. At last by leaning hard on his shoulders, he a little stooped,
and Newport put the Crowne on his head. When by the warning
of a pistoll, the boates were prepared with such a volly of shot, that
the king start up in a horrible feare, till he see all was well, then

remembring himselfe, to congratulate their kindnesse, he gave his old shews and his mantle to Captain Newport. But perceiving his purpose was to discover the Monacans, hee laboured to divert his resolution, refusing to lend him either men, or guids, more then Namontack, and so (after some complementall kindness on both sides) in re-quitall of his presents, he presented Newport with a heape of wheat eares, that might containe some 7 or 8 bushels, and as much more we bought ready dressed in the towne, wherewith we returned to the fort.[67]

Wahunsonacock and the Native people who witnessed the ceremony almost certainly were not laughing. Tribute had been brought, prestige goods displayed, unbalanced reciprocity practiced, and the mamanatowick's power demonstrated.

And "Captain Newport [who] brought them Copper," as the Tsenaco-mocan song called him, once again went off into the Atlantic world, taking Namontack with him and leaving Smith in charge. Namontack would never return. It is likely that, sailing on the *Sea Venture*, flagship of the "Third Supply," he was shipwrecked in Bermuda and then killed in a brawl with a fellow Tsenacomocan named Matchumps.[68] Meanwhile, in the Chesapeake, everything that could have gone wrong in the Anglo-Powhatan relationship, did. Private trade among colonists, mariners, and Indians at Jamestown undercut the authority of both Smith and Wahunsonacock to manage the flow of prestige goods. "Of 2 or 300 hatchets, chissels, mattocks, and pickaxes" brought on the Second Supply, Smith complained, "scarce 20 could be found" six weeks later. All had been illicitly traded to Native people for furs, skins, baskets, and other commodities. Food remained scarce at Jamestown, and Smith, using ever more aggressive tactics to extract it from Indian neighbors, finally "resolved . . . to surprise Powhatan, and al his provision." Almost simultaneously, Wahunsonacock—much as he had the last time Newport sailed away—tested Smith's willingness to maintain the controlled, ritualized flow of prestige goods and allow the mamanatowick to reassert the authority that private trade threatened to undermine. If Smith "would send him but men to build him a house, bring him a grin[d]stone, 50 swords, some peeces, a cock and a hen, with copper and beads," Wahunsonacock's messengers said, "he would loade his shippe with corne." Smith, "knowing there needed no better castel, then that house to surprize Powhatan," quickly shipped off five craftsmen he could not feed anyway to start construction on the mamanatowick's house while he mobilized some thirty-eight troops for an expedition to the Powhatan capital in January 1609.[69]

Smith, told along the way at the town of Weraskoyack that Wahunsonacock "hath sent for you only to cut your throats," needed no convincing. The mamanatowick similarly needed little convincing from the house builders who (perhaps encouraged by their first decent meals since arriving in the Chesapeake) "revealed to him as much as they knew of . . . [English] projects, and how to prevent them." Not surprisingly, the meeting between Smith and Wahunsonacock was strained. The English had to ask for the reception feast that earlier embassies had received as a matter of course, and Wahunsonacock almost immediately inquired when the visitors "would bee gon, faining hee sent not for" them. Multiplying the insult, the mamanatowick both drove a hard bargain and mocked Smith for his insistence that the expedition was about trading for food rather than about alliance and prestige goods. "Neither had hee any corne, and his people much lesse, yet for 40 swords he would procure . . . 40 bushels," Wahunsonacock declared. Indeed he would not trade at all "without gunnes and swords, valuing a basket of corne more pretious then a basket of copper, saying he could eate his corne, but not his copper." When Smith protested that, "as for swords, and gunnes, I told you long agoe, I had none to spare," Wahunsonacock responded bluntly. "Many do informe me, your comming is not for trade, but to invade my people and possesse my Country, who dare not come to bring you corne, seeing you thus armed with your men," he announced. "To cleere us of this feare, leave abord your weapons, for here they are needlesse we being all friends and for ever Powhatans."[70]

The next day, having gotten nowhere with Smith on the incompatibility of arms and petty trade with the status of "being all Powhatans," the mamanatowick starkly outlined the contrast between Smith and Newport:

Captaine Smith, I never used anie of [my] Werowances, so kindlie as your selfe; yet from you I receave the least kindnesse of anie. Captaine Newport gave me swords, copper, cloths, a bed, tooles, or what I desired, ever taking what I offered him, and would send awaie his gunnes when I intreated him: none doth denie to laie at my feet (or do) what I desire, but onelie you, of whom I can have nothing, but what you regard not, and yet you wil have whatsoever you demand. Captain Newport you call father, and so you call me, but I see for all us both, you will doe what you list, and wee must both seeke to content you.

Smith utterly rejected the status of a subordinate weroance: "Powhatan, you must knowe as I have but one God, I honour but one king; and I live not here as your subject, but as your friend."[71] Many specific affronts and skirmishes led up to the bloodbath that J. Frederick Fausz has rightly termed "the First Anglo-Powhatan War" of 1609 to 1614. But Smith's rejection of the basic assumptions of subordination and asymmetrical exchange in a prestige-goods chiefdom may well have served as that war's declaration.[72]

Yet even through the years of fighting, the goods that Namontack and Newport brought from across the Atlantic retained their power for both sides. At least one English raiding party "ransaked" the temple of the subordinate Nansemond chiefdom and "Tooke downe the Corpes of their deade kings from of their Toombes, and caryed away their pearles Copper and braceletts wherewitth they doe decore their kings funeralles." Tsenacomocans, meanwhile, "stopped full of Breade" the mouths of Englishmen they slew.[73] Most suggestive of the continued power of goods, however, was a ceremony described by Henry Spelman, who lived among the Powhatans from late 1609 to late 1610. Spelman explained that Wahunsonacock kept most of the more ordinary "goods and presents that are sent him, as the Cornne," in a house built for that purpose at the village of Oropikes. "But the beades or Crowne or Bedd which the Kinge of England sent him are in the gods' house at Oropikes, and in their houses are all the Kinge ancesters and kindred commonly buried." At least once a year, on the day after the people planted the corn fields that belonged to the mamanatowick, Wahunsonacock

> takes the croune which the Kinge of England sent him beinge brought him by tow [two] men, and setts it on his heade which dunn the people goeth about the corne in maner backwardes for they going before, and the king followinge ther faces are always toward the Kinge exspecting when he should flinge sum beades among them which is his custum is at that time to doe makinge those which had wrought to scramble for them But to sume he favors he bids thos that carry his Beades to call such and such unto him unto whome he giveth beades into ther hande and this is the greatest curtesey he doth his people.[74]

This was a prestige-goods chiefdom in action. That ceremony, that crown, those beads were exactly what Paquiquineo and Namontack hoped to bring home from the Atlantic world, confirming Powhatan's power over Europeans

Early seventeenth-century glass trade beads, most in shades of blue. Jamestowne
Image 126, Courtesy of APVA Preservation Virginia.

and their goods even—perhaps especially—in the midst of war with the
English.

*   *   *

As is well known, the first Anglo-Powhatan war came to an end with the
kidnapping of Pocahontas in 1613, her diplomatic marriage to John Rolfe in
1614, and their voyage to England in 1616.[75] Joining the traveling couple were
several others, including Uttamatomakkin. A high-ranking priest—the pre-
fix *uttama-* connotes "spiritual" or "priestly"—and "an experienced Man and
Counseller to *Opochancanough* their King and Governour in *Powhatans* absence," Uttamatomakkin was, said Samuel Purchas, "sent hither to observe
and bring newes of our King and Country to his Nation."[76] To Wahunsonacock and Opechancanough—the rising chief whose emissary Uttamatomakkin was—the trip to England may have been a final attempt to establish
the kind of relationship envisioned since 1608 or 1561.

Shortly after Pocahontas's marriage, colonist Ralph Hamor had visited Wahunsonacock in hopes he could persuade him to marry off another

daughter to the English. He quickly learned that the mamanatowick had a quite different agenda, focused on prestige goods and his image of the long-absent Christopher Newport. Wahunsonacock's first words were to Hamor's interpreter, Thomas Savage: "You . . . are my child, by the donative of Cap-taine *Newport*, in lieu of one of my subjects *Namontacke*, who I purposely sent to King James his land, to see him and his country, and to returne me the true report thereof." Unaware, as was Hamor, of Namontack's death in Bermuda, the mamanatowick complained that he had "yet . . . not returned, though many ships have arrived here from thence, since that time, how ye have delt with him I know not."[77] If Namontack's quest to harness the power of the Atlantic world for Tsenacomoco's paramount chiefdom remained un-finished, it was the fault of the English.

And at Jamestown, the English also continued to ignore the demands of prestige-goods relationships. Before Wahunsonacock spoke to Hamor, he felt the Englishman's neck and demanded to know "where the chaine of pearle was" that he had sent to his "Brother Sir *Thomas Dale* for a present, at his first arrival" and that was to be worn by any future official English emissary. Having talked his way out of this breach of protocol, Hamor grandiloquently announced that "Sir *Thomas Dale* your Brother, the principal commander of the English men, sends you greeting of love and peace, on his part invio-lable," and presented, "in testimonie thereof . . . a worthie present, *vid*, two large peeces of copper, five strings of white and blew beades, five wodden combes, ten fish-hookes, and a paire of knives." Wahunsonacock expressed polite "thankes" but made it clear that such gifts given in the king's name were "not so ample, howbeit himselfe a greater *Weroance*, as formerly Captaine *Newport*, whom I very well love, was accustomed to gratefie me with." To drive home the point about impudent English stinginess, he announced that the daughter whose hand the English sought was already pledged to "a great *Weroance* for two bushels of *Roanoke* [wampum]." Moreover, he considered "it not a brotherly part of your King, to desire to bereave me of two of my children at once."[78]

After a meager meal of nothing but sodden cornbread, presented with the excuse that Wahunsonacock had not expected guests, the mamana-towick "caused to be fetched a great glasse of sacke, some three quarts or better, which Captain *Newport* had given him sixe or seaven yeeres since, carefully preserved by him, not much above a pint in all this time spent." To each of the English he dispensed "in a great oister shell some three spoone-fuls." After redistributing this powerful substance associated with Newport,

Wahunsonacock sent the emissaries on their way the next day with explicit instructions for Dale. Hamor was

> to remember his brother to send him these particular, Ten peeces
> of copper, a shaving knife, an iron frow to cleave bordes, a grinding
> stone, not so bigge but four or five men may carry it, which would be
> bigge enough for his use, two bone combes, such as Captaine *Newport*
> had given him, the wodden ones his own men can make, an hundred
> fish-hookes or if he could spare it, rather a fishing saine, and a cat, and
> a dogge, with which things if his brother would firnish him, he would
> requite his love with the returne of skinnes.

Wahunsonacock insisted that Hamor repeat each item and, the Englishman said, "yet still doubtful that I might forget any of them, he bade me write them downe in such a Table book as he shewed me, which was a very fair one." Like the bottle of sack and the crown from England, the notebook (which may or may not have come from Newport and which Hamor was not allowed to mark) was a prestige item that ratified the mamanatowick's power. "He tolde me," said Hamor, "it did him much good to shew it to strangers which came unto him."[79]

There is no record that Dale sent the goods Wahunsonacock demanded; this would have been an unlikely course for a man who a few years earlier had directed that some colonists who "did Runne Away unto the Indyans . . . be hanged some burned some to be broken upon wheles others to be Staked and some to be shott to deathe . . . To terrefy the reste for attempteinge the Lyke."[80] That Uttamatomakkin returned from England filled with "rails against England, English people, and particularly his best friend Thomas Dale" suggests Dale did nothing to meet the Powhatans' expectations.[81] So too does Pocahontas's embittered complaint when she met Smith in England that "they did tell us alwaies you were dead, and I knew no other till I came to Plimoth; yet Powhatan did command Uttamatomakkin to seeke you, and know the truth, because your Countriemen will lie much."[82]

Clearly Uttamatomakkin was not impressed with the truths he found in England, where he became the brunt of a running English joke. Wahunsonacock "sent him, as they say, to number the people here, and informe him well what wee were and our state," Smith reported. "Arriving at Plimoth, according to his directions, he got a long sticke, whereon by notches hee did thinke to have kept the number of all the men hee could see, but he was quickly wearie of that task." Purchas said he also tried to count trees, "till his Arithmetike failed, For their numbring beyond an hundred is imperfect, and somewhat confused." Still, Uttamatomakkin held his own in a theological debate with Purchas (who found him "very zealous in his superstition") and presumably sat gamely through the theatrical productions and other events where the Powhatans were paraded. Although the Tsenacomocans had been "graciously used" at the court of James I, Uttamatomakkin vociferously "denied ever to have seene the King," because the monarch acted nothing like a proper chief. When Smith finally persuaded him otherwise, "He replyed very sadly, You gave Powhatan a white Dog, which Powhatan fed as himselfe, but your King gave me nothing, and I am better than your white Dog."[83]

Christopher Newport was probably in England during part of Uttamatomakkin's unsuccessful quest for prestige goods; in November 1616 he sailed for the East Indies, where he died in August of the next year.[84] There is no record that the two men met, although it is hard to imagine that Uttamatomakkin failed to ask after him, to hear talk of him, or to take additional umbrage if there was no response. Whatever the case, he returned home with nothing good to say about the English or Dale. Samuel Argall was convinced that "all his reports are disproved before opachankano and his Great men whereupon (to the great satisfaccion of the Great men) Tomakin is disgraced."[85] Uttamatomakkin's disgrace may have been real, but less because of the rhetorical brilliance of English counterarguments than the plain proof that Powhatan's vision of incorporating the Atlantic world into Tsenacomoco had been so utterly wrong and that Opechancanough would have to build chiefly authority through other means. Those who sang the taunting song of 1611 already realized as much.

* * *

I have speculated here at great length, but also attempted to operate within an accepted model of how chiefdoms work and to stay very close to the texts of the few documents that describe the exploits of Paquiquineo, Namontack, and Uttamatomakkin in the Atlantic world. Those texts glimpse envoys from Tsenacomoco attempting to incorporate European things into their prestige-goods economy, attempting to subordinate representatives of European kingdoms to their paramount chiefdom, attempting to use the new world of the Atlantic to multiply the power of their people, and of themselves. Control of supplies of copper, sacred chalices, exotic crowns, blue glass beads, bottles of sack, volumes of blank paper reinforced the power of the mamanatowick and his subordinate weroances—and in turned displayed to Tsenacomocans their power over Captain Newport and King James. As copper and beads became ever more accessible to ever more ordinary people, the need to display ever more esoteric items—and to send someone like Uttamatomakkin to find out exactly how things worked at the source—became ever more pressing.

This particular Native world of goods perhaps had already died with Pocahontas, Powhatan, and Newport in 1617 and 1618. Perhaps it died with Namontack in 1609. But it certainly died in the devastating Powhatan assault on the English in 1622—an assault that, few have noticed, came within months of the arrival of word about a new Virginia Company scheme. To forestall Dutch exploitation "of a trade of Furrs to be had in Hudsons and De La Ware River," a ship was to be dispatched from Virginia, loaded with trade goods and "two or three [men] skilfull in the languages and maners of the Indians, and expert in those places, wherein the trade is to be, that may serve for guides and Interpreters."[86] Virginia colonists who spoke Algonquian were hardly known for their tight lips. Opechancanough surely overheard their talk and understood what this expedition to competing distant shores meant for the economic basis of his, and his people's, power over the English and their goods.

CHAPTER 2

Brothers, Scoundrels, Metal-Makers: Dutch Constructions of Native American Constructions of the Dutch

Dutch traders had come to North American shores at almost exactly the same time that English people arrived in Tsenacomoco. In 1609, Henry Hudson sailed up what later became his eponymous stream, which the Dutch simply called in their language the "North River." By 1614, one hundred and fifty miles upstream on that river at the future site of Albany, European traders were conducting a thriving annual trade. Algonquian-speaking Mahicans, along with Iroquoian-speaking Mohawks and other people of the Haudeno-saunee Iroquois, or Five Nations, mostly peacefully exchanged beaver skins and varied furs for the copper, glass beads, tools, and other items that caused so much contention at Jamestown. Over the next couple of decades, Dutch traders, and a few agricultural colonists from various spots in Europe, con-solidated the North River outpost as "Fort Orange," surrounded by the pa-troonship, or proprietary manor, of Rensselaerswyck and by the aptly named town of "Beverwyck." Others moved into valleys of the "South" (the English called it *Delaware*) and "Fresh" (*Connecticut*) rivers and into what one his-torian calls "the saltwater frontier" of the perimeters of Long Island Sound. Everywhere the Dutch spread in what they labeled, with various spellings, *Nieu Nederlandt*, they traded with Native people and embedded themselves in Indian systems of power mediated by exchange.[1]

Documentary and archaeological sources provide many clues about what Native people *did* as they traded and contended with New Netherland-ers. It is a tricky business, however, to try to fathom what Indians *thought* about these interactions and about the newcomers. As is often the case, an

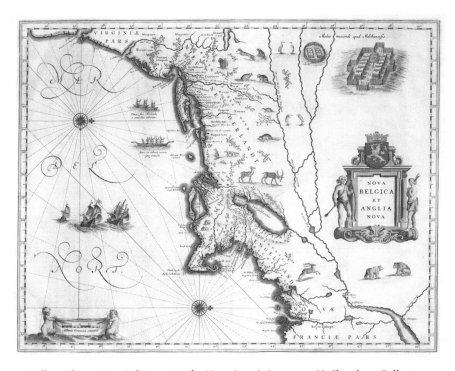

Willem Blaeu, *Nova Belgica et Anglia Nova* (1662). Lawrence H. Slaughter Collection, The Lionel Pincus and Princess Firyal Map Division, The New York Public Library, Astor, Lenox and Tilden Foundations. On this map of what the Dutch called New Netherland, the Mohawk (*Maquaes*) country near the top of the map (westward orientation) is populated by four beavers prized for their fur; two Native villages are illustrated in the upper right corner.

indirect and imprecise approach is the best that can be attempted. Although seventeenth-century Native ideation may be inaccessible, it is possible to say something about what *Dutch* people thought Indian people thought, and what those thoughts might tell us about intercultural relations in New Netherland in particular and eastern North America more generally. The subject, then, is less what Indians may have *really* believed than how a selected group of Dutch authors tried to *make sense of* what they heard Indians say about New Netherlanders. In calling the resulting images "constructions," we remind ourselves that these authors were not just reporting what was done and said but actively shaping knowledge, building meaning for themselves and their readers as they considered the question of who they—and their Native neighbors—were.[2]

* * *

Colonists and visitors wrote about the Native people of New Netherland in any number of ways. Explorers, casual visitors, and new residents recorded brief and usually ill-informed impressions.[3] Court clerks reported Dutch testimony about Indian plaintiffs and defendants and occasionally translated the words of Indians who appeared before them; other government officials recorded speeches by Native leaders on official embassies.[4] Business agents discussed the Indians with whom they dealt in communications with contacts in Europe; private letter writers similarly shared their impressions with equally private correspondents across the ocean.[5] A small group of authors, however, consciously set out to interpret and communicate hard-won firsthand knowledge of Native people, and four of them in particular deserve close attention: Harmen Meyndertsz van den Bogaert, Johannes Megapolensis, Jr., Adriaen Cornelissen van der Donck, and Jasper Danckaerts.[6]

Van den Bogaert's "A Journey into Mohawk and Oneida Country" is the journal of an expedition by three men whom the Dutch West India Company sent to neighboring Iroquois villages during the winter of 1634–1635 to learn why the number of furs being brought to the Fort Orange market had recently declined. Its author's primary purpose was to figure out what Indians expected from the fur trade and to make those expectations understandable to his Dutch superiors.[7] Megapolensis's "Account of the Mohawk Indians" (1644) similarly represents a concerted effort to figure out what made Indians tick. Its author occupied the Rensselaerswyck pulpit from 1642 to 1649 and was the first clergyman in the colony to give serious consideration to converting the Mahican and Iroquois neighbors of Fort Orange to Christianity.[8] Lawyer van der Donck's "Description of New Netherland," composed in Holland in 1653, resulted at least in part from information its writer—who lived in the colony for over a decade, participated in treaty negotiations with Indians, and conversed about their customs with van den Bogaert, French Jesuit missionary Isaac Jogues, and others—had collected to support his side in a dispute with New Netherland Governor Petrus Stuyvesant. He too, then, was consciously constructing his material to communicate a particular understanding to his audience.[9]

Zeelander Danckaerts had less firsthand knowledge of Native Americans than the others. Along with Peter Sluyter, a fellow member of the pietistic Labadist sect, he traveled widely in North America during 1679 and 1680 in search of a site for a colony of his coreligionists. While in what was now known as New York (after the English conquest of New Netherland in 1664), Danckaerts met several Native people at Albany (formerly Fort Orange), spoke extensively with such knowledgeable colonists as trader Robert Sanders, and read van der Donck's book. Despite his brief exposure to his subject matter, as his modern editors note, Danckaerts was "a meticulous diarist" who "recorded detailed accounts of the social, political, economic, geographic, and environmental conditions he encountered" and "was fascinated by Indians." And, like the other authors, he diligently set out to shape his knowledge to explain Native behavior to his readers.[10]

This shared explanatory project places these four works among the few surviving New Netherland examples of two important overlapping genres of colonial writing, genres that literary scholar Gordon M. Sayre labels "exploration narratives and ethnographic descriptions, or simply writing about the land and the act of moving through it, and writing about the inhabitants of the land."[11] Van den Bogaert's journal is clearly an exploration narrative; Megapolensis's and van der Donck's are just as clearly ethnographic descriptions; Danckaerts's partakes of both genres. But what all four have in common—and what Sayre stresses as a shared characteristic of these categories of writing more generally—is their active effort to construct meaning for European audiences from personal observation of Native Americans. In such works, one finds neither straightforward, literal videotapes of what Native Americans said and did, nor mere literary inventions of Europeans so caught up in their imagined mythic tropes that they saw only what they wanted to see. Instead, there is a complex filtering of information—a conscious effort by the author to make sense of Native people to himself and for his audience.[12]

The subject matter of the four authors accordingly tended to be generalized "Indians," rather than the individual Mahicans, Mohawks, and Oneidas they met in and near Fort Orange. And the Indians they constructed tended to employ a cluster of three images of the Dutch, as "brothers," "scoundrels," and "metal-makers." Each image had complicated meanings, and each illuminates how Dutch people understood the nature of cultural difference and intercultural relationships. Together, the three constructions of Indian constructions tell us something about what Indians believed about the Dutch, as well as what the Dutch believed about the Indians whose words and deeds they reported. But mostly these images of brothers, scoundrels, and metal-makers reveal how the four Dutch authors viewed themselves and their Dutch New Netherlanders. In writing about what they thought Indians said, they were holding up a mirror to their own society.

*   *   *

As the four authors understood it, the Indians' first and foremost construction of the Dutch was as brothers and friends. "He told me simply that I was
his brother and good friend," van den Bogaert said of one Indian his party
met. "Friends, I have come here to see you and to speak with you," he had
another exclaim.[13] Not just speech but behavior conveyed images of close,
amicable relationships. Exuberant welcomes, for instance, are a constant
theme in van den Bogaert's account of his party's travels through Mohawk
and Oneida country. As he told it, greetings often spun out of control, as
crowds of people pushed and shoved each other to meet Dutch visitors. "We
caused much curiosity in the young and old; indeed we could hardly pass
through the Indians here," he said of one village. "They pushed one another
into the fire to see us. It was almost midnight before they left us. We could not
do anything without having them shamelessly running about us." In another
town, "the Indians looked on in amazement; for most everyone was at home,
and they crowded in on us so much that we could barely pass among them.
After a long period, an Indian came to us who took us to his house and we
went in it." Again, "they pushed one another into the fire in order to see us."[14]

While van den Bogaert thus unwittingly redefined the phrase *warm welcome*, the other authors also represented Indians who showed by their actions
that they regarded the Dutch as friends, brothers, and kin. "We live among . . .
[the] Indians; and when they come to us from their country, or we go to
them, they do us every act of friendship," wrote Megapolensis. "Though they
are so very cruel to their enemies, they are very friendly to us, and we have
no dread of them," he also observed. "We go with them into the woods, we
meet with each other, sometimes at an hour or two's walk from any houses,
and think no more about it than as if we met with a Christian. They sleep by
us, too, in our chambers before our beds."[15] Danckaerts described a cordial
welcome from "some families of Indians living" near the Cohoes Falls, while
van der Donck—who lacked the Labadist's prudery—stressed more intimate
forms of making Dutch guests feel welcome. "Some, like chiefs and prominent persons, having two or more wives, will readily accommodate a visiting
friend with one of their wives for a night," he noted.[16] In whatever context,
the words *friend* and *brother* tended to go together; for Dutch people as well
for the Mahicans and Iroquois they described, "friends" were almost always
also one's kin, literally or symbolically. In seventeenth-century Dutch culture,
vriendschap thus evoked anything but a casual relationship; it embodied,

according to historian Jaap Jacobs, the kind of "solidarity and support within the family network . . . considered vital for survival."[17]

Yet, at the same time authors depicted Indians who reckoned the Dutch indispensable "friends" and "brothers," they also constructed an image of Indians who considered their European neighbors to be "scoundrels." "One of the councilors came to ask me what we were doing in his country and what we brought him for gifts," van den Bogaert recalled of his sojourn with the Oneida Iroquois. "I said that we brought him nothing, but that we just came for a visit. However, he said that we were worth nothing because we brought him no gifts. Then he told how the French had traded with them here with six men and have given them good gifts. . . . And this councilor derided us as scoundrels, and said that we were worthless because we gave them so little for their furs." Two days later, said van den Bogaert, "an Indian once again called us scoundrels . . . and he was very malicious so that Willem Tomassen became so angry that the tears ran from his eyes."[18] To call someone a "scoundrel"—*schlem*—was a high insult to personal honor in seventeenth-century Dutch culture; as court records indicate, it was literally a fighting word.[19] Still worse, the Mohawk term that comes down to us in English as *scoundrel* evidently was *seronquatse,* which linguist Gunther Michaelson glosses as "a really evil person."[20] In light of both extremely negative connotations, it should not be surprising that—as in the case of Tomassen—fear and anger sometimes entered the equation.[21]

There were many variations on scoundrelity, yet in order to understand them we need first to discuss the third Indian image of the Dutch that appears in these documents. "They call us *Assirioni,* that is, cloth-makers, or *Charistooni,* that is, iron-workers, because our people first brought cloth and iron among them," noted Megapolensis.[22] (While "cloth-maker" no doubt was a name used by Indians, the Mohawk word *assirioni* actually means "axe-maker," and is still used as a name for Europeans by Iroquois people today.)[23] According to van den Bogaert, firearms joined cloth, iron, and axes in the inventory of material items Indians supposedly associated with the Dutch. "We took our leave amid much uproar that surged behind and before us," he wrote. "They repeatedly shouted: 'ALLESE RONDADE,' i.e., 'Shoot!'"[24]

Whether hard goods or soft goods were emphasized, commodities and commerce appear at the core of the perceived relationship between Indians and Dutch. Van den Bogaert certainly conveyed this message; indeed, the main reasons Indians seem to have called his party "scoundrels" was because they didn't bring sufficient trade goods with them and because their compatriots at Fort Orange were insufficiently generous in the prices they paid for beaver pelts. By the same token, when van den Bogaert's Indians welcomed the Dutch as "friends" and "brothers," there was an assumption that trade was what it was all about. Everywhere the travelers went, people showed up with goods to trade or with gifts of the items Indians believed the Dutch most craved, particularly beaver skins.[25] Megapolensis provides a particularly revealing image of Indians who thought the Dutch were scoundrels only interested in trade. "One of their chiefs," he said, "came to me and presented me with a beaver, an otter, and some cloth he had stolen from the French, which I must accept as a token of good fellowship."[26] How better to win friends and influence scoundrels than to give them what they want?

Megapolensis told his readers about the metal-maker image, though, as a mere aside—by way of explanation that Mohawks used a very different word to describe the Dutch than the Dutch used for themselves. *Christians* was the word Europeans of this period most often used as a self-descriptor. Yet, he complained,

> When we pray they laugh at us. Some of them despise it entirely; and some, when we tell them what we do when we pray, stand astonished. When we deliver a sermon, sometimes ten or twelve of them, more or less, will attend, each having a long tobacco pipe, made by himself, in his mouth, and will stand awhile and look, and afterwards ask me what I am doing and what I want, that I stand there alone and make so many words, while none of the rest may speak. I tell them that I am admonishing the Christians, that they must not steal, nor commit lewdness, nor get drunk, nor commit murder, and that they too ought not to do these things; and that I intend in process of time to preach the same to them and come to them in their own country . . . , when I am acquainted with their language. They say I do well to teach the Christians; but immediately add, *Diatennon jawy Assirioni, hagiouisk*, that is, "Why do so many Christians do these things?"[27]

Similarly, van der Donck noted that the Indians

> appreciate hearing about God and our religion, and during our services and prayers they keep very quiet and seem to pay attention, but in reality they have no notion of these matters. . . . When one berates them, individually or generally, for some wicked act or speech on the

ground that it incurs the wrath of God in heaven, they reply, we do not know that God or where he is and have never seen him; if you know and fear him, as you say you do, how come there are so many whores, thieves, drunkards, and other evil doers among you; surely that God of yours will punish you severely, since He warned you of it. He never warned us, and left us in ignorance, therefore we do not deserve such punishment.[28]

These descriptions of Indian images of the Dutch as false Christians amounted to a variation on the theme of the Dutch as scoundrels. Other themes stressed by van der Donck, Megapolensis, and Danckaerts similarly reinforced an impression that Indians thought the metal-makers were "really bad people," even if they were also friends and brothers. The Dutch were, for example, unbearably rude in a variety of ways. According to Danckaerts, the Indians

are not backbiters, and it is a slander to accuse them of it. For when they are sometimes asked, when they come out of the woods, "How fares this or that one of your neighbors?" they say, "I just saw him in the woods and he is still in good health." If they are questioned further, "But weren't you in his house and don't you know what its condition is?" then they would probably respond, "Phew, what kind of talk is that?" "Isn't the man free in his own house?" "Isn't he capable of taking care of his own things?" "Are we supposed to concern ourselves with it?" "Everyone has enough to do with his own things." "No, that would be very bad, so we don't do it, etc."[29]

In a similar vein, Danckaerts said that "the Indians hate the precipitancy of comprehension and judgment, the excited chattering, often without knowing what is being said, the haste and rashness to do something, whereby a mess is often made of one's good intentions" among the Dutch.[30]

Van der Donck, meanwhile, had his Indians view the Dutch as not only as gossipy chatterboxes but sexual hypocrites:

When all is well and they are unattached, . . . [Indians] make light of their virtue, both men and women being extremely liberal and un-inhibited in their relations. But foul and improper language, which many of our people think amusing, they despise. Kissing, romping, pushing, and similar playful frolicking, popularly known as petting, and other suggestive behavior one is unlikely to see among these people. They speak scornfully of it when done in their presence. And if they see Hollanders behaving in that fashion they tell them sarcastically: "Shame on you; if you are so inclined, wait till nighttime or you are alone." Could anything be funnier? Yet at the right time they will decline no proposition, and almost all of them are available and ready to carry on with abandon.[31]

When the Dutch were not playing too hard, in hypocritical ways, they worked too hard. Indians, said van der Donck, "raise so much corn and beans that we purchase these from them in fully loaded yachts and sloops. They know nothing of manuring, fallow seasons, and proper tillage. The labor they devote to farming is all manual, using small adzes that are sold to them for the purpose. Not much more is to be said of their husbandry; yet they regard their methods as better than ours which, in their view, involve far too much bother, care, and effort than is to their liking."[32] Moreover, the Dutch were, according to van der Donck's Indians, status-mad. "Social differences among the Indians are not nearly as great and obvious as among us," he concluded. "They say frankly they are unable to understand why one person is so much higher-placed than another, as they are in our estimation."[33]

Capping these pictures of Dutch scoundrels was, according to Megapolensis, a reputation for avarice. Indian "money consists of certain little bones, made of shells or cockles, which are found on the sea-beach . . . ," he explained. This wampum "they value . . . as highly as many Christians do gold, silver, and pearls; but they do not like our money, and esteem it no better than iron. I once showed one of their chiefs a rix-dollar; he asked how much it was worth among the Christians; and when I told him, he laughed exceedingly at us, saying we were fools to value a piece of iron so highly; and if he had such money, he would throw it into the river."[34] In this context, it is significant that, according to a word list attached to van den Bogaert's journal, the Mohawk term that comes down to us in English as "to trade," *cadadiiene*, means "I am storing it for myself."[35]

Images of metal-making scoundrel friends sometimes went so far as to suggest that Indians thought the differences between them and the Dutch were so great that Europeans perhaps were not people at all—or at least not quite the same sort of people as they. Both Megapolensis and van der Donck portrayed Indians who believed Europeans were the product of a creation separate from themselves. "They think that there are more worlds than one, and that we came from another world," explained Megapolensis.[36] "When we relate the creation of Adam . . . ," echoed van der Donck, "they cannot or will not understand it in regard to their own nation or the Negroes, on account of the difference in skin color."[37]

*　　*　　*

In their efforts to depict Indian depictions of cultural difference, these Dutch writers adopted a familiar form of European discourse usually described as the "noble savage" motif. They used imaginary Indians (or in these cases imagined versions of real Native people) as foils to expose all the vices of European "civilization." Most often associated with eighteenth-century French *philosophes*, the noble savage theme has been traced backward in Western culture as far as Tacitus and forward at least to the film *Dances with Wolves*.[38] The always-and-everywhere quality of this European (or perhaps human) tendency to use cultural Others as mirrors of the Self certainly makes the noble savage trope a problematic explanatory concept for historians. Perhaps, as theorist Hayden White has famously pointed out, it may even be "one of the few historical topics about which there is nothing more to say."[39] Still, its very omnipresence—and its obvious use by Dutch writers considered here— remains to be accounted for. There was something compelling in the literary device of constructing noble savages to explore cultural difference, and to find ways of criticizing one's own society—a process that Sayre has labeled "negation and substitution." The mirrored Other that authors constructed as the negation of the civilized Christian European was, paradoxically, "not necessarily less civilized than the European, for the negation of negative qualities creates a favorable image."[40] So noble savages became critics of the ignoble civilized—the scoundrel Christians.

The Indians who called Dutch people hypocritical Christians fell particularly into this rhetorical tradition. So too did Indians who scorned Dutch insensitivity, talkativeness, sexual hypocrisy, and cupidity. Indeed, Megapolensis, van der Donck, and Danckaerts placed their descriptions of Indian critiques of the Dutch as hypocritical Christians in a context of making the same critiques in their own European voices.[41] "The inhabitants of this country are of two kinds: first, Christians—at least so called; second, Indians," scoffed Megapolensis.[42] "What shall I call them," Danckaerts similarly asked, "not to give them the name of Christians, or if I do, it is only to distinguish them from the others?"[43] As van der Donck bluntly put it, religion had little to do with his usage of the term *Christian*. Most colonists employed it merely "to set themselves apart" from the "foreign nations" they gave "the name of Turks or Mamelukes or Barbarians."[44]

*   *   *

Dutch constructions of Indian constructions of the Dutch reflected European literary conventions and European cultural preoccupations. That does not necessarily mean, however, that they were merely products of Dutch imaginations. As historian Anthony Grafton explains, an author "who sets out to describe another culture embarks on a task as difficult and elusive as it is fascinating. The would-be ethnographer must make a whole series of strategic and tactical decisions: he or she must adopt an attitude toward both the society to be described and the informants who describe it, select a limited number of topics to cover . . . , and choose a literary form to convey the results to a public. In each of these decisions, models matter. Few writers weave whole new tapestries of their own; rather, they make quilts from ready-made ingredients."[45]

Models *do* matter, then, and they seem profoundly to have shaped Dutch images of Indian images of the Dutch. But in their use of noble savage models, these authors were trying to interpret what they actually saw and heard from Mahicans, Mohawks, and Oneidas. Questions of the meaning of intercultural commerce with "metal makers"; of the nature of interpersonal and intercultural relations with those who might be "brothers," or "scoundrels," or both; and of how to make sense of cultural difference when dealing with people who "came from another world" were very pressing—and no doubt weighed heavily on the minds of flesh-and-blood Indians as well as on those of Dutch writers. In observing the intercultural process of constructing identity, we can catch a glimpse of each side as it tried to make sense of the other and of the seventeenth-century North American world they were rebuilding together.

===

"That Europe Be not Proud, nor America Discouraged": Native People and the Enduring Politics of Trade

Like the writings of Harmen Meyndersz van den Bogaert or John Smith, the works of Roger Williams, the founder of Rhode Island, constructed complicated images of Native people. And like those of the others, his images conveyed real, if convoluted, insights. "O the infinite wisedome of the most holy wise *God*, who hath so advanced *Europe* above *America*, that there is not a sorry *Howe, Hatchet, Knife,* nor a rag of cloth in all *America,* but what comes over the dreadfull *Atlantick* Ocean from *Europe,*" Williams wrote in *A Key into the Language of America* (1643). "And yet that *Europe* be not proud, nor *America* discouraged," one need only ask, "What treasures are hid in some parts of *America,* and in our *New English* parts, how have foule hands (in smoakie houses) the first handling of those Furres which are after worne upon the hands of Queens and heads of Princes?"[1] We might well wonder whether divine wisdom had anything to do with it or just which of the trading partners' hands were more foul, but there is no questioning Williams's central point about how early, and how deeply, eastern North American Native people engaged in the world of Atlantic commerce. Opechancanough of Tsenacomoco, no less than van den Bogaert of New Netherland, understood that well.

And so, for historians, Native American involvement with what Timothy Breen calls (in a very different context) "an empire of goods" is a familiar story.[2] It has been difficult, however, to find ways to make Native Americans rather than Europeans central actors in that drama or to tell it as anything other than a relentless progression toward economic dependence, imperial subjection, and cultural decline. The fate of Powhatan's Tsenacomoco chiefdom seems to follow that narrative arc. Yet closer attention to the continued evolving roles of material goods in the political economies of eastern Native North America suggests a different—although not necessarily prettier—plot line. For many generations, for better or worse, imported goods continued to function within Native communities more as flexible sources of power than as markers of creeping dependence on the imperial juggernaut of the Atlantic economy.

* * *

Historian James Axtell, in an essay on "The First Consumer Revolution" (1992), emphasized that Native peoples were participants in a global economy and careful purchasers of not just any hoes, hatchets, knives, and rags but of

Assemblage of Susquehannock Trade Goods, Courtesy of the State Museum of Pennsylvania, Pennsylvania Historical and Museum Commission. Clockwise from the left are a rum bottle, beads, a spoon, a snuffbox, glass beads and a Swedish ceramic bowl, brass kettles, a flintlock musket mechanism, a metal harpoon, a cut Delft ceramic disk, brass arrowheads, iron axe heads, a jaw harp, and tobacco pipes.

tools, weapons, and duffle cloth specifically tailored to their tastes. Earlier, Francis Jennings, in *The Invasion of America* (1975), rightly stressed Native peoples' active roles as producers in a global "extractive industry." Supply as well as demand, then, made Indian people actors in the Atlantic economy. Still, for Axtell, Jennings, and those who followed in their footsteps, Indian agency almost disappeared in a broader tale of Native subordination within a European-dominated global economy. "Most Indians in colonial America . . . were . . . dragged into dependence and debt," Axtell concluded. Similarly, Jennings declared, "Although the trade was as eagerly sought by Indians as by Europeans . . . in the long run it helped to make Europeans dominant and Indians dependent."[3]

"In the long run," the trajectory that Axtell and Jennings traced is correct; the Atlantic world of commerce surely contains what Richard White memorably calls *The Roots of Dependency*.[4] Exchanges that began with the swapping of a few rare glass beads or bits of metal for beaver skins that were nearly as rare to the Europeans who received them seemingly inevitably evolved first into a trade for raw materials such as metal and cloth to be reworked into new forms, then into a commerce in goods that were substituted wholesale for traditional items—copper kettles for earthenware pots, iron axes for stone choppers, firearms for bows and arrows—then ultimately into Axtell's consumer revolution.[5] Everywhere in eastern North America, Native people came rapidly to rely on transatlantic commerce for weapons, ammunition, textiles, tools, household utensils, jewelry, tobacco, liquor—almost everything except the basics of food and shelter, and even the production of those necessities now required the use of imported tools.[6] A dismal tale of indebtedness, cultural decay, and economic dependence seems unavoidable. For Native people of eastern North America, the Atlantic world of goods would appear to be "dreadfull" indeed.

"In the long run." In the shorter run, Roger Williams reminds us, the picture was much more complicated. Far from sliding rapidly into oppressed dependency, at least the Narragansetts that Williams knew best were actually "very desirous to come into debt"—because, he said, they were so adept at avoiding their creditors. "Some are ingenuous, plaine hearted and honest," he admitted, "but the most never pay unless a man follow them to their severall abodes, townes and houses, as I my selfe have been forc'd to doe."[7] And, far from being pitiable junkies addicted to whatever goods were on offer, Williams's Indians were "marvailous subtle in their Bargaines to save a penny: And very suspitious that *English* men labour to deceive them: Therefore they will beate all markets and try all places and runne twenty thirty, yea, forty mile, and more, and lodge in the Woods, to save six pence."[8]

As archaeologist Patricia Rubertone warns us, Williams's comments about Native people (like those of his Dutch contemporaries) need to be taken with more than a grain of salt.[9] Still, Williams's stylized generalizations about Indians as active, savvy consumers demand our attention. It is worth listening to him one last time before leaving behind the book he hoped might "unlocke some *Rarities* concerning the *Natives* themselves, not yet discovered."[10] In exchange for wampum beads, Williams wrote, "the *Indians* bring downe all their sorts of Furs, which they take in the Countrey, both to the *Indians* and to the *English*." Wampum also was something "the *English, French* and *Dutch*, trade to the *Indians*, six hundred miles in severall parts (North and South from *New-England*) for their Furres and whatsoever they stand in need of from them: as Corne, Venison, etc."[11] Among the et ceteras that moved in these intertwined Native and European trading networks were, Williams says elsewhere, "great [tobacco] *pipes*, both of *wood* and *stone* . . . two foot long, with men or beasts carved so big or massie, that a man may be hurt mortally by one of them." These came from the Haudenosaunee Iroquois country, "three or foure hundred miles from" Rhode Island.[12]

What Williams struggled to describe in these passages was a triangular trade that historian Neal Salisbury calls a major "source of peace and stability in southern New England" during the generation after the Pequot War of 1637–1638. "Exchanges of furs, wampum, and European goods . . . linked English traders to the Mohawks via the Indians of Narragansett Bay and the Connecticut Valley." Stretching over vast distances that Williams could only estimate as hundreds of miles, and encompassing connections among "*Indians*" of whose differences in language and nation Williams was only dimly aware, this triangular trade was where the world of Atlantic commerce intersected with the world of Native American exchange like the overlapping space of a Venn diagram.[13]

That, at least in spatial terms, such a Venn diagram existed—that trade networks controlled by Natives intersected with Atlantic trade routes—is not surprising. That European goods spread into the continental interior far in advance of European traders, that Native groups acted as "middlemen" brokering trade between Albany or Charlestown and the Great Lakes or the Mississippi Valley, that ancient North American trade routes were reconfigured to carry new traffic, and that Europeans and colonists who traveled those routes, dealt with those "middlemen," and catered to those customers had to adapt to North American customs of gift-giving, reciprocity, and ceremonial exchange—all these ideas have become historiographical commonplaces.[14] As Salisbury sums it up, "For varying periods of time after their arrival in North America, Europeans adapted to the social and political environments they found, including the fluctuating ties of reciprocity and interdependence, as well as rivalry, that characterized those environments." Yet if Salisbury were to attempt to draw a Venn diagram, it might be one in which Atlantic trade did not so much intersect Native trade as absorb it like some vast hungry Pac-Man. When Europeans "insert[ed] themselves in new networks of exchange and alliance" they "permanently altered the primary patterns of exchange in eastern North America." Systems that, for centuries before European contact, had "channeled exchange in the interior of the continent gave way to one in which growing quantities of goods arrived from, and were directed to, coastal peripheries and ultimately Europe."[15]

"In the long run." But even in the shorter run, current scholarship makes it difficult to conceive of a Venn diagram with chronological and cultural, rather than merely spatial, dimensions—a zone of overlap where the new Atlantic trading genuinely intersected an older, and ongoing, North American pattern of exchange. To understand the nature of the conceptual problem— why the two circles in the Venn diagram seem incapable of sustained coexistence—we need only briefly summarize the argument of an essay that has, justifiably, shaped most scholars' understanding of what happened when the two circles first met.

In a 1987 *Journal of American History* article, Christopher Miller and George Hamell offered "A New Perspective on Indian-White Contact." On the basis of archaeological evidence and oral traditions, they concluded that, before the arrival of Europeans, long-distance exchange in eastern North America concentrated on small quantities of rare items that came from mysterious sources underground or under the water. Shell, crystal, copper, and other minerals "believed to be 'other-worldly' in origin . . . were obtained by real human man-beings through reciprocal exchanges with extremely powerful Other World Grandfathers, man-beings of horned or antlered serpent, panther, and dragon forms." Not surprisingly, then, the European goods that Native Americans initially found most valuable shared similar characteristics with these prestige goods. The glass beads and other "trinkets," "toys," and "trash" that figure so prominently in early European accounts experienced what Miller and Hamell memorably called "transubstantiation . . . into Native American artifacts" and became "ceremonial objects possessing great ideological and symbolic meaning." When such goods ceased to be rare, however—when beads arrived by the bushel instead of the handful and when Native people learned to pursue a good bargain in the ways Williams described—the "ideological world" of early trade "was shattered." This "process of disenchantment . . . pushed intercultural exchange out of the symbolic ceremonial realm and into the realm of the white marketplace." Once historians imagine how "magical crystals turn[ed] into cheap glass beads," it becomes hard to imagine that any semblance of the pre-contact Native American long-distance exchange culture could survive assault by the Atlantic world of goods.[16]

*   *   *

Yet much of that pre-contact world *did* survive, and much longer than the literature focused on disenchantment or dependency would imply. It should be noted, for example, that the specific items Williams identified in the New England triangular trade—wampum and ceremonial pipes—had powerful cultural meanings to Native people, meanings that had far more in common with "magical crystals" than with "cheap glass beads." And, significantly, both were artifacts of Native rather than European manufacture. The fact they were now made with European metal tools may have only increased their symbolic value as expressions of Native identity and power over the Atlantic world from which the tools, but not the products, came. Moreover, similar cultural work continued to be accomplished by goods of strictly European origin as well. Specific European trade items acquired new meanings even as the older ones in which those meanings were rooted seemed to disappear.[17]

Copper kettles, for instance, entered eastern Native exchange networks in much the same way as glass beads. Valued for their similarity to rare native copper and for the cultural associations of their reddish color, copper kettles were almost never used *as* kettles in the sixteenth and early seventeenth centuries but instead as raw material for all manner of Native-made objects such as gorgets, amulets, and beads that fit seamlessly into ancient patterns.[18] Yet, as scholar Laurier Turgeon argues, when Atlantic trade brought vastly increased supplies of copper, nothing so simple occurred as a process of reverse transubstantiation of sacred metal into cheap kitchenware. Instead, well into the 1670s, copper kettles took on new cultural significance, not as mere cooking and storage vessels but as treasured items "hoarded inside the house, where they enhanced the decor" and "were taken off display only for special feasts" emphasizing communal and spiritual unity. Kettles assumed particular importance in mortuary rituals, as grave goods sent with the deceased into the next world. More significant—and more lasting than the literal interment of kettles as grave goods, which seems to have declined before the end of the seventeenth century—were the metaphoric uses of kettles that came to permeate eastern Native American discursive worlds. People spoke of hanging the kettle to welcome guests, of the kettle from which allies all ate with one spoon, of the war kettle hung over the fire as a symbol of unity against one's enemies. "The copper kettle became the rallying point for individuals and groups, because its force of attraction was stronger than that of any other known object," Turgeon concludes. "Around the kettle people gathered for festivals of life and of death; around the kettle they reflected on the community and on what they wanted it to become; around it, too, they rekindled such hopes."[19]

An emphasis on such acts of what Turgeon calls cultural "appropriation" as opposed to "acculturation" not only restores agency to Indian engagement with the Atlantic world of goods but also opens windows on realms of behavior that a focus on Atlantic markets, supply, demand, disenchantment, and dependence obscures. "In the final analysis," Turgeon concludes, "the function of the kettle seems to have been more political than eschatological."[20] (The euphony of the phrase outweighs its literal inaccuracy, in that end times were not really part of the spiritual picture Miller and Hamell evoked.) If we shift perspective to examine how the cultural symbolism associated with items such as copper kettles and glass beads reflects the political systems in which those goods were embedded, we might find additional ways way to trace the persistence, and continued evolution, of Native exchange patterns even as the Atlantic economy would appear to be achieving supremacy. It may well be in the political, rather than what western Europeans would call the economic, realm that Native people "appropriated" rather than became acculturated to the Atlantic world of goods and the Venn circles of North American and Atlantic exchange found an enduring zone of intersection and power.

An attempt to draw this kind of Venn diagram requires attention to the political economy of the eastern Native American societies that, lacking a more technical anthropological vocabulary, Roger Williams called "Monarchicall" and that anthropologists would call chiefdoms.[21] As Karen Kupperman argues, when early European travelers and colonists used that word to describe Indian polities, they knew what they were talking about. "In

England," she observes, "aristocrats and monarchs, knowing that government rested more on honor and credit than on law or force, took care to surround themselves with visual emblems of magnificence . . . , presenting their persons in ways that affirmed their place atop the hierarchy." Such modes of presentation "were designed to convey ideas that mortal minds could not grasp directly; their desired effect was to evoke in the affirming audience a sense of wonder or awe." Nearly everywhere they looked, English travelers described Native leadership in ways that "echoed the language of English aristocratic self-presentation," convinced as they were that "Indians exhibited the same natural courtesy, virtue, and care for their reputations that characterized England's nobility."[22]

Unlike Powhatans or many communities of what colonizers called southern New England, most Iroquoian- and Algonquian-speaking peoples of the northern continental interior were not technically chiefdoms. But, with their local community populations in the hundreds or thousands, with their at least seasonally permanent agricultural villages, with their redistributive economic systems, and with their clear patterns of hereditary ritually charged office-holding, they shared many of the defining characteristics of that political form. Among those were the setting apart of exalted figures whom Haudenosaunee Mohawks called *rotiyanehr*, a term that combines the concepts of "great" or "honored one" with "one who keeps the peace"; using a different orthography, the Jesuit author Joseph-François Lafitau further distinguished "*Roiander Gôa*, meaning 'noble par excellence,' from *gaïander*, the usual [Mohawk] word meaning nobility."[23] In the Southeast, terms like *mico* and "beloved man" carried similar valences, while, everywhere, chiefs displayed their lofty status by wearing rare, spiritually charged goods such as copper or shell on their bodies and living in communal houses that were larger, if not always more elaborate, then those of ordinary folk.[24]

*   *   *

Not least among the common themes across these varied political orders was the symbolic importance of material goods to systems of power. Chiefs displayed their power through artifacts acquired through exchanges with other chiefs, with shamans, or even with spirit-beings. The potency of these things came not so much from their rarity as from their association with distant sources of power. Their significance was, as Turgeon might put it, "more political and eschatological." It was the connection to the power of "Other

World Grandfathers" that crystals represented, more than their inherent material qualities, that made them so valued. Similarly, everywhere, as in turn-of-the-seventeenth-century Tsenacomoco, it was the alliance with—indeed the power over—Europeans that appropriated glass beads, copper kettles, and similar items represented that made these goods so important to Native people. An Algonquin chief in the St. Lawrence Valley expressed the concept perfectly in 1636, when he told a council of Hurons "that his body was hatchets" and "that the preservation of his person and of his Nation was the preservation of the hatchets, the kettles, and all the trade of the French, for the Hurons." This relationship based on the control of goods, the chief proclaimed, made him "master of the French."[25] This is what Turgeon means by "appropriation."

As Powhatan of Tsenacomoco well understood, the political functions of the goods, rather than the goods themselves, were the key. Thus, the symbolism attached to prestige items could take on new meanings and perhaps even lose entirely whatever transubstantiated spiritual qualities they may once have possessed. Similarly, it seems likely that the basic political functions of prestige goods economics could evolve into new forms even as the underlying principle of leaders' ability to mobilize powerful alliances for the benefit of their people endured. Comparative anthropological work on chiefdoms portrays them as inherently unstable political forms, as polities constantly in flux.[26] Precisely this flux is what allows the drawing of a Venn diagram in which Native exchange patterns overlap with the Atlantic economy. Of course chiefdoms reliant on sacralized control of tiny amounts of exotic prestige goods could not long survive the invasion of shiploads of glass beads and copper kettles from the Atlantic world. Indeed, it is far more likely that the particular chiefdoms that Williams observed among the Narragansetts and such neighbors as the Wampanoags were products, rather than survivals, of new patterns of trade providing new goods in unprecedented quantities.[27] And those chiefdoms, too, were not only, like their precedents and parallels elsewhere, prone to inherent flux but also subject to the particular strains of a situation in which chiefs and elite lineages could never hope to control access to and redistribution of a massive influx of goods from Europe.[28] If virtually every man, and perhaps even woman, could trade for beads, hatchets, kettles, and cloth, virtually everyone could claim the powers formerly reserved for chiefs. Clearly, new political forms had to emerge.

Thus, the kinds of hierarchical chiefdoms that existed in the sixteenth century became rare as contact with Europeans accelerated. From the 1630s onward, even the most careful European observers would have seen little evidence of social and economic stratification and hereditary political authority. Powhatan had died in 1618, and the chiefdom over which he had presided was smashed in the wars with Virginia colonists that began in 1622 and resumed in 1644. No Chesapeake Native leader again would ever accurately be described "not onely as a King, but as halfe a God."[29] Much the same fate befell the chiefdoms of southern New England, where epidemics, new patterns of trade, and wars with Native and English colonial foes ensured that, as Salisbury concludes, "in less than a generation, the world into which most surviving Indians had been born, and for which they had been prepared, had vanished."[30] Meantime, epidemics, warfare, population resettlements, and, a generation later, massive slave raiding so transformed the Mississippian-descended chiefdoms of the southeastern interior that, with the famous exception of the Natchez of the lower Mississippi Valley, few traces remained of the kinds of stratification witnessed by Hernando de Soto's *entrada* in the previous century.[31] The transformation seems to be recalled in Cherokee traditions about the violent overthrow of a corrupt, oppressive priestly class known as the *Aní-Kutání* and its replacement by a more egalitarian order.[32]

Few descriptions of early seventeenth-century political leaders could match the trappings attributed to the litter-borne, pearl-garlanded "Lady of Cofitachiqui" who met Soto in 1539 or to Powhatan's ritual storehouse guarded by "foure Images as Sentinels, one of a Dragon, another a Beare, the third like a Leopard, and the fourth like a giantlike man."[33] Nonetheless, even in post-chiefdom polities, there was no doubt about who was a member of the elite. "Although the chiefs have no mark of distinction and superiority so that, except in a few individual cases, they cannot be distinguished from the crowd by the honours due to be paid them, people do not fail to show always a certain respect for them," Lafitau concluded about the Iroquois. "The councils assemble by their orders; they are held in their lodges unless there is a public lodge, like a town hall, reserved only for councils; business is transacted in their names; they preside over all sorts of meetings; they play a considerable role in feasts and community distributions; they are often given presents; and, finally, they have certain other prerogatives resulting from their preeminent status."[34] In some societies, these subtle patterns created a situation in which the clearest marker of social stratification was the *lack* of the forms of ostentatious display that Europeans found familiar. "The chiefs are generally the poorest among them," one seventeenth-century Dutch traveler along the Hudson River reported, "for instead of their receiving anything . . . , these Indian chiefs are made to give to the populace."[35]

For the Iroquoian-speaking peoples of the northeastern interior, the forces undermining chiefly elites everywhere were only just beginning to be felt in 1636, when Jesuit missionary Jean de Brébeuf heard Hurons tell him that "formerly only worthy men were Captains, and so they were called *Enondecha*, the same name by which they call the Country. . . . But today they do not pay so much attention to the selection of their Captains; and so they no longer give them that name, although they still call them *atiwarontas, atiwanens, ondakhienhai*, 'big stones, the elders, the stay-at-homes.'"[36] The mid-century epidemics that would slaughter at least half the Hurons and Iroquois and the wars those epidemics inspired, which would kill or resettle countless thousands of others, had already begun.[37] By the 1690s, when a Mohawk Iroquois spokesman claimed "that we have no forcing rules or laws amongst us," he was not just evoking an already standard trope of cultural difference but describing a reality in which what it meant to be a noble *rotiyanehr* had been profoundly altered.[38]

*   *   *

Still, even as all this was happening, a deep Native political pattern not only persisted but evolved into new forms—forms in which leadership was rooted in, and validated by, the ability to mobilize connections with other peoples and to do so by conspicuous ceremonial redistribution of material goods. More than just words such as *rotiyanehr* and pale reflections of "prerogatives resulting from . . . preeminent status" survived into the eighteenth-century world Lafitau wrote about.[39] Although stratified chiefdoms had virtually ceased to exist in eastern North America, chiefdomship traditions provided an enduring set of political tools for dealing with massive change, for incorporating new peoples into reconfigured communities, for persistence through upheaval. As Rubertone observes, an understanding of the dynamic quality of chiefdoms suggests that, "rather than viewing these 'tribal' groups as remnants of population decline, social turmoil, and economic disruptions which many indeed experienced to varying degrees it might be more useful to consider their emergence as evidence of survival skills that were part of long-standing repertoires of experiences."[40]

This might prove a particularly useful way of looking at things in light of the way studies of prestige-economy chiefdoms emphasize interactions with what Susan Frankenstein and Michael Rowlands call "external systems organ-ised on different economic principles." The same chief whose status "depends on his controlling external exchange of highest status goods . . . in turn acts as a dependant of an external system whose structure may be only vaguely comprehended."[41] In the sixth-century B.C.E. German example on which Frankenstein and Rowlands's sweeping study concentrates, those mysterious differently organized systems were the commercial city-states of the ancient Mediterranean world that provided the prestige goods controlled by central European chiefs. In eastern North America in the thirteenth century C.E., it is likely that emergent chiefdoms on the periphery of Missisippian influences were built on similar control of (or resistance to) prestige goods distributed from differently organized Cahokia, Moundville, and elsewhere.[42]

In the mid-seventeenth century, the "systems organised on different eco-nomic principles" were European empires. If patterns of interaction with such systems had long historical precedents, it is reasonable to assume that they had long historical legacies as well, even as the polities themselves al-tered almost beyond recognition. The dynamic persistence of earlier forms of economic political leadership helps to explain why both the offices and cultural significance of hereditary chiefs also persisted. The perdurability of Haudenosaunee League Chiefs through the years—and the transformations of their roles from the noble *rotiyanehr* described by seventeenth-century missionaries, to the behind-the-scenes cultural integrators of the eighteenth, to the "lords" whose offices were codified in writing at the turn of the twenti-eth, to the political activists many of them became in the twentieth—suggests the flexibility of such traditions.[43]

In a parallel, but very different manner, the ways in which seventeenth- and eighteenth-century New England Algonquian sachems and people ma-nipulated hereditary claims to office to defend their lands and autonomy suggest that we have only begun to understand the importance of chiefdom traditions over time. Chieftainship endured and perhaps even grew in impor-tance, even as chiefdoms themselves disappeared or evolved in ways that little resembled their former selves. Providing a prime example are the southern New England Algonquian chiefdoms that historian David Silverman, follow-ing anthropologist Kathleen Bragdon, calls "sachemships." By the late seven-teenth century, Silverman explains,

The sachemship was at once a territory about the size of an English town and a network of villages encompassing usually no more than five hundred people. The sachem advised by a council of elders and elites was responsible for managing his territory's economic resources hosting prominent visitors, maintaining relations with other communities, caring for the destitute, arbitrating disputes, punishing criminals, and organizing defense. Sachems also collected tribute in food, furs, animal skins, wampum, labor, and military service, but not by and large for strictly personal use. Sachems were hardly better off than most of their followers, as Europeans frequently observed with some puzzlement. Unlike European elites, who could translate accumulated wealth into political power, sachems generated status by applying wealth to public ends, not hoarding it. Poor men could be rich men in a society that paid its leader with deference.[44]

That deference stemmed from patterns of mobilizing connections inside and outside the sachemship, as embodied in the redistribution of material items. Like prestige-good chiefs of an earlier era, late seventeenth-century New England sachems were conduits for the flow of goods and power.

Similar patterns can be seen across the map and across the centuries. Eighteenth- and nineteenth-century Native leaders wore gorgets, peace medals, military jackets, and other tokens of their ability to forge connections with Euro-American governments and bend them to their will. These were direct cultural descendants of prestige goods and perhaps no less (or no more) imbued with spiritual significance than the native copper or crystal ornaments that chiefs had worn hundreds of years earlier.[45] Such practices embedded themselves in the elaborate cultural forms of intercultural treaty diplomacy that flourished in eighteenth-century eastern North America. From Michilimackinac to Montreal, Albany to Philadelphia, Williamsburg to Charleston, hundreds of Native people regularly gathered for ceremonial reenactments of their alliances with provincial governors and royal officials. Gifts of wampum changed hands as speakers for each side rehearsed the history of their relationship and struggled to reconcile controversies. Feasts were shared, and the power that came from strong alliances was made visible to all in the distribution of wagon-loads of kettles, blankets, weapons, liquor, and countless other products of the Atlantic economy.[46] "The giving and receiving of such gifts involved far more than simply a disguised exchange of material goods . . . ," legal historian Robert Williams reminds us. "Reciprocal gift giving established solidarity with others by opening the channels of communication and connection that made relationships strong and reliable."[47]

＊　＊　＊

A spokesman for the Haudenosaunee Iroquois said this to New York lieutenant governor George Clarke during a contentious Albany treaty council in
June 1737:

> In Antient times when our forefathers first met at this place we will
> tell you what then happned; before there was a house in this place,
> when we lodged under the Leaves of the Trees the Christians and
> We Entered into a Covenant of friendship, and the Indians loved the
> Christians on Account the[y] sold them the goods Cheap. [T]his Gov-
> ernment was likened unto a Great Ship which was moared behind a
> great Yper [elm] Tree but because the Tree was perishable the Anchor
> was lifted up and laid behind the Great hill at Onondage and the Six
> Nations are to take Care of that Anchor: that it be not Removed by
> any Enemy.[48]

This speech, one of many recounting the history of the Covenant Chain alliance between the Haudenosaunee and New York, can be read in at least
two ways. From the perspective of the Atlantic economy, it is all about an
arrangement that kept "the goods Cheap." But, from the perspective of North
America—and of the throng of Native people who heard the words in the
public treaty session—note who the active partners in the relationship were
and what they did. The Iroquois seized the initiative when they "entered into
a Covenant of friendship" and assumed responsibility for hauling the metaphorical anchor of the ship that brought trade goods to their capital at Onondaga, where they took "Care of that Anchor: that it be not Removed."

This was language that the chiefs who knew Roger Williams would have
recognized: Native leaders established the alliance, controlled the relationship, and brought the material benefits to their people. These were not their
grandfathers' prestige goods, and the leaders who received and redistributed
them were not, by the eighteenth century, men who presided over polities
that anthropologists would any longer recognize as chiefdoms. But the political and cultural functions they carried out were as deeply rooted in the Native
North American past as they were in the Atlantic world present. The treaty
ground occupied a space in the Venn diagram where the political economy
of Native American exchange intersected creatively with the consumer economy of the Atlantic world.

For historians to emphasize only that sunny creativity, however—or to tell, as the Haudenosaunee orator did in 1737, a peaceful tale of a covenant of friendship based on trade—is to ignore the darker side of the connection between trade and power. "The trade and the peace we take to be one thing," another eighteenth-century Haudenosaunee orator once said.[49] But the importance of trade also led to violent competition for access to furs, goods, and markets. Those, too, were inseparable from power and indeed crucial for avoiding the kind of dependence and decline so often stressed in historical accounts. Combined with other consequences of the European invasion—devastating imported diseases, massive population declines, political upheaval—this darker side of the relationship between trade and power produced bloody warfare on a scale the North American continent had probably never before seen, especially after imported European weapons entered the mix. Looking back on their seventeenth-century past, Haudenosaunee Iroquois people, like most others in Native eastern North America, knew these facts only too well. In the long run, such a revised story of Native involvement in the Atlantic economy becomes no happier than the former tale of dependence and cultural decline. But it does become one in which Indian people are central actors rather than peripheral victims.

CHAPTER 4

War and Culture:

The Iroquois Experience

"The character of all these [Iroquois] Nations is warlike and cruel," wrote Jesuit missionary Paul Le Jeune in 1657. "The chief virtue of these poor Pagans being cruelty, just as mildness is that of Christians, they teach it to their children from their very cradles, and accustom them to the most atrocious carnage and the most barbarous spectacles."[1] Like most Europeans of his day, Le Jeune ignored his own countrymen's capacity for bloodlust and attributed the supposedly unique bellicosity of the Iroquois to their irreligion and uncivilized condition. Still, his observations contain a kernel of truth often overlooked by our more sympathetic eyes: in ways quite unfamiliar and largely unfathomable to Europeans, warfare was vitally important in the cultures of the seventeenth-century Iroquois and their neighbors. For generations of Euro-Americans, the significance that Indians attached to warfare seemed to substantiate images of bloodthirsty savages who waged war for mere sport. Only in recent decades have ethnohistorians discarded such shibboleths and begun to study Indian wars in the same economic and diplomatic frameworks long used by students of European conflicts. Almost necessarily, given the weight of past prejudice, their work has stressed similarities between Indian and European warfare.[2] Thus neither commonplace stereotypes nor scholarly efforts to combat them have left much room for serious consideration of the possibility that the non-state societies of aboriginal North America may have waged war for different—but no less rational and no more savage—purposes than did the nation-states of Europe.[3] This chapter explores that possibility through an analysis of the changing role of warfare in Iroquois culture during the first century after European contact.

The Iroquois Confederacy (composed, from west to east, of the Five Nations of the Senecas, Cayugas, Onondagas, Oneidas, and Mohawks) frequently went

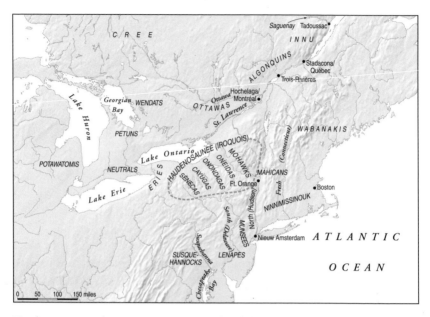

Northeastern North America, c. 1650. Map by Philip Schwartzberg.

to war for reasons rooted as much in internal social demands as in external disputes with their neighbors. The same observation could be made about countless European states, but the particular internal motives that often propelled the Iroquois and other northeastern Indians to make war have few parallels in Euro-American experience. In many Indian cultures a pattern known as the "mourning-war" was one means of restoring lost population, ensuring social continuity, and dealing with death.[4] A grasp of the changing role of this pattern in Iroquois culture is essential if the seventeenth- and early eighteenth-century campaigns of the Five Nations—and a vital aspect of the contact situation—are to be understood. "War is a necessary exercise for the Iroquois," explained missionary and ethnologist Joseph-François Lafitau, "for, besides the usual motives which people have in declaring it against troublesome neighbours . . . , it is indispensable to them also because of one of their fundamental laws of being."[5]

*   *   *

Euro-Americans often noted that martial skills were highly valued in Indian societies and that, for young men, exploits on the warpath were important determinants of personal prestige. This was, some hyperbolized, particularly true of the Iroquois. "It is not for the Sake of Tribute . . . , that they make War," Cadwallader Colden observed of the Five Nations, "but from the Notions of Glory, which they have ever most strongly imprinted on their Minds."[6] Participation in a war party was a benchmark episode in an Iroquois youth's development, and later success in battle increased the young man's stature in his clan and village. His prospects for an advantageous marriage, his chances for recognition as a village leader, and his hopes for eventual selection to a sachemship depended largely—though by no means entirely—on his skill on the warpath, his munificence in giving war feasts, and his ability to attract followers when organizing a raid.[7] Missionary-explorer Louis Hennepin exaggerated when he claimed that "those amongst the Iroquoise who are not given to War, are had in great Contempt, and pass for Lazy and Effeminate People," but warriors did in fact reap great social rewards.[8]

The plaudits offered to successful warriors suggest a deep cultural significance; societies usually reward warlike behavior not for its own sake but for the useful functions it performs.[9] Among the functions postulated in studies of non-state warfare is the maintenance of stable population levels. Usually this involves—in more or less obvious ways—a check on excessive population growth, but in some instances warfare can be, for the victors, a means to increase the group's numbers.[10] The traditional wars of the Five Nations served the latter purpose. The Iroquois conceptualized the process of population maintenance in terms of individual and collective spiritual power. When a person died, the power of his or her lineage, clan, and nation was diminished in proportion to his or her individual spiritual strength.[11] To replenish the depleted power the Iroquois conducted "requickening" ceremonies at which the deceased's name—and with it the social role and duties it represented—was transferred to a successor. Vacant positions in Iroquois families and villages were thus both literally and symbolically filled, and the continuity of Iroquois society was confirmed, while survivors were assured that the social role and spiritual strength embodied in the departed's name had not been lost.[12] Warfare was crucial to these customs, for when the deceased was a person of ordinary status and little authority the beneficiary of the requickening was often a war captive, who would be adopted "to help strengthen the familye in lew of their deceased Freind."[13] "A father who has lost his son adopts a young prisoner in his place," explained an eighteenth-century commentator on Indian customs. "An orphan takes a father or mother; a widow a husband; one man takes a sister and another a brother."[14]

On a societal level, then, warfare helped the Iroquois to deal with deaths in their ranks. On a personal, emotional level it performed similar functions. The Iroquois believed that the grief inspired by a relative's death could, if uncontrolled, plunge survivors into depths of despair that robbed them of their reason and disposed them to fits of rage potentially harmful to themselves and the community. Accordingly, Iroquois culture directed mourners' emotions into ritualized channels. Members of the deceased's household, "after having the hair cut, smearing the face with earth or charcoal and gotten themselves up in the most frightful negligence," embarked on ten days of "deep mourning," during which "they remain at the back of their bunk, their face against the ground or turned towards the back of the platform, their head enveloped in their blanket which is the dirtiest and least clean rag that they have. They do not look at or speak to anyone except through necessity and in a low voice. They hold themselves excused from every duty of civility and courtesy."[15] For the next year the survivors engaged in less intense formalized grieving, beginning to resume their daily habits but continuing to disregard their personal appearance and many social amenities. While mourners thus channeled their emotions, others hastened to "cover up" the grief of the bereaved with condolence rituals, feasts, and presents (including the special variety of condolence gift often somewhat misleadingly described as *wergild*). These were designed to cleanse sorrowing hearts and to ease the return to normal life. Social and personal needs converged at the culmination of these ceremonies, the "requickening" of the deceased.[16]

But if the mourners' grief remained unassuaged, the ultimate socially sanctioned channel for their violent impulses was a raid to seek captives who, it was hoped, would ease their pain. The target of the mourning-war was usually a people traditionally defined as enemies; neither they nor anyone else need necessarily be held directly responsible for the death that provoked the attack, though most often the foe could be made to bear the blame.[17] Raids for captives could be either large-scale efforts organized on village, nation, or confederacy levels or, more often, attacks by small parties raised at the behest of female kin of the deceased. Members of the dead person's household—presumably lost in grief—did not usually participate directly. Instead, young men who were related by marriage to the bereaved women but who lived in other longhouses were obliged to form a raiding party or face the matrons' accusations of cowardice.[18] When the warriors returned with captured men, women, and children, mourners could select a prisoner for adoption in the

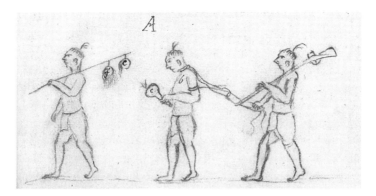

French copy of Iroquois pictograph, c. 1666. Colonies, C11A2, folio 263,
Archives nationales d'Outre-Mer, Aix-en-Provence, France. Iroquois
warriors bearing firearms return home with scalps and a bound captive.

place of the deceased or they could vent their rage in rituals of torture and
execution.[19]

The rituals began with the return of the war party, which had sent word
ahead of the number of captives seized. Most of the villagers, holding clubs,
sticks, and other weapons, stood in two rows outside the village entrance
to meet the prisoners. Men—but usually not women or young children—
received heavy blows designed to inflict pain without serious injury. Then they
were stripped and led to a raised platform in an open space inside the village,
where old women led the community in further physical abuse, tearing out
fingernails and poking sensitive body parts with sticks and firebrands.[20] After
several hours, prisoners were allowed to rest and eat, and later they were made
to dance for their captors while their fate was decided. Headmen apportioned
them to grieving families, whose matrons then chose either to adopt or to execute them.[21] If those who were adopted made a sincere effort to please their
new relatives and to assimilate into village society, they could expect a long
life; if they displeased, they were quietly and unceremoniously killed.

A captive slated for ritual execution was usually also adopted and subsequently addressed appropriately as "uncle" or "nephew," but his status was
marked by a distinctive red and black pattern of facial paint. During the next
few days the doomed man gave his death feast, where his executioners saluted him and allowed him to recite his war honors. On the appointed day
he was tied with a short rope to a stake, and villagers of both sexes and all
ages took turns wielding firebrands and various red-hot objects to burn him

systematically from the feet up. The tormentors behaved with religious solemnity and spoke in symbolic language of "caressing" their adopted relative with their firebrands. The victim was expected to endure his sufferings stoically and even to encourage his torturers, but this seems to have been ideal rather than typical behavior. If he too quickly began to swoon, his ordeal briefly ceased and he received food and drink and time to recover somewhat before the burning resumed. At length, before he expired, someone scalped him, another threw hot sand on his exposed skull, and finally a warrior dispatched him with a knife to the chest or a hatchet to the neck. Then the victim's flesh was stripped from his bones and thrown into cooking kettles, and the whole village feasted on his remains. This feast carried great religious significance for the Iroquois, but its full meaning is irretrievable; most European observers were too shocked to probe its implications.[22]

Mourners were not the only ones to benefit from the ceremonial torture and execution of captives. While grieving relatives vented their emotions, all of the villagers, by partaking in the humiliation of every prisoner and the torture of some, were able to participate directly in the defeat of their foes. Warfare thus dramatically promoted group cohesion and demonstrated to the Iroquois their superiority over their enemies. At the same time, youths learned valuable lessons in the behavior expected of warriors and in the way to die bravely should they ever be captured. Le Jeune's "barbarous spectacles" were a vital element in the ceremonial life of Iroquois communities.[23]

The social demands of the mourning-war shaped strategy and tactics in at least two ways. First, the essential measure of a war party's success was its ability to seize prisoners and bring them home alive. Capturing of enemies was preferred to killing them on the spot and taking their scalps, while none of the benefits European combatants derived from war—territorial expansion, economic gain, plunder of the defeated—outranked the seizure of prisoners.[24] When missionary Jerome Lalemant disparaged Iroquoian warfare as "consisting of a few broken heads along the highways, or of some captives brought into the country to be burned and eaten there," he was more accurate than he knew.[25] The overriding importance of captive-taking set Iroquois warfare dramatically apart from the Euro-American military experience. "We are not like you CHRISTIANS for when you have taken Prisoners of one another you send them home, by such means you can never rout one another," explained the Onondaga orator Teganissorens to Governor Robert Hunter of New York in 1711.[26]

The centrality of captives to the business of war was clear in precombat rituals: imagery centered on a boiling war kettle; the war feast presaged the future cannibalistic rite; mourning women urged warriors to bring them prisoners to assuage their grief; and if more than one village participated in the campaign, leaders agreed in advance on the share of captives that each town would receive.[27] As Iroquois warriors saw it, to forget the importance of captive-taking or to ignore the rituals associated with it was to invite defeat. In 1642 missionary Isaac Jogues observed a ceremony he believed to be a sacrifice to Areskoui, the deity who presided over Iroquois wars. "At a solemn feast which they had made of two Bears, which they had offered to their demon, they had used this form of words: 'Aireskoi, thou dost right to punish us, and to give us no more captives' (they were speaking of the Algonquins, of whom that year they had not taken one . . .) 'because we have sinned by not eating the bodies of those whom thou last gavest us; but we promise thee to eat the first ones whom thou shalt give us, as we now do with these two Bears.'"[28]

A second tactical reflection of the social functions of warfare was a strong sanction against the loss of Iroquois lives in battle. A war party that, by European standards, seemed on the brink of triumph could be expected to retreat sorrowfully homeward if it suffered a few fatalities. For the Indians, such a campaign was no victory; casualties would subvert the purpose of warfare as a means of restocking the population.[29] In contrast to European beliefs that to perish in combat was acceptable and even honorable, Iroquois beliefs made death in battle a frightful prospect, though one that must be faced bravely if necessary. Slain warriors, like all who died violent deaths, were said to be excluded from the villages of the dead, doomed to spend a roving eternity seeking vengeance. As a result, their bodies were not interred in village cemeteries, lest their angry souls disturb the repose of others. Both in burial and in the afterlife, a warrior who fell in combat faced separation from his family and friends.[30]

Efforts to minimize fatalities accordingly underlay several tactics that contemporary Euro-Americans considered cowardly: fondness for ambushes and surprise attacks, unwillingness to fight when outnumbered, and avoidance of frontal assaults on fortified places. Defensive tactics showed a similar emphasis on precluding loss of life. Spies in enemy villages and an extensive network of scouts warned of invading war parties before they could harm Iroquois villagers. If intruders did enter Iroquoia, defenders attacked from ambush, but only if they felt confident of repulsing the enemy without too many losses of their own. The people retreated behind palisades or, if the enemy appeared too strong to resist, burned their own villages and fled—warriors

included—into the woods or to neighboring villages. Houses and corn supplies thus might temporarily be lost, but unless the invaders achieved complete surprise, the lives and spiritual power of the people remained intact. In
general, when the Iroquois were at a disadvantage, they preferred flight or
an insincerely negotiated truce to the costly last stands that earned glory for
European warriors.[31]

That kind of glory, and the warlike way of life it reflected, were not Iroquois ideals. Warfare was a specific response to the death of specific individuals at specific times, a sporadic affair characterized by seizing from traditional
enemies a few captives who would replace the dead, literally or symbolically,
and ease the pain of those who mourned. While war was not to be undertaken gladly or lightly, it was still "a necessary exercise for the Iroquois," for it
was an integral part of individual and social mourning practices.[32] When the
Iroquois envisioned a day of no more wars, with their Great League of Peace
extended to all peoples, they also envisioned an alternative to the mourning
functions of warfare. That alternative was embodied in the proceedings of
league councils and Iroquois peace negotiations with other peoples, which
began with—and frequently consisted entirely of—condolence ceremonies
and exchanges of presents designed to dry the tears, unstop the mouths, and
cleanse the hearts of bereaved participants.[33] Only when grief was forgotten
could war end and peace begin. In the century following the arrival of Europeans, grief could seldom be forgotten.

*   *   *

After the 1620s, when the Five Nations first made sustained contact with
Europeans, the role of warfare in Iroquois culture changed dramatically. By
1675, European diseases, firearms, and trade had produced dangerous new
patterns of conflict that threatened to derange the traditional functions of the
mourning-war. Before most Iroquois had ever seen a Dutchman or a French-
man, they had felt the impact of the maladies the invaders inadvertently
brought with them.[34] By the 1640s the number of Iroquois (and of their Indian neighbors) had probably already been halved by epidemics of smallpox,
measles, and other European "childhood diseases," to which Indian populations had no immunity.[35] The devastation continued through the century. A
partial list of plagues that struck the Five Nations includes "a general malady"
among the Mohawks in 1647; "a great mortality" among the Onondagas in
1656–1657; a smallpox epidemic among the Oneidas, Onondagas, Cayugas,

and Senecas in 1661–1663; "a kind of contagion" among the Senecas in 1668; "a fever of . . . malignant character" among the Mohawks in 1673; and "a general Influenza" among the Senecas in 1676.[36] As thousands died, ever-growing numbers of captive adoptees would be necessary if the Iroquois were even to begin to replace their losses; mourning-wars of unprecedented scale loomed ahead. Warfare would cease to be a sporadic and specific response to individual deaths and would become instead a constant and increasingly undifferentiated symptom of societies in demographic crisis.

At the same time, European firearms would make warfare unprecedentedly dangerous for both the Iroquois and their foes, and would undermine traditional Indian sanctions against battle fatalities. The introduction of guns, together with the replacement of flint arrowheads by more efficient iron, copper, and brass ones that could pierce traditional Indian wooden armor, greatly increased the chances of death in combat and led to major changes in Iroquois tactics. In the early seventeenth century Champlain had observed mostly ceremonial and relatively bloodless confrontations between large Indian armies, but with the advent of muskets—which Europeans had designed to be fired in volleys during just such battles—massed confrontations became, from the Indian perspective, suicidal folly. They were quickly abandoned in favor of a redoubled emphasis on small-scale raids and ambushes, in which Indians learned far sooner than Euro- Americans how to aim cumbersome muskets accurately at individual targets.[37] By the early 1640s the Mohawks were honing such skills with approximately three hundred guns acquired from the Dutch of Albany and from English sources. Soon the rest of the Five Nations followed the Mohawk example.[38]

Temporarily, the Iroquois' plentiful supply and skillful use of firearms gave them a considerable advantage over their Indian enemies: during the 1640s and 1650s the less well armed Hurons and the poorly armed Neutrals and Khionontateronons (Petuns or Tobacco Nation) succumbed to Iroquois firepower. That advantage had largely disappeared by the 1660s and 1670s, however, as the Five Nations learned in their battles with such heavily armed foes as the Susquehannocks. Once muskets came into general use in Indian warfare, several drawbacks became apparent: they were more sluggish than arrows to fire and much slower to reload, their noise lessened the capacity for surprise, and reliance on them left Indians dependent on Euro-Americans for ammunition, repairs, and replacements. But there could be no return to the days of bows and arrows and wooden armor. Few Iroquois war parties could now expect to escape mortal casualties.[39]

While European diseases and firearms intensified Indian conflicts and stretched the mourning-war tradition beyond previous limits, a third major aspect of European contact pushed Iroquois warfare in novel directions. Trade with Europeans made economic motives central to American Indian conflicts for the first time. Because iron tools, firearms, and other trade goods so quickly became essential to Indian economies, struggles for those items and for furs to barter for them lay behind numerous seventeenth-century wars. Between 1624 and 1628 the Iroquois gained unimpeded access to European commodities when Mohawk warriors drove the Mahicans to the east of the Hudson River and secured an open route to the Dutch traders of Albany.[40] But obtaining the furs to exchange for the goods of Albany was a problem not so easily solved. By about 1640 the Five Nations perhaps had exhausted the beaver stock of their home hunting territories; more important, they could not find in relatively temperate Iroquoia the thick northern pelts prized by Euro-American traders.[41] A long, far-flung series of "beaver wars" ensued, in which the Five Nations battled the Algonquian nations of the Saint Lawrence River region, the Hurons, the Khionontateronons, the Neutrals, the Eries, and other western and northern peoples in a constant struggle over fur supplies. In those wars the Iroquois more frequently sought dead beavers than live ones: most of their raids were not part of a strategic plan to seize new hunting grounds but piratical attacks on enemy canoes carrying pelts to Montreal and Trois-Rivières.[42]

The beaver wars inexorably embroiled the Iroquois in conflict with the French of Canada. Franco-Iroquois hostilities dated from the era of Champlain, who consistently based his relations with Canada's Natives upon promises to aid them in their traditional raids against the Five Nations. "I came to the conclusion," wrote Champlain in 1619, "that it was very necessary to assist them, both to engage them the more to love us, and also to provide the means of furthering my enterprises and explorations which apparently could only be carried out with their help."[43] The French commander and a few of his men participated in Indian campaigns against the Five Nations in 1609, 1610, and 1615, and encouraged countless other raids.[44] From the 1630s to the 1660s, conflict between the Five Nations and Canadian Indians intensified, and Iroquois war parties armed with guns frequently blockaded the Saint Lawrence and stopped the flow of furs to the French settlements. A state of open war, punctuated by short truces, consequently prevailed between New France and various of the Five Nations, particularly the Mohawks. The battles were almost exclusively economic and geopolitical—the Iroquois were not much interested in French captives—and in general the French suffered more than the Iroquois from the fighting.[45] Finally, in 1666, a French army invaded Iroquoia and burned the Mohawks' fortified villages, from which all had fled to safety except a few old men who chose to stay and die. In 1667, the Five Nations and the French made a peace that lasted for over a decade.[46]

While the fur trade introduced new economic goals, additional foes, and wider scope to Iroquois warfare, it did not crowd out older cultural motives. Instead, the mourning-war tradition, deaths from disease, dependence on firearms, and the trade in furs combined to produce a dangerous spiral: epidemics led to deadlier mourning-wars fought with firearms, the need for guns increased the demand for pelts to trade for them, the quest for furs provoked wars with other nations, and deaths in those conflicts began the mourning-war cycle anew. At each turn, fresh economic and demographic motives fed the spiral.

Accordingly, in the mid-seventeenth-century Iroquois wars, the quest for captives was at least as important as the quest for furs. Even in the archetypal beaver war, the Five Nations-Huron conflict, only an overriding—even desperate—demand for prisoners can explain much of Iroquois behavior. For nearly a decade after the dispersal of the Huron Confederacy in 1649, Iroquois war parties killed or took captive every starving (and certainly peltry-less) group of Huron refugees they could find. Meanwhile, Iroquois ambassadors and warriors alternately negotiated with, cajoled, and threatened the Huron remnants living at Quebec to make them join their captive relatives in Iroquoia. Through all this, Mohawks, Senecas, and Onondagas occasionally shed each other's blood in arguments over the human spoils. Ultimately, in 1657, with French acquiescence, most of the Huron refugees filed away from Quebec—those of the Arendaronon nation to the Onondaga country and of the Attignawantan nation to the Mohawk country.[47]

Judging by the number of prisoners taken during the Five Nations' wars from the 1640s to the 1670s with their other Iroquoian neighbors—the Neutrals, Khionontateronons, Eries, and Susquehannocks—these conflicts stemmed from a similar mingling of captive-taking and fur trade motives. Like the Hurons, each of those peoples shared with the Iroquois mixed horticultural and hunting and fishing economies, related languages, and similar beliefs, making them ideal candidates for adoption. But they could not satisfy the spiraling Iroquois demand for furs and captives; war parties from the Five Nations had to range ever farther in their quest. In a not atypical series of raids in 1661–1662, they struck the Wabenakis of the New England region, the

Algonquians of the subarctic, the Siouans of the Upper Mississippi area, and various Indians near Virginia, while continuing the struggle with enemies closer to home.[48] The results of the mid-century campaigns are recorded in the *Jesuit Relations*, whose pages are filled with descriptions of Iroquois torture and execution of captives and note enormous numbers of adoptions. The Five Nations had absorbed so many prisoners that in 1657 Le Jeune believed that "more Foreigners than natives of the country" resided in Iroquoia.[49] By the mid-1660s several missionaries estimated that two-thirds or more of the people in many Iroquois villages were adoptees.[50]

By 1675 a half-century of constantly escalating warfare had at best enabled the Iroquois to hold their own. Despite the beaver wars, the Five Nations still had few dependable sources of furs. In the early 1670s they hunted primarily on lands north of Lake Ontario, where armed clashes with Algonquian foes were likely, opportunities to steal peltries from them were abundant, and conflict with the French who claimed the territory was always possible.[51] Ironically, even the Franco-Iroquois peace of 1667 proved a mixed blessing for the Five Nations. Under the provisions of the treaty, Jesuit priests, who had hitherto labored in Iroquois villages only sporadically and at the risk of their lives, established missions in each of the Five Nations.[52] The Jesuits not only created Catholic converts but also generated strong Christian and traditionalist factions that brought unprecedented disquiet to Iroquois communities. Among the Onondagas, for example, the Christian sachem Garakontié's refusal to perform his duties in the traditional manner disrupted such important ceremonies as dream guessings, the roll call of the chiefs, and healing rituals.[53] And in 1671, traditionalist Mohawk women excluded at least one Catholic convert from her rightful seat on the council of matrons because of her faith.[54] Moreover, beginning in the late 1660s, missionaries encouraged increasing numbers of Catholic Iroquois—particularly Mohawks and Oneidas—to desert their homes for the mission villages of Canada; by the mid-1670s well over two hundred had departed.[55] A large proportion of those who left, however, were members of the Five Nations in name only. Many—perhaps most—were recently adopted Hurons and other prisoners, an indication that the Iroquois were unable to assimilate effectively the mass of newcomers their mid-century wars had brought them.[56]

Problems in incorporating adoptees reflected a broader dilemma: by the late 1670s the mourning-war complex was crumbling. Warfare was failing to maintain a stable population; despite torrents of prisoners, gains from adoption were exceeded by losses from disease, combat, and migrations to Canada.

Among the Mohawks—for whom more frequent contemporary population estimates exist than for the other nations of the confederacy—the number of warriors declined from 700 or 800 in the 1640s to approximately 300 in the late 1670s. Those figures imply that, even with a constant infusion of captive adoptees, Mohawk population fell by half during that period.[57] The Five Nations as a whole fared only slightly better. In the 1640s the confederacy, already drastically reduced in numbers, had counted over 10,000 people. By the 1670s there were perhaps only 8,600.[58] The mourning-war, then, was not discharging one of its primary functions.

Meanwhile, ancient customs regarding the treatment of prisoners were decaying as rituals degenerated into chaotic violence and sheer murderous rage displaced the orderly adoption of captives that the logic of the mourning-war demanded. In 1682 missionary Jean de Lamberville asserted that Iroquois warriors "killed and ate . . . on the spot" over six hundred enemies in a campaign in the Illinois country; if he was even half right, it is clear that something had gone horribly wrong in the practice of the mourning-war. The decay of important customs associated with traditional warfare is further indicated by Lamberville's account of the return of that war party with its surviving prisoners. A gauntlet ceremony at the main Onondaga village turned into a deadly attack, forcing headmen to struggle to protect the lives of the captives. A few hours later, drunken young men, "who observe[d] no usages or customs," broke into longhouses and tried to kill the prisoners whom the headmen had rescued. In vain, leaders pleaded with their people to remember "that it was contrary to custom to ill-treat prisoners on their arrival, when They had not yet been given in the place of any person . . . and when their fate had been left Undecided by the victors."[59]

Nevertheless, despite the weakening of traditional restraints, in the 1670s Iroquois warfare still performed useful functions. It maintained a tenuous supply of furs to trade for essential European goods, it provided frequent campaigns to allow young men to show their valor, and it secured numerous captives to participate in the continual mourning rituals that the many Iroquois deaths demanded (though there could never be enough to restock the population absolutely). In the quarter-century after 1675, however, the scales would tip: by 1700 the Anglo-French struggle for control of the continent would make warfare as the Five Nations were practicing it dangerously dysfunctional for their societies.

*   *   *

During the mid-1670s the Five Nations' relations with their Indian and European neighbors were shifting. In 1675 the Mohawks and the Mahicans made peace under pressure from Albany and ended—except for a few subsequent skirmishes—over a decade of conflict that had cost each side heavily.[60] In the same year the long and destructive war of the Oneidas, Onondagas, Cayugas, and Senecas against the Susquehannocks concluded as the latter withdrew from Pennsylvania to Maryland. The end of hostilities with the Mahicans and Susquehannocks allowed the Iroquois to refocus westward their quest for furs and captives. In the late 1670s and early 1680s conflicts with the Illinois, Miamis, and other western peoples intensified, while relations with the Wyandots (composed of remnants of the Hurons and other Iroquoian groups forced to the west in earlier wars with the Five Nations) and with various elements of the Ottawas alternated between skirmishes and efforts to cement military alliances against other enemies of the Iroquois.[61]

As the Onondaga orator Otreouti (whom the French called *La Grande Gueule*, "Big Mouth") explained in 1684, the Five Nations "fell upon the Illinese and the Oumamies [Miami], because they cut down the trees of Peace that serv'd for limits or boundaries to our Frontiers. They came to hunt Beavers upon our Lands; and contrary to the custom of all the Savages, have carried off whole Stocks, both Male and Female."[62] Whether those hunting grounds actually belonged to the Five Nations is questionable, but the importance of furs as an Iroquois war aim is not. And captives were also a lucrative prize, as the arrival in 1682 of several hundred Illinois prisoners demonstrated.[63] But this last of the beaver wars—which would melt into the American phase of the War of the League of Augsburg (King William's War)—was to differ devastatingly from earlier Iroquois conflicts. At the same time that the Five Nations began their fresh series of western campaigns, the English and French empires were also beginning to compete seriously for the furs and lands of that region. The Iroquois would inevitably be caught in the Europeans' conflicts.[64]

Until the mid-1670s the Five Nations had only to deal, for all practical purposes, with the imperial policies of one European power, France. The vital Iroquois connection with the Dutch of New Netherland and, after the 1664 conquest of that colony, with the English of New York had rested almost solely on trade. But when the English took possession of the province for the second time in 1674, the new governor, Sir Edmund Andros, had more grandiose designs for the Iroquois in the British American empire. He saw the Five Nations as the linchpin in his plans to pacify the other Indian neighbors

of the English colonies, he hoped to make the Five Nations a tool in his dealings with the Calverts of Maryland, and he sought an opportunity to annex
land to New York from Connecticut by encouraging the Iroquois to fight
alongside New England in its 1675–1676 war on the Wampanoag Metacom
("King Philip") and his allies.[65] After Andros, New York–Iroquois relations
would never be the same, as successors in the governor's chair attempted to
use the Five Nations for imperial purposes. Thomas Dongan, who assumed
the governorship in 1683, tried to strengthen New York's tenuous claims to
suzerainty over the Five Nations—in 1684 he ceremoniously distributed the
duke of York's coat of arms to be hung in their villages—and he directly challenged French claims in the west by sending trading parties into the region.[66]

Meanwhile, the French had begun their own new westward thrust. In
1676 Canadian governor Louis de Buade de Frontenac established a post at
Niagara, and a few years later René-Robert Cavelier de La Salle began to construct a series of forts in the Illinois country. The French had long trodden a
fine line in western policy. On the one hand, Iroquois raids in the west could
not be allowed to destroy Indian allies of New France or to disrupt the fur
trade, but, on the other hand, some hostility between the Iroquois and the
western Indians helped prevent the latter from taking their furs to Albany
markets. In the late 1670s and the 1680s Frontenac, and especially the governors during the interval between his two tenures, Joseph-Antoine Le Febvre
de La Barre and Jacques-René de Brisay de Denonville, watched that policy
unravel as they noted with alarm New York trading expeditions in the west,
Iroquois raids on Indian hunters and *coureurs de bois*, Iroquois negotiations
with the Wyandots and Ottawas, and the continual flow of firearms from
Albany to the Five Nations.[67] As Iroquois spokesmen concisely explained to
Dongan in 1684, "The French will have all the Bevers, and are angry with us
for bringing any to you."[68]

French officials, faced with the potential ruin of their western fur trade,
determined to humble the Five Nations. For over a decade, Canadian armies
repeatedly invaded Iroquoia to burn villages, fields, and corn supplies. Although the first French attempt, led by La Barre against the Senecas in 1684,
ended in ignoble failure for the French and diplomatic triumph for the Iroquois, later invasions sent the Five Nations to the brink of disaster. In 1687
La Barre's successor, Denonville, marched against Iroquoia with an army of
over 2,000 French regulars, Canadian militia, and Indian warriors. Near Fort
Frontenac his troops kidnapped an Iroquois peace delegation and captured
the residents of two small villages of Iroquois who had lived on the north

shore of Lake Ontario for nearly two decades. Denonville sent over thirty of the prisoners to France as slaves for the royal galleys, and then proceeded toward the Seneca country. After a brief but costly skirmish with Seneca defenders who hid in ambush, the invaders destroyed what was left of the Seneca villages, most of which the inhabitants had burned before fleeing to safety. Six years later, after war had been declared between France and England, the Canadians struck again. In January 1693, 625 regulars, militia, and Indians surprised the four Mohawk villages, captured their residents, and burned longhouses and stores of food as they retreated. Then, in 1696, the aged Frontenac—again governor and now carried into the field on a chair by his retainers—led at least 2,000 men to Onondaga, which he found destroyed by the retreating villagers. While his troops razed the ripening Onondaga corn, he received a plea for negotiation from the nearby Oneida village. The governor dispatched Philippe de Rigaud de Vaudreuil and a detachment of 600 men, who extracted from the few Oneidas who remained at home a promise that their people would soon move to a Canadian mission. Vaudreuil burned the village anyway.[69]

The repeated French invasions of Iroquoia took few lives directly—only in the campaign against the Mohawks in 1693 did the invaders attack fully occupied villages—but their cumulative effect was severe. One village or nation left homeless and deprived of food supplies could not depend on aid from the others, who faced similar plights. And as the Five Nations struggled to avoid starvation and to rebuild their villages, frequent raids by the Indian allies of the French levied a heavy toll in lives. In December 1691 a Mohawk-Oneida war party sustained fifteen deaths in an encounter on Lake George—losses significant beyond their numbers because they included all of the two nations' war chiefs and contributed to a total of 90 Mohawks and Oneida warriors killed since 1689. The Mohawks, who in the late 1670s had fielded approximately 300 warriors, in 1691 could muster only 130.[70] Combat fatalities, the continued exodus of Catholic converts to Canada, and the invasion of 1693 had, lamented a Mohawk orator, left his nation "a mean poor people," who had "lost all by the Enemy."[71] Fighting in the early 1690s had considerably weakened the three western Iroquois nations as well. In February 1692, for example, 50 Iroquois encountered a much larger French and Indian force above Montreal, and 40 suffered death or capture; a month later, 200 met disaster farther up the Saint Lawrence, when many were "captured, killed and defeated with loss of their principal chiefs."[72] Through the mid-1690s sporadic raids in and around Iroquoia by Canada's Indian allies kept the Five Nations on the defensive.[73]

The Five Nations did not meekly succumb. In 1687, soon after Denonville's capture of the Iroquois settled near Fort Frontenac and his invasion of the Seneca country, a Mohawk orator declared to Governor Dongan his people's intention to strike back at the French in the tradition of the mourning-war. "The Governor of Canada," he proclaimed, "has started an unjust war against all the [Five] nations. The Maquase [Mohawks] doe not yet have any prisoners, but that Governor has taken a hundred prisoners from all the nations to the West. . . . Therefore the nations have desired to revenge the unjust attacks."[74] Iroquois raids for captives kept New France in an uproar through the early 1690s.[75] The warriors' greatest successes occurred during the summer of 1689. That June a Mohawk orator, speaking for all Five Nations, vowed "that the Place where the French Stole their Indians two years ago should soon be cut off (meaning Fort Frontenac) for to steal people in a time of Peace is an Inconsiderate work."[76] Within two months the Iroquois had forced the temporary abandonment of Frontenac and other French western posts, and, in an assault at Lachine on Montreal Island, had killed twenty-four French and taken seventy to ninety prisoners.[77]

Later in the 1690s, however, as the Five Nations' losses mounted, their capacity to resist steadily diminished. They repeatedly sought military support from governors of New York, but little was forthcoming. "Since you are a Great People and we but a small, you will protect us from the French," an Iroquois orator told Dongan in 1684. "We have put all our Lands and ourselves, under the Protection of the Great Duke of york."[78] Yet as long as the crowns of England and France remained at peace, the duke's governors largely ignored their end of the bargain. England's subsequent declaration of war against France coincided with the Glorious Revolution of 1688, which unleashed in New York the period of political chaos known as Leisler's Rebellion. In 1689 Mohawks visiting Albany witnessed firsthand the turmoil between Leislerians and anti-Leislerians, and soon the Iroquois observed the resulting English military impotence. In February 1690, a few miles from the easternmost Mohawk village, a party of French and their Indian allies destroyed the sleeping town of Schenectady, whose Leislerian inhabitants had ignored warnings from anti-Leislerian authorities at Albany to be on guard.[79] Soon after the attack, the Mohawk headmen visited Albany to perform a condolence ceremony for their neighbors' losses at Schenectady. When they finished, they urged prompt New York action against the French. But neither then nor during the rest of the war did the Iroquois receive a satisfactory response. New York's offensive war consisted of two ill-fated and poorly supported invasions of Canada: the first, in 1690, was a dismal failure, and the second, in 1691, cost nearly as many English casualties as it inflicted on the enemy.[80] After 1691 New York factional strife, lack of aid from England, and the preoccupation of other colonies with their own defense prevented further commitments of English manpower to support the Iroquois struggle with the French. The Five Nations received arms and ammunition from Albany—never as much or as cheap as they desired—and little else.[81]

What to the Five Nations must have seemed the most typical of English responses to their plight followed the French invasion of the Mohawk country in 1693. Though local officials at Albany and Schenectady learned in advance of the Canadian army's approach and provided for their own defense, they neglected to inform the Mohawks. In the wake of the attack, as approximately 300 Mohawk prisoners trooped toward Canada, Peter Schuyler assembled at Schenectady a force of 250 New Yorkers and some Mohawks who had escaped capture, but he was restrained from immediate pursuit by his vacillating commander, Richard Ingoldsby. At length Schuyler moved on his own initiative and, reinforced by war parties from the western Iroquois nations, overtook the French army and inflicted enough damage to force the release of most of the captive Mohawks. Meanwhile, when word of the invasion reached Manhattan, Governor Benjamin Fletcher mustered 150 militia and sailed to Albany in the unprecedented time of less than three days; nevertheless, the fighting was already over. At a conference with Iroquois headmen a few days later, Fletcher's rush upriver earned him the title by which he would henceforth be known to the Five Nations: *Cayenquiragoe*, or "Great Swift Arrow." Fletcher took the name—chosen when the Iroquois learned that the word *fletcher* meant arrow-maker—as a supreme compliment. But, in view of the Mohawks' recent experience with the English—receiving no warning of the impending invasion, having to cool their heels at Schenectady while the enemy got away and Schuyler waited for marching orders, and listening to Fletcher rebuke them for their lax scouting and defense—the governor's political opponent Peter De La Noy may have been right to claim that Cayenquiragoe was a "sarcasticall pun" on Fletcher's name, bestowed for a showy effort that yielded no practical results.[82]

Yet if the English had been unable—or, as the Iroquois undoubtedly saw it, unwilling—to give meaningful military aid to the Five Nations, they were able to keep the Indians from negotiating a separate peace with the French that might leave New York exposed alone to attack. Although after 1688 ambassadors from several Iroquois nations periodically treated with the Canadians,

New Yorkers maintained enough influence with factions among the Five Nations to sabotage all negotiations.[83] New York authorities repeatedly reminded their friends among the Iroquois of past French treacheries. At Albany in 1692, for example, Commander-in-Chief Ingoldsby warned the ambassadors of the Five Nations "that the Enemy has not forgot their old tricks." The French hoped "to lull the Brethren asleep and to ruine and distroy them at once, when they have peace in their mouths they have warr in their hearts."[84] Many Iroquois heeded the message. Lamberville complained in 1694 that "the english of those quarters have so intrigued that they have ruined all the hopes for peace that we had entertained."[85] The repeated failure of negotiations reinforced Canadian mistrust of the Iroquois and led French authorities to prosecute the war with more vigor. By the mid-1690s, with talks stymied, all the Five Nations could do was to accept English arms and ammunition and continue minor raids on their enemies while awaiting a general peace.[86]

For the Iroquois that peace did not come with the Treaty of Ryswick in 1697. At Ryswick, the European powers settled none of the issues that had provoked the conflict, yet they gained a respite that allowed each side to regroup. Paradoxically, however, a truce between the empires precluded an end to conflict between the French and the Five Nations; jurisdiction over the Iroquois and their territory was one of the sticking points left unsettled. Accordingly, Frontenac and his successor, Louis-Hector de Callière, refused to consider the Iroquois—whom they called unruly French subjects—to be included in the treaty with England and insisted that they make a separate peace with New France. Fletcher and his successor, Richard Coote, earl of Bellomont, argued equally strenuously that the Iroquois were comprehended in the treaty as English subjects. Thus they tried to forbid direct Franco-Iroquois negotiations and continued to pressure their friends among the Five Nations to prevent serious talks from occurring.[87] While Iroquois leaders struggled to escape the diplomatic bind, the Indian allies of New France continued their war against their ancient Iroquois enemies. In the late 1690s the Ojibwas led a major western Indian offensive that, according to Ojibwa tradition, killed enormous numbers of Senecas and other Iroquois. Euro-American sources document more moderate, yet still devastating, fatalities: the Onondagas lost over ninety men within a year of the signing of the Treaty of Ryswick, and the Senecas perhaps as many. Such defeats continued into 1700, when the Senecas suffered over fifty deaths in battles with the Ottawas and Illinois. All along at Albany, authorities counseled the Five Nations not to strike back, but to allow Bellomont time to negotiate with Callière on their behalf.[88]

*   *   *

By 1700 Iroquois warfare and culture had reached a turning point. Up to about 1675, despite the impact of disease, firearms, and the fur trade, warfare still performed functions that outweighed its costs. But thereafter the Anglo-French struggle for control of North America made war disastrous for the Five Nations. Conflict in the west, instead of securing fur supplies, was cutting them off, while lack of pelts to trade and wartime shortages of goods at Albany created serious economic hardship in Iroquoia.[89] Those problems paled, however, in comparison with the physical toll. All of the Iroquois nations except the Cayugas had seen their villages and crops destroyed by invading armies, and all five nations were greatly weakened by loss of members to captivity, to death in combat, or to famine and disease. By some estimates, between 1689 and 1698 the Iroquois lost half of their fighting strength. That figure is probably an exaggeration, but by 1700 perhaps 500 of the 2,000 warriors the Five Nations fielded in 1689 had been killed or captured or had deserted to the French missions and had not been replaced by younger warriors. A loss of well over 1,600 from a total population of approximately 8,600 seems a conservative estimate.[90]

At the turn of the century, therefore, the mourning-war was no longer even symbolically restocking the population. And, far from being socially integrative, the Five Nations' current war was splitting their communities asunder. The heavy death toll of previous decades had robbed them of many respected headmen and clan matrons to whom the people had looked for guidance and arbitration of disputes. As a group of young Mohawk warriors lamented in 1691 when they came to parley with the Catholic Iroquois settled near Montreal, "all those . . . who had sense are dead."[91] The power vacuum, war weariness, and the pressures of the imperial struggle combined to place at each other's throats those who believed that the Iroquois' best chance lay in a separate peace with the French and those who continued to rely on the English alliance. "The [Five] Nations are full of faction, the French having got a great interest among them," reported the Albany Commissioners for Indian Affairs in July 1700. At the town of Onondaga, where, according to Governor Bellomont, the French had "full as many friends" as the English, the situation was particularly severe. Some sachems found themselves excluded from councils, and factions charged one another with using poison to remove adversaries from the scene. One pro-English Onondaga headman, Aquendero, had to take refuge near Albany, leaving his son near death and supposedly bewitched by opponents.[92] Their politics being ordered by an interlocking structure of lineages, clans, and moieties, the Iroquois found such factions, which cut across kinship lines, difficult if not impossible to handle. In the 1630s the Hurons, whose political structure was similar, never could manage the novel factional alignments that resulted from the introduction of Christianity. That failure perhaps contributed to their demise at the hands of the Five Nations.[93] Now the Iroquois found themselves at a similar pass.

As the new century opened, however, Iroquois headmen were beginning to construct solutions to some of the problems facing their people. From 1699 to 1701 Iroquois ambassadors—in particular the influential Onondaga Teganissorens—threaded the thickets of domestic factionalism and shuttled between their country and the Euro-American colonies to negotiate what one scholar has termed "The Grand Settlement of 1701."[94] On 4 August 1701, at an immense gathering at Montreal, representatives of the Senecas, Cayugas, Onondagas, and Oneidas, also speaking for the Mohawks, met Governor Callière and headmen of the Wyandots, Algonquins, Wabenakis, Nipissings, Ottawas, Ojibwas, Sauks, Fox, Miamis, Potawatomis, and other French allies. The participants ratified arrangements made during the previous year that provided for a general peace, established vague boundaries for western hunting territories (the Iroquois basically consented to remain east of Detroit), and eschewed armed conflict in favor of arbitration by the governor of New France. A few days later, the Iroquois and Callière reached more specific understandings concerning Iroquois access to Detroit and other French western trading posts. Most important from the French standpoint, the Iroquois promised neutrality in future Anglo-French wars.[95]

A delegation of Mohawks arrived late at the Montreal conference; they, along with ambassadors from the western Iroquois, had been at Albany negotiating with Lieutenant Governor John Nanfan, who had replaced the deceased Bellomont. The Five Nations' spokesmen had first assured Nanfan of their fidelity and told him that the simultaneous negotiations at Montreal were of no significance. Then they had agreed equivocally to perpetuate their military alliance with the English, reiterated that trade lay at the heart of Iroquois–New York relations, consented to the passage through Iroquoia of western Indians going to trade at Albany, and granted the English crown a deed to the same western hunting territories assured to the Five Nations in the Montreal treaty. In return, Nanfan promised English defense of Iroquois hunting rights in those lands. Meanwhile, at Philadelphia, yet a third series of negotiations had begun, which, while not usually considered part of the Grand Settlement, reflected the same Iroquois diplomatic thrust; by 1704 those talks would produce an informal trade agreement between the Five Nations and Pennsylvania.[96]

On one level, this series of treaties represented an Iroquois defeat. The Five Nations had lost the war and, in agreeing to peace on terms largely dictated by Callière, had acknowledged their inability to prevail militarily over their French, and especially their Indian, enemies.[97] Nevertheless, the Grand Settlement did secure for the Iroquois five important ends: escape from the devastating warfare of the 1690s, rights to hunting in the west, potentially profitable trade with western Indians passing through Iroquoia to sell furs at Albany, access to markets in New France and Pennsylvania as well as in New York, and the promise of noninvolvement in future imperial wars. The Grand Settlement thus brought to the Five Nations not only peace on their northern and western flanks but also a more stable economy based on guaranteed western hunting territories and access to multiple Euro-American markets. Henceforth, self-destructive warfare need no longer be the only means of ensuring Iroquois economic survival, and neither need inter-Indian beaver wars necessarily entrap the Five Nations in struggles between Euro-Americans.[98] In 1724, nearly a generation after the negotiation of the Grand Settlement, an Iroquois spokesman explained to a delegation from Massachusetts how the treaties, while limiting Iroquois diplomatic and military options, nevertheless proved beneficial. "Tho' the Hatchett lays by our side yet the way is open between this Place and Canada, and trade is free both going and coming," he answered when the New Englanders urged the Iroquois to attack New France. "If a War should break out and we should use the Hatchett that layes by our Side, those Paths which are now open wo[u]ld be stopped, and if we should make war it would not end in a few days as yours doth but it must last till one nation or the other is destroyed as it has been heretofore with us[.] . . . [W]e know what whipping and scourging is from the Governor of Canada."[99]

After the Grand Settlement, then, Iroquois leaders tried to abandon warfare as a means of dealing with the diplomatic problems generated by the Anglo-French imperial rivalry and the economic dilemmas of the fur trade. Through most of the first half of the eighteenth century the headmen pursued a policy of neutrality between the empires with a dexterity that the English almost never, and the French only seldom, comprehended. At the same time the Iroquois began to cement peaceful trading relationships with the western nations. Sporadic fighting continued in the western hunting grounds through the first decade and a half of the eighteenth century, as the parties to the

1701 Montreal treaty sorted out the boundaries of their territories and engaged in reciprocal raids for captives that were provoked by contact between Iroquois and western Indian hunters near French posts. Iroquois headmen quickly took advantage of Canadian arbitration when such quarrels arose, however, and they struggled to restrain young warriors from campaigning in the west.[100] As peace took hold, Alexander Montour, the son of a French man and an Iroquois woman, worked to build for the Iroquois a thriving trade between the western nations and Albany.[101]

The new diplomatic direction was tested between 1702 and 1713, when the imperial conflict resumed in the War of the Spanish Succession (Queen Anne's War). Through crafty Iroquois diplomacy, and thanks to the only half-hearted effort each European side devoted to the western theater, the Five Nations were able to maintain their neutrality and avoid heavy combat losses. Only between 1709 and 1711 did the imperial struggle again threaten to engulf the Five Nations. In 1709 Vaudreuil, now governor of New France, ordered the murder of Montour to prevent further diversion of French western trade to the Iroquois and the English. As a result, many formerly pro-French Iroquois turned against the Canadians, and most Mohawk and Oneida warriors, with many Onondagas and Cayugas, joined in the plans of Samuel Vetch and Francis Nicholson for an intercolonial invasion of Canada. Only the Senecas, who were most exposed to attack by Indian allies of the French, refused to participate.[102] The army of colonists and Iroquois, however, never set foot in Canada because Whitehall reneged on its promise of a fleet that would simultaneously attack Canada from the east. After the 1709 fiasco, Iroquois-French relations continued to deteriorate. The Senecas determined on war with the French in 1710, when they were attacked by western Indians apparently instigated by the Canadians. Then, in the spring of 1711, a party of French came to the Onondaga town and, spouting threats about the consequences of further Iroquois hostility, attempted to build a blockhouse in the village. When Vetch and Nicholson planned a second assault on Canada in the summer of 1711, large war parties from all Five Nations eagerly enlisted. Once more, however, the seaborne wing of the expedition failed, and the land army returned home without seeing the enemy.[103] The debacles of 1709 and 1711 confirmed the Iroquois in their opinion of English military impotence and contributed to a chill in Anglo-Iroquois relations that lasted for the rest of the decade.[104] Iroquois leaders once again steered a course of neutrality between the empires, and after the peace of Utrecht, trade once again flourished with the western Indians.[105]

In addition to its diplomatic benefits, the Grand Settlement of 1701 provided a partial solution to Iroquois factionalism. Iroquoian non-state political structures could not suppress factional cleavages entirely, and in the years after 1701 differences over relations with the French and the English still divided Iroquois communities, as each European power continued to encourage its friends. Interpreters such as the Canadian Louis-Thomas Chabert de Joncaire and the New Yorker Lawrence Claeson (or Claes) struggled to win the hearts of Iroquois villagers. Each side gave presents to its supporters, and on several occasions English officials interfered with the selection of sachems in order to strengthen pro-English factions. As a result, fratricidal disputes still occasionally threatened to tear villages apart.[106] Still, in general, avoidance of exclusive alliances or major military conflict with either European power allowed Iroquois councils to keep factional strife within bounds. A new generation of headmen learned to maintain a rough equilibrium between pro-French and pro-English factions at home, as well as peaceful relations with French and English abroad. Central to that strategy was an intricate policy that tried to balance French against English fortified trading posts, Canadian against New York blacksmiths, and Jesuit against Anglican missionaries. Each supplied the Iroquois with coveted aspects of Euro-American culture—trade goods, technology, and spiritual power, respectively—but each also could be a focus of factional leadership and a tool of Euro-American domination. The Grand Settlement provided a way to lessen, though hardly eliminate, those dangers.[107]

The Iroquois balancing act was severely tested beginning in 1719, when Joncaire persuaded pro-French elements of the Senecas to let him build a French trading house at Niagara. Neither confederacy leaders nor Senecas opposed to the French encroachment attempted to dislodge the intruders forcibly, as they had done in the previous century at Fort Frontenac. Instead, Iroquois headmen unsuccessfully urged New York authorities to send troops to destroy the post, thus hoping to place the onus on the British while avoiding an open breach between pro-French and pro-English Iroquois. But New York Governor William Burnet had other plans. In 1724 he announced his intention to build an English counterpart to Niagara at Oswego. With the French beginning to fortify Niagara, league headmen reluctantly agreed to the English proposals. In acquiescing to both forts, the Iroquois yielded a measure of sovereignty as Europeans defined the term; yet they dampened internal strife, avoided exclusive dependence on either European power, and maintained both factional and diplomatic balance.[108]

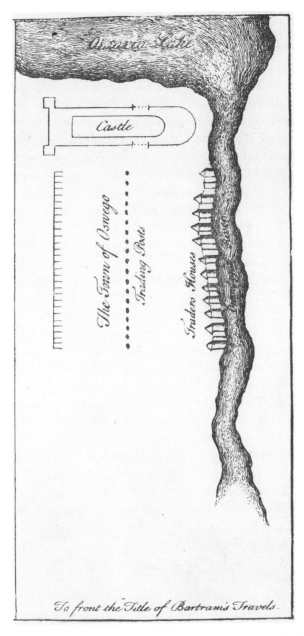

Plan of English Fort Oswego, 1743, John Bartram, *Observations . . . on His Travels from Pensilvania to Onondago, Oswego, and the Lake Ontario . . .* (London, 1751). Rare Book and Manuscript Library, University of Pennsylvania. The layout of Oswego, built in the Onondaga country in 1727, was intended to control the trading environment by confining all transactions to public stalls supervised by the post's military commander.

The years following the Grand Settlement also witnessed the stabiliza-tion of Iroquois population. Though the numbers of the Iroquois continued to decline gradually, the forces that had so dramatically reduced them in the seventeenth century abated markedly after 1701. The first two decades of the seventeenth century brought only one major epidemic—smallpox in 1716—while the flow of Catholic converts to Canadian missions also slowed.[109] The missions near Montreal had lost much of the utopian character that had pre-viously attracted so many Iroquois converts. By the early eighteenth century, drunkenness, crushing debts to traders, and insults from Euro-American neighbors were no less characteristic of Iroquois life in Canada than in Iro-quoia, and most of the Jesuit priests serving the Canadian missions had be-come old, worn-out men who had long since abandoned dreams of turning Indians into Frenchmen.[110]

As the population drain from warfare, disease, and migration to mission villages moderated, peaceful assimilation of refugees from neighboring na-tions helped to replace those Iroquois who were lost. One French source even claimed, in 1716, that "the five Iroquois nations . . . are becoming more and more formidable through their great numbers."[111] Most notable among the newcomers were some 1,500 Tuscaroras who, after their defeat by the English and allied Indians of the Carolinas in 1713, migrated north to settle on lands located between the Onondaga and Oneida villages. They were adopted as the Sixth Nation of the Iroquois Confederacy about 1722. There are indications that the Tuscaroras—who, according to William Andrews, Anglican mission-ary to the Mohawks, possessed "an Implacable hatred against Christians at Carolina"—contributed greatly to the spirit of independence and distrust of Europeans that guided the Six Nations on their middle course between the imperial powers. The Tuscaroras, concluded Andrews, were "a great Occa-sion of Our Indians becoming so bad as they are, they now take all Occasions to find fault and quarrel, wanting to revolt."[112]

*   *   *

The first two decades of the eighteenth century brought a shift away from those aspects of Iroquois warfare that had been most socially disruptive. As the Iroquois freed themselves of many, though by no means all, of the de-mographic, economic, and diplomatic pressures that had made seventeenth-century warfare so devastating, the mourning-war began to resume some of its traditional functions in Iroquois culture. As the Five Nations made peace with their old western and northern foes, Iroquois mourning-war raids came to focus on enemies the Iroquois called "Flatheads"—a vague epithet for the Catawbas and other tribes on the frontiers of Virginia and the Carolinas.[113] Iroquois and "Flathead" war parties had traded blows during the 1670s and 1680s, conflict had resumed about 1707, and after the arrival of the Tuscaroras in the 1710s Iroquois raiding parties attacked the "Flatheads" regularly and almost exclusively.[114] The Catawbas and other southeastern Indians sided with the Carolinians in the Tuscarora War of 1711–1713, bringing them into further conflict with warriors from the Five Nations, who fought alongside the Tuscaroras.[115] After the Tuscaroras moved north, Iroquois-"Flathead" warfare increased in intensity and lasted—despite several peace treaties—until the era of the American Revolution. This series of mourning-wars exasperated English officials from New York to the Carolinas, who could conceive no rational explanation for the conflicts except the intrigues of French envoys who delighted in stirring up trouble on English frontiers.[116]

Canadian authorities did indeed encourage Iroquois warriors with arms and presents. The French were happy for the chance to harass British settlements and to strike blows against Indians who troubled French inhabitants of New Orleans and the Mississippi Valley.[117] Yet the impetus for raiding the "Flatheads" lay with the Iroquois, not the French. At Onondaga in 1710, when emissaries from New York blamed French influence for the campaigns and presented a wampum belt calling for a halt to hostilities, a Seneca orator dismissed their arguments: "When I think of the Brave Warriours that hav[e] been slain by the Flatheads I can Govern my self no longer. . . . I reject your Belt for the Hatred I bear to the Flatheads can never be forgotten."[118] The "Flatheads" were an ideal target for the mourning-wars demanded by Iroquois women and warriors, for with conflict channeled southward, warfare with northern and western nations that, in the past, had brought disaster could be avoided. In addition, war with the Flatheads placated both Canadian authorities and pro-French Iroquois factions, since the raids countered a pro-English trade policy with a military policy useful to the French. And, from the perspective of Iroquois-English relations, the southern campaigns posed few risks. New York officials alternately forbade and countenanced raids against southern Indians as the fortunes of frontier war in the Carolinas and the intrigues of intercolonial politics shifted. But even when the governors of the Carolinas, Virginia, Pennsylvania, and New York did agree on schemes to impose peace, experience with English military impotence had taught the Iroquois that the governors could do little to stop the conflict.[119]

While the diplomatic advantages were many, perhaps the most important aspect of the Iroquois-Flathead conflicts was the partial return they allowed to the traditional ways of the mourning-war. By the 1720s the Five Nations had not undone the ravages of the preceding century, yet they had largely extricated themselves from the socially disastrous wars of the fur trade and of the European empires. And though prisoners no longer flowed into Iroquois villages in the floods of the seventeenth century, the southern raids provided enough captives for occasional mourning and condolence rituals that dried Iroquois tears and reminded the Five Nations of their superiority over their enemies. In the same letter of 1716 in which missionary Andrews noted the growing independence of the Iroquois since the Tuscarora had settled among them and the southern wars had intensified, he also vividly described the reception recently given to captives of the Onondagas and Oneidas.[120] Iroquois warfare was again binding Iroquois families and villages together.

CHAPTER 5

Dutch Dominos:
The Fall of New Netherland and the
Reshaping of Eastern North America

At the height of the seventeenth-century Iroquois wars, Jesuit missionaries in New France attributed much of the violence to unscrupulous Dutch firearms traders.[1] Yet, despite such firsthand testimony to New Netherland's impact on power relationships in mid-seventeenth-century North America, historians have remained unimpressed with the colony's role. Its most thorough and sympathetic recent scholar admits that "New Netherland was not of prime economic importance," and authors of both newer and older general studies agree; Alan Taylor, for example, calls New Netherland "a relatively minor enterprise in an especially wealthy, ambitious, and far-flung empire." C. R. Boxer's classic *The Dutch Seaborne Empire* devotes only four index entries to the colony and only seventeen to its parent, the Dutch West India Company.[2] That company, another historian writes, was "an enfeebled giant," whose "grandiose illusion of strength" masked the fact that it was the undercapitalized weak sibling of the mighty East India Company. Deeply divided over whether its North American holdings were to be trading outposts or settlement colonies (or if they were worth the trouble at all), the West India Company's board of directors, the Heren XIX (literally the Nineteen Lords), dithered while New Netherland remained underpopulated, underfinanced, and subject to excessive profit-taking by private Amsterdam merchants operating both in- and outside the company's framework. Grand schemes for neo-feudal patroonships never got off the ground, with the exception of Rensselaerswyck on the upper Hudson. Even what should have been New Netherland's greatest strength—its trades in furs and wampum with Native people—collapsed

Arnoldus Montanus, *De Nieuwe en Onbekende Weereld, of Beschrijving van America* (Amsterdam, 1671). Rare Book and Manuscript Library, University of Pennsylvania. The Netherlands receive tribute from the nations of the world.

spectacularly in the last years before the English conquest, to the point that the colony came to export more value in tobacco than in furs.[3]

Such underwhelming performance evaluations might not have been news to the Heren XIX, but they would have surprised almost everyone in eastern North America who did not speak Dutch in the middle years of the seventeenth century. Modern-day criticisms would also have puzzled the courts of England and France, which watched the American activities of their northern European rivals with dismay. To the Iroquois as to Native Americans and Euro-Americans alike from New England through the mid-Atlantic region through the upper Chesapeake, New Netherland appeared to be an economic colossus. Indeed, it *was* a comparative titan in the then-puny emergent Atlantic economy, and the impact of its mere 9,000 colonists on the geopolitical landscape of eastern North America was profound. Perhaps the best measures of New Netherland's significance are the falling dominos set in motion by its erasure from the map after it was conquered by the forces of James, duke of York, in 1664 and, after a brief Dutch reconquest, confirmed to the English in the Treaty of Westminster of 1674. It is not too much to say that the Dutch collapse set in motion processes that greatly shaped—perhaps even caused—the disastrous turn that Iroquois warfare took after 1664, the gradual emergence of the "Middle Ground" in the Great Lakes, the violent outbreak of King Philip's War in New England, and the chaotic eruption of Bacon's Rebellion in Virginia.

∗   ∗   ∗

By 1650, the Dutch West India Company—or, more precisely, merchants and ships' captains in one way or another affiliated with it—had created six Atlantic and continental trades crucial to the intertwined economies of Native and European colonial North America. First was the West African slave trade, poorly developed anywhere north of the Caribbean in this period, but almost entirely carried on by Dutch ships and large enough to make enslaved people approximately 20 percent of the population of New Amsterdam on the eve of the English conquest.[4] More significant economically, but harder to quantify, is the role of the Dutch in the general carrying trade of English colonies in the Caribbean, New England, and the Chesapeake. In colonial ports everywhere, Dutch ships were nearly as likely to be found as English ones, and colonists extended them a hearty welcome. Virginia Governor William Berkeley, for example, was an outspoken supporter of commerce with the Dutch from the time of his arrival in the Chesapeake in the early 1640s through his endorsement of formal "Articles of Amitie and commerce" with New Netherland in 1660. As a result, even when the royalist Berkeley was banished from office during the English Commonwealth period of the 1650s, Batavian ships seem to have hauled at least as much leaf directly from the Chesapeake to Europe as from New Amsterdam—whose tobacco shipments in turn were mostly re-exports from Maryland and Virginia.[5]

From the perspective of the English and French metropoles, the Dutch Atlantic slaving and carrying trades appeared the greatest threat, and as mid-century rulers attempted to impose centralized governmental and economic regulation on far-flung collections of privately founded colonies, the propensity of those colonies to traffic with the Dutch was their main specific target. The Navigation Acts passed by the Commonwealth Parliament in 1651 and the Restoration Parliament in 1660 (both vigorously opposed by Virginia's Berkeley), the Anglo-Dutch wars of 1652–1654, 1664–1667, and 1672–1674; the English conquest of New Netherland during the second of those conflicts in 1664; and the establishment of what became known as the Royal African Company in 1663 were all part of a concerted English campaign to destroy the West India Company and "cripple the carrying and entrepôt trade of the Dutch."[6] So, too, despite France's alliance with the Netherlands in the first two Anglo-Dutch wars, were its crown's assumption of direct government of New France and all other French colonies in 1663, its imposition of regulations similar to the Navigation Acts beginning in the same year, and its chartering of a West India Company in 1664, a Senegal Company in 1673, and a Guinea company in 1685.[7]

Less clearly understood in Whitehall and Versailles than the slaving and carrying trades were four overlapping networks that linked the Atlantic to both Indians and colonists across much of eastern North America. The first (and indeed all the others) involved wampum. In the earliest days of their exploratory commerce on New England coasts, Dutch traders discovered the value that Native people attached to the shell beads that were produced with imported European tools from quahog and whelk shells plentiful along Long Island Sound. By the early 1630s, traders at New Amsterdam and on the Connecticut River were exchanging cloth and metal goods for wampum produced by Native peoples of the Sound, which the Dutch in turn sold to other Native and European customers. After the Pequot War of 1637–1638, in which the Dutch as well as their Pequot trading partners were driven from the Connecticut Valley, the wampum trade became more diffused. By the

1650s, New Netherland purchased most of its wampum from English colonists, who acquired much of it through tribute payments from southern New England Natives; an estimated seven million beads, worth perhaps £5,000 New England currency, entered the regional economy this way between 1634 and 1664. Meanwhile, the Mohawks had established their own source of wampum through indirect trade with the Narragansetts and direct commerce with English traders on the Connecticut. Nonetheless, the basic flows of wampum continued through a network established, and still largely mediated by, New Netherland, where, as in New England, the beads served as the primary medium of exchange in the internal Euro-American economy.[8]

At one end the wampum trade connected both colonists and Native Americans to the Dutch Atlantic. At the other it connected them to two networks that tapped major sources of furs in the continental interior. To the north, on the upper Hudson, Dutch wampum, trade goods, and weapons lured to Fort Orange, Beverwyck, and Rensselaerswyck thousands of pelts hunted and looted from lands that Haudenosaunee Iroquois warriors overran in their mid-century wars, conflicts that in turn severely disrupted the trading networks of the French on the St. Lawrence. French government officials and Jesuit missionaries alike complained in the 1640s that Iroquois people could "obtain all things very cheaply: each of the Dutch outbidding his companion, and being satisfied, provided he can gain some little profit." French colonists thus rightly feared they would be the next target for the guns that Iroquois warriors acquired on the Hudson. "Fifty Hiroquois are capable of making two hundred Frenchmen leave the country," missionary Paul Le Jeune wrote, but "fifty Frenchmen would rout five hundred Hiroquois, if the Dutch did not give them firearms."[9]

To the south, on the Delaware River, another network connected the Dutch Atlantic to one of the chief enemies of the Haudenosaunee—and one of the few Native peoples able to fight Iroquois warriors to a draw in this period—the Susquehannocks. This trade had been established not by the West India Company but by dissident Dutch merchants (including former New Netherland Director Peter Minuit) who dominated the short-lived colony of New Sweden from its founding in 1638 to its conquest by the Company in 1655. The connection between Dutchmen and Swedes was such an open secret that even French Jesuit missionary Isaac Jogues heard during his brief sojourn in New Netherland after he escaped Iroquois captivity in 1643 "that these Swedes are maintained by Amsterdam merchants, incensed because the Company of the west Indies monopolizes all the trade of these regions." New

Sweden seems never to have come close to dominating the region's trade. Historian Karen Kupperman has aptly described the colony as a protectorate of the much stronger Susquehannocks, who off and on also maintained contentious and sometimes violent relationships with English traders from Virginia and Maryland and with the Dutch who competed with the Swedes on the Delaware. Nonetheless, commerce with New Sweden was every bit as important to Susquehannock military success as the more flourishing Fort Orange trade was to the Haudenosaunee. Thanks to this trading connection, as Francis Jennings put it, "to outward appearances . . . the Susquehannocks were the Great Power in their part of the world."[10]

The Swedes were particularly successful in convincing the Susquehannocks that they "could sell them powder, lead and guns enough," while "the Netherlanders, being poor tatterdemalions, could not do so."[11] But, like the Dutch trade with the Haudenosaunee, Swedish trade with the Susquehannocks ultimately depended on the flow of wampum (or, as Dutch and Swedes labeled it in various spellings, *seawant*) out of southern New England. "If *sevant* is not always on hand here . . . , it is difficult to trade with the savages," Swedish Governor Johan Printz explained in 1644, "hence we must buy *sevant* from Manathans and of the North English, where *sevant* is made." Ships from the New Haven colony in particular brought substantial supplies of wampum (along with grain and manufactured goods for the colonists and, presumably, firearms and other trade items for Native people) to exchange for Susquehannocks' furs. The Swedes were "obliged to pay to the English and Hollanders a double price in good beavers" compared with what the beads cost at their source, "because the savages always want *zewandt*."[12]

The dependence of New Sweden on overpriced wampum from New England was part of a broader set of economic difficulties that placed the Delaware Valley colony at the center of the final Dutch continental trading network of mid-century, a weakly developed but nonetheless significant commerce that drew England's Chesapeake colonies into a vast wampum-mediated web spanning the mid-Atlantic and New England coasts. The key factor was the almost complete inability of the New Sweden Company to provide for its handful of traders and colonists on the Delaware, who once went more than two years and another time nearly six years without a visit from a Scandinavian ship.[13] Thus, trade with the Dutch—both clandestine and with the winking consent of New Netherland's Director Willem Kieft—was crucial to the survival of New Sweden. Just as important was commerce with traders from New Haven and elsewhere in New England who carried more than just

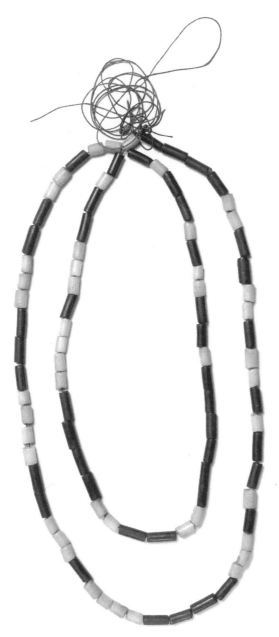

Strings of wampum, from archaeological site at Bainbridge, Pennsylvania. Courtesy of the University of Pennsylvania Museum (Penn Museum object 70-9-304, image #147810).

wampum. Most notably, Hartford merchant Richard Lord and the ubiquitous New Englander Isaac Allerton sold the Swedes much-needed foodstuffs on credit in the early 1650s. All of this trade took place in a tense environment of repeated Dutch and English efforts to establish competing trading posts and settlements in the Delaware Bay and River Valley.[14]

New Sweden also conducted a substantial trade in Chesapeake tobacco, particularly from the Eastern Shore and the Severn River area. On the rare occasions when official New Sweden Company ships sailed homeward, much of their cargo consisted of leaf from "Virginia," which no doubt also included Maryland: over 15,000 Swedish pounds in 1644, over 24,000 in 1647, and over 13,000 in 1654. This was three to four times as much weight as was legally exported by New Sweden's own farmers, who seem to have virtually stopped growing tobacco after 1646. Other Chesapeake leaf, joined by some from "Cribitz" (the Lesser Antilles) and New England, probably sailed illegally on Dutch ships to New Amsterdam or directly to the Netherlands. Additional clandestine commerce allowed goods to move in and out of New Amsterdam and the Dutch posts that periodically occupied locations on the Delaware.[15]

Thus, everywhere one looked from the Chesapeake northward in eastern North America, traders affiliated with, or once affiliated with, the West India Company created economic networks that knit together Indian and European peoples and tied them into the nascent Atlantic economy. As Jennings observed, "At the center of everything were the Dutch. . . . When something happened to the Dutch, therefore, whether its source lay in Europe, colonies, or Indian country, its effects reverberated through the tribes"—and, I would add, through the English and French colonies as well.[16] Yet, dominant as the Dutch appeared to be, the West India Company lacked the economic resources, the political will, and the human capital to defend the economic networks its people had created. The troubles began long before the passage of the English Navigation Acts and the conquest of the Dutch colony.

*   *   *

Just as the wampum trade connected the Atlantic and continental networks of the Dutch trading empire, so too its fate epitomizes the inherent weaknesses of the Dutch position and the profound consequences of that weakness for all involved. An irony here is that what would appear to be a major victory for the West India Company—the Dutch conquest of New Sweden in 1655—may have turned out to be the key to the Company's North American demise. The conquest provoked the Susquehannocks and their allies to attack New Amsterdam in what became known as the "Peach War," beginning a decade of almost constant bloodshed between the Dutch colony and Native peoples of the lower Hudson Valley.[17]

More important, the conquest of New Sweden seems to have almost destroyed the New England wampum trade to the Delaware. This contraction of the bead market must have been a key factor in the rapid inflation of the value of wampum against specie that plagued New Netherland during this period. To the Heren XIX, Dutch North America seemed populated with hapless traders, unable to acquire either furs or trade goods, "sitting meanwhile on their boxes full of wampum." The Hudson River colony saw its primary medium of exchange fall in value by as much 60 percent between 1641 and 1658 and by more than 200 percent during the following decade, particularly after 1660, when the beads ceased to be accepted for payment of taxes in the New England colonies. Historians disagree on the precise impact of the great wampum inflation, but it is clear that economic disruption was severe, both for the internal economy of the Dutch colony and for the ability of traders to supply Indian customers with other goods at Fort Orange. At the very least, the inflation further weakened an already ailing New Netherland economy and helps explain the alacrity with which Dutch colonists surrendered to the English.[18]

In the decade after the fall of New Netherland to the English, dominos fell in every direction traced by the wampum trades, with dramatic effects on the Indian peoples of Iroquoia, southern New England, and the Susquehannock country, and ultimately on the European colonial neighbors of each region as well. The Haudenosaunee, whose military success in their far-flung mid-century wars depended on their trade with Fort Orange, simultaneously confronted the efforts of both the English and French crowns to centralize their colonial possessions and to seize trade from the Dutch. While most of the individual Dutch people with whom Iroquois people traded at the town now known as Albany remained on the scene despite the English conquest, the already strained economic relationship of the last years of New Netherland became much worse as most Atlantic connections to the Netherlands shut down and the Anglo-Dutch wars of 1664–1667 and 1672–1674 made European weapons, tools, and cloth increasingly scarce. Especially difficult years for the Albany marketplace were 1665 and 1673, when French Jesuit missionary Jacques Bruyas reported "stuffs to be so dear, that our Iroquois are resolved to provide themselves with these at Montreal."[19]

In 1673 Bruyas was able to employ the word "our" because the scarcity of

Hudson River goods after the fall of New Netherland enabled an aggressive French campaign to deal with the Iroquois and the Dutch believed to be behind them. This effort culminated in the peace treaties between New France and the Haudenosaunee in the mid-1660s and the decade of uneasy peace that followed.[20] Meantime, a pax Gallica in the Great Lakes region not only opened hunting territories and settlement frontiers north of Lake Ontario to the Haudenosaunee. It also allowed Iroquoian- and Algonquian-speaking former enemies of the Five Nations to regroup and relocate under the political protection and economic auspices of the French "Father," who established posts at Cataraqui on Lake Ontario (established with Garakontié's blessing in 1673), Michilimackinac (also in 1673), Niagara (1676), and elsewhere. As historian Richard White has shown, these posts were the nodes around which Ottawas, Wyandots, Miamis, and other Great Lakes peoples created the eighteenth-century "Middle Ground." Of course the Pax Gallica did not last much beyond 1676, when the duke of York's governor, Edmund Andros, made a concerted effort to reinvigorate the Albany trade and win over anti-French Iroquois toan alliance with New York. Thus the Middle Ground was just as much a product of the new round of western wars the Iroquois were able to wage once they escaped the French yoke as it was of the period of Iroquois retreat. Still, it is safe to say that none of this would have worked out quite as it did had New Netherland remained on the scene.[21]

Andros's alliances with the Haudenosaunee and other Native peoples were designed not only to challenge the French but to impose some coherence on the shambles into which English-Indian relations everywhere seem to have fallen in the wake of King Philip's War in New England and Bacon's Rebellion in the Chesapeake. These transformative events of 1675–1676 were extraordinarily complicated, and certainly did not trace their sole origins to the fall of New Netherland. Nonetheless, in both cases dominos falling away from New Amsterdam gave a major push to already fragile structures. As with events in the Great Lakes region, had New Netherland and the Dutch West India Company remained a potent force, things would surely have turned out much differently than they did.

Nearly every recent study of King Philip's War has traced its roots not to some inherent clash of civilizations or of races but to the collapse of a functional—if asymmetrical—political and social order that had allowed Algonquian-speaking communities to survive, and sometimes even prosper, in an English-dominated landscape for a generation from the end of the Pequot War in 1638 to the mid-1660s. Close ties with rivalrous New England colonies allowed Mohegans, Niantics, Narragansetts, and Wampanoags to prosper economically and to remain largely in control of their own political and cultural lives during that period. As Neal Salisbury concludes, this "was not a war between strangers but rather one between neighbors," who, over the course of two generations, "had learned much about each other in the course of trading, working, negotiating, socializing, suing, complaining to their leaders about one another, occasionally fighting, and—in a few cases— attending school and church and even living together."[22]

For Native peoples, wampum was key to these relationships, as the price to be paid in tribute to the governments of Plymouth or Connecticut, as the primary commodity that could be sold to English and Dutch traders, and (somewhat incongruously with these mundane economic functions) as a prestige good that marked the spiritual and political power of sachems and the people they protected. The great wampum inflation, the demonetization of the beads in New England, relentless pressure on the land base from an expanding English population, and the removal of any possibility that a Dutch government might be played off against the English put Native communities in an almost impossible bind.[23] People like the Wampanoags were now "dependents on, rather than partners in, New England's business," one knowledgeable popular writer on King Philip's War puts it. "And that business . . . was strictly land development."[24]

The immediate cause of the conflagration that ripped New England apart came in June 1675, when Plymouth officials tried and executed the Wampanoags who allegedly killed Philip's aide John Sassamon for informing the English of Native military preparations.[25] But, as Philip himself explained to Rhode Island lieutenant governor John Easton on the eve of the war, the problems went much deeper. English courts, missionaries, and governments wielded such power that Native people "now . . . had not so much land or muny, that thay wear as good be kiled as leave all ther liveflyhode" and "had no hopes left to kepe ani land."[26] Had the West India Company remained a significant countervailing force in the region, things would not have reached such a pass, at least not so quickly. Dutch trade would have continued to structure a regional balance of power rooted in exchange.

Much the same might be said of the contemporaneous situation in the Chesapeake. As Edmund Morgan observes, Bacon's was "a rebellion with abundant causes but without a cause," and no simple explanation will do. Still, to the extent that the economic distress of small tobacco farmers was very real—as no one denies it was—the success of the Navigation Acts in shutting down the sale of tobacco to the Dutch and enforcing the payment of duties on tobacco sent to England had a major impact. More important than the mere passage of legislation was the closing of the alternative outlets for Chesapeake tobacco provided by New Sweden and New Netherland. Under the new English-only regime, tobacco prices plummeted to a half penny per pound of leaf in 1666 and hovered around one penny for the next decade, less than half of what they had been in the 1650s when the Swedes and Dutch were major purchasers.[27] As a result, among the many worries of Governor Berkeley in 1673 was that the "large part of the people" who were "so desperately poor" might be tempted to welcome a Dutch invasion "in hopes of bettering their condition."[28]

Instead, an aristocratic English newcomer to the colony named Nathaniel Bacon raised those hopes. Many of Bacon's followers sought relief from their economic distress not by growing less tobacco but finding means to grow more, by conquering lands from Native people protected by Governor Berkeley's much-detested treaties. Thus Virginians and their Maryland neighbors found themselves in a war with Indian peoples nearly as brutal as that simultaneously wracking New England. The war, far more than economic distresses or systemic political grievances, dominated contemporary understandings of the Rebellion. "The common cry and vogue of the Vulgar was . . . wee will have warr with all Indians," the royal commissioners sent to investigate the conflagration concluded in 1677. "We will spare non, and [if] wee must be hang'd for Rebells for killing those that will destroy us, let them hang us, wee will venture that rather than lye at the mercy of a Barbarous Enemy" and endure "the calamity that befell New England by them."[29]

Most potent among the Native peoples in the line of English fire were none other than the Susquehannocks, and it was the fall of New Sweden and the collapse of New Netherland that placed them in that targeted position. Already in 1652, after years of on-and-off warfare with English people on the Chesapeake, the Susquehannocks had made peace with Maryland (then actually governed as part of Virginia by the English Commonwealth government that temporarily replaced Berkeley). Apparently this was an effort to hedge their bets on the unstable Swedish trade as well as to protect their southern flank during a period of heightened conflict with the four western Iroquois nations. The peace briefly gave Susquehannocks access to Virginian William Claiborne's trading posts on Kent and Palmer's islands at the head of the Chesapeake Bay, but it collapsed in 1657 when the Calvert family regained control of Maryland.[30] Meantime, in 1655, the Dutch had conquered

New Sweden. Most of the mixed group of Europeans who had settled under Swedish rule remained on the scene. Many continued to participate in trade with Susquehannocks and Lenapes as best they could, while the most linguistically talented among them offered their services to the new regime. The major Dutch entrepôt, however, shifted south from Fort Christina (today's Wilmington, Delaware) to New Amstel (today's New Castle), a post that was not controlled by the West India Company but instead was an independent project of the city of Amsterdam. Thus, New Amstel recreated the awkward relationship that New Sweden had maintained with the Company, which continued to operate separately on the Delaware as well.[31]

By the late 1650s, all of these developments created sufficient insecurities to force the Susquehannocks to try to open direct trade with Manhattan by making peace with the Dutch and ending support for the lower Hudson Valley Native peoples who had been at war with New Netherland since the fall of New Sweden; the Susquehannocks found it necessary, they confessed, "to submit to the Dutch or hide."[32] That submission became somewhat less pressing after 1661, when the Maryland assembly, fearing the consequences for their frontiers of Iroquois attacks, declared the Susquehannocks "a Bullwarke and Security of the Northern parts of this Province" and authorized a Susquehannock-speaking defector from New Amstel named Jacob Claeson to trade with them on Maryland's behalf. From Claeson and other English and Dutch sources, the Susquehannocks acquired sufficient arms—including artillery reportedly manned by Marylanders—to repulse a major Iroquois attack on their main town in 1663.[33]

That was only a year before the English conquest of New Netherland threw all the trading connections of both the Susquehannocks and the Iroquois into disarray. Devastating as the conquest was for the economy of the Haudenosaunee, it seems to have been much worse for the Susquehannocks. New Amsterdam, Fort Orange, and Beverwyck surrendered without a shot and thus enjoyed favorable terms that allowed the traders with whom Native people had long dealt to stay in place under the new regime—including ultimately the right to send three ships per year to the Netherlands despite the prohibitions of the Navigation Acts.[34] Although New Amstel put up some armed resistance and its defeated garrison was shipped off into virtual slavery in Virginia, the remaining civilian Delaware Valley European population enjoyed privileges similar to those granted on the Hudson. Still, under English rule, tense hostility punctuated by occasional murders on either side replaced peaceful trade as the norm for interactions between Europeans and their Lenape neighbors, if not with the Susquehannocks. "Wee are in a sad condition," local officials complained to the duke's governor, John Lovelace; "it is most uncertain living under the power of the Heathens," who "give for reason of there warre that they threaten to make upon the Christians . . . [that] where the English come they drive them from there lands and bring for instance the North Virginia and Maryland."[35] That at least some Scandinavians were no more comfortable with English rule than were the Lenapes

Richard Blome, *Nouvelle carte de la Pensylvanie, Maryland, Virginie, et Nouvell Jarsey* (1688). Lawrence H. Slaughter Collection, The Lionel Pincus and Princess Firyal Map Division, The New York Public Library, Astor, Lenox and Tilden Foundations. The English conquest imposed new boundaries on the former New Netherland and its Native trading partners.

is indicated by a poorly documented rebellion led by a man known as "the Long Swede" in 1669.[36]

The exact scale of the distress that these developments caused for the Susquehannocks is unclear. But there are various hints in European records: from New York City both under the English and under the Dutch in the brief period when it was reconquered and renamed "New Orange" in 1673–1674; from the Chesapeake, where it was rumored in 1675 that they had been "driven from their Habitations, at the head of Chesepiack Bay, by the Cineka-Indians" (the Senecas and other Iroquois); from Jesuit missions in Haudeno-saunee territory, where they were similarly reported "utterly defeated."[37] The fact that we do not know much about what the Susquehannocks were doing during this period is probably the best indicator of the limited trade they were able to maintain with Europeans and the major problems they faced as a result. "Here live Christians and there live Christians," one of their frustrated spokesmen supposedly said to Lenape neighbors who pondered an escalation of their violence against the Delaware Valley English in 1670. "As they were surrounded by Christians," the Susquehannock man continued, "if they went to war, where would they get powder and ball?" There was no more potential to play one European colonial market against another.[38]

By 1675, the Susquehannocks had seemingly concluded that their only real option was to throw in their lot with the Marylanders who for twenty years had provided an alternative to the Swedes on the Delaware. In February of that year, responding to an invitation apparently issued at a treaty with the colony's governor several months previously, what was reputed to be the entire surviving population of the nation arrived at St. Mary's City and "desired to know what part of the Province Should be allotted for them to live upon." They had hardly settled into an abandoned Piscataway village on the Potomac River when militiamen from Virginia and Maryland (one of whose commanders was none other than trader Isaac Allerton) laid siege to it, murdered five of their chiefs during a sham peace conference, and provoked the long months of Indian-English conflict that were inextricable from the internal political upheaval of Bacon's Rebellion. Had New Sweden and New Netherland never fallen, those militiamen—despite higher tobacco prices—might still have been itching for a fight, might still have been convinced that Virginia Governor Berkeley, "for the lucre of the Beaver and otter trade etc. with the Indians, rather sought to protect the Indians than them."[39] But they would never have encountered a foe as able to do them military damage as the Susquehannocks, who would have continued to thrive and battle Iroquois enemies from homes that would have remained well north of Virginians' reach.[40] And Allerton and others might still have been hauling wampum and other goods between Connecticut and the Delaware watershed.

*   *   *

As Joni Mitchell could have said of New Netherland, "You don't know what you've got till it's gone." Yet nothing ever completely goes away. Dutch finance, Dutch merchants, and Dutch shipping—both legal and contraband—remained crucial parts of the Atlantic economy long after New Netherland itself ceased to exist. In particular, five of the six trade networks that the Dutch created would be reinvigorated by the English in the late seventeenth and early eighteenth centuries. English slavers and an English carrying fleet would take over routes the Dutch had once dominated. English New Yorkers—or rather Dutch traders living in English New York—would reinvigorate commerce between the Hudson and Iroquoia and the Great Lakes. Pennsylvania, with the assistance of veterans of New Sweden, would restore trade westward from the Delaware with a variety of Indian peoples, including some descendants of the Susquehannocks. Philadelphia would recreate New Sweden's many intercolonial trades on a scale the Swedes could never have imagined. But these English reinventions really only began to take hold after 1676. And, for a crucial twelve years after the conquest of New Netherland in 1664, all of the networks had fallen into disarray.

Yet one network—the wampum trade—never would be revived in anything like its original form. This was the one that had most distinctively unified the many trade networks of New Netherland, knit Native and European people most firmly together, and caused the most widespread disruption when it collapsed. It is tempting to conclude that all the Dutch dominos were made of those black and white shell beads.

CHAPTER 6

Brokers and Politics:
Iroquois and New Yorkers

Building on the wreckage left by the departure of the Dutch West India Company from North America in the late 1670s and early 1680s, English governors
of New York and Haudenosaunee leaders of the Five Nations forged what was
known as the Covenant Chain, an alliance that became the centerpiece of
diplomatic relationships across much of eastern North America. Relying on
these relationships, in the early 1690s the Iroquois and the English fought,
independently but in concert, against New France and its Indian allies in the
conflict colonials called King William's War. Whether understood in terms
of the patterns of the mourning-war, or of the nexus of exchange and power
the Delaware leader Teedyuscung would later call *Whish-shicksy*, or of the
geopolitics of European diplomacy, for the Haudenosaunee the experience
was an almost unmitigated military disaster. Although the Covenant Chain
remained and would be reinterpreted in the eighteenth century, the New
York–Iroquois alliance that was originally at its core mutated into a quite different form at the turn of the eighteenth century, when neutrality rather than
exclusive alliance became the dominant strategy of the Five (and later Six)
Nations of the Haudenosaunee.

From a distance, the story seems a simple tale of alliance and defeat, spiced
with a touch of English betrayal. But, when the viewpoint shifts to the community level of Albany and the Haudenosaunee villages, the image becomes
a kaleidoscope of local and supra-local leaders working at cross purposes,
struggles and alliances among competing interest groups, and tangled family quarrels on all sides. Far from comprising unitary polities, the Mohawks,
Oneidas, Onondagas, Cayugas, and Senecas of the late seventeenth-century
Haudenosaunee each were clusters of virtually autonomous kin-based,

factionally divided communities. Within and among the diverse villages, ceremonial gift exchanges among hereditary sachems and less highly structured personal alliances among charismatic local headmen provided a primary means of political integration and the mobilization of power.[1] The province of New York as it emerged from conquered New Netherland was similarly a bundle of localized communities held together by intricate networks of personal and familial political connections. In the late seventeenth century, it was less a single colony than three—one centered on the cosmopolitan but Dutch-dominated town on Manhattan Island, another on the almost exclusively Dutch fur trading outpost at Albany, and a third on the Long Island villages settled by immigrants from New England. Over all of these presided English governors charged with making the fractious province a cornerstone of imperial power in North America and somehow incorporating the Five Nations into that edifice.

Thus, for both sides, large-scale diplomacy rested upon the internal politics of diverse local communities. As anthropologists and political scientists have long understood, connections between large- and small-scale politics often depend on highly personal relationships centered on individuals called, in the language of social network theory, *brokers* or *mediators*. Simultaneously members of two or more interacting networks (kin groups, political factions, communities, or other formal or informal coalitions), brokers are nodes of communication; with respect to a community's relations with the outside world, they "stand guard over the crucial junctures or synapses of relationships which connect the local system to the larger whole." This intermediate position allows considerable room for maneuver. One step removed from final responsibility in decision making, brokers may occasionally promise more than they can deliver. By using their maneuvering room to promote the aims of one group while protecting the interests of another, skillful mediators can become nearly indispensable to all sides.[2] In North America, brokers also served as the primary conduits for the exchanges of prestige goods and more mundane items that symbolized strong alliances. But, as the rise and fall of the late seventeenth-century Iroquois–New York Covenant Chain alliance illustrates, the relationships thus created were fragile for the same reasons they were functional. Much like a Mississippian prestige-good chiefdom, such an alliance cycled in and out of existence during the lifetimes of the individuals upon whom it depended.

*   *   *

For both New York and the Five Nations, basic patterns of personal connections among brokers for kin groups, political factions, and local communities
had been set long before the English conquered New Netherland. The key
broker in the mid-seventeenth-century Dutch-Iroquois relationship was the
fur trader and agent of the van Rensselaer family Arent van Curler ("Corlaer"), who on countless occasions beginning in the 1630s mediated disputes
between Mohawks and colonists.[3] Corlaer drowned in 1667; by then the relationships he personified had perished as well. Since the late 1650s New Netherland's economic and other woes had turned the mood in the Fort Orange
marketplace nasty, as hard-pressed traders regularly cheated their Native customers and employed strong-armed *boslopers* to steal furs outright from Indians bound for market.[4] In the interval between the first English takeover in
1664 and the confirmation of the duke of York's rule in 1674 after a brief Dutch
reconquest, Haudenosaunee people learned how fragmented the politics of
the newly barely-English Hudson River colony were. The French-led armies
that invaded the Mohawk country in 1666 received a hearty welcome from
Dutch residents of Schenectady and Albany who nursed Frenchmen's wounds
and replenished their supplies. No one entertained the attackers more lavishly than van Curler himself. After the second invasion, he and other Albany
Dutch were "very forward towards . . . [the Mohawks'] makeinge of peace,"
because, suspected the town's English commander, French forces would then
be able to "Martch Which way they please Thurrow" Iroquoia and remove the
English duke's men from the Hudson.[5]

In the late 1660s and early 1670s, the short-lived peace with New France
and its Native allies provided a partial respite from conflict but hardly a solution to the economic and military problems of the Five Nations. Abroad,
debilitating wars with Mahicans, New England Algonquians, and Susquehannocks continued, while at home conflict of another sort brewed. Under the
terms of the 1667 peace treaties, French Jesuit missionaries settled in most
of the major villages of the Five Nations and created sizeable followings
for whom conversion to Christianity and close political ties to the French
were virtually inseparable. The francophile Christians were reviled by other
Iroquois who saw their policies and religion as abject capitulations to the
enemy, but, with connections to the Hudson in disarray, there was no viable
alternative.[6]

That changed after the final English takeover of New York in 1674. By
the early 1680s a triangular brokerage system emerged to link the English
government based in Manhattan, the Dutch trading community at Albany,

and the Iroquois villages of the Five Nations. Individual mediators rose to prominence in both Albany and Iroquoia through their membership in specific political networks and their ability to deal with forces in other corners of the triangle. The principal architect of the new arrangements was the duke's governor from 1674 to 1682, Edmund Andros. A loyal servant of the Stuart family and a paradigm of the vigorous imperial style known as "garrison government," Andros was instructed to pacify the turbulent frontiers of the English colonies. His improvised efforts created the Covenant Chain system of diplomacy and, knowingly or not, provided a focus around which demoralized anti-French Iroquois factions could regroup. Early in his tenure, the governor struck a military partnership with the Mohawks and encouraged them to intervene against New England Algonquians in King Philip's War. Simultaneously he and his agents at Albany worked to end Iroquois conflicts with Mahicans and with Susquehannocks enmeshed in the fighting associated with Bacon's Rebellion. By 1677 the wars to the south and east of Iroquoia were over on terms favorable to the Five Nations, many Susquehannocks and New England Indians had relocated under the protection of New York and the Iroquois, the Mohawks had emerged as the principal Indian power in the Albany area, and all of the nations of the confederacy had assumed new prominence in the diplomacy of the colonial Northeast. Anti-French Iroquois could now dream of security on their eastern and southern borders and of thousands of prospective allies among Englishmen, Mahicans, and Indian refugees united in the chain of English-Indian and Indian-Indian alliances that Andros had helped to construct.[7]

Iroquois enemies of the French could also rest assured of a secure market at Albany, where the confirmation of ducal rule and the conclusion of the Anglo-Dutch wars ended shortages and provided an attractive option to commerce with New France. Meantime, the regional peace Andros's government had sponsored freed the Five Nations' hunters to seek new sources of furs in the west and allowed their traders unmolested access to the Albany marketplace, which itself became physically safer than it had been in over a decade. Under Andros's government, the worst abuses of the mid-seventeenth-century abated dramatically when strictly enforced new local ordinances confined legal trading to residents of Albany and to public areas inside the town palisade. It is hard to imagine that unscrupulous practices disappeared or that Indians received very attractive prices in an environment tightly controlled by local magistrates who also happened to be fur traders, but the improvement over the beatings and thefts of earlier years was plain.

Native traders could now expect to get something in exchange for their pelts and to return home in one piece.[8]

The changes at Albany, of course, could not have occurred without the cooperation of local residents. Just as in Iroquoia specific anti-French political factions profited from connections to the English government, so in the Dutch community a particular group rose to prominence under the new regime. In the late 1670s, Peter Schuyler, Dirck Wesselse Ten Broeck, Evert Bancker, and other young fur traders cultivated ties to Sylvester Salisbury (Andros's commander of the Albany garrison and the town's chief magistrate) and to such other newcomers as the Dutch-speaking Scot Robert Livingston. Their compromises with the conquerors allowed members of this rising "anglicizer" elite to gain offices and preferment at the expense of such dominant figures of the old regime as trader and Mohawk language interpreter Arnout Cornelisz Vielé and merchants Johannes Cuyler and Johannes Wendell.[9]

Despite the real divisions between them, the anglicizers and the traditionalists—interlinked by ties of kinship, debt, and trade—melted together in what outsiders (and most historians) took to be an undifferentiated and unassimilated Dutch subculture in the English colony. The surface calm stemmed partly from the anglicizers' success as brokers between their community and the English regime at Manhattan, from which they garnered an enhanced position for the town and its fur trade economy as well as for themselves. In 1686 the leaders secured from Andros's successor, Thomas Dongan, a city charter that, among other things, confirmed Albany's traditional monopoly of the province's northern and western Indian trade and installed Schuyler as mayor, Livingston as town clerk, and other prominent anglicizers as aldermen. Although all of the town's merchants prospered from the monopoly, the anglicizers benefited most. Several of the anglicizers' rivals, for example, had hoped to gain an advantage by investing in lands at Schenectady, sixteen miles closer than Albany to the Mohawk villages. The anglicizers' confirmation of the Albany monopoly brought that plan to naught.[10]

At the same time that members of the anglicizer elite consolidated their economic and political dominance at Albany and their positions as mediators between the Dutch community and the English government, they also emerged as brokers between the Five Nations and the duke's government at Manhattan. This role evolved easily from their control of key local offices, their dominant position in the town's Indian trade, their resulting connections to anti-French Iroquois, and their simple presence on the scene; of necessity Andros and Dongan left day-to-day Indian affairs in the hands of local authorities. Schuyler, as mayor and chief spokesman for the town, and Livingston, as town clerk and by extension Indian affairs secretary, played particularly important roles. In recognition of the independent intermediary functions the Albany elite had assumed, in the mid-1680s Iroquois spokesmen modified the ceremonial language of diplomacy to distinguish between propositions to be relayed to their "Brother" the governor at Manhattan and those intended primarily for their "Brethren" of Albany and "Quider," a Mohawk pronunciation of Peter Schuyler's first name.[11]

The intercultural influence of Quider and the other Albany anglicizers increased after 1683, when Dominie Godfridius Dellius arrived from the Netherlands to take a pulpit at Albany. From the start, the clergyman allied himself with the English government and the Schuyler faction and thus earned the hearty distrust of the orthodox Dutch Calvinist burghers who were the anglicizers' chief opponents. Nonetheless, he was a great success among anti-French Iroquois, for he offered an alternative for those who were attracted to Christianity but who feared the political power that French missionaries and their followers exercised in many villages of the Five Nations. "Wee cannot forbear to acquaint you how greatt Pains the Jesuit Takes and what Diligence he uses to draw away and Entice our Indians to Canada upon Pretence to Convert them to his Religion, [and we] Desyre that itt may be hindred," the Mohawk headman Tahiadoris pleaded at Albany in 1687.[12] In the late 1680s, Dellius answered Tahiadoris's prayer by systematically cultivating Iroquois religious converts and political allies. For Dellius, as for Tahiadoris, politics and conversion went hand in hand to strengthen personal ties between Indians and members of the Albany elite; the latter often served as sponsors at converts' baptisms. From such connections emerged a coterie of Mohawks—most notably three young men with the Christian names Joseph, Jurian, and Lawrence—who in coming years would mediate with varying degrees of success between their communities and Albany.[13]

Because Dellius never mastered an Iroquoian language, he could not have succeeded without the assistance of another newcomer to Albany, the interpreter Hilletie van Olinda. In the Mohawk village where she was reared—her mother was Mohawk and her father Dutch—she had been impressed by the teachings of French priests. Ridiculed for her beliefs, she moved to Schenectady, and sometime before 1673 she became one of a handful of Indians who received baptism at Albany before the arrival of Dellius. Soon thereafter officials began to take advantage of her bicultural background and linguistic talents. Although her twin handicaps as a woman and a *métis* prevented

Peter Schuyler (1657–1724), by Nehemiah Partridge. Collections of the Albany
Institute of History & Art.

her from ever becoming an equal to Schuyler, Livingston, and Dellius, van
Olinda possessed ideal credentials to mediate between Dutch anglicizers and
Iroquois anglophiles. As the anglicizers' alternative to Vielé, she shared with
her rival interpreter official translating duties at Albany treaty sessions with
the Iroquois.[14]

The impact of van Olinda, Dellius, and the anglicizers on politics in the
Five Nations is difficult to pinpoint, but the effect of English policies when
combined with Iroquois concern about French western expansionism and
internal political influence can be traced. "Let the *Maques* [Mohawk] Indyans
know . . . ," Andros instructed Albany officials in early 1675, "that if they bee
not wanting themselves, I shall not [be wanting] on my part, in continuance
of the Friendship . . . and also [in] interposing with the *French*, or any other
Neighbour, in any just matter." Through such pledges of aid, often delivered in
person in Iroquois villages, Andros and his Albany allies won wide support.[15]
"Wheras wee have alwyes had ane firm Covenant with this Goverment which
haith bein fayt[h]fuly Keeped by this Governor Generall . . . ," the Seneca
leader Adondarechaa proclaimed in 1677, "wee doe give him harty thankes,
whom wee have taken to be our greatest Lord."[16]

The word *Lord*, of course, is European, not Iroquoian, although it has
frequently been used to translate Iroquois terms for civil chiefs. Yet, whatever
Seneca phrase Adondarechaa actually employed, the interpreter's translation
suggests a final key to support for Andros and his intermediaries at Albany
in Iroquois villages. Around the formal diplomacy and day-to-day dealings
of Iroquois and Euro-Americans at Albany developed a rich body of intercultural rituals that, like *Lord*, had different meanings for Indians and colonists.
The regular meetings that Andros initiated with headmen of the Five Nations
quickly evolved into periodic ritual "brightenings" of the Anglo-Indian Covenant Chain, which were modeled after Iroquois ceremonies. When Andros
visited the Mohawk country in 1675, his hosts bestowed on him the council
title "Corlaer," installing him in the position formerly held by van Curler. The
name would be inherited by Andros's successors in the governor's chair in
the same way that Iroquois sachems passed their traditional names from one
generation to the next. Such practices infused the practical benefits of ties to
New York with personal relationships and cultural meanings that ordinary
Iroquois could understand. For many, the combination was irresistible. By
the early 1680s strong anglophile factions emerged in most Iroquois villages.[17]

As enthusiasm for the English regime and the Albany leadership waxed,
tolerance for the French and their religion waned. One crucial factor was the

departure of hundreds of francophiles for mission villages in Canada. The exodus by no means included all Iroquois Catholics, but it did remove many of the most dedicated, while the depopulation further angered their foes who remained behind. During the mid-1670s francophile ranks were further weakened by the deaths of several of their most prominent leaders. As francophile support evaporated, the days of the French Jesuits were numbered. By early 1684, missionaries' lives were in danger throughout the Five Nations, and a mere handful of Iroquois still openly practiced Roman Catholicism. That summer, with the anglophiles apparently in complete control, most of the priests serving Iroquoia abandoned their posts. As they left, French governor Joseph-Antoine Le Febvre de La Barre prepared to invade the Seneca country in retaliation for challenges to French interests in the west. During the weeks and months preceding his expedition, anglophile Iroquois, in collaboration with Governor Dongan and the Albany elite, had greatly strengthened the Covenant Chain alliance when they announced that they had "Put all our Land and our Selves under the Protection of the great Duke of York the brother of your great Sachim," King Charles II.[18]

Most Iroquois probably welcomed that protection, but many believed the anglophiles were paying too high a price in acknowledging English claims to their lands. A delegation of Onondagas, Cayugas, and Oneidas therefore ignored a prohibition from Dongan and met the French governor at La Famine on Lake Ontario to deal with matters in their own way. In the French camp, the Onondaga headman Otreouti (*La Grande Gueule*)—a neutralist who remained aloof from both French and English and had doubts about Dongan's promises—publicly humiliated La Barre, whose army was too short of supplies and too weakened by disease to travel any further. La Barre came to terms, and open war with New France was postponed for the present. Subsequently, Iroquois raiders and traders, encouraged by both anglophiles and neutralists and openly supported by Dongan and the Albany leadership, redoubled their western offensives. Leading anglophiles during this period included the Mohawk headmen Rode and Odianne, the Oneida Oheda, and the Onondaga war chief Cannadakte (Chaudière Noire, or Black Kettle). By 1687 their initiatives provoked a successful French invasion of the Seneca country and the outbreak of general conflict in King William's War two years later.[19]

The English colonists joined the Iroquois-French war as a result of the Glorious Revolution of 1688, which brought William of Orange to the throne to rule jointly with James II's daughter Mary. When the Albany officials announced that William would soon bring his new domains into his ongoing

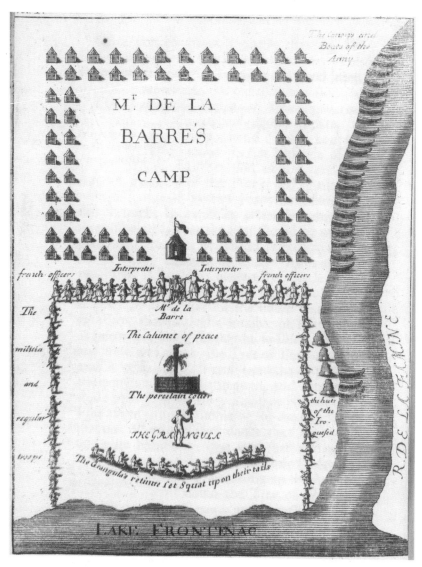

Otreouti's speech at La Famine, 1684. From [Louis Armand de Lom d'Arce], Baron [de] Lahontan, *New Voyages to North-America* . . . (London, 1703). Robert Dechert Collection, Rare Book and Manuscript Library, University of Pennsylvania. Despite its uncomplimentary captions, this illustration based on firsthand information portrays both the ceremonial aspects of Native diplomacy and the audacity of an Onondaga Iroquois orator who faced down a French army that attempted to invade his country in 1684.

conflict against the French, anglophile Iroquois had great hopes for the future of the Covenant Chain, "in which . . . ," proclaimed the Mohawk Tahiadoris, "are Included all there Majesties Subjects from the Sinnekes Countrey quite to the Eastward as farr as any Christian Subjects of our great king lives and from thence Southward all along New England quite to Virginia." For anglophiles, whatever they understood the term "Subjects" to mean, the Covenant of friendship now became a reciprocal military alliance, binding on both English and Indian partners: "Wee Esteem your Enemies ours," Tahiadoris, Adondarechaa, and several other leaders declared at Albany in September 1689. Yet Iroquois opinion was hardly unanimous. In all five nations, though "there Majesties Subjects" were apparently in control, many people remained skeptical of English promises. Tahiadoris and Adondarechaa made their declaration in a secret session with a few magistrates, for fear, they said, "by Some falsehearted Persones our DeSigne should be carried to our Enemies."[20]

The anglophiles' need for secrecy indicates the degree to which relationships between New York and the Five Nations were dependent upon the outcome of the internal political struggles that had brought the Indian and Euro-American mediators to power. Yet on only a few occasions do the formal records of intercultural diplomacy allow glimpses of Iroquois or Dutch opposition to the anglophile-anglicizer alliance. In 1671, during one of the earliest Iroquois efforts to strengthen ties with New York, two Mohawks got into an open dispute before the Albany magistrates. A few years later, while Andros and his Albany friends were enlisting Mohawks to fight in King Philip's War, rumors persisted that Dutchmen were selling arms to New England Algonquians and urging Iroquois not to enter the conflict. Significantly, Vielé, foe of the Schuyler faction, was mentioned in both connections. The interpreter also figured prominently in attempts to thwart a key part of Dongan's plans for the Five Nations during 1683 and 1684: William Penn's agents relied on him to bargain with Iroquois for the purchase of Susquehanna River lands claimed by the Onondagas and Cayugas. Schuyler, Wesselse, and the Cayuga leader Ourehouare (Taweeraet) quickly intervened to turn the episode to the advantage of Dongan and Iroquois anglophiles and to secure the territory for the duke's governor instead of for Pennsylvania. The partnerships struck on such occasions were crucial to the Anglo-Iroquois alliance; French missionary Jean de Lamberville complained that, after the Susquehanna deal, Ourehouare came home to make his Albany friends "the never-ending subject of his praise."[21]

*   *   *

Throughout King William's War, the fates of anglophiles and anglicizers remained linked. The intricacies became vitally apparent in early 1689, when the Glorious Revolution and the presence of a Dutch king on the English throne inspired disgruntled Dutch New Yorkers to take action against local forces they identified with Stuart tyranny. By June, Jacob Leisler, a German-born longtime champion of Calvinist orthodoxy and opponent of the province's anglicizers, had emerged as leader of a revolt that seized control of Manhattan and ousted the Stuarts' government. In November Leisler sent his son-in-law Jacob Milborne upriver to take over Albany, which was governed by a provisional "convention" dominated by Schuyler and Livingston. Leading opponents of the anglicizers, supported by much of the populace at large, gave Milborne a warm reception. But for the anglicizers the day was saved by a group of anglophile Mohawks, "who were come . . . for the assistance of there Majesties Subjects Standing upon the hill neer the fort and being Spectators to all these tumolts." When Milborne and his troops attempted to seize the town garrison, the Indians sent word to the beleaguered members of the convention "that Since they were in a firm Covenant chain . . . , and Seeing that the People of New Yorke [City] came in a hostile manner to Disturbe their Brethren . . . if any of those men came without the gates to approach the fort they would fyre upon them." Milborne withdrew, and Albany remained under the control of anti-Leislerian forces for two more months.[22]

The dramatic rescue of the anglicizer leaders by their Indian friends not only revealed the extent to which factions in Iroquoia and Albany had become intertwined and interdependent, but, unbeknownst to the participants, it also marked the beginning of the collapse of their system of brokered relationships. As Leisler's Rebellion unfolded, Louis de Buade, comte de Frontenac, returned to New France for a second term as governor, bringing with him a peace offer for the Five Nations. At the end of the year, Native messengers traveled toward the confederacy's seat at Onondaga to present the governor's terms. En route, they stopped at the Oneida village to deliver letters to resident French Jesuit priest Pierre Millet and were met by some of Dellius's Mohawk protégés—"to wit, those of the Dominie's side"—who argued that Millet's papers should be seized and burned. "The more cunning sachems," including a recently released Oneida prisoner of the French named Cohank, proposed instead to read the letters at the Onondaga council, where the French treacheries they presumably contained could be revealed. The latter plan prevailed, and headmen invited Schuyler and other Albany leaders to attend the meeting at Onondaga and press the English cause.[23]

The political situation at Albany ensured that things would not work out as "those of the Dominie's side" had hoped. Milborne's recent visit had placed the anglicizers in a perilous situation; Schuyler and his friends dared not leave their besieged posts. Moreover, to go to Onondaga and perhaps watch the Iroquois make peace with New France could be politically fatal, for that would seem to substantiate Leislerian charges that anglicizers were—as their supposed Stuart mentors were alleged to be—secret papists plotting to deliver the province into French hands. No one felt the pressure more than Dellius, who was religiously and politically anathema to Leislerians. Within a few weeks he had to flee to Boston when Albany leaders, panicked by a French raid on nearby Schenectady, nominally submitted to Leisler. Ironically, in light of the scene at the Oneida village, the dominie's foes charged that he conspired with Father Millet.[24]

Because of the crisis at Albany, the only men the anglophile Iroquois could pry loose to attend the council at Onondaga were Vielé and Robert Sanders, a major fur trader whose long-standing ties to Mohawks had developed independently of the anglicizer elite and who was apparently sympathetic to Leisler. These two, apparently at the behest of Leislerian Albany merchant Johannes Wendell, convinced a traveling companion, Dellius's Mohawk convert Jurian, to peddle trade goods at the sacred council fire. This scandalous breech of Iroquois political and diplomatic etiquette undermined the credibility of all involved and thus botched a prime opportunity to forge an anglophile consensus among the Five Nations; at this date there was little chance that the Iroquois—who were winning the war—would have made peace on Frontenac's terms. To compound the problems of anglophile forces, a public reading of Millet's letters revealed nothing incriminating. In the end, although confederacy leaders stridently rejected the French proposal, they ignored English demands that they refuse to answer Frontenac at all.[25]

This episode, embarrassing for Iroquois anglophiles and members of both Albany factions, was a harbinger of worse things to come. In April 1691 Leisler and Milborne were hanged by King William's new royal governor Henry Sloughter. Understandably, in consolidating his power, Sloughter allied himself with groups throughout the province who had opposed Leisler, and thus he restored the anglicizers to authority at Albany. With them in the summer of 1691 he made hasty plans to inspire New York's wavering Iroquois allies with a dramatic assault on Canada. The campaign, like a more elaborate invasion Leisler's government had attempted the previous year, was an almost total fiasco that could hardly have done less to impress the Five Nations. Nor, conversely, did either effort foster much English confidence in the Iroquois: in 1690 the anglophiles could convince few of their skeptical confederates to enlist, and in 1691 the death of Tahiadoris prevented the participation of mourning warriors from his village. This awkwardly timed demise led a disgruntled Wesselse to call the Mohawk anglophile "a Sachim who never did good in his Lifetime and his death it self was prejudiciall to a good Design."[26]

Whatever else the 1691 "Design" did, it destroyed prospects for limiting the Five Nations' involvement in the continental war. In an attempt to salvage something from the debacle, Schuyler had led a raid into Canada, during which a few confederacy Mohawk scouts exchanged fatal shots with some Mohawks from the Catholic mission village of Caughnawaga. Hostilities quickly escalated, and Mission Iroquois and confederacy Iroquois of all five nations were soon attacking each other mercilessly, widening and deepening the conflict in which most French- and English-allied Natives were already engaged. By the end of the century, two French invasions of Iroquoia, relentless attacks by Ojibwas, Ottawas, Wyandots and other western and northern Indians, and parsimonious English aid had reduced the Iroquois to a position reminiscent of that of the early 1660s; again they were besieged by foes too numerous and well armed to handle. "We are dayly in great Terrour, and very uneasie, . . . our Wives and Children being daily Exposed to fresh assaults," the exasperated Onondaga anglophile Sadekanaktie (Aquendero) informed his New York friends.[27]

That any Iroquois at all remained in the English interest was due largely to the efforts of the brokers at Albany. Amid warfare and political rebellion, Quider and his fellow magistrates retained steady control of New York–Indian relations and proved loyal allies. In 1690, as the first joint invasion of New France crumbled before it began, Schuyler's brother Johannes had led a band of Mohawks in a successful attack on the French settlement at La Prairie. The next summer Quider slogged to Canada and fought his way home at the side of his Iroquois friends. Two years later, after a French and allied Indian invasion of the Mohawk country, he defied orders and organized a rescue of prisoners from the retreating attackers. The same year, Wesselse and the younger Schuyler secured the release of two Mohawks falsely accused of murdering several residents of Deerfield, Massachusetts.[28]

Such actions were not the only things that endeared the Albany mediators to their Iroquois friends. On crucial occasions, Schuyler and other magistrates traveled to Onondaga to make their case in person and to support their Iroquois allies in confederacy councils. There and at home, Schuyler's,

Livingston's, and Wesselse's positions in local and provincial government provided them with material resources with which to support and reward Iroquois clients. Like country squires at militia musters and election days in another time and place, they knew well the value of "treating" the common folk whom they wanted to keep in their interest. Such behavior coincided nicely with Iroquois expectations about generous headmen and the ratification of political ties through ritual exchanges of gifts. As providers and patrons, the Albany leaders acted in ways that Indians understood and respected.[29]

Dellius too earned Iroquois respect and influence. Governor Sloughter had concluded that the clergyman's work was essential and had lured him home with the promise of stipends from the province and the New England Company for the Propagation of the Gospel. The dominie plunged deeply into intercultural diplomacy, and in late 1696 and early 1697, while Livingston attended personal affairs in England, he emerged as chief recorder and manipulator of treaty sessions with Iroquois ambassadors. Meanwhile, with van Olinda's aid, he translated a number of religious texts into Mohawk, and by the end of the century he had baptized at least 131 Indians, most of them Mohawks. The religious sincerity of many of these conversions is open to question, but their political import is not. Anglophile groups existed in each of the Five Nations—for internal political reasons, Sadekanaktie's Onondaga faction was particularly strong—but the English had no more staunch friends than the Protestant Mohawks. Through most of the 1690s, they worked closely with Sadekanaktie, Dellius, Schuyler, Wesselse, van Olinda, and a young new interpreter named Jan Baptist van Eps to thwart increasingly popular Iroquois movements for peace.[30]

*   *   *

The pounding that the Five Nations took from Indian foes in the closing years of the 1690s was the principal reason that Iroquois diplomats would defy English demands and come to terms with their French and Indian enemies in treaties of "the Grand Settlement of 1701."[31] The process was aided mightily, however, by a precipitate decline in the influence of the Albany anglicizers and their anglophile Iroquois friends. Though Albany's problems hardly compared to those of the Five Nations, its residents suffered greatly during the war of the 1690s. French and Canadian Indian raids harassed the countryside, the fur trade dried up, and inhabitants fled. Feeling just as alone and betrayed by the English government in the war as did the Iroquois, many Albany residents—Leislerian and anti-Leislerian alike—began to repudiate the diplomatic and economic policies on which the anglicizing elite had risen to power. By the mid-1690s the town's leading merchants were convinced "that success against the French depended upon concerted action by all the colonies backed by English assistance," one historian concludes. "Failing that, . . . [they] preferred to maintain a neutrality which enabled them to continue their trade and spared them both loss of life and the cost of defensive measures."[32]

With regard to the fur trade and relations with the Iroquois, merchants of both political persuasions sought to broaden their reach beyond the Five Nations, who were, of course, in no position to supply pelts for the starving Albany market. In 1692, Vielé, whom Governor Sloughter had recently removed from his interpreter's post, headed west in search of new trading partners. Two years later he returned triumphantly at the head of a virtual army of Shawnees eager to bypass Iroquois middlemen. After the Peace of Ryswick, the anglicizers made their own contribution to diminishing the economic importance of their Iroquois friends. On an official diplomatic visit to Montreal in 1698, Schuyler and Dellius invited Mission Iroquois to trade directly at Albany. In subsequent years, various Albany leaders repeatedly renewed the invitation, and countless Canadian Indians accepted, firmly establishing an illegal trade between Albany and Montreal that would thrive for much of the next century.[33]

As the Iroquois, their wars, and their beaver pelts became less vital to Albany than they had been in the early 1680s, personal ties between Yorkers and Iroquois withered. A turning point in intercultural politics came in 1698, with the exposure of one of many questionable land grants made by Benjamin Fletcher, who had become governor in 1692 after the death of Sloughter. Late in his administration, Fletcher gave Dellius, Schuyler, Wesselse, Bancker, and New York merchant William Pinhorne title to most of the Mohawk Valley and to an enormous tract surrounding Schaghticoke on the upper Hudson—acreage including most of the Mohawk homeland; with help from van Olinda, Dellius somehow convinced eight Mohawks to sign a confirmatory deed. Leislerian Albany merchants, who feared the economic threat of Euro-American settlements on the tract and were eager to undermine the anglicizers' power, sought to void the transaction and gained the support of Fletcher's successor, Richard Coote, Earl of Bellomont. When Schuyler, Wesselse, and Bancker sensed the direction of the political winds, they resigned their shares, laying the blame for any deception on Dellius. Finally, in the spring of 1699, Bellomont pushed through the New York assembly a bill that invalidated the Mohawk Valley grant along with several others. At the legislators' insistence, the same bill removed Dellius from his pulpit.[34]

The damage to New York–Iroquois relations was considerable. Not only did Dellius's influence vanish from Iroquois councils, but van Olinda too lost her position. Bellomont, convinced that she was a principal reason Indian diplomacy was "managed, with extraordinary division and jealousy," dismissed her from provincial service and tried to banish her from Albany. In her place he reinstated that "good and faithful interpreter, name[d] Arnout Cornelissen Vilé."[35] Most other anglicizers also left or were forced from political office; only Schuyler and Livingston, whose expertise in Indian affairs was irreplaceable, remained in positions to mediate effectively between the provincial government and the Iroquois. Yet, as Vielé's return shows, both now had to share power in local politics and intercultural diplomacy with prominent Albany Leislerians, many of them members of the same Dutch merchant families that had presided over the collapse of New Netherland–Iroquois relations in the 1660s.[36]

As the influence of the anglicizers who had mediated between Albany and Iroquoia declined, English political leverage in the Five Nations reached a nadir. During the war, New York's failure to provide the military protection Dongan had promised undermined the credibility of anglophile brokers. And after the European peace Dellius's Mohawk converts must have further lost the trust of their confederates because of their role in the land deal. A measure of the weakness of anglophile factions is contained in the reports of Schuyler, Livingston, and Albany Leislerian Hendrick Hansen, who visited Iroquoia on Bellomont's instructions in the spring of 1700. In the Onondaga country, the travelers found many of the nation's men dispersed to fishing camps, as was usual at that time of year. Also fishing were many of the headmen, including the anglophile Sadekanaktie and the influential Onondaga neutralist Teganissorens. The leaders' absence apparently had as much to do with politics as with subsistence: when the New Yorkers tracked down Sadekanaktie, he told a rambling tale of factional intrigue strongly suggesting that men of anglophile views were no longer welcome in his village. At Onondaga, the New Yorkers found neutralists and anglophiles in retreat and Francophiles led by the headman Aradgi firmly in charge. Within a few months, Sadekanaktie and some twenty-five supporters had to flee their country entirely and take up residence on Schuyler's land near Albany.[37]

The eclipse of the anglophile factions paved the way for peace negotiations with western Indians and the French in 1700 and 1701, negotiations from which the remaining anglophiles were frequently pointedly excluded. During Sadekanaktie's exile from Onondaga, a council of leaders of the Five Nations surrendered to a delegation of Ojibwas. A few weeks later, over the objections of Teganissorens and his neutralist followers, Aradgi and a Seneca named Aouenano led an embassy to Montreal, where they capitulated to New France and all its Indian allies on behalf of the Senecas, Cayugas, Onondagas, and Oneidas. The dual surrenders of 1700 were not the last act in the drama. Later that year both Sadekanaktie (who would live only a few more months) and Teganissorens (who had briefly retired from leadership after the death of his wife) regained influence and worked collectively with francophiles to reunite the factionally divided confederacy, to bring the Mohawks into the peace, and to salvage some shreds of Iroquois independence. The next summer, their efforts culminated in the simultaneous treaties at Montreal and Albany and in Iroquois acceptance of neutrality between the European empires under the terms of the Grand Settlement.[38]

Of these events, New Yorkers had little control and less understanding. After a pivotal 1701 meeting at Albany, the deceased Bellomont's successor, Lieutenant Governor John Nanfan, was convinced that he had "intirely . . . fix'd our Indians in their obedience to his Majesty." In reality, the Mohawk anglophile Onnucheranorum, speaking at the conference for all Five Nations, had substantially redefined his people's relationship with New York. "Wee doe assure you of our reall intentions to cleave close to you and never to separate our interest nor affections from you," Onnucheranorum, perhaps protesting too much, told the lieutenant governor. "If a warr should break out between us and the French, wee desire you . . . to assist and defend us." The headman said nothing about Iroquois assistance and defense of the English. The bond of friendship between the colony and the confederacy remained, but it was no longer the reciprocal military alliance Iroquois anglophiles and Albany anglicizers once believed it to be.[39]

Nanfan's misreading of Iroquois sentiments, like his virtual ignorance of the negotiations occurring between the Five Nations and New France and its Indian allies, was symptomatic of the breakdown in communications that political upheavals in Albany and Iroquoia had produced. In the first decade of the eighteenth century, the brokerage system further decayed. Schuyler increasingly devoted his attention to provincial rather than local politics, and Livingston was in England from 1703 to 1706. In their absence, their political foes at Albany repeatedly—and presumably therefore ineffectively—promulgated ordinances against the abuse of Indian fur traders; the Hudson River market-place was returning to the chaos of the mid-seventeenth century. Meanwhile, royal governor Edward Hyde, Lord Cornbury (1702–1708), consistently ignored and insulted Iroquois diplomats. He alternately missed appointments and called snap treaty sessions, he failed to distribute customary diplomatic presents, and he only once formally "brightened" the Covenant Chain during his tenure.[40]

The close partnership between Albany anglicizers and Iroquois anglophiles had collapsed, and with it the triangular system of political brokerage and the reciprocal alliance created in the administrations of Andros and Dongan. There would be no more scenes like the Mohawk rescue of embattled anglicizer leaders in 1689. A "fire of prudence and friendship" had been kindled "at the habitation of Quider," the Mohawk leader named Abraham informed latter-day broker William Johnson in 1755. "This fire never burnt clear and was almost extinguished."[41] For more than a generation until Johnson was able to fan the flames and re-enlist Mohawk warriors in Great Britain's imperial struggles with the French, the English-Iroquois alliance blazed brightly only in the fertile minds of such imperialist politicians as Cadwallader Colden, who wove the elaborate fiction that the Covenant Chain was an Iroquois empire of Native peoples and their lands all "Dependent on the Province of New-York" and thus all subject to British, rather than French, suzerainty. The Five Nations—struggling to preserve their independence and political unity as their various headmen cultivated a tangled and often contradictory web of economic, military, and diplomatic relationships with New York, Pennsylvania, New France, and a host of Native friends and foes—knew better.[42]

*   *   *

The rise and fall of the late seventeenth-century Anglo-Iroquois alliance and of the political factions and mediators who helped to create it illustrate the complexities of interactions among the peoples and polities of colonial North America. A reconstruction of the larger whole that the Native and European peoples of early America shared requires simultaneous attention to the broad North American context, to the internal dynamics of local communities, and to links between the two levels of experience. The Albany anglicizers and the Iroquois anglophiles exemplify those connections. As members of local political networks and as brokers between their communities and the outside

world, they struggled and allied with imperial officials and with similar individuals elsewhere to serve the interests of their compatriots, their particular
political factions, and themselves. In all this, their short-lived successes were
just as important as their long-term failures. Trade and peace, exchange and
power, depended, as they had for centuries previously in Native North America, on personal connections among leaders.

PART II

European Power and
Native Land

CHAPTER 7

Land and Words:
William Penn's Letter to the
Kings of the Indians

Among the major figures in seventeenth-century European-Indian relations, one is usually portrayed standing alone above the messy everyday business of politics, brokers, and deal-making, somehow exempt from the matrix of trade, land, and power. "William Penn told the Indians that he loved them all; their Men, Women and Children, and that he held Councils with them to perpetuate the Remembrance of his Affection towards them," said the Conestoga chief Tawenna in 1729. Echoing a refrain sung repeatedly by Indians and English alike in the early eighteenth century, Tawenna hoped "that all those things which Governour Penn Spoke to them may ever be remembred and imprinted on our and their hearts, so as to be observed inviolably."[1]

Nothing seems more in keeping with such memories than a remarkable document that dates almost—but not quite—to the very founding of Penn's North American experiment. On 18 October 1681—a little over eight months after Penn received the royal charter for his colony and, as it would turn out, just about a year before he first visited the place—he wrote a letter "to the Kings of the Indians." Two period copies bearing Penn's signature along with several manuscript versions made in later years can be found today at the Historical Society of Pennsylvania. The document has also appeared in print many times, most recently and authoritatively in the scholarly edition of the Penn Papers edited by Mary Maples Dunn and Richard S. Dunn.[2] Although it is thus well known to historians, Penn's letter has not received much close attention, perhaps because it seems to consist mostly of airy declarations of good will. Those declarations are what the historians who *have* noticed the document have emphasized. As Francis Jennings observed, the letter "is an earnest and moving statement, unique in the literature of Indian-European relations."[3]

Addressing the Native leaders as "My Freinds," the Quaker proprietor announced that

> There is one great God and Power that hath made the world and all things therein, to whom you and I and all People owe their being and wellbeing, and to whom you and I must one Day give an account, for all that we do in this world: this great God hath written his law in our hearts, by which we are taught and commanded to love and help and do good to one an other, and not do harme and mischeif one unto one another: Now this great God hath been pleased to make me concerned in your parts of the World, and the king of the Countrey where I live, hath given unto me a great Province therein, but I desire to enjoy it with your Love and Consent, that we may always live together as Neighbours and freinds, else what would the great God say to us, who hath made us not to devoure and destroy one an other but live Soberly and kindly together in the world? Now I would have you well to observe, that I am very Sensible of the unkindness and Injustice that hath been too much exersised towards you by the People of thes Parts off the world, who have sought themselvs, and to make great Advantages by you, rather then be examples of Justice and Goodness unto you, which I hear, hath been matter of trouble to you, and caused great Grudgeings and Animosities, sometimes to the shedding of blood, which hath made the great God Angry. But I am not such a Man, as is well known in my own Country: I have great love and regard towards you, and I desire to Winn and gain your Love and freindship by a kind, just and peaceable life; and the People I send are of the same mind, and shall in all things behave themselvs accordingly; and if in any thing any shall offend you or your People, you shall have a full and Speedy Satisfaction for the same by an equall number of honest men on both sides that by no means you may have just Occasion of being offended against them; I shall shortly come to you my self. At what time we may more largely and freely confer and discourse of thes matters; in the mean time, I have sent my Commissioners to treat with you about land and a firm league of peace. Lett me desire you to be kind to them and the People, and receive

thes Presents and Tokens which I have sent to you, as a Testimony of my Good will to you, and my resolution to live Justly peaceably and friendly with you. I am your Friend.

William Penn[4]

As Jennings concluded, "Penn meant what his letter said, and while he exerted effective control over his province, the Indians had good reason for gratitude."[5] But at least one hard-headed practical clause embedded itself in all the expressions of good will. Added as an interlineation—if not as an afterthought, at least as a second thought—was the notice that "in the mean time I have sent my Commissioners to treat with you about land and a firm league of peace." The passage as originally drafted read simply, "in the mean time, lett me desire you to be kind to my People." Without questioning the sincerity of Penn's "resolution to live Justly peaceably and friendly with" his Native American neighbors, this chapter suggests that the inserted clause "about land" holds a key to the very existence of this remarkable letter, to the precise time at which it was drafted, to broader trends in English imperial ideas, and to the non-Indian as well as Indian audiences the document was meant to impress. It also roots William Penn—for all his great virtues—more deeply in the everyday politics of the struggle for trade, land, and power in seventeenth-century North America.

*   *   *

The existence of the letter at all should be a matter of some surprise. Jennings may have overstated the uniqueness of the document's prose, but I am not aware of any previous English proprietor, representative of a chartered trading company, or royal governor who found it necessary to try to communicate in advance, in writing, with Native people whose lands were about to be colonized. In 1587, it apparently never occurred to Sir Walter Ralegh's colonists to seek Native permission to establish an English beachhead on Roanoke Island or that there might be any difficulty in fulfilling Ralegh's pledge to grant five hundred acres of Indian land to each colonist who paid his own way. Similarly, in 1607 John Smith and the Virginia Company's colonists asked no one's leave before setting up shop on Jamestown Island, and Smith pointedly ignored Powhatan's efforts to get them to resettle in a more suitable part of Tsenacomoco.[6] In 1620, William Bradford and the Plymouth colonists made no particular effort to contact their Native neighbors at all

William Penn to the Kings of the Indians, 18 October 1681 (DAMS 8044), Penn Family Papers (045A), Box 7, folder 48, Historical Society of Pennsylvania (HSP). Note the inserted phrase on the second page.

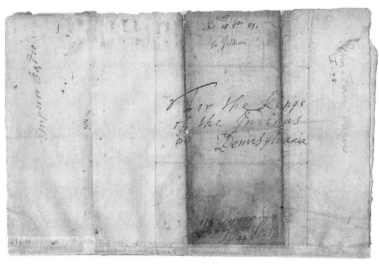

At what time we may more largely and freely confe[r]
[I] have sent my Commissioners to treat with you about land and a
league of freindshippe &c:discourse of thes matters, in the mean time, lett the desir[e]
them &c to be kind to my People, and receive thes Presents a[nd]
Tokens which I have sent to you as a Testimony of m[y]
Good will to you, and my resolution to live Justly p[eace]
-ably and freindly with you, I am your Freind

Wm Penn

Sr: 18. 8br: 81.
to Indians

For the Kings
of the Indians
in Pennsylvania

until the English-speaking Samoset came walking out of the woods to greet them months after their landfall. In Robert Cushman's words, the newcomers had long since concluded that it was "lawfull . . . to take a land which none useth, and make use of it."[7]

Not all early seventeenth-century English commentators fully agreed on that point, however. True, in 1609 Virginia promoter Robert Gray had argued that "Savages have no particular proprietie in any part or parcell of that Countrey, but only a generall recidencie there, as wild beasts have in the forrest." But, by contrast, a year later William Crashaw had insisted that "A Christian may take nothing from a Heathen against his will, but in faire and lawfull bargaine."[8] The debate continued in 1629, when John Winthrop and others planning to emigrate to Massachusetts Bay circulated among themselves various drafts of a document that ultimately concluded that, "As for the Natives in New England . . . , if we leave them sufficient for their use, we may lawfully take the rest, there being more than enough for them and us."[9] Still, whatever position English writers took in these controversies, none of them seems to have seriously considered discussing the matter with Native people or communicating a decision to them, in writing or otherwise.

Perhaps the closest precedent for Penn's letter was the reading of the *requerimiento,* a practice that no self-respecting English person steeped in the "Black Legend" of Spanish cruelty would admit to be following. Although by Penn's day the practice had long since gone out of use, sixteenth-century Spanish conquistadors had once been required to read to Native people a formal document announcing that the pope, "who succeeded . . . St. Peter as lord of the world . . . made donation of these islands and mainland to the . . . king and queen [of Castile] and to their successors, with all that there are in these territories." If you will submit to your new rulers, the conquistadors were to inform the Natives, "we in their name shall receive you in all love and charity" and gently encourage, but not force, conversion to Christianity. "But if you do not do this or if you maliciously delay in doing it . . . we shall forcefully enter into your country and shall make war against you in all ways and manners that we can, and shall subject you to the yoke and obedience of the Church and their highnesses." With a properly notarized record that the requerimiento had been read, the Spaniards, when they returned home to Iberia, hoped to be absolved of suspicion that their warfare had been unjust. Ultimately, then, the audience for the practice was European rather than American.[10]

Penn's letter had an entirely different tone, but not an entirely different message—and not an entirely different audience. The belligerent threats of the requerimiento were nowhere to be seen, and of course there was no reference to the pope, but the Quaker proprietor did make it clear to the Natives that "God hath been pleased to make me concerned in your parts of the World, and the king of the Countrey where I live, hath given unto me a great Province therein." There is no doubting the sincerity of Penn's "desire to enjoy" that province with the Indians' "Love and Consent," but also no doubting the certainty of his belief that divine and civil authority alike made Pennsylvania legitimately his to enjoy. Nonetheless, Penn's letter placed an extraordinary emphasis on voluntary negotiation and an extraordinary lack of emphasis on Native submission to European government. English and Indians, Penn proclaimed, were to "live together as Neighbours and freinds," not rulers and ruled, and, "if in any thing any shall offend you or your People, you shall have a full and Speedy Satisfaction for the same by an equall number of honest men on both sides."[11]

This language of friendship, more than any other aspect of Penn's policies, struck an enduring chord with Native people. Nothing so perishable as a Covenant Chain bound him to his Indian neighbors, later orators insisted. "They are not to be as People bound together to each other, tho' the Bonds were ever so strong, tho' they were of Iron," Tawenna proclaimed in 1728, "but they and we, as William Penn said, must be as the same Body, half the one and half the other, that cannot be divided." Not even kinship terms would do for describing the relationship, another Conestoga chief had insisted in 1720. "When Governour Penn first held Councils with them, he promised them so much Love and Friendship that he would not call them Brothers, because

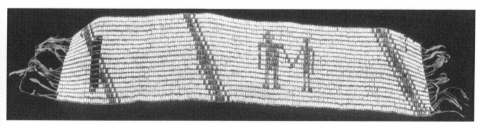

Penn Treaty Wampum Belt, Courtesy of the Philadelphia History Museum at the Atwater Kent, The Historical Society of Pennsylvania Collection. Said to represent the agreement made between William Penn and the Lenapes in 1682, the imagery is usually interpreted to portray a stout European with a broad Quaker hat clasping hands with a Native American. It is just as likely that the stout figure is a strong Indian wearing chief's regalia welcoming a weak early colonist.

Brothers might differ, nor Children because these might offend and require Correction, but he would reckon them as one Body, one Blood, one Heart, and one Head."[12]

In its insistence on asserted equality and unity, Penn's late seventeenth-century proposal "to treat with you about land and a firm league of peace" could not, for all its echoes of the requerimiento, have traveled further from the spirit of its sixteenth-century Spanish predecessor. In several important ways, that journey was a product of the historical moment in which the words were composed. Penn was a leading figure in the second generation of Quakers who perfected the use of public letters to promulgate the theological and other decisions of the London Yearly Meeting to a network of supposedly equal, but in fact subordinate, gatherings of Friends elsewhere in the world. "These regional and local meetings," as historian John Smolenski explains, "sent letters in response, vocally assenting to the Yearly Meeting's decrees," simultaneously reinforcing spiritual harmony, organizational unity, and hierarchical discipline among the Society of Friends—while also setting Quakers firmly apart from their spiritual and political enemies.[13] Surely Penn's letter to the Indian kings—addressed to his "Freinds," infused with themes of harmony, of love, and of a god who writes laws in human hearts—grew from this Quaker discursive mode. Such a letter was the rhetorically egalitarian mechanism by which a Quaker hierarchy communicated authority and exercised discipline. This was how a Friend whose god and king had given him "a great Province" might be expected to evoke the "Love and Consent" of that province's Native inhabitants, in contrast to the "unkindness and Injustice" inflicted by other Europeans unguided by the Inward Light.

The contexts for Penn's letter extended far beyond the discursive practices of his Quaker coreligionists, however, to reflect more worldly ideas circulating at Charles II's court. Although "imperial" and "policy" may be words too strong to describe the often contradictory thinking of those who envisioned English colonial expansion during the Restoration period, several trends had become clear during the 1660s—trends that make Penn's Holy Experiment seem a bit less new under the sun than it does when viewed in isolation. Among other developments, the early 1660s saw the creation of the Company of Royal Adventurers into Africa (later reorganized as the Royal African Company), the granting of a vast tract of land claimed by Spanish Florida to the eight Lords Proprietors of Carolina, and of course the conquest of New Netherland with its rechristening as "New York" under the personal proprietorship of James, duke of York. In every case, these enterprises were either under the control of a closely held trading company dominated by members of the royal family or, more often, by proprietorships composed of one or more influential courtiers who had either remained loyal to the Stuarts during the interregnum or aided the return of Charles II to the throne in 1660. The financial rewards for these men were expected to be immense (although few of those expectations proved realistic). James, for instance, planned on at least £10,000 per year in customs revenues from the furs and other commodities exported from New York. This would be a drop in the bucket for a man who spent nearly a quarter-million per year to live in the way a king's brother should, but enough to make a significant dent in annual deficits approaching £30,000, particularly when combined with rents, fees, taxes, and other emoluments from the European colonists already living in his newly conquered province.[14]

Among those to whom the crown owed favors was William Penn's father, Sir William Penn. Despite his service to Oliver Cromwell's regime, the elder Penn had nonetheless been instrumental in paving the way for Charles II's Restoration, had subsequently held several high offices, and had loaned the Stuart house at least £11,000 before his death in 1670. In payment of that debt, the younger Penn had received his proprietary grant in 1681. Like his proprietary counterparts in the Carolinas, New York, and New Jersey, Penn hoped to make substantial profits from land rents and other duties, to pay off not only the debt he had inherited from his father but the many thousands of pounds he had spent in extracting his charter from the royal bureaucracy and launching the colony.[15]

But also like his counterparts, Penn dreamed of far more than mere personal enrichment, and thus saw no contradiction between his financial needs and his plan for a Holy Experiment in religious toleration under the benign Quaker rule of himself as "True and Absolute Proprietary." In ways deeply rooted in the oft-thwarted hopes of those surrounding the Stuart family, others also dreamed of social perfection under aristocratic guidance. Nowhere were such dreams more on display than in the gloriously impractical "Fundamental Constitutions" that Anthony Ashley Cooper and John Locke drew up for the Carolina proprietors in 1669. Among its many feudal fantasies, it envisioned almost complete religious toleration for all colonists, including those who were enslaved. Similarly, the governor of the duke of York's domain in North America promulgated a form of toleration in the voluminous "Duke's Laws" that governed much of New York beginning in 1665. Those laws also reveal an interethnic order that James and his circle placed at the center of their imperial vision and that brings us back to the context for Penn's letter of 1681. No land was to be purchased from Indians without prior permission from the governor and a personal appearance before him by both buyer and seller. Trade was to be strictly controlled by licenses, with particular attention to the sale of firearms, ammunition, and liquor. Colonists were required to assist Native people in building fences to protect their cornfields from wandering livestock, and "all injuryes done to the Indians of what nature whatsoever shall upon their Complaint and proofe thereof in any Court have speedy redress gratis . . . , as if the Case had been betwixt Christian and Christian."[16]

These provisions of the Duke's Laws reflect a more general English reconsideration of the question of Native land rights during the generation before Pennsylvania received its charter. As legal historian Stuart Banner explains, while there had never been wholesale agreement or much intellectual coherence among early seventeenth-century figures such as Cushman, Gray, and Winthrop, early English promoters had generally subscribed to the twin doctrines later known as *vacuum domicilium* and *terra nullius*—that lands empty of "civilized" inhabitants and unowned by Christian monarchs were free for the taking under the so-called rights of "first discovery" or "first possession." But, despite the blustering of theorists writing in European capitals, on the ground in North America, all who dreamed of asserting their rights under *vacuum domicilium* quickly came up against two important facts. First, the land self-evidently *was* already owned, and colonists who pretended otherwise could not long enjoy anything like peaceable possession; self-preservation, if nothing else, required that colonists at least go through the motions of negotiating with Native owners to purchase the territory they planned to occupy. Second, and often more important, hardly an inch of North American real estate was not contested by various European powers who claimed first discovery or possession—and questioned by internal critics within each power who raised pesky moral qualms about the whole imperial enterprise. The best resolution to all such contests came to be seen as possession of a written deed from a Native leader who transferred clear title to a particular European claimant.[17]

As with so much else in the colonization of North America, the Dutch seem to have grasped this concept first and most wholeheartedly, if only because every outpost they established intruded on competing claims of the English, French, Swedish, Spanish, or Portuguese. Thus, in 1625 the Director-General of New Netherland was instructed to record purchases of Indian land in "a contract being made thereof and signed by them in their manner." But the English were not far behind the Dutch in appreciating the virtues of what Jennings called "the deed game."[18] As early as 1610, an apologist for the Virginia Company justified English occupation of Tsenacomoco in a long list of ways, "but chieflie because *Paspehay*, one of their Kings, sold unto us for copper, land to inherit and inhabite."[19] By the 1630s Roger Williams had articulated a powerful moral defense of Native land rights. "We have not our Land by Pattent from the King," he asserted; "the Natives are the true owners of it."[20] Soon Williams and rival New England colonial rulers were using deeds signed by Indians to strengthen their claims against each other and against the Dutch. And, for their part, as Jennings observed, "when the Dutch became embroiled . . . with Swedes and assorted English provincials, they pulled out their deeds."[21] Penn was personally acquainted with the importance of Indian deeds from his experiences as one of the proprietors of West New Jersey, which—struggling with the problem of multiple overlapping Dutch and English alleged purchases from Natives—appears to have been the first English colony to make systematic provisions for keeping a central record of the documents and attempting to place the process of negotiations firmly under the control of the proprietors, rather than individual colonists.[22]

Largely as a result of such experiences in North America, by the 1680s not just Penn but most English imperial planners agreed that colonial territory had to be purchased from Native owners—and that no land could be sold to colonists that had not first been duly bought and paid for as documented with an Indian deed.[23] Very recent events drove this conclusion forcefully home. In 1681, no English person interested in North America could have been unaware of the disastrous wars between colonists and Native people that had recently wracked the continent. Penn may not have known about the Pueblo Revolt that, a year before he wrote his letter, had banished the Spanish from their colony of New Mexico. But he and Charles II's courtiers were well aware of King Philip's War, which convulsed southern New England from 1675 to 1676.[24] Also familiar were postmortems on the battles that pitted Virginians and Marylanders against Susquehannocks and other Native peoples during Bacon's Rebellion in 1676–1677, events that occurred just to the south of Penn's new colony. Along with a pamphlet called *Strange News from Virginia*, readers in 1677 could pick up a copy of the Treaty of Middle Plantation, which gave the impression that all had been set right between English and Indians in the Chesapeake, in large part because Native territorial boundaries were at least formally acknowledged, although the lands protected were alleged to be held by grant from the king, rather than by indigenous right.[25]

As Penn's charter worked its way through the Court bureaucracy and as he drafted his letter to the Indian kings, such publications helped the planners of a reformed Stuart empire to conclude that poorly governed colonists had brought the simultaneous catastrophes on themselves and that a rethinking of policies toward Native Americans was vital. As New York Governor Edmund Andros put it, conflicts such as King Philip's War and Bacon's Rebellion were what the English "must expect and bee lyable to, so long as each petty colony hath or assumes absolute power of peace and warr."[26] Such thinking explains why, at the last minute, Penn's charter was amended to strike a clause allowing his government to "make Peace or Warr with the Indians as they shall think fitt," in favor of the more restrictive emergency-only war powers granted to "any Captain General of an Army."[27] Like others observing from the metropole, Penn understood the need to make a new start, to set himself apart from earlier colonizers who, as his letter to the Indians admitted, had "caused great Grudgeings and Animosities, sometimes to the shedding of blood, which hath made the great God Angry." His Quaker inclination toward pacifism was central to his vision of that new start, but it was also very much in line with broader thinking within imperial circles. It was almost a given that, as; Penn succinctly put it when explaining his process for acquiring Indian land and selling it to colonists, "I clear the kings and Indians Title. The Purchasser pays the scrivener and Surveyor." Both titles—royal and Native—needed to be dealt with before immigrants could complete the deal.[28]

*   *   *

Placing Penn's letter against the immediate backdrop of King Philip's War and Bacon's Rebellion and the longer-term development of English thinking about Native land rights thus helps us understand its emphasis on establishing "a firm league of peace." Yet a more finely grained timeline raises an important question. If the primary purposes of Penn's letter to the kings of the Indians were to proclaim the proprietor's legitimate authority over Pennsylvania, to declare a fresh start in relations with the region's Native people, and to base that start on fair purchases of land, one might expect it to have been sent very shortly after the colony's charter was issued in March 1681. Indeed, within a month, ships were already carrying two letters to the existing *Euro*-American inhabitants of Pennsylvania, one from King Charles in both wax-sealed manuscript and printed broadside forms, and the other in multiple manuscript copies from Penn himself. These documents announced the new regime, promised the existing colonists a government "by laws of your own makeing," required obedience to the proprietor's deputy, and instructed the people to "pay him those dues (that formerly you paid to the order of the Governour of new york) for . . . [Penn's] use and benefitt."[29]

Yet apparently no letter to the Indians accompanied these April 1681 documents; the letter to the kings did not go out until October, when it was accompanied by two others, discussed below, reiterating to particular European inhabitants Penn's claims to authority. Joining the October communications was a sometimes cryptic series of instructions to Deputy Governor William Markham and the commissioners whom Penn had appointed to allot land to the colony's "first purchasers" and to lay out the city of Philadelphia.[30] These were the men to whom Penn's letter to the Indians referred when it announced that he had "sent . . . Commissioners to treat with you about land and a firm league of peace."

And the proprietor's instructions to the commissioners indeed said as much about land as about peace. "Be tender of offending the Indians, and hearken by honest spyes, if you can hear that anybody inveighs the Indians not to sell, or to stand off and raise the value upon you, you cannot want those that will inform you," Penn wrote. "To soften them to mee and the people, lett them know that you are come to sit downe Lovingly among them. Let my Letter . . . about just dealing with them be read in their Tongue, that they may see, wee have their good in our eye, equall with our own Interest." The commissioners were, Penn instructed, "from time to time in my Name and for my use, [to] buy Land of them where they justly pretend, for they will sell one anothers, if you be not Carefull, that so such as buy and come after these Adventurers may have Land ready."[31] A separate additional memorandum to Markham and the commissioners put things more urgently. They were "First, To Act all in my Name as Proprietary and Governor[;] Secondly To buy Land of the true owners which I thinke is the Susquehanna People; Thirdly To treat Speedily with the Indians for Land before they are Furnisht by others with things that Please them." The proprietor urged his agents to "take advice in this."[32]

The urgency stemmed from the fact that the territory encompassed by Penn's royal charter was subject to a confusing set of overlapping European claims. The dilemmas of attempting to "clear the kings and Indians Title" began with the wording of Penn's charter itself. As the duke of York's secretary confessed to the secretary to the Lords of Trade when asked to comment on an early draft, "I beleeve the Description by Lines of Longitude (especially) and of Latitude, are very uncertaine, and soe allsoe is it, under what Meridian the head of De La Ware River lyes; which I doe beleeve hath never yet beene observed, by any Carefull Artist."[33] Assigned to arbitrate the limits of Pennsylvania, Lord Chief Justice Francis North had frankly to confess his confusion about the exact course of the Delaware River. Pennsylvania's eastern boundary, he said, should follow the river north to the forty-third parallel, "if the said River doth extend so farre Northward. Butt if the said River shall not extend so farr Northward, thereby the said River so farr as it doth extend and from the head of the said River, the Eastern bounds are to be determined by a Meridian line to be drawne from the Head of the said River unto the said three and fortieth degree." By modern reckoning, this would have included most of today's New York State, except that the justice's document elsewhere set the northern boundary not at the forty-third parallel but at "the begining of the three and fortieth degree," which most lawyers understood to mean just past the forty-second parallel, where the Pennsylvania border would in fact much later be set. With seemingly more precision, Justice North placed the western boundary at five degrees of longitude inland, far into an Indian country that no Englishman had mapped but that everyone presumed to include the Susquehanna River Valley.[34]

The greatest and most enduring confusion that Justice North sowed, however, involved the southern limits of Penn's grant, defined by "a Circle drawne at 12 Miles distance from Newcastle Northward and Westward then to the begining of the fortieth degree of Northern latitude, and then by a straight line Westwards to the limitt of Longitude abovementioned."[35] In that one tangled phrase lay the origins of the dispute between Penn's family and its proprietary neighbors to the south, the Lords Baltimore, for Maryland's royal charter set its northern boundary at a line that "lieth under the fortieth degree." "Begining" and "under" were the key words of contention, for either could be construed to put the boundary closer to the thirty-ninth than the fortieth parallel; if so, Maryland would virtually cease to exist. On the other hand, although no one knew it at the time, the actual location of the fortieth parallel was well north of what would become Philadelphia. (The twelve-mile circle around Newcastle also lay well south of the accurate line.) Both Justice North and William Penn, however, seem genuinely to have believed that the parallel lay much farther south than we now know it does, and that Penn and Baltimore could easily negotiate the relatively small difference encompassed by "begining" and "under" between themselves. This London-based geographical misunderstanding influenced a highly inaccurate map that Penn had published in 1681, which placed the mouths of the Delaware and Susquehanna Rivers firmly within

Pennsylvania and relatively close together, while, with equal inaccuracy, making each stream's serpentine course appear to flow almost straight from north to south.[36] Similarly, if a bit more tentatively, Penn's first promotional tract, *Some Account of the Province of Pennsilvania* (which in some bindings included a copy of the map), announced that, "for *Navigation*," the colony was "said to have two conveniences; the one by lying Ninescore miles upon *Delaware* River" and "the other . . . through *Chespapeak-Bay*" to the Susquehanna.[37]

The struggle with Baltimore over these water routes alone would have been

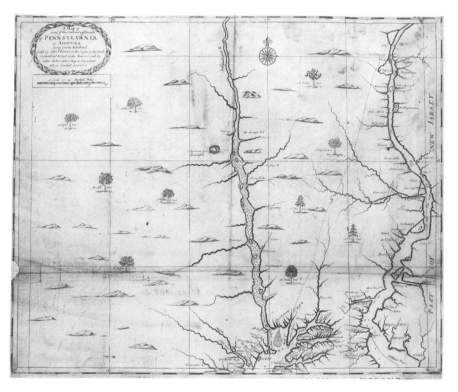

A Map of Some of the South and East Bounds of Pennsylvania in America, Being Partly Inhabited (London, 1681). The Historical Society of Pennsylvania (HSP). The map's misleading depiction of the courses of the Susquehanna and Delaware Rivers may have reflected genuine geographical ignorance. The accompanying text says that "the Intention of this *Map*, is to give an account . . . , so far as the Relations received from persons that have been upon the place, could give any light towards it." Nonetheless, it shows the importance Penn attached to securing access to the mouths of waterways contested by Maryland.

enough to turn Penn's mind toward negotiating with the Native inhabitants to gain clear title to the contested territory. Yet there were additional complications. Whatever claims the duke of York (and the English crown) possessed to New Castle and any other points on the west shore of the Delaware River and Bay derived from the 1664 conquest of New Netherland from the Dutch, as ratified in the 1674 Treaty of Westminster. The English crown, of course, had never recognized the legitimacy of the Dutch claim in the first place; the military campaigns of 1664 thus could be christened not conquests but the king's "remedyes" for "the Intrusion of such monsters and the exceeding damage to his subjects by this bold usurper."[38] Further complicating things, the Dutch claim to the lower Delaware in turn rested on their conquest of the territory from the Swedes, whose territorial legitimacy the Dutch West India Company had never recognized. Moreover, the duke of York's 1664 royal patent to New York (from which New Jersey had quickly been carved out, later to be split into separate East and West Jersey proprietorships) stopped at the *east* bank of the Delaware. Neither New Castle nor anyplace else on the west bank had ever been clearly granted him by royal charter from his brother King Charles II. And, in any case, James, in exile because of the recent Exclusion Crisis, in which Parliamentary opponents sought to bar him and any other professed Catholic from the throne, was, despite his trappings of royalty, in a weak position to defend his claims.[39]

At the time Penn's charter was issued, then, the only Englishman with an unambiguous royal title to *any* lands west of the Delaware River was Penn's rival Baltimore. Within the past decade, Baltimore had aggressively asserted his claims in a way that hardly endeared him either to the duke of York or to anyone else at Court. In 1669, a Maryland surveying party determined that the western shore of the Delaware Bay and River to a point well north of New Castle lay within Baltimore's boundaries. Shortly thereafter, Maryland proclaimed the area to be a county of the province and began to dispatch more surveying parties. In 1672, when one of these met armed resistance from rival colonists at the place known as Whorekills (modern Lewes, Delaware), Baltimore sent a troop of horse to plunder the settlement. Before this audacious assault on a territory ruled by the king's brother could be sorted out, the Dutch reconquest occurred, adding some legitimacy to Baltimore's next move on the Whorekills, a brutal December 1673 raid in which Maryland troops burned every structure except a single barn and left the starving and freezing Dutch and Swedish inhabitants to rely on their Native trading partners to get through the winter. When the duke of York regained his colony in 1674 and reasserted his shaky authority over the west bank of the Delaware

River and Bay, the contest had thus already moved far beyond poorly drawn maps, confusing royal patents, and lawyerly hairsplitting. And in 1677, Baltimore reasserted his claims by offering land grants in the Whorekills area. Penn's 1681 charter placed him deep in these struggles, as the third, and politically weakest, of the rival English claimants.[40]

*   *   *

By September 1681, when Penn wrote his letter to the Indians, he already knew he was in danger of losing to Baltimore control of the mouths of both the Delaware and Susquehanna "conveniences" for his colony—and thus of all import and export revenues. At the heart of the controversy, he explained, "was not the love or need of the land, but the water." He did not yet know that, in August 1682, he would succeed in extracting from the duke four documents that transferred title to what would later become the state of Delaware to him, that when he finally got to North America in 1682 among his first acts would be to claim that title through ritual enactments of receiving "one turf with a twigg upon it" from the European inhabitants, or that the king would formally ratify Penn's possessory rights in 1683.[41]

In that year, as the multi-sided controversy reached a peak, Penn explained his understanding of the complicated issues of clearing the king's and the Indians' title in a memorandum to Markham on how Baltimore's claims should be countered. In 1632, Penn argued, Charles I had granted the first Lord Baltimore "a Country in Ameri[ca] . . . being all of it Uncultivated and unplanted, saving by a few Savage Natives: which was a misinformation to the King" because "part of the Eastern Shore and Delaware Bay, was before, and at the passing of this Patent, claimed and planted, and purchased of the Natives by the Dutch, a Christian and European State; in peace with the Crown of England." Even if the Dutch were illegally encroaching on territory claimed by the English crown, Baltimore still could not assert possession of the territory because "his Patent gives him only Land in the Possession of the Savages, and not planted by Christians." Moreover, even if Baltimore did have "a Right to it, yet his plainly Suffering Invaders to live above 30 years there, and *not under the English Soveraignty* while he had it as part thereof, is a Treachery to the Crown, and so a forfeiture of his Patent." His belated attempts to "take the Whorekills" counted for nothing, because it occurred "about 7 Years after it had been first in the Duke's Possession."[42]

Yet, in the end, none of this mattered as much as that

the Dutch had the Title of the Civil Law, by which the Crown of England holds these Parts of the World, to witt, quæ nullius sunt, in bonis, dantur occupanti, That which is no body's is the Right of him that occupieth and enjoyeth it; for there was no Christian Body there at the time the Dutch seated it, to prevent them by a prior Clame. . . .

The Dutch had the Natives Right, of whom they fairly purchased it, who, if allow'd to be natural Lords of the Soil (that are as exact Preservers of Property as we are) it doth indeed over throw the Dutch Clame, by that maxim of the Civil Law; but then it establisheth it by another, which is also the Law of all Nations, that whosoever buyeth any thing of the true Owner, becomes rightful Owner of that which he bought; and that the Indians are true rightful Lords of the Soil, there are 2 Reasons; 1st, because the Place was never conquer'd. 2dly That the Kings of England have alwaies commanded the English to purchase the Land of the Natives, as appears by many Letters sent to Governors and Colonies, to that Effect, which, it is supposed they would never have done, to the prejudice of their own Title, if the Right of the Soil had been in them, and not in the Natives.[43]

For Penn, then, in both ideal and practice, possession ultimately had to be traced to documented purchases from Indians. When he wrote his letter in September 1681, he was not just articulating an abstract ideal of justice and peace to an ill-defined generic set of "kings of the Indians" but announcing to a very specific (if vaguely known) group of chiefs his intention to purchase lands on the west bank of the mouth of the Delaware claimed by Maryland. This practical aim is demonstrated by the two letters to specific European inhabitants that accompanied the letter to the Indians. In language echoing the Indian letter, Penn hastily instructed Markham to "strive to give Content to the Planters, and with meekness and Sweetness, mixt with Authority, carry it so as thou mayst honour me as well as they selfe; and I do hereby promess thee I will effectually answear it to thee and thyn. Give the Inclosed in sweed, to the sweeds Preis[t] to read to the sweeds; it comes from the sweeds embassador in england the Lord Liembergh, whos lady is lately dead. Also myn to the Natives and the Inhabitants. And be tender of my Creditt with all, watching to prevent all fals storyes; and inculcate all the honest and advantageous things on my behalfe that may be, in which be diligent."[44]

The Swedish letter to the Swedish Lutheran priest (presumably Lars Carlsson Lock) appears not to have survived, but the one to "the Inhabitants" has. Addressed to James Frisby and five others with English names "at their plantations in Pennsylvannia" and signed "your real friend, William Penn," the letter warned the recipients "(if within my bounds as I am ready to believe; but I desire no more than my own) that none of you pay more taxes or assessments by any law or order of Maryland, for if you do it will be greatly to your own wrong as well as my prejudice, though I am not conscious to myself of such an insufficiency of power here with my superiors as not go be able to weather that difficulty if you should."[45]

This heavy-handed concern for asserting authority over the existing European inhabitants—which Baltimore, in a nice inversion of Quaker rhetoric, called "unkind and unneighbourly"—illuminates the otherwise puzzling urgency of Penn's instructions to Markham and the commissioners "to treat Speedily with the Indians for Land before they are Funisht by others with things that Please them." The "others" were Marylanders who held patents from Baltimore. Penn's concern with their competition—and with delays in getting the land transaction completed and in getting himself to North America—provide background for a second letter he sent to the Indians in April 1682, assuring them that "when the Great God brings me among you, I Intend to order all things in such manner, that we may all live in Love and peace one with another." (The surviving copy of this letter is endorsed by Thomas Holme: "I read this to the Indians by an Interpreter the 6th month 1682.")[46]

The same concern for besting Maryland's competition perhaps explains an opaque memorandum attached to at least one copy of the first land sale treaty finally concluded with Lenape chiefs in July 1682. Although English rivals are not mentioned in the text of the treaty, the note refers to "Remembring our neighbouring Collonies."[47] Heading off Maryland's competition more certainly lies behind a declaration Penn himself issued in October 1683, announcing that he had "bought of Machaloha all his Land lying between Delaware River the Bay of Chesapeake bay [sic] and Susquahannah River; And . . . warn[ing] all Persons, that they presume not to settle there on without" his permission.[48] Like latter-day pacifist requirimientos, all of these documents were aimed at persuading a European, not an Indian, audience of the legitimacy of the acts they described. And they allowed Penn to argue that, like the Dutch before him, he had "bought the natives right, which the Lord Baltimore never did."[49]

*   *   *

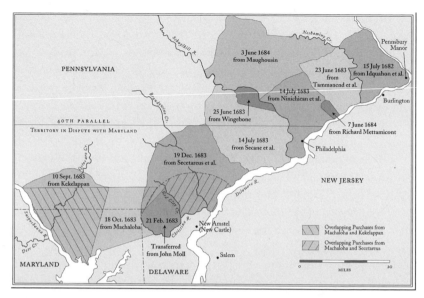

Approximate boundaries of William Penn's purchases from the Lenapes, 1682–1684. Map prepared by Adrienne Gruver, as revised with the assistance of Luis M. Waddell from Richard S. Dunn and Mary Maples Dunn, eds., *The Papers of William Penn* (Philadelphia, 1982), 2:491. Note the concentration of purchases in the area disputed between Pennsylvania and Maryland.

Penn's letter to the kings of the Indians, then, was very much a part of the time, the place, and the politics in which it was written. We are rightly captivated by its vision of "Love and freindship by a kind, just and peaceable life." That vision is also enshrined in folk memories of the legendary Treaty of Shackamaxon in 1682 as portrayed in the art of Benjamin West and the later Peaceable Kingdoms paintings by Edward Hicks. But fond recollections that, as eighteenth-century Native orators put it, Penn "took none of their Lands without purchasing and paying for them" can obscure the founder's practical need nonetheless to secure clear title to the land on which his Holy Experiment rested.[50] Lenape diplomats called Penn and his successors *Miquon*; their Iroquoian neighbors used the title *Onas*. Both names translate as "quill," and thus are puns on the proprietor's name.[51] Perhaps in light of the many purposes of Penn's 1681 letter, we might suspect a deeper level of meaning. Penn's pen was in many ways at the heart of his dealings with Native people and their lands.

CHAPTER 8

"No Savage Should Inherit":
Native Peoples, Pennsylvanians, and the
Origins and Legacies of the Seven Years War

The global war that began nearly three-quarters of a century after William
Penn wrote his letter—the war whose origins the Delaware leader Teedyuscung struggled both to explain and bring to an end when he negotiated with
Pennsylvanians in the 1750s—has usually been called the "French and Indian
War." Native peoples certainly would not have used that term. How could
they, when few recognized more than a uneasy alliance of convenience with
the French king and none could deny deep differences among the many communities that Euro-Americans lumped together as "Indians"? And who was
their enemy? Europeans and Euro-Americans in general? The Pennsylvania
governors they called, in memory of the founder, by the council title *Miquon* or *Onas*? The Virginians usually referred to as *Shemockteman* or "Long
Knives"? The British Crown as represented by the invading army of Major
General Edward Braddock? The Scots-Irish and German squatters who, often
without the consent of any European government, lived in ever-greater numbers along the Susquehanna and to the west? Or were the Indians' real enemies the Native people who collaborated with the Europeans, who somehow
continued to believe that the continent could be shared with the invaders?
Few things were simple or clear-cut, at least not in 1754, at the beginning of
the conflict many historians prefer to call by its European name, the "Seven
Years War."

Teedyuscung had a better name for these times. He called them "gloomy
and dark days."[1] Despite the gloom, at least two things *were* clear, however.
First, while long-standing imperial rivalries between Britain and France

provided an overarching structure for the conflict, the immediate origins of the Seven Years War lay in the disputed territory known as "the Ohio country," radiating westward from the confluence of the Monongahela and Allegheny Rivers at the site of modern-day Pittsburgh. Second, these North American roots of the global conflict are inseparable from the breakdown in relations between Native peoples and the province of Pennsylvania in the generation before the 1750s.

With the benefit of historical hindsight, a third thing also becomes clear. The crisis in Native-Pennsylvania relations established a pattern that would endure throughout the next half-century, during which British colonists would declare their independence and create a republic in which they would envision no permanent place for independent Native peoples. The vision of a continent reserved for descendants of Europeans pre-dated the Declaration of Independence and was hardly unique to settler colonizers. In 1755, when the Irish-born and English- and Dutch-trained Braddock began his doomed march to try to dislodge the French from the Ohio country, he met with six Native chiefs. One of them, the Delaware Shingas, recalled several years later that the Indians had "applied to General Braddock and Enquired what he

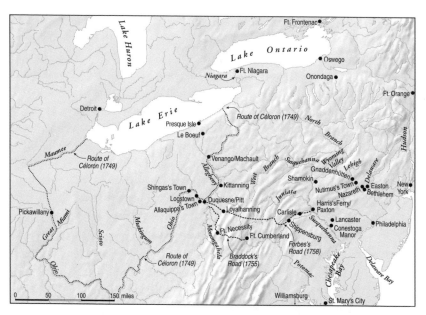

The Ohio country, 1748–1760. Map by Philip Schwartzberg.

intended to do with the Land if he Could drive the French and their Indians away. To which General Braddock replied that the English Shoud Inhabit and Inherit the Land, on which Shingas asked General Braddock whether the Indians that were Freinds to the English might not be Permitted to Live and Trade Among the English and have Hunting Ground sufficient To Support themselves and Familys as they had no where to Flee Too. . . . On which General Braddock said that No Savage Should Inherit the Land."[2]

*   *   *

Whoever would inherit its land, the Pennsylvania that Native people knew in the 1750s was very different from the place that William Penn had envisioned. Yet the same kinds of controversies over real estate that shaped the colony's early relations with Indians drove much of the transformation. The founder left North America for the last time in 1701, suffered a stroke in 1712, and remained in poor health until his death in 1718. During this period, he exercised little influence over what transpired in his province. His second wife, Hannah Callowhill Penn, and after her death in 1726, their sons John, Thomas, and Richard (none of whom, as converts to Anglicanism, shared their parents' commitment to Quaker values) struggled to pay the family's huge debts. The three sons also had to counter challenges to their authority from their half-brother William, offspring of the founder and his first wife, Gulielma Springett Penn. As the legal struggle continued and the family's financial deficit mounted, John, Thomas, and Richard Penn began making major speculative land grants in hopes of recovering some of the losses through quitrents, the annual fees due (but seldom actually paid) from property holders to the proprietor. Meanwhile, they deeded thousands of additional acres to themselves as private persons, from which they hoped to profit directly. But much of the granted territory had not yet been purchased from its Indian owners, and adherence to their father's policies about such purchases ensured that no revenues could be realized until it was.[3]

Apart from the desperate financial straits of Penn's sons (in 1734 John actually had to flee England to avoid imprisonment for debt), several factors made acquiring paper title to large Indian tracts ever more pressing. One derived from a fundamental cultural conflict with Indians over the nature of rights to what the English called *real property*, over the nature of the relationship among trade, land, and power. It was not that Native people had no concept of property ownership or of the transfer of that ownership to another party. But, when Lenapes first encountered Europeans, they—like virtually all Native people in eastern North America—conceived of property rights more in terms of active use for specific purposes than of static possession for all time. In their earliest transactions with Swedes, Dutch, and English, and perhaps even in their first treaties with Penn himself, Lenape leaders probably thought they were merely granting colonists privileges to employ land for sowing crops, building houses, and pursuing other activities, rather than permanently transferring what Europeans, with their very different views, considered exclusive possessory rights.[4]

With their drastically reduced numbers, post-epidemic Lenapes had plenty of territory to spare and thus agreed to numerous such grants. Perhaps they even saw these arrangements as the kind of strength through gifting that Teedyuscung would later describe by the term *Whish-shicksy*. But they had little reason to expect that they would have to leave their homes after transferring some rights to the newcomers or that the privileges they granted would not have to be renewed through additional gift payments in subsequent years. Moreover, among the decentralized Lenapes—particularly as their population reshuffled in the wake of epidemics—spokesmen for multiple kin groups in various villages might well assert legitimate claims to payment for the right to use a particular patch of ground that their ancestors had shared. One result of such confusion was that colonists claimed to have paid repeatedly for what they thought should be clear-cut, one-time transactions. Another was that, as late as the 1750s, Teedyuscung could still argue that the English "ought to have reserved some place for the Indians" within territories ceded by previous treaties.[5]

Still, as early as the turn of the eighteenth century, historical experience must have taught Lenape people that when English men made a purchase, the land was transferred in perpetuity, in the European sense. So, in the way that often happened in colonial North America, what were initially cultural misunderstandings became creative fictions subject to deliberate manipulation by all sides.[6] Treaties written in English that most Lenapes could not read for themselves described boundaries with deliberate ambiguity to allow the most capacious English interpretation. Meanwhile, Native leaders sometimes asserted claims to lands Europeans thought they had already purchased— perhaps because boundaries legitimately overlapped, perhaps in a deliberate effort to play a game similar to that of the colonizers. As William Penn had complained in the earliest days of his colony, "they will sell one anothers [land], if you be not Carefull."[7] More often, Indians rightly protested, the chicanery festered on the Euro-American side. "When one Man had formerly

Liberty to purchase Lands, and He took the Deed from the *Indians* for it, and then dies, after his Death, the Children forge a Deed like the true One, with the same *Indian* Names to it, and thereby take Lands from the *Indians* which they never sold," Teedyuscung explained in 1756. "This is Fraud."[8]

A generation later, Moravian missionary John Heckewelder recorded a more metaphorical traditional Delaware story about fraud:

> As the whites became daily more familiar with the Indians, they at last proposed to stay with them, and asked only for so much ground for a garden spot as, they said, the hide of a bullock would cover or encompass, which hide was spread before them. The Indians readily granted this apparently reasonable request; but the whites then took a knife, and beginning at one end of the hide, cut it up to a long rope, not thicker than a child's finger, so that by the time the whole was cut up, it made a great heap; they then took the rope at one end, and drew it gently along, carefully avoiding its breaking. It was drawn out into a circular form, and being closed at its ends, encompassed a large piece of ground.[9]

By the 1730s, the suspicions and confusions proliferated because Lenapes were no longer the only Native people involved. In the past half-century, various groups had resettled much of the watersheds of the upper Delaware, the Susquehanna, and the more western streams of the Ohio country, territories that had been almost entirely depopulated during the Native American wars of the 1600s. Among the recent arrivals were bands of Munsees and other Algonquian speakers who joined the Lenapes in communities coming to be known, and to identify, as *Delawares*. Pushed out of lands stretching from what is now New Jersey to southwestern New England, Delawares collected in portions of their peoples' ancestral territories on the west side of the upper Delaware River or in new homes along the Susquehanna and points farther west. Also prominent among the Indian settlers were Shawnees, Algonquian-speaking people whose ancestral homes may have been in the Cumberland and Tennessee River Valleys but who had dispersed widely during the seventeenth-century conflicts. Delawares and Shawnees were joined by an array of other migrants from almost every point on the compass: Mahicans from the Hudson River valley; Nanticokes, Conoys, and others from the Chesapeake region; Tuscaroras from the Carolinas who had migrated northward to join the Iroquois League as the Sixth Nation of the Haudenosaunee;

families from other Iroquois nations who moved southward and westward. Some of these people were returning to lands on which their ancestors had lived. Others, defeated in conflicts with Euro-Americans or deprived of their homes by treaties they considered unjust, were seeking refuge wherever they could find it. Some settled in ethnically defined villages, others in mixed places that could only be described as "Indian." Few of them recognized any central authority, Native or European, and none were in the mood to sell their lands and move again—although many were quite willing to grant privileges to traders and individual European settler families who could profitably share the territory with them.[10]

And those European families vastly complicated the situation for Pennsylvania authorities trying to assert legal title to lands occupied by diverse Indian peoples. In the years after William Penn's death, thousands of Scots-Irish and German immigrants streamed through the port of Philadelphia seeking freedom from economic privation and religious persecution in their homelands—this at the very moment that the battle among Penn's heirs for control of the province's lands had virtually halted formal distribution of property titles to immigrants. Even if the Pennsylvania land distribution system had been fully functioning, these two immigrant groups would have presented particular problems. The Scots-Irish, many of them fleeing rapacious English landlords in Ulster, were hardly eager to embrace the Penn family as their new masters. Many moved west into either proprietary or Indian lands with little regard to the niceties of legal paperwork and no intention of paying quitrents. Not for them was William Penn's orderly system for clearing in advance the claims of both the king and the Indians. Meanwhile, Germans were not legally entitled to own land in an English province at all without special dispensation from the legislature prior to 1740, when Parliament passed a general naturalization act. Yet by the thousands, Germans, too, occupied lands in the 1720s and 1730s. As early as 1728, the Delaware chief Sassoonan complained to Pennsylvanian James Logan that "he was grown old and was troubled to see the Christians settle on Lands that the Indians had never been paid for."[11]

Logan, as the proprietors' personal agent, as secretary of the province, and as commissioner of property for three decades after William Penn's departure in 1701, was a central figure in Pennsylvania's early eighteenth-century relations with Native people. A land speculator and fur trader in his own right, he had mixed his private interests with those of the Penn family to engage in vast real estate ventures, some of which involved territories not yet purchased from their Indian owners—so he had strong personal, as well as official, motives to solve the vexing problem of acquiring legal title before any more land was unofficially occupied by European immigrants. "As the numbers of these People encrease upon us, so will the Difficulties of settling them," he understated in 1728.[12]

The problem was pressing. In the late 1720s and early 1730s, the Penn family still owned clear Indian and royal title only to a triangular sliver of what would ultimately become the state of Pennsylvania. This was between the Delaware and Susquehanna Rivers, south of Tohickon Creek and South Mountain, and north of the fortieth parallel, below which Maryland would bitterly dispute Pennsylvania's claim until the 1760s, when Mason and Dixon surveyed their famous line at 39° 43'. Logan repeatedly complained that Maryland was prepared to legitimate its claims by issuing titles to immigrant squatters and endorsing armed resistance to Pennsylvania officials. From 1736 to 1738, rival militias from the two colonies chased each other through the lower Susquehanna Valley in the shooting match known as "Cresap's War" or the "Conojocular War." The conflict with Maryland highlights the practical reason that Logan and the younger Penns had to adhere at least

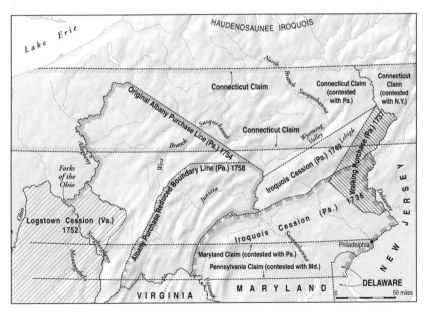

Pennsylvania's contested land claims, 1736–1758. Map by Philip Schwartzberg.

to the external forms of William Penn's insistence on clearly documented Indian land cessions. New York, Virginia, and even Connecticut—not to mention New France—all asserted claims to Indian territories that Pennsylvania considered within the bounds of its royal patent. As the founder had understood well, in European courts, the colony that possessed a plausible deed signed by Native leaders gained powerful ammunition in such controversies.[13]

While the younger Penns worked with Logan to produce an appropriate paper trail, they faced several related problems. The Indian communities living on the coveted lands not only were disinclined to sell, but the sheer diversity of their recently arrived residents made the structure of authority even at the most local level problematic. And even if a few alleged chiefs could be persuaded, bribed, or liquored into signing a land-cession, the extremely localized political traditions of the Lenapes, Munsees, Shawnees, and others ensured that those leaders could speak for only a fraction of the interests involved. No single political entity, or even a manageable set of such entities, existed with whom the Penns might have negotiated a legitimate treaty of cession. The problems of mediating among all these groups—indeed of any European agent safely navigating through the literal and metaphorical woods of the territory west of the Schuylkill—were daunting.[14]

Logan, however, devised a brilliant solution to the take-me-to-your-leader problem by identifying a central authority that, in his and the Penns' minds, could claim to speak for all the Indians concerned. As the brokered relationships that originally forged the Covenant Chain decayed in the early eighteenth century, factions among the Haudenosaunee Iroquois sought a closer alliance with Pennsylvania to counterbalance the diplomatic, military, and economic vise in which their powerful neighbors in the colonies of New York and New France threatened to trap them. Although Haudenosaunee lands lay well to the north and west of those of the Lenapes, seventeenth-century warfare had given the Iroquois a claim to the Susquehanna River territories of the Susquehannocks, or, as those who remained in that watershed were known in the eighteenth century, the Conestogas. Moreover, since the 1670s, the Covenant Chain treaties had established the principle (more in image than in reality) that, in dealing with the British, Iroquois chiefs served as master brokers for all the Indians of the Northeast. In keeping with this principle, by 1728, Logan was assuring Governor Patrick Gordon and the Pennsylvania provincial council that the Iroquois "have an absolute Authority of all our Indians, and may command them as they please." At least some hard-pressed

Haudenosaunee spokesmen were eager to validate Logan's fictions in hopes of gaining advantages for their own communities.[15]

Yet the relationship of Delaware peoples to the Anglo-Iroquois Covenant Chain was hardly clear. Munsees and Lenapes had apparently never been conquered by, and may never even have engaged in significant warfare with, the Iroquois. Still, in 1728 Sassoonan of the Delawares acknowledged that Haudenosaunee spokesmen had "often told them that they were as Women only, and desired them to plant Corn and mind their own private Business, for that they would take Care of what related to Peace and War." References to the Delawares as *women* appear in English records at least as early as the 1690s, and outside observers have puzzled over the meaning of that usage ever since. Such gendered terminology was evidently not limited to Sassoonan's and Teedyuscung's Delawares; in 1732 a Shawnee chief told Pennsylvania Governor Patrick Gordon that the Iroquois had "told the Delawares and us, Since you have nott hearkened to us nor Regarded whatt we have said, now wee will [put] pettycoatts on you, and Look upon you as women for the future, and nott as men."[16] Gunlög Fur, the most recent and sensitive scholar to examine the evidence, stresses the impenetrability of Native gendered rhetoric and practice at a historical distance of three centuries and the rapidly changing meaning of such things in colonial context. But it is almost certain that in the early eighteenth century when Delaware men referred to their nation as *women*, the primary meaning of the term was not pejorative. Instead, it placed the Delawares in an exalted position above the fray of masculine-denominated warfare among other peoples. "Delawares," Fur concludes, "used the metaphor to argue for nonintervention and a role as peaceful mediators."[17]

Despite—or rather because of—these ambiguities, as historian Francis Jennings showed, Logan and the Penns seized upon the diplomatic fictions of the Covenant Chain to go over the heads of the allegedly emasculated Delawares to get the land cessions they needed from the Haudenosaunee. As Logan put it in a letter to John Penn in 1731, "there will be an absolute necessity of treating with the Five [Iroquois] Nations and Securing their friendship more effectually."[18] Seeing in Pennsylvania the potential benefits of a powerful diplomatic protector and economic trade partner, at least some Iroquois leaders obliged. The key events in this Pennsylvania-Iroquois partnership were two treaties in 1736, one made publicly in a ceremonial visit of Haudenosaunee chiefs to Philadelphia and the other secured less decorously by Pennsylvania's agent Conrad Weiser at Shamokin as the Iroquois

James Logan (1674–1751). Portrait by Thomas Sully (after Gustavus Hesselius), 1831. The Library Company of Philadelphia. More than any other individual, Logan shaped early eighteenth-century Pennsylvania policy toward Native peoples and their lands.

delegation headed homeward. In the Philadelphia treaty, the Six Nations formally ceded all claims to lands on both sides of the Susquehanna River from North (Blue) Mountain southward, a cession that provided Pennsylvania vital paper ammunition in the Conajocular War with Maryland. The second agreement focused on lands farther east, to which Maryland held scant pretense. In this treaty, the Iroquois "released to John Penn, Thomas Penn, and Richard Penn, Proprietors of Pennsylvania, and to their Heirs and successors, ALL our Right, Claim and Pretentions whatsoever" between the Delaware and Susquehanna Rivers south of North Mountain. Although the Iroquois apparently made clear to Weiser that in relinquishing these pretensions, they could not speak for those, such as the Lenapes, whose claims were stronger, Logan and the Penns translated the document into a clear and positive grant of the territory to Pennsylvania.[19]

This grant was news to the people who lived on one particularly important tract, known to the Penns as "the Forks of the Delaware" and to the Lenapes as *Lechauwekink*, a word that colonists rendered as *Lehigh*. In recent decades, this area had become a magnet for Lenapes who tried to remain within their ancient territory rather than move farther westward. Among these were the then young Teedyuscung, who had emigrated from near today's Trenton, New Jersey. Although his family had no hereditary title to office, Teedyuscung's speaking talents allowed him to rise quickly to a prominent, though still junior, position, and the transactions with Pennsylvania he witnessed in the late 1730s shaped many of his subsequent actions.[20]

The more senior leader at the Forks, a chief named Nutimus, had announced his intention to defend his lands and the people gathering on them from English expansion decades earlier. In 1700, William Penn had agreed with another Lenape chief named Mechkilikishi upon terms for surveying lands that he had previously purchased to the south of the Forks. An elaborate plan called for two Europeans and two Indians to stroll along the banks of the Delaware River and its Tohickon Creek tributary as far as possible in a day and a half—while making sure to stop for a leisurely lunch during which their pack horse was to be unloaded and then reloaded. From the stopping point, a line was to be drawn toward the setting sun to define the purchase boundary. Midway through the first afternoon of the walk, a dispute arose when Penn's men insisted on crossing Tohickon Creek into territory over which Nutimus claimed jurisdiction. Nutimus refused to let them pass, the survey party broke up with its work uncompleted, and, for all intents and purposes, Tohickon Creek—twenty miles or so south of the Forks—remained the northern boundary of Pennsylvania. This affair constituted the first, and by far least controversial, "walking purchase" that affected the Delawares.[21] It also created the geographical dilemma that confronted land-deprived Logan in the 1730s.

The second, and far more famous, Walking Purchase, of 1737, originated in 1732. That year, Thomas Penn claimed to have discovered in the province's papers an early draft of the first walking purchase treaty his father had made with Mechkilikishi in 1700—a draft that omitted such important pieces of information such the date of the agreement and the direction in which the survey walkers were to go. It may well have been an outright forgery. Probably because Thomas Penn knew Nutimus could contradict him if he dated the document to 1700, he claimed that it referred to a land sale made between Lenapes and William Penn in 1686, long before Nutimus's time. The proprietor's story, then, was that the second Walking Purchase was not really a purchase at all, but instead merely the implementation of a half-century-old agreement that now needed only to be reconfirmed by re-strolling the boundaries originally agreed upon. In pursuit of this interpretation, the Pennsylvanians sent scouting parties into the woods to blaze a trail likely to take in the most territory in a thirty-six-hour trek. Nutimus's repeated objections finally produced a blunt Pennsylvania declaration in 1735 that the walk would take place whether he approved or not.[22]

The 1736 agreements with the Iroquois gave the Penns the legal cover they needed for their scheme and—more importantly—robbed Nutimus of any political and diplomatic support he might have received from the Iroquois. Under pressure from both Pennsylvania and the Six Nations, and undercut by other Delaware chiefs who had been courted by the Penns, the Forks leader had almost no choice but to agree in August 1737 that the walk could take place. But even that agreement could be achieved only through an act of almost incredible Pennsylvania audacity. At a treaty council in Philadelphia, Thomas Penn showed Nutimus and other Delaware headmen a poorly drawn map that led them to believe they were agreeing to only a very limited survey of lands along Tohickon Creek. English-language labels (which may have been added after the council was over) identified the stream that the Indians thought was the Tohickon as the "West Branch River Delaware," or what is today called the Lehigh. Before producing this map, Thomas Penn reminded the Delawares "that all the Indians must be fully sensible as well of the Justice of William Penn as of his great Love for al the Indians, since he made it Rule, constantly to be observed, neither to take possession himself, nor suffer other to possess themselves of any Lands without first purchasing them from the Indians, who had a Right to them."[23]

When the walkers (or, one might say with only slight exaggeration, sprinters) hired by the province to carry out the charade had completed their day-and-a-half journey—variously estimated by scholars at between fifty-five and sixty-five miles—they had enlarged the province by something on the order of twelve hundred square miles. The territory encompassed all of the lands on which Nutimus's people lived and the sites of today's cities of Bethlehem, Allentown, and Easton. All that was left to the Forks Indians was a tract of about 6,500 acres surrounding the village known as Nutimus's Town, but even this was legally defined as a proprietary manor belonging to the Penns, rather than to the Indians themselves, who were merely permitted to dwell on it as non-paying tenants. Euro-American settlers quickly moved into the Walking Purchase, occupying lands long since granted them by the Penn family. By 1740, more than one hundred households had taken up residence in the area. A year later, these were joined by the first of several German-speaking religious communities of the *Unitas Fratrum*, or Moravians, established at Bethlehem. Teedyuscung lived among these Christian newcomers for several years at the village called Gnadenhütten ("Huts of Grace"), where he acquired the baptismal name *Gideon*.[24]

Meanwhile, Nutimus and the Forks Indians continued to deny the right of any of the European migrants to invade their lands. The political forces arrayed against them became clear at a treaty council that the Penns' lieutenant-governor George Thomas called at Philadelphia in 1742, a council at which Nutimus hoped for a fair hearing of his grievances. Thomas declared to the Six Nations delegations present that he expected them to "cause these Indians to remove from the Lands in the Forks of Delaware, and not give any further Disturbance to the Persons who are now in Possession." In response, the Onondaga Iroquois orator Canasatego thunderingly asked the Delawares, "How came you to take upon you to sell land at all? We conquered you, we made women of you. You know you are women, and can no more sell land than women. . . . We charge you to remove instantly. We don't give you the liberty to think about it. . . . We, therefore, assign you two places to go—either to Wyoming [the modern Wilkes-Barre area] or Shamokin. You may go to either of these places, and then we shall have you more under our eye, and shall see how you behave."[25] This remarkable harangue—designed more for Thomas's ears and Euro-Americans' written documents than for the Delawares' enlightenment—is in several ways as brazenly mendacious as the map deception perpetrated on Nutimus five years earlier. The formerly respectful characterization of the Lenapes as peacemaking women became a slur. And most remarkable of all was Canasatego's claim that females had no right to sell land. In his own Haudenosaunee tradition, women—the farmers who controlled a village's cornfields—were the only ones who *could* convey use rights to others. *Men* were the ones who had no right to sell land on their own.[26]

Nonetheless, the message recorded in Euro-American documents was clear. Most of the Forks Lenapes had little choice but to move on. As Canasatego directed, many went to new homes at Shamokin or Wyoming, where Teedyuscung, having left the Moravians, emerged as "King of the Delawares" and repeatedly protested the travesty of 1737. He found vocal allies in the colony among Quaker political opponents of the Anglican Penns. Other Delawares followed Nutimus to new homes in the Susquehanna Valley. Still others went to the Ohio country, where they would nurse grudges against both the government of Pennsylvania and the Six Nations and watch as more and more German and Scots-Irish immigrants took up lands in their midst. The Forks Delawares, meanwhile, were not the only ones dispossessed by the diplomatic maneuvers of the Penn family government and its Iroquois allies. Two additional treaties between Pennsylvania and the Six Nations—at Philadelphia in 1749 and at the Albany Congress of 1754—transferred title to vast additional territories without the consent of the diverse Indians who lived there. Pennsylvania diplomacy triumphed on paper, but at the cost of destroying any legitimacy for the province's claim to William Penn's dream of "kind, just, and peaceable" relations.[27]

With such experiences scarring its newly arrived Indian residents, with so many parties contesting for control, with so little agreement among them, with so few overarching structures of authority to keep the peace—the territories from the Susquehanna River westward became a powder keg waiting to explode. The sparks that set it off came from outside the region. But everyone concerned was, to one degree or another, an outsider, and that was the crux of the issue. Delawares who hated Pennsylvanians, Shawnees whose ancestral territories may have lain to the southwest, Wyandots who lived to the northwest and granted permission for some of the Indian newcomers to settle lands there, and Six Nations Haudenosaunee Iroquois who lived to the north and asserted rights of conquest—all of these had, of course, far stronger claims than any Europeans to the land. Yet all were newcomers to the Ohio country, and all jostled for control in an arena of extraordinary ethnic and political complexity. Traders from Pennsylvania, meanwhile, followed the Indian migrants from the Delaware and Susquehanna into their new homes and were soon joined by rivals from Virginia. Their activities attracted the attention of British land speculators, British provincial governments, and the rulers of New France, adding more powder to the mix.

In 1749, alarmed by what were rightly perceived as British schemes for expansion west of the Appalachians and threats to the French network of Native trading alliances, the governor of New France sent an expedition from Montreal through the Ohio country to Detroit under the command of Pierre-Joseph Céloron de Blainville. Far from rallying Indian trading partners to the Gallic cause, the expedition alienated those concerned about rights to their lands when it made a great show of hanging metal plaques on trees and burying lead plates at strategic spots to assert Louis XV's claims. In subsequent years, the French pressed their assertions with a chain of posts that would culminate with the establishment of Fort Duquesne, at the site of modern Pittsburgh. Although many of the region's Indian inhabitants at least be-grudgingly welcomed the French as an alternative source of trade goods and a counterbalance to British power, others deeply resented them. As a result, in 1754, when Virginia Governor Robert Dinwiddie sent a troop of militia under George Washington to halt construction at Fort Duquesne, some Ohio Indians welcomed the intrusion. Indeed, the Ohio Iroquois Tanaghrisson struck the decisive blow against the French in what nonetheless turned out to be a humiliating defeat for Washington at the place since known as Jumonville's Glen. Braddock and his supposedly crack troops were subsequently sent from the British Isles to complete the job the Virginians had poorly started.[28]

*   *   *

These events were the beginnings of the Seven Years War, a conflict that in North America would last far longer than its eponymous global name implies. Bloodshed had been going on for nearly two years before hostilities between the French and British empires were officially declared in 1756. Indeed, news of that declaration arrived in North America even as Teedyuscung and his Pennsylvanian foes were beginning the first of many peace talks at Easton in 1756. One would think that the choice of sides in the imperial conflict would have been plain for most of the Delawares, Shawnees, and other Indians of the Susquehanna and Ohio countries. Braddock's arrogance (and military ineptitude), decades of embittered experiences as the government of

Pennsylvania pushed them from homes in the east, distrust of the Iroquois Six Nations who had consented to their dispossession—all apparently created a compelling case for the French as the least distasteful option.[29]

Iroquois opposition to a French alliance, especially when phrased in renewed gendered taunts, can only further have driven resentful Delawares, at least, in that direction. According to the Seneca leader known to the English as Newcastle, the council of the Iroquois confederacy gave Teedyuscung a wampum belt and told Delaware people to

> remember that you are our Women; our Forefathers made you so, and put a Pettycoat on you, and charged you to be true to us and lye with no other man; but of late you have suffered the String that tyed your petticoat to be cut loose by the French, and you lay with them and so became a common Baud, in which you did very wrong and deserved chastisement, but notwithstanding this, we have still Esteem for you, and as you have thrown off the cover of your Modesty and become Stark naked, which is a Shame for a Woman, We now give you a Little [Prick] and put it into your private Parts, and so let it grow there 'till you shall be a compleat Man, but be first instructed by us, and do as we bid you and you will become a Noted man. Cousins the English and French fight for our Lands, let us be strong and lay our Hand on it. In the mean Time turn your Eyes and Ears to us, and the English our Brethren and you will live as well as we do.[30]

This message supposedly accompanied the same wampum belt, with its image of "a Square in the Middle, meaning the Lands of the *Indians*," that Teedyuscung (with no mention of Newcastle's story) presented to Pennsylvania's governor as he tried to patch things up at Easton in 1756.[31]

Meanwhile, Teedyuscung reported of his Delawares "that the French had made exceeding much of them, were very open and free with them." A few weeks before the meeting at Easton, the French commander at Niagara had shown Teedyuscung an alleged letter to New France "from the King of England." Pointing out that "we the English live on one side and you the French live on the other Side and we have all the Indians in the midst of us," King George said that the Europeans should "join together at a certain Time and squeeze the Indians all to Death at once and then we will divide the Country betwixt us." The proposal, which the French of course supposedly rejected, showed "plainly ... what People the English are and what you are to expect from their Hands."³² A similar message about British intentions had long been circulating among Native communities. In 1754, a spokesman for one of the allies of New France had put it this way to Ohio country Indian people: "Brethren, are you ignorant of the difference between our [French] Father and the English? Go see the forts our Father has erected, and you will see that the land beneath his walls is still hunting ground, having fixed himself in those places we frequent, only to supply our wants; whilst the English, on the contrary, no sooner get possession of a country than the game is forced to leave it; the trees fall down before them, the earth becomes bare, and we find among them hardly wherewithal to shelter us when the night falls."³³

Yet Teedyuscung and most other Native people knew that such demonization of land-hungry invaders from the British colonies was a vast oversimplification. The same intrusion of Scots-Irish and German settlers into the west that was such a major grievance also meant that many Euro-Americans had deep personal ties with Indians. Some had settled at Indian invitation and even paid rent for their land. Mutual trading, drinking, and eating occurred in countless cabins. Moreover, many Indians had, like Teedyuscung, spent time with Moravian or other missionaries, been baptized, and bore Christian as well as Native names. Dozens still lived within the bounds of the Walking Purchase at Moravian Gnadenhütten and elsewhere. In- and outside the missions, Indian and non-Indian people used many of the same material goods, hunted in the same woods with the same kinds of weapons, and spoke the same Germanic-, Celtic-, or Algonquian-inflected English tongue. As one young man recalled, the Native Americans who captured him "mostly all spake English, one spake as good English as I·can."³⁴ The war, when it came, was deeply personal and fraught with conflicting emotions.

And therefore bloodily brutal. As late twentieth-century Bosnia and Rwanda would demonstrate, ethnic conflicts can become most ruthless when the parties have long lived side by side and know each other well. Precisely *because* antagonists share personal histories, it apparently becomes necessary to dehumanize the enemy in the starkest ways, to draw clear and uncrossable lines between an *us* and a *them* that had long been blurred. When Delawares, Shawnees, and others took up arms, therefore, they did not engage in random acts of violence or broad strategic sweeps. Instead, they struck very specific targets, at particular homesteads of Euro-Americans who had settled on the lands the Six Nations had sold out from under them in the Walking Purchase and in the treaties of 1749 and 1754. Often they attacked people whose names they knew and against whom they had specific grievances. Corpses

were not just scalped in accordance with long tradition, but sometimes brutally mutilated in ways that were at once transgressive expressions of rage,
symbolic messages to those who would discover the devastation, and statements to those who misunderstood what it meant to call Native men women.
When one Euro-American man's body was discovered, his "brains were beat
out, . . . he had two Cuts in his breast, was shott with a bullett in his back, and
his privities [were] cut off and put into his mouth." Another was found "lying
the Road shott and scalped his Scull split open and one of the Provincial
Tom[a]hawks sticking in his private parts."[35]

Euro-Americans returned the violence in kind—scalping Indian women
and children, desecrating corpses, venting revenge for what they had seen
done to their neighbors and kin—but seemed to do so in less focused ways,
finding *any* Native American an appropriate target. In a way, the random
brutality was a perverse, unintended by-product of Pennsylvania's history of
Quaker pacifism. Although prominent Quakers had resigned from public
participation in government in 1755, allowing the provincial assembly for the
first time to vote funds to build frontier forts, raise troops, and supply arms,
Pennsylvania's lack of any preexisting military infrastructure or supervised
system of local militia forced western settlers to devise their own cruder, ad
hoc, means of striking back. A bounty system that the provincial government offered in 1756 validated the pattern; "the Scalp of every Male Indian
Enemy above the age of Twelve Years" earned 130 Spanish dollars, and "the
Scalp of every Indian Woman" earned 50.[36] Yet the sources of brutality ran
still deeper, drawing on the same wells of personal knowledge of the enemy
that infected Native Americans. Ironically, the personal nature of the violence
made those Indians who professed to be friends of Pennsylvania—Christians
who lived with the Moravians, the handful of seemingly innocent people at
Conestoga—especially suspect. Had not other Indians who had visited Euro-
American homes, spoken German or English, and worn imported clothes
turned out to be killers? So the frontiers of a colony founded by pacifists became killing fields.[37]

A few on each side tried to remain above the general carnage, but those
who advocated peace were vilified and pressured to choose. After repeated
threats, the forty or so Christian Indians who remained at Gnadenhütten had
to flee to Bethlehem in late 1755 when Delawares burned the mission town to
the ground. At the same time, among Euro-Americans, the Moravians who
had established Gnadenhütten became increasingly suspect for their shelter-
ing of Indians and their unwillingness to fight. Similarly, Israel Pemberton

and other prominent Philadelphia Quakers, who formed a "Friendly Association for Regaining and Preserving Peace with the Indians by Pacific Measures" that often worked at cross-purposes to the proprietary government,
earned the scorn of many non-Quaker colonists. Nonetheless, heroic efforts
by Teedyuscung, the Friendly Association, the Moravian missionary Christian Frederick Post, and the Ohio country Delaware leader Pisquetomen
patched together a truce by 1758—a truce greatly encouraged by French set-
backs on the battlefield. In October of that year, at Easton, the Pennsylvania
government agreed to prohibit further Euro-American settlement west of the
Appalachians and to surrender much of the western land acquired in the 1754
Albany purchase. Significantly, however, those lands were returned to the Six
Nations, not to Teedyuscung, the Delawares, and other Indians who lived on
them and who had fought so hard to regain them.[38]

✳   ✳   ✳

The 1758 Treaty of Easton was just a hiatus. On both sides, racial hatred
smoldered, and violence was never far from the surface. For years in the
war-scarred Indian communities of the Susquehanna and Ohio countries,
religious prophets had been preaching a message of pan-Indian unity that
transcended ethnic and linguistic differences. Already a few years before
Braddock's campaign, Presbyterian missionary John Brainerd had heard the
core of the message. It had been revealed to a young woman in a trance

> that the great God first made three men and three women, viz.: the
> Indian, the negro, and the white man. That the white man was the
> youngest brother, and therefore the white people ought not to think
> themselves better than the Indians. That God gave the white man a
> book, and told him that he must worship him by that; but gave none
> either to the Indian or negro, and therefore it could not be right for
> them to have a book, or be any way concerned with that way of wor-
> ship. And, furthermore, they understood that the white people were
> contriving a method to deprive them of their country in those parts,
> as they had done by the sea-side, and to make slaves of them and their
> children as they did of the negroes.[39]

This doctrine of separate creations—this harder-edged variant of ideas heard
by Dutch visitors to the Mohawk country more than a century earlier—found

new militance in the teachings of a seer named Neolin, who Euro-Americans called the "Delaware Prophet." Many of Neolin's disciples believed that North America was meant solely for Indians. "As to those who come to trouble your lands—drive them out, make war upon them," the Master of Life supposedly told Neolin in a vision. "I do not love them at all; they know me not, and are my enemies, and the enemies of your brothers. Send them back to the lands which I have created for them and let them stay there."[40]

Neolin's message took on ever greater appeal after British forces defeated the French at Quebec in 1759, for it quickly became apparent that pledges made to Indians during the war meant little. As late as 1762, Delawares had been assured that "the English have no intention to make settlements in your hunting country beyond the Allegheny hills, unless they shall be desired for your conveniency to erect store houses in order to establish and carry on a trade."[41] Yet the British army dug into a string of posts from Fort Pitt (which replaced Duquesne) to Detroit to Michilimackinac, and squatters crossed the mountains into Indian country at the first opportunity. Meanwhile, in 1761, the commander-in-chief of British forces, Sir Jeffrey Amherst, placed severe restrictions on commerce with Indians in the Ohio country and the Great Lakes region. He also made it clear that he had no intention of seriously negotiating with Indians he considered conquered enemies or of following traditional customs of diplomacy that involved "purchasing the good behavior of Indians, by presents." The product of Amherst's aversion to presents was the violence of what is usually termed Pontiac's War, or, better, "the War called 'Pontiac's.' "[42]

In the Ohio and Susquehanna countries, Indians—while they may have derived inspiration from Pontiac's activities—fought independently, and, essentially, resumed the war that had been put on hold at Easton a few years earlier. Their immediate provocation seems to have been the murder of Teedyuscung at Wyoming in April 1763. Persons unknown burned down around him the house that the Pennsylvania government had built for him as a reward for his services in the peace negotiations of 1756 and 1758. When that house and those nearby caught fire, whatever Delaware trust in British guarantees of Native land claims remained also went up in smoke. Within weeks of the murder, across a vast stretch of trans-Appalachian territory bordering Virginia northward through Pennsylvania, colonists who had squatted in Indian country or settled under patents Indians did not recognize were slaughtered or sent fleeing to the east by Delawares and their allies among the Ohio country Shawnees, Cherokees, and Iroquois. Euro-Americans responded to the Indian renewal of violence in kind. The Conestoga Massacre by the "Paxton Boys" a few months after Teedyuscung's murder was a particularly gruesome example of the racial brutality that had become all too familiar in the past decade. Indeed, against the background of the Seven Years War, the Paxtonians' slaughter of a defenseless community of Indians who professed to be friends of the provincial government and treasured their memories of the Quaker William Penn seems almost predictable.[43]

And so it went for a generation. Some years would be bloodier than others, marked by a few brutal murders on either side rather than all-out carnage, but everywhere in the Susquehanna and Ohio countries, race war became the norm. When colonial resistance to British imperial authority turned the corner to revolution, the hatreds burst into the open again. This time, the European ally that Ohio country Indians reluctantly embraced was not the French but the British. The region's people of European stock who claimed for themselves the name *American,* meanwhile, fought primarily—and brutally—not so much against the British as against the same Indian foes they had been battling for many years.[44]

*   *   *

In his 1889 history, Theodore Roosevelt observed that "the revolutionary contest" had a "twofold character" as "a struggle for independence in the east, and in the west a war of conquest."[45] Two decades letter, making no reference to Native Americans and their land, historian Carl Lotus Becker also attributed a dual character to the American Revolution. In words now familiar to nearly every scholar of the subject, Becker posited that

The American Revolution was the result of two general movements: the contest for home-rule and independence, and the democratization of American politics and society. Of these movements, the latter was fundamental; it began before the contest for home-rule, and was not completed until after the achievement of independence. . . .

From 1765 to 1776, therefore, two questions [were] about equally prominent. . . . The first was whether essential colonial rights should be maintained; the second was by whom and by what methods they should be maintained. The first was the question of home rule; the second was the question, if we may so put it, of who should rule at home.[46]

Becker and Roosevelt disagreed, then, on the character of the duality, but for both the struggle for the independence of the United States was inseparable from more important contests, over "who should rule at home" or (to apply Becker's words to Roosevelt's insight) who should rule the continent. In Braddock's words, the question was, who "should Inherit the Land."

Roosevelt, then, understood (and no doubt Braddock, had he lived long enough, would have too) that two wars for independence took place simultaneously on the North American continent: the victorious one by the United States, and the unsuccessful (at least in Euro-American minds) one by Native peoples. What none of these men was able to appreciate, however, was the extent that Native Americans' wars for independence—for "home rule"—were also inseparable from "the question, if we may so put it, of who should rule at home." Indians, too, were engulfed in constant, multi-sided, contests over land, trade, and power within and among indigenous communities. Those struggles inevitably involved huge and divisive questions about who, exactly, their people were—a clan, a village, a confederacy, or all the Creator's Red children—and about who, precisely, among other Native people was to blame when things went wrong. These contests over who should rule at home were something that Teedyuscung must have comprehended, as he tried, from his fragile position as "king" of one small Delaware community among many, to wage the battle for independence. After his murder, Native and European Americans alike would prove time and again that the struggle for eastern North America had a twofold character as they insisted that only one people should inherit the land.

CHAPTER 9

The Plan of 1764:
Native Americans and a British
Empire That Never Was

For a brief moment after the Seven Years War, a handful of British officials on both sides of the Atlantic struggled to imagine an empire where Native Americans and Europeans might coexist. Their ideas spawned an ill-starred document known as the "Plan for the future Management of Indian Affairs," which the British ministry circulated for transatlantic comment in 1764. To set this "Plan of 1764" in context, and to explain both the logic of its vision and the reasons for its failure, requires an eighteenth-century back story reminiscent of the period's popular novel *Tristram Shandy*, for the perceived problems that the Plan tried to address are as significant as the flawed prescription it offered. As both perception and prescription, the Plan reveals tensions at the heart of the British Empire as it was, even as it struggled to envision an empire that never was to be. Paradoxically, the Plan's utter rejection—the apparent irrelevance of its scheme for British-Indian coexistence—may be its greatest historical relevance, and a further key to the racial violence of the intertwined U.S. and Native American wars for independence.[1]

*   *   *

The secrets to a successful imperial relationship with Native Americans, as Superintendent for Indian Affairs William Johnson once complained, lay in "a Terra Incognita, inaccessible to the Generality of even enquirers."[2] Yet, as the Seven Years War drew to a close, Britons who approached that mysterious landscape agreed on four basic principles. First was the need for an enforceable boundary to defend Native lands from unregulated Euro-American expansion. "The Indians ought to be redressed or satisfied, in all their reasonable and well founded complaints of enormous and unrighteously obtained Patents for their Lands and Treaties of Limitations with the respective Provinces agreed upon and religiously observed," Johnson breathlessly concluded as early as 1759.[3]

The second principle was particularly vital for an empire whose national identity was deeply rooted in commerce: the need to find some workable system to regulate trade. Among what South Carolina's agent to the Creeks called the "several irregular Practices and Abuses" that had "crept into the Indian Trade" were shoddy goods, rigged scales, usurious debts, and outright theft. Alcohol, as the key weapon in crooked traders' arsenals, the most lucrative of commodities, and the lubricant of murderous violence when things went wrong, compounded Native grievances. The persistence of non-capitalist ideas about reciprocity and redistribution and the Indian expectation that much of what Europeans considered commerce should take the form of gift-giving only deepened Native perceptions that the entire system was corrupt. The real or imagined presence in Indian country of competing French and Spanish traders who were presumably eager to capitalize on British lapses to divert merchandise to New Orleans multiplied the potential for trouble.[4]

And trouble, in all its varied forms, undergirded the third great issue in British-Indian relations: boundary lines and trade regulations would remain meaningless unless some mutually acceptable system of resolving disputes between Native people and Europeans—some workable mechanism of cross-cultural justice—could be found. Finally, none of the other issues could be addressed effectively without centralized administration in the hands of agents who could speak reliably on behalf of the empire as a whole. It was vital, said Johnson, for "the Superintendency and Direction of Indian Affairs and Trade, to be under an Authority from the Crown" rather than the fractious individual provinces.[5]

Most Native Americans of the continental interior probably would have agreed with this four-part analysis. Paradoxically, the utter breakdown of Indian-British relations in "the War called 'Pontiac's'" demonstrates the importance Native people attached to boundaries, trade regulation, dispute resolution, and centralized imperial authority.[6] The religious teachings of the Delaware prophet Neolin—the ideological glue binding the varied Indian attacks on British forts in the Great Lakes and Ohio countries in 1763—centered on what a more secular vocabulary would call the need for a clear

Sir William Johnson (1715–1774). Portrait by John Wollaston, Jr. Collections of the Albany Institute of History & Art. As British Superintendent of Indian Affairs for the Northern Department, Johnson—along with his counterpart for the Southern Department, John Stuart (1718–1779, of whom no portrait is known to exist)—long struggled with the problems the Plan of 1764 attempted to address.

territorial boundary. "This land where ye dwell I have made for you and not
for others. Whence comes it that ye permit the Whites upon your lands?"
the Master of Life supposedly demanded of Neolin.[7] Such rhetoric mobilized very real grievances, as the British violated their pledges not to expand
into the Ohio country and Great Lakes regions. "They say We mean to make
Slaves of them, by Taking so many Posts in their Country," the commandant
at Detroit reported in April 1763. Indians were convinced "that they had better Attempt Something now, to Recover their Liberty, than Wait till We were
better Established."[8]

Trade grievances inevitably intertwined with threats to Indian lands.
Neolin prophesied a future in which Indians would abandon their addiction
to European goods, and many of his followers ritually purged themselves of
foreign corruption. Yet for most of those who went to war in 1763 the crucial
questions involved the quantity, quality, and price of British commodities and
the behavior of those who supplied them. "It is important for us, my brothers,
that we exterminate from our lands this nation which seeks only to destroy
us," Pontiac reputedly told his followers. "The English sell us goods twice as
dear as the French do, and their goods do not last . . . ; and when we wish to
set out for our winter camps they do not want to give us any credit as our
brothers, the French, do."[9]

Commander-in-Chief Jeffrey Amherst's policies for the Ohio country and
Great Lakes regions exacerbated the commercial squeeze. Trade was to take
place only at British army posts—Fort Pitt, Niagara, Detroit, Michilimackinac, and about a dozen smaller garrisons—and only those provincials who
held licenses from Superintendent Johnson and pledged to follow price lists
drawn up for each station were to engage in commerce.[10] Rum was, in theory,
completely banned from the marketplace. Powder and lead, Amherst rea-
soned, should purposely be kept "scarce, . . . since nothing can be so impoli-
tick as to furnish them with the means of accomplishing the Evil which is so
much Dreaded."[11] The "Evil" that broke out in 1763 only became more likely
when both French voyageurs (whom Great Lakes Indians had long trusted)
and British traders (whom Ohio country Indians seldom had) ignored Amherst's and Johnson's regulations and flocked into Native villages. Floods of
rotgut rum and shoddy goods at high prices combined with shortages of officially sanctioned alcohol and of the ammunition crucial for hunting to convey an impression of British mean-spiritedness, if not outright aggression.[12]

That impression took deeper root as Amherst also abandoned the cen-
tury-old diplomatic tradition of using ritual largesse to demonstrate the

Sir Jeffrey Amherst (1723–1792). Portrait by James Watson, published by John Boydell. NPG D7002, copyright © National Portrait Gallery, London. As commander-in-chief in North America, Amherst was largely responsible both for the British victory over New France in the Seven Years War and for provoking "the war called 'Pontiac's.'"

benefits of alliance with imperial power. "All the Indian Nations were . . . become verry Jealous of the English, who had erected so many Posts in their Country, but were not so generous to them as the French, and particularly gave them no Amunition, which was the cheif cause of their Jealousy and Discontent," Johnson's subordinate George Croghan reported from Fort Pitt in early 1763.[13] The failure of British beneficence had long since made it impossible for Native headmen who had formerly relied on French patronage to use their own powers of redistribution to restrain warriors inclined to seek justice through violence. In the months leading up to Pontiac's War, chiefs repeatedly showed up at British posts, desperately seeking some token of generosity they could take back to their people to convince them that a workable political order was possible with the British. At Fort Pitt, Croghan reported that Indian visitors were "very unesey att our Not Suplying them with Amunishion and Nesereys." Attempts to make up for the shortfall personally cost Croghan "above a years Salery within this twelf Months in trifles, More then the officer Coimmanding heer wold aLow them In order to keep them In Temper."[14]

In the effort to cool tempers, the same alcohol that at other times caused grief assumed particular significance. In April 1762, the commandant at Niagara, having locked up in his storehouse a "very Large" cache of rum confiscated from traders, had an awkward conversation with an unnamed Native leader who was an "old friend" of William Johnson. "Beging" for an order to "allow the traders to sell their people a Little Rum for their Refreshment," the Indian man refused to take no for an answer. Finally, in consideration of the "great number of his Tribe with him," the officer "made him a preasent of three two-gallon Cags of rum to take whome with him."[15] A little over a year later, as war was breaking out, "Wapackcamigat, the Chief of all the Indians here abouts," enacted a similar scene at Niagara. The commandant reported that when the headman was denied the gift he sought, he "said he would come here once more, and if he was Refused Rum (as he only asked a little) We must take Care of the consequence . . . and he was afraid that We should soon hear bad News." That news arrived soon enough; a few days later, as the entire region erupted in violence, a party of Chippewas attacked six traders' boats near the fort, killed three of the passengers, and took several others prisoner.[16]

That many such local scenes combined to spark regionwide bloodshed points to the final dilemma of British-Indian relations during Pontiac's War: the need for an empire that spoke in a single voice. Thus Indians also shared with the handful of British officials who thought about such matters the desire for centralized administration, albeit an administration whose responsibilities Native people defined very differently than did their imperial counterparts. The desire was just as strong among Native people who had remained allied to the British as among those who had fought against them in the Seven Years War and the battles of 1763. Indeed, disinterested royal mediation was the great hope of many who despaired of dealing with land-hungry provincials through any other means. Teedyuscung, for example, in making peace with the king's Pennsylvania subjects in 1757, had "desired that all Differences between the Indians and Your Majesty's Subjects might be referred to Your Majesty's Royal Determination, and that the same might be publish'd throughout all your Majesty's Provinces."[17] In the 1760s Mohawks, Narragansetts, Wappingers, and others all similarly tried to go over the heads of provincial officials in hopes that their land claims and other grievances might gain a more impartial hearing at Whitehall.[18] As Johnson explained later, such petitions to the crown were "founded on a certainty that they could expect no redress elsewhere."[19]

*   *   *

In late 1763, as Pontiac's War began sputtering to an end and British and Native leaders began to rebuild their uneasy connection, none of the basic problems had been solved. Only the most rudimentary skeleton of a centralized administration existed. Since the early days of the Seven Years War, the right to speak in the name of the crown had in theory rested in two regional Superintendents of Indian Affairs. Johnson had held the northern post since 1756. John Stuart of South Carolina had succeeded to the southern office in 1762 after the death of Edmund Atkin, whose proposals had convinced Whitehall to create the superintendencies in the first place. Yet independent diplomacy by provincial governors and especially the military's control of the superintendents' budgets stymied many of Johnson's, Atkin's, and Stuart's efforts to keep Indians in the British camp. This was most powerfully demonstrated when Amherst overruled Johnson's objections to the policies that helped provoke the carnage of 1763. In September of that year, the Board of Trade concluded that Amherst's decisions were "the causes of this unhappy defection of the Indians" and that "nothing but the speedy establishment of some well digested and general plan for the regulation of our Commercial and political concerns with them can effectually reconcile their esteem and affections."[20]

On that, there may have been widespread consensus in government circles, but less agreement prevailed on what should, or could, be done about boundaries, trade, and keeping the peace. To the extent that British officials supported the general concept of a boundary between Natives and Europeans, they seemed motivated less by a quest for justice toward Native Americans than by a desire to impose some order on land titles among Euro-Americans. A coherent land tenure system would capture for provincial and imperial governments the filing fees and quitrents, and for large proprietors the purchase prices and land rents, that they so much desired and that squatters and freelance purchasers so frequently denied them. Talk of a British-Indian boundary line was almost always inseparable from schemes to remove the authority to make future purchases (or uncompensated expropriations) of Indian lands from individual colonists and colony governments and instead place it safely in centralized imperial hands.[21]

The stress on Euro-American rather than Native American real estate rings clearly in the royal Proclamation of October 1763. Although it was issued a few days after Whitehall learned about Pontiac's War, the Proclamation had been in the works for months before the ministry knew anything about the troubles in the Great Lakes and Ohio country.[22] The text of the Proclamation begins not with lands belonging to Indians but with "the extensive and valuable Acquisitions in *America,* secured to Our Crown by the late Definitive Treaty of Peace" that brought the Seven Years War to an end. The bulk of the document deals with establishing the new colonies of Grenada, East Florida, West Florida, and Quebec and with annexing conquered territory to Newfoundland, Nova Scotia, and Georgia. Next comes a scheme for distributing lands to war veterans in both new and old colonies.[23]

Only then, not quite as an afterthought, does the final third of the Proclamation turn its attention to "the several Nations or Tribes of *Indians,* with whom we are connected, and who live under Our Protaction, [and] should not be molested or disturbed in the Possession of such Parts of Our Dominions and Territories as, not having been ceded to or purchased by Us, are reserved to them . . . as their Hunting Grounds." Royal and proprietary governors must not "pass any Patents for Lands beyond the Bounds of their respective Governments, as described in their Commissions" or "beyond the Heads or Sources of any of the Rivers which fall into the *Atlantick* Ocean from the West and North-West, or upon any Lands whatever, which, not having been ceded to or purchased by Us as aforesaid, are reserved to the said *Indians.*" British subjects "who have either wilfully or inadvertently seated themselves upon" the reserved lands were "forthwith to remove themselves." In future, "no private Person" would be allowed to purchase lands from Indians on either side of the line. Instead, the crown directed that, "if at any Time, any of the said *Indians* should be inclined to dispose of the said Lands, the same shall be Purchased only for Us, in Our Name, at some Publick Meeting or Assembly of the said *Indians* to be held for that Purpose by the Governor or Commander in Chief of our Colonies respectively, within which they shall lie." Clear British legal titles were a principal objective, and, with the continental interior off limits, Euro-American expansion could be more profitably channeled into such places on the Atlantic rim as Nova Scotia and the Floridas. Imperial aims and the exclusion of Europeans from Indian country ("reserved to" but not technically owned by its inhabitants) happily converged.[24]

The Proclamation's language revealed the multiple complications that would bedevil every British effort to envision, much less enforce, a boundary line. In 1763, Euro-American squatters already lived west of the Proclamation Line and would continue to do so despite royal edicts, threats of forced removal, and even the occasional cabin-burning by provincial or regular troops.[25] Moreover, powerful interests in every province had long been speculating in western lands and in schemes to plant entire new colonies in the continental interior. These men (who of course had no sympathy for the squatters who already occupied some of the lands in question) were those for whom the otherwise toothless edict of 1763 had a real impact. They could not obtain legal possession of the lands they coveted and, just as important, faced tough questions about their titles to tracts east of the line privately purchased from Indians under questionable circumstances.[26] Yet they were patient and determined. "The majority of those who get lands, being persons of consequence in the Capitals, . . . can let them lye dead as a sure Estate hereafter," observed Johnson. "Tho' Proclamations are issued, and orders sent to the several Governours[,] experience has shewn that both are hitherto ineffectual and will be so, whilst the Gentlemen of property and Merchants are interested in finding out evasions or points of Law against them."[27]

The lands in question were not only vast but almost impossible to map coherently. One of the most problematic phrases in the Proclamation was its seemingly simple prohibition on the various governors granting lands "beyond the Bounds of their respective Governments, as described in their Commissions." Those commissions almost universally conflicted with each other. On the northern half of the continent alone, nearly every inch of territory east of the Proclamation Line and west of what provincials called "the settled parts" was subject to bitter intercolonial dispute. The Penn and Calvert families had recently agreed to end their decades-long controversy over the boundary between Pennsylvania and Maryland, but all conceptual clarity broke down when the border line reached the headwaters mentioned in the Proclamation of 1763. There Pennsylvania and Maryland both transgressed Virginia's extensive land claims—the same claims that in 1754 had led George Washington to Fort Necessity and ignited the Seven Years War. The crossroads then known as "Redstone"—around modern-day Bedford, Pennsylvania—was a particularly contentious place, claimed by both Pennsylvania and Virginia and inhabited by a thriving community of squatters on lands never publicly purchased from Indian owners. Thus, at precisely the geographic point where Whitehall most needed a neat division between the British and the Indians, rival British provinces bitterly contested ownership in a way that mocked the crown's vision of orderly real estate transactions.[28]

Northward along the east side of the Proclamation Line the situation was just as confused. Pennsylvania and New York had for decades contested a sixty-mile swath of what would eventually become part of the Empire State. More pressing, however, was Connecticut's pretension, under the terms of its 1662 sea-to-sea charter, to territory that now comprises the northern third of Pennsylvania. This Connecticut claim was the basis for the aggressive efforts of the Susquehanna Company, chartered in 1753, to plant colonists in Teedyuscung's Wyoming Valley. To stave off the New Englanders, at the Albany Congress of 1754, Pennsylvania delegates secured a purported deed to the lands, signed by a handful of headmen who apparently had no authority to engage in the transaction, and worded in a way that appeared to include not only Wyoming but much of the territory southwestward to Virginia's claims at Redstone and on the Ohio River.[29]

Similar controversy reigned in the Hudson Valley. Tenant uprisings that had occurred between 1751 and 1757 and that would erupt again in 1766 capitalized on long-standing border disputes among New York, Massachusetts, and the Stockbridge Indians to call into question the manorial titles of New York grandees.[30] The upper Hudson and Lake Champlain watersheds were likewise a legal no-man's-land contested by New York and New Hampshire, the fate of which would not be decided until after white inhabitants proclaimed the independent state of Vermont in 1777.[31] To the west, in the Mohawk Valley, New York's legal authority was unchallenged by any other British province, but real-estate chaos nonetheless remained the order of the day as a result of massive, overlapping, and often fraudulent land grants made earlier in the century. The mother of all such controversies centered on the 800,000-acre Kayaderosseras Patent, a half-century-old legal quagmire that threatened to dispossess the Mohawk Iroquois of almost their entire home-land and to provoke war between the Six Nations and New York.[32]

And so it went, wherever one looked. The only semblance of legal order emerged at the forty-fifth parallel, where governors Henry Moore of New York and Guy Carleton of Quebec would amicably meet to settle the boundary between their jurisdictions in late 1766. But the orderly scene was neverthe-less troubled by "several French Gentlemen . . . from Quebec" who requested that Moore confirm their pretensions to seigneuries well south of the border, "which were granted to them before the conquest of Canada" and included at least two tracts of 100,000 acres or more.[33] Similar problems could be found almost anywhere along the Appalachians from that point south to the Caro-linas, even in areas where the claims of provinces and grandees were not in dispute. For smallholders, land titles were difficult to acquire, clear patents rare, rules stacked in favor of well-connected easterners, quitrents paid only by the excessively scrupulous, property rights defined variously by ethnic tra-ditions, leases available from a variety of Indians and Europeans with a vari-ety of claims to ownership.[34] For British officials, then, the boundary problem rested on nothing so simple as mere land hunger. It sank into a quicksand that made the bounds of any individual Euro-American farm—much less any-thing so grandiose as a line tracing "the Heads or Sources of any of the Rivers which fall into the *Atlantick* Ocean"—profoundly unstable.

*   *   *

The nightmares plaguing enforcement of a boundary line were matched by those afflicting rational regulation of British-Indian trade. On a local scale, the commercial problems were quite old, and various British provinces had long attempted to deal with them. New York and South Carolina—not co-incidently the homes of superintendents Johnson and Stuart—had the most experience and, between them, provided a range of tested options. Since the 1670s, New York had relied with some success on a plan that required all mer-chants to set up shop in public markets at specific military posts, first Albany and then Oswego. In theory, Indians came to the traders, not vice versa, and the worst excesses of price-gouging, short measures, and transactions under the influence of alcohol could be policed, although hardly eliminated. Yet the viability of the New York system depended on three distinctively local factors that did not apply to the broader continental stage: leaders of the Six Nations, New York's primary trading partners, almost universally agreed that pedlars were best kept out of their villages; Albany and Oswego were close enough to those villages that shopping trips were not a major inconvenience; and any traders who might venture elsewhere had to enter hostile territory dominated by the French and their Native allies.[35]

The stay-at-home New York model contrasted strikingly with the policies that South Carolina had attempted to enforce on its much more far-flung commercial system in the early eighteenth century. Traders had to apply for licenses issued by a board of commissioners that granted each the right to set up shop only at a particular Indian town. Provincial oversight rested on requirements that traders appear annually in Charleston to renew their permits and post bond for compliance with regulations. In addition, a government agent, instructed to spend at least ten months a year traveling in Indian country, was armed with a justice of the peace's powers to mete out penalties in minor cases, take testimony under oath, and send major offenders to Charleston for trial.[36] On occasion, the Carolinians had superimposed on this basic model a government monopoly over particular trades. Most recently, in the wake of the Cherokee War of 1759 to 1761, a board of "Directors of the Cherokee Trade" assumed control of commerce with that nation and appointed a factor to manage its operations in the town of Keowee. A regular but almost impossible to enforce feature of both South Carolina systems was an official "tariff," or price list for staple items.[37]

Amherst's approach to trade in the Great Lakes and Ohio countries on the eve of Pontiac's War attempted to combine New York's military posts with South Carolina's licenses and tariff schedules. But neither of the two British provincial models was familiar to most of the region's Native peoples. For over half a century, the French had managed the region's trade as a set of local monopolies controlled by those who held government office. These officers in turn contracted with companies of merchants and with the voyageurs who transported goods into the continental interior and fanned out from military posts to deal with Indian customers. For New France as a whole, a company of merchants leased the right to export beaver furs and the concomitant obligation to buy at a fixed price all the pelts offered. Those who transported goods westward from Montreal similarly purchased the right to do so, under licenses that minutely described their destinations and privileges. Forts Frontenac, Niagara, and Detroit had been "king's posts" that often operated at a loss in order to keep prices competitive with the British. At smaller forts, the commandant usually leased the right to trade, which he then exercised in partnership with a few merchants and by contract with those who traveled to surrounding villages; these establishments were supposed to support themselves from the profits. Only at Michilimackinac did anything resembling free trade exist, on the theory that competition might lower the price of goods otherwise inflated by the vast costs of transportation to that distant post and its far-flung hinterland. Everywhere in the French system, the pursuit of private profit was subordinated to the need to maintain strong alliances with Native people.[38]

As Pontiac's War demonstrates, no one recognized the virtues of such a system more than Indians themselves. Yet after the British conquest, several unprecedented factors made the French trading model only slightly more workable than those of New York or Carolina. First was the sheer geographical scale of the problem that confronted British policy makers. Johnson— rightly concluding that "Traders will be more cautious of committing Frauds under the Eye of a Commanding officer of some Rank"—never quite seemed to grasp the ludicrousness of attempting to export the New York system of military marketplaces to the wide expanses of the Great Lakes and Ohio countries. Native people, he kept trying to convince himself and Whitehall, would "think nothing of comeing to the Posts," no matter how long the trip.[39]

New France had confronted the problem of geography by combining trading posts with mobile voyageurs, all loosely supervised by the interlocking quasi-governmental monopolies that tied the *pays d'en haut* to Quebec City. After the conquest, however, competing lines of authority crisscrossed the continental interior. Traders from Quebec, New York, Pennsylvania, Virginia, the Carolinas, Georgia, and the Floridas all considered themselves free to enter the fray. The Proclamation of 1763 made the problem worse when it opened commerce "to all . . . Subjects whatever; provided that every Person, who may incline to Trade with the said *Indians*, [d]o take out a Licence for carrying on such Trade from the Governor or Commander in Chief of any of . . . [the] Colonies respectively, where such Person shall reside." Governmental monopolies such as that still in effect for the Carolina-Cherokee trade became illegal, and licenses granted under the Proclamation, unlike those previously issued by South Carolina or New France, placed no restrictions on where traders could peddle their wares. This, combined with the availability of permits in any province, rendered nearly meaningless the Proclamation's proviso that licensees "give Security to observe such Regulations as . . . Commissaries to be appointed for this Purpose" might contrive.[40] To make matters worse, Pennsylvania and Virginia, in contrast to Quebec, New York, or South Carolina, had almost no tradition of effective regulation of Euro-Americans who ventured into Indian country. Employed by politically influential eastern merchants, vagabond traders from those two provinces operated much as they pleased.[41]

*   *   *

So the hope of policing the trade took up residence in the same fantasy land as the dream of enforcing boundary lines. Joining them there was any vision of peacefully resolving disputes. A solution to this problem would have to depend either on the British crown somehow exerting real sovereignty over Native Americans or on a successful attempt to blend two very different cultures of justice. Pontiac's War had demonstrated the folly of treating Indians like British subjects. "Many mistakes arise here from erroneous accounts formerly made of Indians," Johnson pointed out. "They have been represented as calling themselves subjects, although, the very word would have startled them, had it been ever pronounced by any Interpreters; they desire to be considered as Allies and Friends." The British had to play along with the rhetoric of alliance at least "until in a few years we shall become so formidable throughout the country, as to be able to protect ourselves." Or perhaps much longer. Indians "can not be brought under our Laws, for some Centuries, neither have they any word which can convey the most distant idea of subjection," Johnson observed on another occasion. "Should it be fully explained to them, and the nature of subordination punishment ettc, defined, it might produce infinite harm, but could answer no purpose whatever."[42]

Hope for permanent peace therefore depended on accommodating European and Native American ideas about justice: on the one hand, the requirement that courts try, punish, and perhaps execute the perpetrator and, on the other, the demand that victims receive compensation either through revenge or, preferably, condolence gifts. At various times and places—early eighteenth-century Pennsylvania, occasionally on the frontiers of South Carolina—the two systems had achieved a fragile balance, resting on a usually unstated agreement that each side would police its own and that, when Europeans killed or robbed Indians, both condolence gifts and judicial trials would have their day.[43] With sufficient diplomatic skill and financial resources, the condolence gifts necessary for such satisfaction could be managed. But the real British problem centered on the need to police their own in a way that would minimize the need for such gifts—and the potential for warfare that each such need represented.

The problem was fundamental. How could Euro-Americans who cheated, robbed, or killed Indians be forced to face charges in a British court and be convicted by a jury of their peers? The political support the Paxton Boys enjoyed in Pennsylvania after their massacre of the Conestoga Indians in 1763, along with numerous other examples of whites who literally got away with murder in the 1760s, demonstrate the enormous barrier that racial hatreds placed in the way of Indians seeking redress from British-American juries. When no one in Lancaster professed to know who broke into the town workhouse and gruesomely slaughtered those who escaped the attack on Conestoga, and when a similarly mysterious mob sprang Frederick Stump and John Ironcutter from the Carlisle jail before they could stand trial for the murder of ten other Indians, the prospects for justice east of the Proclamation Line, much less west of it, were slim indeed.[44]

But even if racism were tamed, vigilantes restrained, and juries forced to do their job, daunting systemic problems stood in the way of bringing what Commander-in-Chief Thomas Gage referred to as "Lawless Banditti" to justice.[45] If perpetrators effortlessly escaped justice in Pennsylvania's Lancaster and Cumberland counties, how much more easily could they vanish into the *pays d'en haut* or the Creek country, where legal pursuit would require direct exertion of the British sovereignty that Indians almost universally resisted? And even if the perpetrator were somehow arrested at a military post, he would still have to be shipped east to be tried in a proper court—preferably far to the east in a provincial capital where there was more hope for an impartial jury than in places nearer the line. "In the course of a long a tedious journey," it was more than likely that the accused would be "suffered to escape either by the neglect or connivance of their conductors," New York Governor Henry Moore complained.[46] But even if the trip could be safely made, which provincial capital should be the destination? A good lawyer could easily make the case that a New York court, for instance, had no jurisdiction in Indian country, which the Proclamation of 1763 had purposely "taken out of the Jurisdiction of the civil Government."[47]

Whatever the destination, not only the perpetrator but witnesses would have to undertake the voyage. Often, the most important evidence would have to come from Indians who—even if they swallowed their scruples about sovereign British courts and endured the journey—were almost universally barred from testifying, largely due to racial prejudice but also because, as non-Christians, they were presumed to have no fear of the divine power behind the oaths that guaranteed nothing but the truth. Oaths were only one of myriad aspects of the common law that stacked the deck in favor of Anglo-Americans who knew them and who could support their arguments with written documents, however tainted those might be.[48] "Is it possible to suppose that the Indians, to whom (according to the account of the Traders) it is not at all convenient to come even to the outposts to Trade, should be able to go at least 5 or 600 miles, still farther to the capitals for Justice; and admitting that some of them should know of this method, and do so, how are they to obtain Justice?" Johnson rightly asked. "The Courts of Law, cannot admit of their evidence, nor is there any reason to expect it from many Jurys, the prejudices against Indians being too strong, and their regard for their friends to[o] powerful, if these insurmountable bars did not exist."[49]

There were only three possible, and unpalatable, solutions. Traders in Indian country could be subjected to courts martial at the western posts, but this was a dangerous proposition to make in a British-American climate of protests in the streets against admiralty courts and in a culture where everyone cherished the rights of Britons. More realistic would have been to grant British officials in Indian country the powers of justices of the peace, as had long been the case with South Carolina's agent. But justices had summary powers only in minor cases. The capital crimes most likely to provoke an Indian war would still need to be bound over to courts in the provinces. And the rights of Britons required that any case have the right of appeal. "As the Indians come from a great distance, to Trade, and at all times lead an ambulatory Life in Hunting, any delay of Justice, is in effect a denial of justice as to them," concluded New York Lieutenant Governor Cadwallader Colden. "Allowing of appeals, cannot be proper in controversies, between the Traders and Indians themselves," because "there is reason to suspect, that . . . when the judgment goes against the Trader he will on any pretence appeal."[50] The third option—seriously if desperately advocated by Johnson—would be to erect full-fledged British provinces with their structure of courts and juries in the Illinois country, at Detroit, and perhaps elsewhere. How this might be reconciled with protecting Indian lands was never made clear.[51]

*   *   *

These were the convoluted problems the Board of Trade hoped to solve with the Plan of 1764. Drafted in the summer of that year under the leadership of

Wills Hill, First Marquess of Downshire, after unknown artist, line engraving (1781). NPG D6602, copyright © National Portrait Gallery, London. As the Earl of Hillsborough, Hill twice served as president of the Board of Trade and Plantations during the 1760s and was largely responsible for both drafting and abandoning the Plan of 1764.

the Earl of Hillsborough, building upon Atkin's scheme for regional superin-tendencies, and drawing on advice in countless wartime letters from Johnson, Stuart, provincial governors, and others, it had "for its object the regulation of Indian Affairs both commercial and political throughout all North America, upon one general system, under the direction of Officers appointed by the Crown, so as to sett aside all local interfering of particular Provinces, which has been one great cause of the distracted state of Indian Affairs."[52]

The Plan assumed "that all laws now in force in the several Colonies for regulating Indian Affairs or Commerce [would] be repealed." In their stead, the eastern half of the continent would be divided into two administrative dis-tricts, defined less by geography than by lists of Indian nations that the Board of Trade, with minimal ethnographic knowledge, presumed to live north and south of the Ohio River. Each district would be the responsibility of one of the existing superintendents, appointed directly by the crown to "have the con-duct of all public Affairs relative to the Indians." Except in emergencies, the commander-in-chief of the British army and the provincial governors were to be forbidden to conduct treaty councils or send official messages to Indians without the consent of the superintendents, who would nonetheless "advise and act in Council" with the governors and sit as provincial "Councillors ex-traordinary within each Colony in their respective Districts."[53]

A similarly awkward rationalization of lines of authority would extend outward into Indian country. In the south, each Native town was to choose, subject to the approval of the superintendent, "a beloved man . . . to take care of the mutual interests both of Indians and Traders." These town representa-tives would in turn "elect a Chief of the whole Tribe" to act "as Guardian for the Indians and protector of Their Rights." In the north, parallel arrange-ments were to be made to the extent "the nature of the civil constitution of the Indians in this District and the manner of administering their civil Affairs will admit."[54] This system envisioned something vaguely similar to the form of indirect imperial government being worked out at the same time around the globe in South Asia, and the result might well have evolved into some-thing more resembling the raj than the rez.[55]

Within the system of centralized communication and indirect author-ity thus established, the crucial business of negotiating workable boundar-ies between Native and Euro-American territory was to fall into place. With "the consent and concurrence of the Indians," the superintendents were "to ascertain and define the precise and exact boundary and limits of the lands which it may be proper to reserve to them and where no settlement whatever shall be allowed." On either side of the line, private and corporate purchases of Indian lands were to be forbidden and, east of it, restricted to proprietors or corporations who held grants from the crown. New purchases on behalf of the crown or any of the colonies were to be negotiated only by the superintendents in open councils with "the principal Chiefs of each Tribe claiming a property in such lands." To prevent fraud, any ceded territories were to be "regularly surveyed by a sworn surveyor in the presence and with the assistance of a person deputed by the Indians to attend" and platted on "an accurate map . . . entered upon record with the Deed of conveyance."[56]

Within the newly defined limits of Indian country, commerce would "be free and open to all his Majestys Subjects," but allowed only at specified Indian towns in the south and forts in the north—thus extending the oversight systems traditionally used by South Carolina and New York to their respective districts. Traders would have to apply for annual licenses from the governors of the provinces from which they imported and exported. Licenses would be valid only for specifically named traders at a single location and subject to bonds for good behavior. Each trading town or post would be staffed by a commissary, interpreter, and smith who reported to the regional superintendent. These were to be civil officers, independent of military command, and forbidden to engage in trade on their own behalf. The commissaries would enforce prices according to tariffs established in consultation with both the traders and their Indian customers, prohibit the sale of "rum, or other spirituous liquors, swan shot or rifled barralled Guns," and nullify the debts of any Indian to whom traders extended credit beyond the sum of fifty shillings.[57]

In enforcing these regulations, commissaries would act as justices of the peace. They would bear the "full power of combating offenders in capital Cases in order that such offenders may be prosecuted for the same" and the capacity to declare summary judgments in civil cases between Indians and traders and among traders to the value of ten pounds sterling. Appeals would be allowed only to the superintendents, whose decisions were to be final. Indians were, "under proper regulations and restrictions," to be allowed to testify in cases tried by the superintendents and commissaries, as well as in trials before provincial courts. The elected national chiefs would have the right "to be present at all meetings and upon all hearings or tryals relative to the Indians." The annual costs of the entire administrative and judicial apparatus—wildly underestimated at £20,000—would be funded by "a duty upon the Indian Trade, either collected upon the exportation of skins and furs (Beaver excepted) from the Colonies or payable by the Traders at the Posts and Places of Trade."[58]

As requested, Johnson and Stuart filed detailed comments on the Plan. The northern superintendent's main reservation concerned the unworkable scheme for Indians to elect national representatives. Attempting to explain to the Board of Trade that in Native polities multiple clan headmen had equal voices in consensual councils, he suggested that a scheme for inviting "A Chief of every Tribe [clan] in a Nation to attend occasionally for the purposes in this article, would . . . appear more satisfactory."[59] Stuart was somewhat more critical than Johnson, setting the Board of Trade straight on the ethnography and geography of the Indian nations assigned to his district, objecting to the provision allowing individual governors to issue licenses—which, he feared, would encourage "Competition and Jealousy between the provinces or the Trading people . . . incompatible with good Order and Government among Indians"—and proposing that the number of permits be strictly limited to avoid the "Confusion arising from Crowds of Traders and Packhorsemen being Sent indiscriminately from the different Provinces."[60]

Yet despite these imperfections (and others that Native people, had they been asked, might easily have pointed out), the superintendents enthusiastically supported the basic outlines of the Plan, which seemed to address comprehensively all four of the great issues in British-Indian relations. With excessive optimism about the proposal's Parliamentary prospects and with Gage's encouragement (and cautious expenditure of military funds), the superintendents set about their work as if the Plan was certain to become law, and waited for Whitehall to confirm their authority to do so.[61]

In the interim, the superintendents devoted much of their attention to undoing the damage Amherst had inflicted on relations with Native people late in the Seven Years War. Already at the Treaty of Augusta in November 1763, Stuart had resurrected something like the prewar system of diplomacy. Governors from Virginia, Georgia, and both Carolinas and spokesmen for substantial segments of the Catawbas, Cherokees, Creeks, Chickasaws, and Choctaws confirmed peace, exchanged gifts, discussed trading arrangements, and made considerable progress toward fixing a boundary line between the Creeks and Georgia and the Carolinas.[62] In the north, meanwhile, peaceful diplomacy also reemerged as the troops Gage dispatched to pacify Indian country in 1764 negotiated more often than fought and presided over a series of treaty councils with Great Lakes and Ohio country Natives. In the spring of 1765 at Johnson's Mohawk Valley home, headmen from throughout the region brought Pontiac's War to a formal end. A year later, Pontiac himself participated in a treaty with Johnson at Oswego and subsequently pronounced himself a great friend of the British.[63]

Beyond the treaty grounds over which the two superintendents presided, however, there was little evidence of friendship. In July 1765, the same month Johnson hosted his grand peace conference, he complained that "the Frontier Inhabitants of *Pensilvania, Mary Land* and *Virginia*" had attacked convoys carrying Indian trade goods to Fort Pitt, "form[ed] themselves into partys threatning to destroy all Indians they met, or all White People who dealt with them," and attacked "a small party of His Majesty's Troops on the Road." With similar mayhem occurring on the Carolina frontiers, Indians everywhere saw "themselves attacked, threatened and their property invaded by a sett of ignorant misled Rioters who defy Government itself."[64]

Thus, when the superintendents were not trying to patch things up with increasingly frustrated Native leaders, they were writing letters "home," bewailing their inability to implement the rest of the plan and their nearly complete loss of control over the Proclamation boundary, trade regulations, and disputes between Indians and Europeans. What Johnson and Stuart most desired was a clear grant of the royal powers they needed to exert their authority over Indians, colonists, and provincial governors alike. Until "the plan formerly proposed by your Lordships Board be carried in to Execution . . . ," Johnson concluded in the summer of 1766, "I cannot see how it is possible to remedy the foregoing evils."[65]

The lack of royal power in North America was, of course, the great issue of a period marked by the chaos of the Stamp Act and Townshend Duties crises in the provinces, the Wilkes affair in Britain, and revolving-door Whitehall ministries too consumed by domestic politics to concentrate on the vexing, but to them relatively minor, question of relations with Native Americans. Even before the Plan of 1764 had been drafted, George Croghan, who was in London to press the importance of Indian affairs (and the interests of speculators in Indian lands), lamented that "No one thing has been Don Except the affairs of Mr. Wilks and Liberty which Draw the attension of the Nation and has Imbarrest the pres[e]nt Ministry Much." With "the Grate ones but Squbeling and fighting [to] See who will keep in power[,] the publick Intrest is Neglected to Serve privet Intrest," and the ministers appeared to be "all R—g—e—s aLicke."[66]

Rogues or not, the members of the Board of Trade confessed in July 1766 that "a great variety of considerations of the most difficult and extensive nature" had made it "impossible for us, amidst the other pressing business that has occur'd, so to prepare our thoughts and opinion upon this important Subject." A year later, the Secretary of State, the earl of Shelburne, still professed that "the System of Regulations" in Indian relations was "a measure of so great Importance as to require the utmost Deliberation." Whenever a moment could be spared for the project, ministers were bombarded with protests from merchants against any restrictions on Indian trade and from governors—particularly James Murray and his lieutenant and successor Carleton of Quebec—against infringements on the powers of their provinces.[67] As a result, four years of vital time was lost in North America, and squatters and free traders imposed an irreversibly chaotic regime on the landscape that made the Plan of 1764 a dead letter. "Had it been put in execution immediately, I am of opinion, it would have had all the effects expected from it," Johnson bemoaned; "the longer it continues unsettled, the greater will be the opposition."[68]

The Stamp Act crisis, in particular, was an important factor in both the delays in implementing the Plan and the inability of Johnson and Stuart to control the situation, if only for the ways in which it paralyzed the machinery of government. In New York in 1766, for example, Governor Moore refused to issue any trading licenses because they could not be engrossed on stamped paper. As a result, the province's traders either went to Quebec to get the permits allegedly handed out by the sheaf there or, more likely, headed west with no papers at all. "I am under no small difficulty in preparing such regulations for the ensuing season as I think can be enforced," Johnson confessed in the spring of the next year. "The Traders have got such a habit of late of passing the Posts, and trading where they please, that it is impossible for me to prevent them."[69] For varying periods in many colonies, meanwhile, courts were closed, preventing prosecutions of unlicensed traders, and the proroguing of rebellious assemblies prevented legislation that might have established effective licensing systems, punished squatters, or otherwise strengthened the hands of Johnson and Stuart—not that there would have been much hope for such action anyway.[70]

Perhaps most important, the Stamp Act crisis instilled habits of contempt for royal authority that doomed any efforts to police British frontiers. "I do not apprehend the Colonists are extremely fond of supporting officers immediately under the direction of the Crown," Johnson understated.[71] The superintendent learned his lesson firsthand in late 1766, when he tried to evict a man who had squatted on Mohawk land. Johnson had, he said, "repeatedly (at the earnest request of the Indians) wrote to him, and personally shewn him His Majesty's Proclamation of 1763, and laid the matter before the Governour in Council and the Attorney General, all which he laughs at, well knowing the party that is ready to suport him, in so much, that it would only weaken the prerogative to prosecute him, as may be evinced in many similar cases."[72]

No wonder that, as Thomas Penn reported from London, when the topic of Indian affairs came up, "Every one" was "out of Humour with the Americans."[73] In early 1768, in the midst of the Townshend Duties crisis, another shuffling of the British ministry brought Hillsborough into the government as Secretary of State for the Colonies, a new post assuming functions formerly exercised by the secretary for the Southern Department. One of his first acts was to help kill the Plan he had originally sponsored. Several months earlier, the ministry, "observing the expences of North America to be enormous, and to arise in a great measure from the present manner of manageing Indian Affairs, by the intervention of Superintendants who necessarily have a power of drawing for such sums as they shall judge expedient," had urged the Board of Trade to pull the plug.[74]

In March 1768 it obliged, and a month later Hillsborough announced the cabinet's final decision. Of the comprehensive program envisioned in 1764, only the negotiation of a boundary line with the Indians (which would be completed by Johnson at the Treaty of Fort Stanwix and by Stuart at the Treaty of Hard Labor later that year, only to be torpedoed by lack of provincial cooperation) remained a goal "essentially necessary to . . . preserving the tranquility of the Colonies." Otherwise, the powers of the superintendents would henceforth be limited to matters that, "as they have reference to the general interests of the Indians, independent of their connection with any particular Colony, cannot be provided for by the Provincial Laws." Among these were "the renewal of antient Compacts or Covenant-Chains . . . ; the reconciling Differences and disputes between one body of Indians and another; the agreeing with them for the sale or surrender of Lands for public purposes not lying within the limits of any particular Colony; and the holding interviews with them for these and a variety of other general purposes which are merely objects of Negotiation between your Majesty and the Indians."[75]

The key word was "merely." Individual provinces now regained the upper hand in nearly everything that mattered. Determining "that no one general Plan of Commerce and Policy . . . can be applicable to all the different Nations of Indians of different interests and in different situations" and "that the confining Trade to certain Posts and Places" was "evidently disadvantageous

inconvenient and even dangerous," the government concluded that "intrust-
ing the entire Management of that Trade to the Colonies themselves" would
"be of great advantage . . . as a means of avoiding much difficulty, and saving
much expense." Admitting that in the past provincial mismanagement of the
trade had "contributed not a little to involve us in the enormous expences of
an Indian War," the Board of Trade somehow found confidence that "the ill
effects of such inattention and neglect, will induce all of them to use more
caution and better management for the future." Moreover, with trade free and
decentralized, there would be no need for the vast expense of western forts,
the majority of which could be dismantled. The few that remained, "being
formed under Military Establishments and ever subjected to Military Authority," did not "require any other Superintendance than that of the Military
commanding at these Posts." This was as close as the new non-plan came to
dealing with the vital issue of judicial powers. Concerning mechanisms for
resolving everyday disputes between Natives and Euro-Americans, the ministry was silent.[76]

*   *   *

On the surface, the demise of the Plan of 1764 is easily explained by its cumbersome features, by pre-revolutionary chaos in British North America, by
political pique in Whitehall, and by empty purses everywhere. Yet deeper still
(although no one at the time apparently made the connections), the scheme
engaged nearly every great constitutional and ideological issue that defined
the imperial crisis. Funding for the Plan—the ballooning annual figure that
provided the excuse for killing it—was to come from a levy on fur and hide
exports, a form of taxation without representation not unlike the Townshend
Duties that nearly brought the empire to its knees. The Plan's tariff schedules, licenses, and trade regulations flowed from the same basic mercantilist
assumptions as the Navigation Acts, assumptions to which Euro-Americans
were only just beginning to articulate their gut-level revulsion. The Plan's
grant of justice-of-the-peace powers to officials outside the purview of assemblies, its limitations on judicial appeals, and its requirements that provincial
laws regarding Indian testimony be overridden would—if anybody seriously
examined them—have horrified those who cherished the common law, the
independence of courts, and the power of juries. And the shortest of the forty-
three articles in the Plan was in some ways the most explosive in its implications. What could more fully assault the privileges of provincial assemblies,

more deeply threaten the powers of Euro-American elites, more thoroughly undermine the ambitions of merchants and traders, landlords and landless, speculators and squatters—more concisely sum up the issue of imperial centralization—than the bald assertion "that all laws now in force in the several Colonies for regulating Indian Affairs or Commerce be repealed"?[77]

Beyond these political and ideological issues, the Plan of 1764, in its ham-handed even-handedness toward Indians, also cut to the heart of an emerging British-American racial identity. Like the Proclamation that preceded it, the Quebec Act that followed it, and the vetoes of schemes for western colonies that surrounded it, the Plan suggested that at least some British imperial officials in both Whitehall and North America actually considered Native people to be something resembling subjects of the Crown who had rights and interests that had to be protected, even if those rights and interests came into conflict with subjects of European extraction. Taking root in the 1760s, this alarming potential for imperial racial fairness would convince many provincials that the crown was not only guilty of an unpopular program to keep Native American lands out of their hands but enmeshed in an unholy alliance with racial others to deny them their lives, liberty, and property. Accordingly, Thomas Paine would assert in 1776 that there were "thousands, and tens of thousands, who would think it glorious to expel from the continent that barbarous and hellish power, which hath stirred up the Indians and Negroes to destroy us."[78]

The Plan of 1764, then, was not just any vision of a British empire that never was, not just a bureaucratic fantasy in which centralized administration would allow trade to flourish, property to be protected (at least until it accumulated in proper elite hands), and peace to be preserved between Euro-Americans and Indian subjects (although the latter were not to be openly called by that name). The flood of petitions lodged against the Plan, and the constitutional, economic, and racial issues it so thoroughly engaged, suggest instead that it reflected a vision of empire deeply threatening to Euro-Americans who would ultimately come to reject any imperial future that they themselves could not control. This was indeed an empire that never was. That it never was speaks volumes about the imperial structures that actually did emerge, and then collapse, in America as well as in Britain, during the generation after 1763.

CHAPTER 10

Onas, the Long Knife:
Pennsylvanians and Indians
After Independence

In April 1792 the war chief Red Jacket led a delegation of Seneca Iroquois to the Federal capital at Philadelphia. Their main business was with the President and Congress, but the Native leaders also paid a courtesy call on Pennsylvania Governor Thomas Mifflin. Standing beneath Benjamin West's portrait of Penn's Treaty in the statehouse council chamber, Red Jacket addressed his host as "Brother Onas Governor," using the Iroquoian translation of the Pennsylvania founder's surname that had long been employed to refer to governors of the province and state. The sight of Onas's portrait, Red Jacket declared, "brought fresh to our minds the freindly conferences that used to be held between the former governor of Pennsylvania and our tribes and the love which your forefathers had of Peace." It was, the Seneca leader told Mifflin, "still our wish, as well as yours to preserve peace between our tribes and you and it would be well if the same Spirit [prevailed] among the Indians to the Westward and thro' every part of the United States."[1]

A little over a year later, the fragility of such hopes for peace on the frontiers of the United States became apparent in another encounter between Indians and Pennsylvanians; then a quite different name was used to describe William Penn's successors. On what started as a pleasant afternoon stroll near the British post at Detroit, Philadelphia Quakers William Hartshorne and John Parrish heartily greeted a half-dozen young Ojibwas who had recently arrived from Michilimackinac. Perhaps amused at the Pennsylvanians' awkward attempt at saying "How do you do?" in trade pidgin, the Indians initially returned the salutation, but when Parrish and Hartshorne extended

Back of the Statehouse, William Birch, *The City of Philadelphia, in the State of Pennsylvania North America; as It Appeared in the Year 1800* (Philadelphia, 1800). Library Company of Philadelphia. An Indian delegation peacefully interacts with Pennsylvanians outside the building later known as "Independence Hall."

their arms, they "drew back and refused to shake hands, and said 'Shemockteman Boston.'" The word that Parrish rendered *Shemockteman* meant, he explained, "'Long knives,' a name . . . given to the Virginians, as a warlike people, which is now spread throughout the whole country[;] as the States unite in one they are all looked upon to be 'Shemocktemen.'" Seeking to set the record straight, the Quakers—true children of the idealized Onas if ever there were any—protested that they were "from Philadelphia," but the Indians would hear nothing of it.[2] The Ojibwas "soon grew furious," Hartshorne recalled, "calling us in their way, long knife, and with furious countenances, and violent gestures." The Quakers believed themselves lucky to escape the conversation alive.[3]

The names and imageries applied to Pennsylvanians in these two encounters—*Onas* the just founder and *Shemockteman* the treacherous killer—could not contrast more starkly. Clearly, in the early 1790s some disagreement

existed between Pennsylvanians who wrapped themselves in the mantle of
Onas and Indians who insisted they were Long Knives. But Red Jacket's invo-
cation of the memory of William Penn also suggests a more profound contest
between Pennsylvania officials and Indian leaders and among Native peoples themselves over the very meaning of the title *Onas*. During the decade
after the close of the American War for Independence, Indians seeking some
way to live, hunt, and trade on lands claimed by Pennsylvania repeatedly attempted to call the commonwealth back to the supposed ideals of its founder.
Despite their efforts, however, and despite Pennsylvania officials' preference
for the pen to the knife in deeds as well as rhetoric, little distinguished the
state's basic policies from those of the Confederation and Federal governments. Thus, in the view of many Native people, Onas took his place among
the other Long Knives of the new republic.

*   *   *

Not surprisingly, most Pennsylvanians who wielded political power or cultural influence in the 1780s and 1790s liked to think that they remained true
to the spirit of Onas. "We hope," Mifflin told a delegation of Creek leaders
visiting Philadelphia in 1790, "the conduct of Pennsylvania, from the land-
ing of William Penn to this day, has unequivocally proved *her* love of justice,
her disposition for peace, and *her* respect for the rights and happiness of her
neighbors."[4] Yet citizens of the commonwealth, then as now, were a diverse
lot, and one suspects that the reputation of Long Knife was embraced proudly
by such western frontierfolk as those who, in 1787, found quaint "an old law
of the Provence of Pennsylvania, which prohibited any person from shooting
at an Indian until the Indian should first shoot at him"—not to mention by
those who participated in such atrocities as the massacre in 1782 of dozens of
Christian Delawares at the Ohio country Moravian community of Gnadenhütten, named for the predecessor community destroyed during the Seven
Years War.[5] Understandably, then, on the Native side of the frontier, the Ojibwas at Detroit were not alone in their contemptuous refusal to distinguish
among Pennsylvanians, Virginians, and Bostonians. As Detroit trader Isaac
Williams told Parrish, "The Indians had in time past had confidence in the
People of Pennsylvania, but since the different governments centered in one,
as the thirteen United fires, they now look upon them all under the denomi-
nation of Virginians, and called the whole, Bigknives."[6]

The shift in terminology was not trivial. To Native people, it mattered a

great deal whether Pennsylvanians were called "Brother Onas" or lumped together with backcountry Virginians as "Long Knives" with whom Indians had
no familial ties. Such words were part of a rich eighteenth-century vocabulary of intercultural diplomacy in eastern North America, in which the names
leaders used for each other—known as "council titles"—were key symbols in
a discourse about who peoples were and the nature and history of their relationships. Typically, council titles consisted of two parts. The first expressed
a fictive kinship relationship, which established terms of authority, deference,
and intimacy. Traditionally, for instance, the Senecas and others of the Six
Nations Iroquois had been "brothers" of English colonies, but "children" of
their "father," the governor of New France. Other Indian nations might be
either "brothers," "nephews," or "children" of their Iroquois "brothers," "uncles," or "fathers" and assume a corresponding status as either "children" or
"brothers" of the English in turn. The matrilineal kinship systems of many
Native societies gave such terms meanings that patrilineal Euro-Americans
seldom fathomed. In a society in which descent was traced through the female line and divorce was frequent, brothers, uncles (mothers' brothers), and
nephews—as members of the same lineage—were closer and more deeply
obligated kin than were fathers and children. Thus, an uncle commanded far
greater obedience from the younger generation than did a father, who should
be respected for his age and wisdom and could be a source of advice and protection in times of trouble, but was not due unquestioned allegiance.[7]

The second element of a council title was often the name of a historical
personage who, like "Brother Onas," was believed to have established the relationship between two peoples on its proper footing. Such a name served two
functions: it embodied an ideal standard of behavior that tended to be elaborated through time as positive aspects were stressed and negative ones sup-
pressed, and it gave a relationship historical depth and continuity, for the title
was applied from generation to generation almost regardless of the personal
qualities of current office-holders.[8] In the Pennsylvania case, as Red Jacket's
speech shows, *Brother Onas* evoked an idealized memory of honest treaties
among equals in which Euro-Americans scrupulously paid Native owners a
fair price for the lands they occupied. That memory—whatever the accuracy
of its original historical referent—assumed particular relevance in light of the
perversion of the treaty process by which William Penn's sons and their agent
James Logan defrauded the Delawares of most of their Pennsylvania lands
during the mid-eighteenth century.[9]

Such historical experiences ensured that the meanings of council titles could be highly contested. To a certain degree, the fact that they *were* contested actually contributed to the stability of intercultural relationships; what historian Richard White calls "the middle ground" on which eighteenth-century Natives and Euro-Americans interacted was built of shared fictions and deliberate misunderstandings that allowed each culture to believe what it wanted about the other.[10] But the *open* contest over titles that occurred at Detroit in 1793 suggests that shared fictions were breaking down, that the image one group constructed of itself could no longer be reconciled to the image current in the discourse of the other. To avert such a crisis, a diplomat could, as Red Jacket did in Philadelphia in 1792, try to use a traditional council title to *educate* the other side—to outline its responsibilities and call it back to the historical principles the name evoked. "You particularly expressed that . . . your disposition is that for which the ancient Onas Governor[s] were remarkable," the Seneca leader thus reminded Governor Mifflin.[11]

In the 1780s, lessons about William Penn, about treaties among equals, and about fair purchase prices assumed far more than antiquarian interest, as Pennsylvania officials used the treaty process to acquire legal title to a massive tract of land in the northwestern third of what became the modern state. The territory lay beyond the boundary line between Natives and colonists that British and Iroquois diplomats had agreed upon at the first Treaty of Fort Stanwix in 1768. By the time Great Britain acknowledged the independence of the United States in the Treaty of Paris of 1783, most of these lands were devoid of Indian inhabitants, although the Penn of memory would not have approved of the way that situation came about. Some of the most brutal fighting of the War for Independence had destroyed the many ethnically mixed Indian villages of the upper Susquehanna watershed and the Wyoming Valley; there the real jurisdictional struggle in the 1780s was not between Euro- and Native Americans but between armed groups of Whites who claimed patents under Connecticut and Pennsylvania. Similarly, the Ohio and Big Beaver Valleys near Pittsburgh had long swarmed with immigrants from Pennsylvania and Virginia, although governments of the Keystone State and the Old Dominion vigorously competed with the squatters and each other for title to the real estate there.[12]

Only in the Allegheny River and French and Conewango Creek watersheds of the extreme northwestern corner of the tract Pennsylvania claimed did any substantial communities of Natives remain. Indian populations were in great flux as refugee communities resettled after the War for Independence, but in the mid-1780s, the core residents of that area and the neighboring portion of what became New York State consisted of about five hundred Seneca Iroquois and a small number of Munsee Delawares led by the Seneca war chiefs Guyasuta (Great Cross), Half-Town (Hachuwoot), Great Tree (Keandochgowa or Karontowanen), and, most prominently, Cornplanter (John O'Bail, Kayentwahkeh). Like nearly all members of their nation, these "Cornplanter" or "Allegany" Senecas had fought in the War for Independence beside the British, or perhaps more accurately, against the United States.[13]

Following the Peace of Paris, however, a variety of geographical and historical factors inclined them southward toward Pennsylvania rather than northward toward the British posts of Niagara and Detroit that kept many other Senecas in the British orbit. Since before the era of European contact, the western Seneca communities in the Allegheny and Genesee River watersheds had been socially and politically distinct from eastern members of their nation whose pre-war homes clustered around Seneca Lake.[14] After Continental troops commanded by John Sullivan and James Clinton destroyed their towns in 1779, most eastern Senecas—of whom Red Jacket was the leader best known to Whites—lived for nearly two years as refugees at Niagara, almost entirely dependent on that post's storehouses for food, clothing, and weapons. By 1781, many were resettling nearby in new villages along Cattaraugus and Buffalo Creeks, where they maintained close economic and political links with the British military.[15]

All of the major western Seneca towns had also been razed by the Sullivan-Clinton campaign and a simultaneous invasion of the Allegheny country by the Pennsylvania troops of Daniel Brodhead, and many of their residents also fled temporarily to Niagara. Two Allegheny villages, however, escaped destruction to provide an alternative locus of resettlement in a region that contained many of the traditional hunting territories, cemeteries, and ceremonial centers of the western Senecas. Yet, even on this familiar ground, trade with Euro-Americans remained crucial to any real hopes for an Indian future, and at least a hundred miles and a ridge of cliffs separated that portion of Pennsylvania and extreme southwestern New York from Niagara. The relatively easy river route to Pittsburgh was far superior to the overland trek to the British post and held out an attractive alternative to the clientage facing the many Cattaraugus and Buffalo Creek men and women still drawing military provisions from Niagara in the immediate postwar years. So the Allegany Senecas pinned their hopes for survival and independence on ties to Pennsylvania.[16]

But Onas's descendants had other ideas about rights to lands within what they called, in a nicely passive-voiced phrase, "the acknowledged limits of this State."[17] In their view, Native land claims had to be extinguished rapidly, and in a way that left no questions about legal ownership of title to the real estate. In part, the need stemmed from Pennsylvania's boundary disputes with neighboring states. Other factors were schemes to dominate trade between the Atlantic coast and the Great Lakes and the influence of "land jobbers" eager to profit from western speculations.[18] Yet the primary motive for quickly acquiring legal title to Indian lands stemmed from the commonwealth's financial situation. Strapped for cash, in 1780 the Pennsylvania legislature had voted to fulfill many monetary obligations to its troops with promises of land: a "donation" of acreage would serve in lieu of an enlistment bounty, and "depreciation certificates" redeemable at the state land office were to compensate officers and men for the lost purchasing power of their paper-money pay. By war's end, the depreciation certificates comprised an enormous portion of the state's debt: entries in the Supreme Executive Council minutes between 1783 and 1785 approve interest payments alone of at least £37,487 ($116,585), and as late as 1790, the outstanding principal was calculated at nearly $1.5 million, roughly three-quarters of the remaining obligations incurred by the state on its own, rather than the Continental government's, behalf.[19]

The beauty of the depreciation certificate plan was that redemption of this substantial liability would cost the commonwealth and its taxpayers next to nothing, provided sufficient "free" real estate was available; as one historian puts it, for Pennsylvanians, "land" promised to be "the path to solvency."[20] Depreciation certificates could be used to purchase any unpatented acreage, and a significant portion of them paid for newly platted city lots in Philadelphia. But clearly, given the size of the financial obligation the certificates represented and the overwhelmingly agricultural nature of the late eighteenth-century economy, much larger and more rural tracts seemed necessary. Accordingly, in March 1783 the Pennsylvania legislature declared most of the southern half of the territory west of the Allegheny River to be "Depreciation Lands" set aside for redemption of the certificates and instructed surveying parties to lay out lots for sale. Meanwhile, plans were being drafted to set aside the northern half of the region as "Donation Lands" for war veterans.[21] As a mutiny by unpaid Pennsylvania soldiers rocked the capital in June of that year and as squatters pouring across the Allegheny and Ohio threatened to overrun the region before it could be distributed to law-abiding citizens who would help to cancel the commonwealth's liabilities, the rapid— and cheap—acquisition of legal title to the remaining Indian lands within "the acknowledged limits of this state" assumed vital importance.[22]

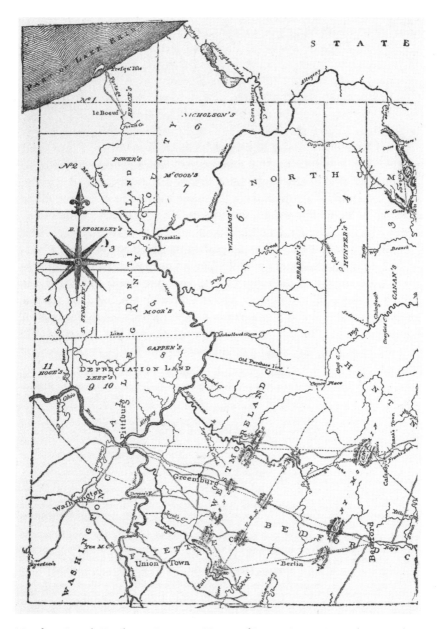

Map from Joseph Henderson Bausman, *History of Beaver County, Pennsylvania and its Centennial Celebration* (New York, 1904), 2:856. University of Pennsylvania Library. To pay its debts to Revolutionary War soldiers, in the mid-1780s, the Pennsylvania government hastened to acquire coerced title to Indian land west of the Allegheny River, to be granted to veterans as "Donation Lands" and "Depreciation Lands."

Yet none of the territory beyond the 1768 treaty line had yet been purchased from Native owners. Indeed, peace had not even been made between
the United States and the Senecas or any other Native peoples, and raids and
counterraids between Indians and frontier Whites threatened to reignite full-
scale warfare at any moment. Some forty Pennsylvanians reportedly lost their
lives in early 1783 alone. "The particular Circumstances of this state render an
attention to Indian affairs indispensably necessary," John Dickinson, president of the commonwealth's Supreme Executive Council, thus concluded in a
letter to his state's Congressional delegation in April of that year. The Council, he said, "earnestly desire[d] that" Congress would "adopt without Loss
of Time, the most effectual measures, for making Peace with all the Indian
nations."[23]

Later that month, Dickinson clarified to the delegates a vision of a peace
imposed on defeated enemies rather than negotiated with independent powers: Congress should notify the Indians "that Peace has been made with Great
Britain . . . ; that the Back Country with all the Forts is thereby ceded to us; that
they must now depend upon us for their Preservation and, that unless they immediately cease from their outrages . . . we will instantly turn upon them our
armies that have conquered the king of Great Britain . . . and extirpate them
from the Land where they were born and now live." This "conquest theory," of
which Dickinson was one of the earliest articulators, rested upon a peculiar
interpretation of the fact that the Treaty of Paris, in declaring all lands south
of the Great Lakes and east of the Mississippi to be within the boundaries of
the United States, failed to mention Britain's Indian allies at all, much less any
rights they may have had to the lands in question.[24]

Native leaders, of course, utterly rejected the conquest theory. "They
never could believe," a British Indian agent explained, "that our King could
pretend to Cede to america What was not his own to give, or that the amer-
icains Would accept from him What he had no right to grant."[25] Nonetheless,
Pennsylvania's position was clear. "If any Indians converse with you on this
Business," Dickinson informed his Surveyor General, "you may assure them
that those Lands are within the Boundary of Pennsylvania . . . , and we have
full power to maintain our title by force of arms." "Yet," the council president added immediately, "we sincerely intend to treat them, as our ancestors
treated their Forefathers, and to deal friendly with them, if they will suffer us
to do so." Like Dickinson's two sentences, the Pennsylvanian as Long Knife
and the Pennsylvanian as Onas stood uneasily together.[26]

Pennsylvania's attempts to "deal friendly with" the Indians under the auspices of the Continental government moved at a glacial pace. Congress almost immediately adopted verbatim Dickinson's articulation of the conquest theory, but the membership took six months to resolve "that a convention be held with the Indians . . . who have taken up arms against the United States, for the purpose of receiving them into the favour and protection of the United States and of establish[ing] boundary lines of property for seperating and dividing the settlements of the Citizens from the Indian Villages and hunting grounds." The resolution invited Pennsylvania to send its own representatives to make "a treaty for the purchase of the Indian Claim to lands within the jurisdiction of that State," and in February 1784 the Supreme Executive Council appointed Samuel J. Atlee, William Maclay, and Francis Johnston to perform the chore.[27] Reflecting the state's priorities, the legislation authorizing the appointments placed them in the context of preparations for "laying off and surveying the lands appropriated for the redemption of the military depreciation certificates." According to state House of Representatives Speaker Frederick Muhlenberg, "The custom of Pennsylvania has always been, to purchase the right of possession, from the Indian nations, as being more consonant to Justice and less expensive, than force," yet neither the Indians' asking price nor even their willingness to sell entered a picture framed by the conquest theory. In August when the assembly appropriated slightly less than $10,500 "worth of such goods, merchandize and trinkets as are known to be very acceptable among the Indians" as the amount to be paid "for the purpose of finally purchasing the said territory agreeable to ancient usage," the only recorded debate was over a proposal to raise the payment to £9,000 ($27,990).[28]

After many additional delays that led Pennsylvania officials to consider seriously proceeding independently of the Confederation government, Congressional commissioners Richard Butler, Arthur Lee, and Oliver Wolcott finally met over six hundred Iroquois men, women, and children at Fort Stanwix (present-day Rome, New York) in October 1784. Atlee, Maclay, and Johnston amicably observed the proceedings and waited their turn "in perfect harmony with the Continental Commissioners," who extolled them as an example of the commonwealth's "Wisdom and Confederal Policy." In this, the Pennsylvanians stood in stark contrast with their counterparts from New York, whose unilateral negotiations with the Iroquois led Butler, Lee, and Wolcott to post armed guards to exclude the Empire State's agents from the grounds.[29]

When the treaty council opened, the Congressional commissioners informed the Iroquois that they were "ready on their part if desired to give

peace . . . upon just and reasonable terms and to receive them into the friendship favour and protection of the United States." As a mark of that friendship,
the Iroquois should propose a mutually satisfactory boundary between their
territory and that of the Euro-Americans.[30] Mohawk Iroquois leader Joseph
Brant—whose comprehension of spoken English was excellent—reported a
few days later that the commissioners assured the Indians that the United
States did "not claim any part of" Iroquois lands falling within the boundaries described by the Treaty of Paris. "We wanted," the commissioners said,
according to Brant's account, "to have a part of your lands to pay our troops
with, which we owe to them and mean to pay you for it, if you let us have it."[31]

Yet when Cornplanter took the commissioners at their word and suggested a modification of the 1768 treaty line that would have yielded much of
the area bounded by the present-day Pennsylvania–New York border and the
Allegheny River, the offer was privately derided as, in the words of one Pennsylvanian, "a nice farce upon the design, attempting to cede great [part] of the
State of Pennsylvania long ago purchased." After considerable debate among
themselves, Butler, Lee, and Wolcott dropped their conciliatory façade in
favor of a blunt explication of the conquest theory. "You are mistaken in sup-
posing that having been excluded from the treaty between the United States
and the King of England you are become a free and independent nation and
may make what terms you please," Lee declared in what one observer called "a
most spirited grand speech." Indians who allied themselves with the British in
the War for Independence were, the commissioner said, "a subdued people,"
and any patches of ground the United States chose to give to them would
belong to them not by right but by through the "magnanimity and mercy" of
the conquerors. Ignoring the Iroquois headmen's protestations that they had
no authority from their peoples to cede additional lands, the commissioners
then dictated a boundary that deprived the Six Nations of the western tip of
New York State and any pretensions to territory beyond the western boundary of Pennsylvania.[32]

The conquest theory propounded at Fort Stanwix dominated the dealings
of the United States with Native peoples throughout the Confederation's existence and guided the treaties forced upon a group of Wyandots, Delawares,
Ottawas, Chippewas, and Potawatomis at Fort McIntosh on the Ohio in 1785
and upon some Shawnee leaders at Fort Finney at the mouth of the Great
Miami River in 1786. It was no coincidence that all these negotiations—if
the term is even appropriate to describe them—took place under the guns of
United States military posts and that Congress took pains to raise substantial

troops in preparation for them.[33] The treaties of Forts Stanwix and McIntosh in particular were among the most notoriously fraudulent in the sordid history of such affairs. White traders kept the Native participants drunk much of the time, while the Congressional commissioners practiced various forms of psychological and military intimidation during the headmen's sober moments. As a University of Pennsylvania professor understated during a visit to Fort McIntosh a few months after the treaty was signed there, "It was the 'general' opinion of the American officers, who were at the treaty, that the proceedings of the whites were unfair, and, indeed, that the Indians were, in a manner, 'compelled' to sign the articles."[34]

The Pennsylvanian commissioners who followed the Congressional delegation from Fort Stanwix to Fort McIntosh made no recorded protests against the tactics and can hardly have escaped the prevailing climate of sleaze. One wonders whether moral, more than physical, exhaustion undergirded Atlee's complaint that the Fort Stanwix experience was "the most fateaguing piece of Business" he "ever undertook" and that his "Western Duty" at Fort McIntosh promised to "be much more disagreeable than the former."[35] Whatever the case, he and his colleagues secured at Fort Stanwix a deed—signed by two Mohawks, three Oneidas, two Onondagas, one Cayuga, three Senecas, and two Tuscaroras on 23 October 1784—that surrendered to Pennsylvania "all that part of the said Commonwealth not yet purchased of the Indians within the acknowledged Limits of the same." In return for a stated payment of $5,000 in goods, the Six Nations were to renounce "any Right Title Interest or property of . . . the said Tract," from which they were to "be forever ban[ned] and excluded."[36] Six years later, Cornplanter (who was present and signed the Congressional treaty but not the Pennsylvania deed) asserted that the Pennsylvanians offered only $4,000, and the commissioners' minutes confirm his statement. Whatever the figure—even when added to the approximately $2,000 given to Wyandot and Delaware leaders for the same lands several weeks later at Fort McIntosh—it was well under the legislative mandate of $10,500, of which the Natives were never informed.[37]

In striking their deal, the Pennsylvanians apparently replayed scenes previously acted out by the Congressional commissioners and, long before that, by the perpetrators of the Walking Purchase. "I have the great pleasure," wrote Atlee, "of reporting that, that part of our mission that respected the Northern Tribes has been concluded to our utmost wish."[38] According to Cornplanter's later recollections, the Iroquois had refused to sell all the territory the Pennsylvanians claimed "for the use of their warriors" and instead offered of "a part of it, which we pointed out to them in their map," probably repeating the proposal made to the Congressional commissioners earlier. In response, Atlee, Maclay, and Johnston invoked the conquest theory to declare that "they must have the whole; that it was already ceded to them by the great king . . . and was *their own*." Yet the Pennsylvanians departed from the Congressional script in evoking, as Dickinson had done earlier, the spirit of Onas: "they would not take advantage of" their conquest rights to the land "and were willing to pay . . . for it, after the manner of their ancestors." The intimidated Iroquois were, said Cornplanter, "unable to contend, at that time," and so several of them affixed their marks to the document.[39]

Things were not that clear-cut, however. Two long days of bargaining had been necessary, the Pennsylvania delegation's secretary confessed, before "we brought them to accept of our offer" and "had our deed executed and our business concluded to our great satisfaction, [and] credit, and to the advantage of the state."[40] As a result, Atlee, Maclay, and Johnston left Fort Stanwix with not one, but five documents, and the sheaf of papers allowed the Allegany Senecas some hope for the future. In his negotiations with the Pennsylvanians, Cornplanter recalled, "I begged of them to take pity on my nation and not buy [the land] . . . forever." The commissioners responded that "they would purchase it forever, but that they would give me further one thousand dollars in goods when the leaves were ready to fall"; thus the deed of cession was joined by a second document that pledged delivery of an additional payment the following October at Tioga on the New York state line. That paper secured Cornplanter's reluctant agreement to the bargain, but he recalled that he then further "requested, as they were determined to have the land[,] to permit my people to have the game and hunt upon the same, which request they complied with, and promised me to have it put upon record."[41] Accordingly, a third document explained "that it is not to be understood that the said Six Nations are by the same sale excluded from the privelege of hunting," which was "expressly reserved to them." Further caveats came from the Mohawk leader Aaron Hill (given up as a hostage to ensure compliance with the Congressional treaty), who insisted upon a fourth text that detailed conditions for delivery of the additional payment and formalized an earlier offer from the Pennsylvanians to allow a Seneca leader to witness the survey of the Commonwealth's northern boundary. A final document pledged delivery to Cornplanter and Hill of "two good Rifles of neat workmanship . . . in consideration of their services."[42]

*   *   *

Seneca Chief, Ki-On-Twog-Ky, also known as Cornplanter, painting by F. Bartoli, 1796. Collection of The New-York Historical Society.

Seizing the small opening that these concessions afforded, during the next several years Cornplanter and his fellow Allegany Seneca leaders cultivated ties to Pennsylvania in order to secure a place for their people within a North American landscape dominated by the new republic. Their persistent goals were to retain possession of their village sites, to secure Native hunting rights in northwestern Pennsylvania, and to establish trading privileges at

Pittsburgh. "I think Brother," Cornplanter had explained to the Congressio-
nal commissioners at Fort Stanwix, "that we Warriors should have a large
Country to range in, as our subsistence will depend on our having much
hunting ground—and as it will also bring in money to you, it will tend to
our mutual advantage."[43] In a message to Congress in May 1785, the Allegany
Seneca leader announced that he and his political allies had "published the
Articles of peace made between you and us, to Our Chiefs and Warriors,
And we have all agreed to become the fourteenth State, and keep you by the
Hand as Brothers if you mean [to abide] by the Agreement the Commissioners made at Fort Stanwix." For himself, he "intend[ed] settling on one of
the Branches of the Allegany, to prevent (if possible) all Mischief that may
accidentally arise" between Pennsylvanians and Senecas. "I wish," he continued, "my Friend General Butler with a Deputy from Virginia could meet me
at Fort Pit[t] with all speed to settle a peace, that we may again Hunt and
Trade with Our Ancient Friends without Molestation" and complete the work
begun with the Pennsylvania commissioners at Fort Stanwix.[44]

Indeed, much work remained to be done, and the Allegany Seneca leaders faced substantial criticism in their own and other Seneca communities. In
July Cornplanter and Guyasuta arrived at Fort Pitt in the company of a fellow
Seneca named Hockushakwego (All Face). "It is hard with me," Cornplanter
admitted to Colonel Josiah Harmar, who, as commander of the Continental
troops in the region, received the delegation in the absence of Butler. "I was
a chief man at Fort Stanwix and my people blame me much, for the English
have told our people that the great king never sold our lands to the thirteen
fires." Hockushakwego brandished a copy of the Treaty of Fort Stanwix and
protested the inadequate Native representation both there and at Fort Mc-
Intosh. Nonetheless, he blamed "the great king our father" for the sad state
of relations between the Six Nations and the United States. "Now we take no
advice from him and wish to sit in council with the Americans as we formerly
did," he announced. "You told us we should live in peace on the lands you
allowed us[;] Now brother we wish everything that was done at those councils to be strictly attended to." What the Allegany Senecas needed most was
peace and trade on the western Pennsylvania frontier, and, for that, regular-
ized channels of communication to Pittsburgh were crucial. "The council fire
was always kindled here," Guyasuta recalled. "I was the man who had the fire
removed from Fort Pitt[;] now I wish it brought back."[45]

Yet, on the issue of trade at Pittsburgh or Tioga, as on many other matters,
Pennsylvanians did little to fulfill the Allegany Senecas' hopes. Of the five

Fort Stanwix documents, only the deed of absolute cession ever made its way into the legislative journals or land office books in Philadelphia. Although the state Assembly initially acknowledged the right of a Seneca to witness the marking of the commonwealth's northern boundary and the Indians were allegedly "in a perfect good humour" at the prospect, Pennsylvania and New York surveyors worked for three summers to complete the chore, "without sending for that man" (who nonetheless did join part of the second year's activities on his own initiative). Moreover, Cornplanter later complained, the line the surveyors marked ran several miles north of the location to which the Iroquois thought they had agreed.[46] Meanwhile, the "elegant rifles" promised Cornplanter and Hill by April 1785 arrived in Iroquoia only in September, after having been damaged en route. State officials neglected the pledge to deliver the Six Nations an additional $1,000 in goods until July, when Johnston prodded Dickinson to "a strict and punctual observance of every promise made to the Savage Nations."[47]

In the fall, when the Council president sent Maclay to Tioga to fulfill the obligation, he made clear his government's very limited interpretation of the hunting rights Cornplanter believed he had extracted from the commissioners at Fort Stanwix: "We wish you to avail yourself of the opportunity . . . of reading the Treaty to the Indians as it is entered on the public Journals of the General Assembly, of explaining the Expressions relating to the Privilege of hunting on the Lands *untill they are improved*, of demonstrating the absurdity of constructing those Expressions so as to overthrow the strong words of Conveyance in their Deeds." On Maclay's return, the Supreme Executive Council declared his dealings with the Iroquois at Tioga to be "another instance to the experience of Pennsylvania, that the friendship of Indians is only to be secured by treaties founded upon reciprocal advantage fairly conducted and strictly adhered to."[48]

Despite the self-congratulations of those who claimed the heritage of Onas, however, Seneca discontent with the commonwealth's deceptions—and their leaders' acquiescence in them—mounted. Cornplanter "refused" to meet with a party of Pennsylvanians surveying the Donation Lands near Venango in January 1786, and Hockushakwego advised them to turn back if they valued their lives. "Brother of the Big Knife," he said to people he failed to call *Onas*, "Many of our young Warriors are dissatisfied with . . . the Reward we received for the Lands Thinking it inadequate for so large a Body; it not being one pair of Mokosons a piece."[49] That spring, Cornplanter left his family at Pittsburgh and, fearing that his Seneca opponents might take his life, set off for New York in an unsuccessful effort to seek relief from Butler and the Confederation Congress meeting there.[50]

While he was gone the situation deteriorated further. In late April Hock- ushakwego arrived at Pittsburgh with nearly fifty Allegany Senecas from French Creek who, after "several Days trading" and drinking, "took away with them" Cornplanter's kin. When asked why, one "laughed, [and] said the Cornplanter was not coming back this way." As the party left Pittsburgh, Half-Town warned trader Thomas Gibson to leave his store at Slippery Rock because war was likely. Taking his own advice, the Seneca leader announced his intention to move with his family from French Creek to Cattaraugus until things settled down. "He parted with me in friendship," Gibson re- ported, "and said he might see me in friendship again and perhaps not."[51] Such warnings were well taken. On the Muskingum River a few weeks later, a party of Mingos and Cherokees living in the Ohio country killed four em- ployees of the Pittsburgh traders William Dawson and Charles McClain "because the[y] have had their Goods from the United States."[52] That attack was one of many that, in the years after the Fort Stanwix and Fort McIn- tosh treaties, demonstrated the utter failure of the conquest theory to bring about peace through force. And the militancy of freelance raiders such as those Mingos and Cherokees represented the extreme wing of a stiffening resistance to the United States that a new Western Confederacy—in which the Mohawk leader Brant was a central figure—was attempting to channel into a systematic defense of Indian lands against incursions from Kentucky, Virginia, and Pennsylvania.[53]

Resisting intense pressure to join the Confederacy, the Allegany Senecas remained committed to their alliance with Pennsylvania and regularly re- ported to Butler and other state and Continental officials on the Western- ers' plans. Nevertheless, their hopes of using the alliance to foster economic ties with Pittsburgh were almost completely dashed as attacks on Indians by frontier Whites joined attacks by Indians on White traders to stifle western Pennsylvania's sputtering Indian trade. Even if, as Butler claimed in the win- ter of 1786 to 1787, Indians who reached Pittsburgh were "very civilly treated by the inhabitants," the roads to and from that market were anything but safe. A few miles outside town, for example, one of Cornplanter's kinsmen was reportedly murdered simply because "he had a very fine riding horse; . . . was richly drest, and had about him a good deal of silver; and . . . had with him a very fine rifle." In separate incidents in the same neighborhood at about the same time Half-Town and an Indian informer en route to report on Western

Confederacy councils each lost two horses to local thieves.[54] No wonder Half-Town, along with Great Tree and many other Senecas, fled northward to Cattaraugus and other Iroquois communities with trading ties to Niagara or New York State. Cut off from Pittsburgh, the shrinking numbers of Senecas who remained on the Allegheny struggled to survive on the meager stock of trade goods available from a poorly supplied and understaffed United States military post called Fort Franklin, established on French Creek in 1787.[55]

* * *

But Cornplanter and his fellow leaders were not yet ready to abandon their hopes for hunting rights, trade, and secure homes in western Pennsylvania. In 1788, the commonwealth's desire for land once again provided an opportunity. As lawyers, politicians, and surveyors completed their messy work of determining the Keystone State's boundaries with New York and the Northwest Territory, it became apparent that only about four miles of Lake Erie shoreline fell within Pennsylvania. Worse still, that brief stretch contained nothing remotely resembling a harbor to serve as an entrepôt for trade with the Great Lakes and points west. The excellent port of Presque Isle, however, lay within a vaguely defined tract known as the Erie Triangle, which New York had ceded, along with its other western claims, to the Confederation in 1781. In 1788 Pennsylvania officials thus began intensive negotiations for its purchase and within a few months agreed upon a price of seventy-five cents in Continental securities per acre. Upon final survey in 1791 the total came to a little over $150,000.[56]

As the bargaining with Congress proceeded, the legislature also made plans for "the purchase of the Country from the Indians, agreeably to the Policy and Justice which have ever marked the Conduct of Pennsylvania in such Cases." The price ordered to be paid to the Iroquois was £375 worth of goods, then equal to about $1,000, or roughly one-half cent an acre.[57] With Congressional commissioners again preparing to hold a land-cession treaty with the Western Indians—this time at Fort Harmar on the Ohio River—the assembly deemed it "proper and oeconomical to take advantage of this Circumstance" and avoid "the Expence and delay of a particular Treaty" to complete the purchase of Native claims. Butler and John Gibson received commissions to carry out the task.[58]

More than pious rhetoric, familiar personnel, and a tight purse made Fort Harmar a replay of the Fort Stanwix and Fort McIntosh treaties. Cornplanter and his Iroquois political allies again played a prominent and, in the eyes of many Native people, entirely too accommodating role in helping to get signatures on documents ratifying an Indian-White boundary line unilaterally proclaimed by the United States. Guyasuta, Great Tree, and Half-Town were among more than two hundred Allegany Senecas and other Iroquois who had traveled with Cornplanter to Fort Harmar under the protection of a United States army escort. The Allegany leaders strove mightily to thwart the efforts of the Mohawk Brant to prevent the negotiations, although territorial governor Arthur St. Clair, who conducted the proceedings on behalf of Congress, refused even such modest requests as their proposal that he release a few Delaware prisoners as a sign of good faith. The Fort Harmar "treaty was effected altogether by the Six Nations; who seduced some of our young men to attend it," the Miami Little Turtle recalled six years later.[59]

But to the Allegany Senecas, the dealings with Pennsylvania seemed anything but a sham. As at Fort Stanwix, they believed they had extracted significant concessions from the state's commissioners in exchange for selling land the Long Knives were determined to have anyway. "For *and in behalf* of the State of Pennsylvania, (Onas)," Butler and Gibson joined twenty-four Indians—the vast majority of them from the Allegany villages—in affixing signatures and seals to a document stating that, "as they have no country to remove to from where they now live, the said chiefs do reserve for their own and their people's residence, hunting and fishing, all that part of the tract . . . passing from Allegany River along the middle of the Cononwago Creek, the Chadochque [Chautauqua] Lake and a meridian line from the North end of the said lake to Lake Erie." In addition to nearly complete rights to a tiny chunk of the land sold to the commonwealth at Fort Stanwix, the Allegany Senecas were to retain "full and peaceable liberty to hunt and fish within any part of the [Erie Triangle] . . . , they demeaning themselves peaceably towards the inhabitants."[60]

Having gained these significant concessions, Cornplanter rose on the final day of the Fort Harmar proceedings to paint a picture of interracial economic cooperation and harmony in which the weak would thrive under the protection of a stronger people they no longer addressed by the council title of *Brother*. "Father!" he said to St. Clair,

> We now the Six nations acquaint you that our opinion is, we are one people and we will live as such, and unite ourselves like children to a father.

Father! Now that we are settled in the midst of you, you will have pity on us, and if we should want clothing you will supply us.

Father! We shall see you upon our Lands, and they will be planted with corn, and we will be hunting about for Deer; we also shall plant corn, and we shall want our hoes and other articles mended, and for that purpose we shall want a blacksmith to settle amongst us upon the Land, that we have now agreed to live with our brothers upon.

Father! You will remember that a few days ago, we gave you the Belt of Friendship, and desired you to hold it fast; we now remind you of what we said then, and hope that it will not be forgotten by either of us.[61]

Cornplanter's dream of protection by Father Onas quickly became a nightmare. Surveys soon revealed that almost none of the land that the Fort Harmar agreement reserved to the Senecas actually lay within the Erie Triangle and that most of it was within the limits of New York, which was not bound by the acts of Pennsylvania's commissioners. Moreover, Gibson and Butler had repeated the multiple document strategy first used at Fort Stanwix; their guarantees of Allegany Seneca rights appeared in a paper separate from a deed of cession that contained far more absolute language. The codicil did not find its way into the commonwealth's files until 1794, long after surveyors, speculators, road builders, and squatters had made a mockery of the hunting rights it supposedly guaranteed.[62]

Before all this became apparent, more immediate problems arose. The Pennsylvania commissioners did not bring to Fort Harmar the goods they promised in payment, for the state coffers lacked the unfunded Assembly allocation of $1,000 (not, as stated in the text of the deed, $2,000). When the Supreme Executive Council finally found sufficient funds, their agents could not locate suitable merchandise in Philadelphia warehouses; lacking both strowdwater cloth and match coats—long standard components of diplomatic presents to Indians—they voted to substitute "some blankets now at Pittsburgh, which are said to be suitable for Indians."[63] In the cold of January, then, some 170 Allegany Senecas had to trudge away from Fort Harmar without a guide or military escort "thro' the wilderness through heaps of briars" to collect their payment. At least three times along the way, Whites robbed the nearly starving band of rifles and other of their meager possessions. When the travelers finally reached Pittsburgh, they found that "one hundred of the blankets were all moth eaton and good fornot'g." According to Cornplanter, no interpreter was present, and the Senecas—who needed the blankets simply to keep warm, could find no one to listen to their protests against Gibson, whom they blamed for the fraud.[64]

When the Allegany Senecas finally reached their homes, their leaders dictated to a literate White (probably interpreter Joseph Nicholson) a letter of protest. On receipt of it, the Supreme Executive Council—its Onas self-image severely shaken—invited the headmen to come to Philadelphia and seek redress during the September 1790 legislative session. "It gives us pain to hear from you that some bad people have plundered your camps and taken your property," the councilors said. "Our laws do not permit one man to injure another." As if to mock that statement, while Cornplanter and his colleagues prepared for their trip, three Pennsylvanians murdered a pair of Allegany Senecas on Pine Creek in Northumberland County on the New York border. Despite a show of state and Federal government activity, only one of the perpetrators was ever caught, and he evidently never stood trial.[65]

In this tense atmosphere, Cornplanter, Half-Town, Great Tree, Guyasuta, and two other Senecas arrived in Philadelphia in October 1790, armed with testimonials to their good faith and services to the commonwealth written by officials at Fort Franklin, Pittsburgh, Greensburg, and Shippensburg. The Seneca leaders stayed in the capital until early March 1791 and negotiated extensively with state and Federal officials, prominent Quakers, and speculators in their lands. "In former days when you were young and weak I used to call you brother, but now I call you father," Cornplanter told the Supreme Executive Council in a reprise of his redefinition of the relationships at Fort Harmar. "Father, I hope you will take pity on your children, for now I inform you that I'll die on your side."[66] Similar themes of allegiance in exchange for fatherly protection ran through a message of Guyasuta to the city's Quakers: "When I was young and strong our country was full of game . . . and the People of my Nation had enough to eat and always something to give to our friends when they entered our Cabins," he recalled. But now "the game is driven away by the white people, so that the young men must hunt all day long to find game for themselves to eat. . . . [W]e are old and feeble and hungry and naked, and that we have no other friends than you, the children of our beloved Brother Onas."[67]

But governmental changes initially allowed the Children of Onas to profess powerlessness. Cornplanter's delegation had arrived in Philadelphia after the dissolution of the last legislature elected under Pennsylvania's expired 1776 constitution. A new frame of government would not take effect until December, and in the interim the Supreme Executive Council could spend no money. Thus Cornplanter's reiterated plea "that a store be established at Fort Pitt for the accommodation of my people" received no response, and even his request for "a loan of one hundred and ninety dollars on account, to procure supplies," had to be denied. A promise Butler had made to Cornplanter shortly after the Fort Harmar Treaty regarding confirmation of the headman's personal title to three tracts of land totaling some 1,500 acres similarly lay in financial limbo, despite legislative approval a year and a half earlier.[68]

Once the new state constitution took effect, officials essentially tried to buy the Allegany Seneca leaders' silence. In compensation for the additional land acquired through what Cornplanter alleged to be the erroneous survey of the New York–Pennsylvania boundary, the legislature and governor paid Cornplanter, Half-Town, and Great Tree $800 "in trust for the use of the whole Seneca Nation of Indians and in full Satisfaction of all claims and demands whatsoever . . . against this Commonwealth."[69] Additionally, Cornplanter received his long promised land patents, and Great Tree obtained a deed to the island in the Allegheny River on which he resided. These private tracts—rather than a reservation vested in the nation as a whole—would be the only territories to which the Allegany Senecas ever acquired clear title from the state.[70]

While the Native leaders waited for the Pennsylvanians to act, major governmental shifts were also under way on the continental level as the new Federal Constitution went into effect. The Indian Trade and Intercourse Act, passed by Congress in August 1790, stripped the states of many powers they had previously claimed in dealing with the Natives. And, already at the Fort Harmar Treaty, United States officials had begun to abandon the conquest theory in favor of at least the pretext of negotiated land purchases. Thus, what the Fort McIntosh Treaty had described merely as gifts "in pursuance of the humane and liberal views of Congress" became in the Fort Harmar Treaty "consideration" paid, in combination with additional, much larger amounts, for lands east of the boundary. Moreover, in contradiction of its earlier declarations of absolute territorial sovereignty, the United States "relinquish[ed] and quit claim" to Native country west of the line.[71] Then, in 1790 and 1791 the Western Confederacy's successive defeats of Federal armies led by Harmar and St. Clair forced a further moderation of Federal policy, to the extent that minor modifications of the United States–Indian boundary lay on the table through the period of Anthony Wayne's defeat of the Western Confederacy at the Battle of Fallen Timbers in 1794 and his reaffirmation and extension of the 1784 Fort Stanwix line in the 1795 Treaty of Greenville.[72]

Yet, despite the changes that were beginning to take place in Federal policy during the Senecas' 1790 to 1791 sojourn in Philadelphia, negotiations with President Washington and Secretary of War Henry Knox in December and January produced no dramatic breakthroughs. Even Cornplanter's suggestion that the trusted interpreter Joseph Nicholson be stationed at Pittsburgh, where Senecas still hoped to trade on a large scale, was rejected. Washington did, however, pledge to prevent future fraudulent land purchases, to open Federal courts to Iroquois grievances, to station a government agent in the Senecas' country as "their friend and protector," and to provide educational and economic assistance. "Continue to be strong in your friendship for the United States, as the only rational ground of your future happiness," the President advised the Senecas, "and you may rely upon their kindness and protection."[73]

Nothing encouraged the Allegany Senecas to rely on the kindness and protection of the Children of Onas. Cornplanter and his party left Philadelphia carrying an additional present from the commonwealth of a little over £65 (about $175); just north of Pittsburgh, militiamen from Virginia attacked the boat on which the party was traveling and stole all of the merchandise those funds had purchased. A few months earlier, another group of Virginians, who were never caught, had murdered four Senecas in the same neighborhood. On the upper Allegheny, meanwhile, Pennsylvania surveyors accompanied by armed militia were completing an exploration of waterways in preparation for the occupation of Presque Isle, and an agent for Philadelphia merchant Robert Morris was plotting in the Senecas' village to attempt a massive private land purchase in the area.[74]

By 1794 the rapid occupation of the Erie Triangle had so trampled the Allegany Senecas' hunting and fishing rights that even Cornplanter had lost his patience; early that year he expelled a Pennsylvania storekeeper from his town and reportedly sought British aid "to Clear French Creek, By killing the White people and taking the Posts." Some young Allegany Seneca men, meanwhile, moved from talk to action and took the lives of several White Pennsylvanians in the area.[75] All of this occurred just at the point when Wayne's campaign against the Western Confederacy and President Washington's efforts to quell the Whiskey Rebellion left the Federal government no troops to spare; nonetheless, it took a personal appeal from Washington to convince Mifflin to order a brief suspension of state-sponsored activities in the Triangle.[76]

At the height of the tensions, Pennsylvania surveyor John Adlum traveled from Pittsburgh to Fort Franklin intending to survey a million-acre tract of Allegheny River Valley land to which Pennsylvanian James Wilson had recently acquired title. Escorted by Half-Town, Adlum's flotilla of canoes received a strained ceremonial reception at Cornplanter's village, during which the welcoming shots fired by Seneca young men whizzed suspiciously close to the surveyor's head. Shortly thereafter, in a crowded council house where Adlum sought permission to conduct his surveys, he attempted to read elaborately beribboned messages he carried from Secretary of War Knox and Governor Mifflin. His interpreter had barely finished the first paragraph of Knox's letter when "the young indians" sitting in the rafters "saluted" Adlum with "an univer[sal] roar, *vulgarly called farting*" and the women seated below joined in with cries of "*shame, scandalous.*" Cornplanter "reprimanded" the rude music-makers, who, Adlum said, then "descended from their roosts, and sneaked off." Next morning, in a more decorous meeting, Adlum received begrudging permission to plat approximately half the territory he intended, but not before Cornplanter informed him "that all persons who encroached on their lands were their enemies."[77]

*   *   *

Onas, Long Knives, Enemies: three Indian names for Pennsylvanians. Despite the repeated attempts of Seneca leaders to hold up the first as a model of behavior for Pennsylvania government officials, the last two were the ones that stuck. In Native eyes, Onas's descendants were no different from all the other Long Knives of the new republic. Nearly a decade of dealing with the Pennsylvania had secured the Allegany Senecas title to precisely 1,500 acres of land and one island; their hopes for hunting and fishing rights inside the state's borders and for a flourishing trade with Pittsburgh remained unfulfilled. And, by the early nineteenth century only a handful of Senecas would remain within the commonwealth, the rest having joined their kin across the state line on the New York Allegany reservation.[78] Long before, Senecas had apparently given up their hopes that accommodation with the commonwealth's government might help them achieve their goals of a secure land base, hunting rights, and trading privileges. The legacy of the commonwealth's Indian policies lived on, however, as the Federal government embraced techniques the commonwealth had perfected and applied them widely in the years of the early republic: legalistic adherence to treaty documents, forced purchases of Indian territory, resales of the land acquired to its own citizens to pay government debts, and rhetoric that wrapped the process in professions of philanthropic justice.[79] In more ways than one, Onas became the Long Knife.

CHAPTER 11

"Believing That Many of the Red People Suffer Much for the Want of Food": A Quaker View of Indians in the Early U.S. Republic

In the spring of 1804, Gerard T. Hopkins traveled from Baltimore to Fort Wayne, in Indian country. As secretary of the Baltimore Yearly Meeting of Friends and a member of its Committee on Indian Affairs, he carefully kept a journal, which he later edited to "convey inteligibly, both the route we took and the various circumstances attendant upon our Journey"; his traveling companions were fellow committee member George Ellicott and a young man named Phillip Dennis, who had been employed to live with the Indians and "instruct them in Agriculture and other useful knowledge." Hopkins's journal records that, when the three travelers reached Fort Wayne, they appeared before a council of chiefs convened by Miami leader Little Turtle. Speaking with the assistance of resident Federal agent and interpreter William Wells, they announced that, "in coming into the Country of our Red brethren, we have come with our eyes open and . . . are affected with sorrow in believing that Many of the red people suffer much for the want of food and for the want of Clothing." If only the Miamis would "adopt our mode of Cultivating the earth and of raising useful animals," they would, the Quakers assured them, "find it to be a mode of living not only far more plentif[ul] and much less fatiguing but also much more Certain . . . than is now attendant upon hunting."[1]

Eyes may have been open, but brains apparently were not processing much of what was seen. For Hopkins also noted that a few days before the Quakers delivered their speech, one of the supposedly starving Native women—Wells's wife and Little Turtle's daughter, Sweet Breeze—treated them to "an excellant dinner" featuring "a very large well roasted wild Turkey [and] also a wild Turkey boiled," both accompanied by "a large supply of Cramberry Sauce." Later, the Marylanders visited a camp where Miami women and their "very fat and healthy looking children" dressed in "very costly silver ornaments" were producing maple sugar for Euro-American markets.[2] Hopkins did not know it, but it is likely that the Indians engaged in that commercial activity because it was early April and not yet time to plant the corn, beans, and squash that their agriculturalist ancestors had known how to grow for at least eight hundred years before Dennis was born. To insist that these people were ill-fed and ill-clad was a remarkable triumph of ideological construction over visual and gastronomical evidence.

As Hopkins tried to "convey inteligibly" his experiences, he relied less on what he had actually seen than on what he thought he knew before he began his journey. An easterner whose knowledge of Native people came largely from eighteenth-century books—most of them published by European authors who themselves had not even visited North America—he deployed a powerfully wrong-headed analysis of who Indians were and what kind of problems they faced as the new republic assumed control of the continent. Despite a maize of evidence, this analysis insisted that Indians were not really farmers. Despite the economic importance of the trade in fur and hides (and, at Fort Wayne, maple sugar), it similarly insisted that they did not participate in the modern commercial economy in any significant way, except to purchase rotgut liquor and other self-destructive luxuries. Supposedly hunters living hand-to-mouth in a world where game lands were rapidly shrinking, these imagined Indians *had* to be facing starvation because their way of life was doomed by the presence on the continent of an allegedly more advanced society based, unlike theirs, on agriculture and commerce. Their only earthly salvation was to take up the plow that Hopkins and his companions offered them.

The *belief* "that Many of the red people suffer[ed] much for the want of food"—and that such abstract categories as "red people" and "hunters" provided in themselves sufficient explanation for the economic and social distress of Indians whose particular circumstances need not be considered—proved almost impervious to contradictory evidence, in part because it so conveniently justified Euro-American expropriation of Indian land and resources. But for Hopkins and his fellow turn-of-the-nineteenth-century Quakers, the noble work of turning starving hunters into sturdy subsistence farmers held greater appeal because it addressed their own unease with the emerging economy of the new republic, an economy in which commercial activity in particular threatened to undermine morality. Thus blinded to the possibility that plows may not have been the answer, they could not translate their genuinely humanitarian impulses into any kind of meaningful assistance for Native people who sought not mere subsistence but to preserve a place for themselves on their own terms in the expanding market economy of early nineteenth-century North America.

*   *   *

The background and results of Hopkins's trip to Fort Wayne can quickly be summarized. The Indian Affairs Committee of the Baltimore Yearly Meeting first convened in 1795, at much the same time as a similar group took shape in Philadelphia and as urban Friends throughout the United States were beginning to concentrate on the agricultural transformation of Native Americans. The two committees agreed on a division of labor: the Philadelphians would concentrate on Indian communities in New York state and the Marylanders on those of the Old Northwest, a responsibility the latter exercised until the Ohio Yearly Meeting took over in 1813. Small-scale as it was, the effort to establish a model farm at Fort Wayne was by far the most ambitious project the Baltimore organization attempted in its less than two decades of existence.[3]

The mission had its origins in a visit to Washington, D.C., by Little Turtle, the Potawatomi chief Five Medals, and several other Miami and Potawatomi leaders in December and January 1801–1802. En route, the delegation stopped in Baltimore, where it met with members of the Indian committee. A year later, the Friends sent "a considerable number of implements of husbandry; such as *Ploughs, Hoes, Axes,* etc. etc." to Fort Wayne for distribution to the two nations.[4] In February 1804, the committee received a letter of thanks that Little Turtle and Five Medals had sent the previous September. "It is our wish that the Great Spirit will enable you to render your red Brethren that service which you appear to be so desirous of doing them and their women and children are so much in need of," the Native leaders said. "We will try to use the Articles you have sent us and if we should want more we will let You know it," but "we are sorry to say that the minds of our people are not so much inclined towards the cultivation of the earth as we could wish them." Nonetheless, Little Turtle and Five Medals expressed a "hope that the Great Spirit will permit some of you to come and see us when you will be Able to know whether you can do any thing for us or not." On the basis of that ambiguous invitation, the committee appointed Dennis and asked Hopkins and Ellicott, along with two other Friends who declined the call, to see that he got safely to Fort Wayne.[5]

The spot Miami leaders chose for Dennis to set up operations was not, as the Quakers had hoped, at an established village, but at an uninhabited, though fertile, riverside locale eighteen miles from the nearest Indian town. After Hopkins and Ellicott returned to Maryland, Dennis went about his work of clearing, plowing, and fencing twenty acres of ground, from which he said he reaped "about 400 bushels of corn, besides a quantity of turnips, pota-toes, cucumbers, water melons, pumpkins, beans, parsnips and other garden vegetables." When he returned to Maryland in the fall, he left the fruits of his harvest, along with perhaps two dozen hogs and a log house, with the few Miamis who had agreed to work with him. Neither Dennis nor anyone else in the Baltimore Yearly Meeting could be induced to resume the mission the next year, although agent Wells reported that ten Miami families had moved in and were raising bumper crops on the land. (He was vague about whether they used plows or more traditional Indian methods to do so.) In 1806, the Baltimore committee employed a man named William Kirk, who, though a Friend, was not a member of their Yearly Meeting, to take over the work Dennis began. The newcomer promptly alienated Wells, by refusing to take his advice, and Little Turtle and other Miamis by appearing to pocket funds meant for them. By 1808 he had moved on to start an agricultural mission among the Shawnees at Wapakoneta, Ohio, which continued to receive sup-port from Baltimore and Ohio friends after the War of 1812.[6]

*   *   *

The tactless Kirk and the sorry end he brought to the feckless efforts of a well-meaning group of eastern humanitarians tells us something about the problems facing those who tried to bridge the increasingly wide racial divide of turn-of-the-nineteenth-century America. But the language and imagery through which Hopkins composed his narrative of those efforts reveals much more about the evolution of racial categories during that crucial period. In his journal, Hopkins stressed not only his pity for the Indians' supposedly starv-ing present, but also his awareness of a very different Indian past he believed to be irrevocably doomed by a great, ongoing historical transition. Repeat-edly in his travels, he noted reminders of bygone epochs. A stone fish weir that spanned the Monongahela River caught his attention because it was so old "that the Indians who resided upon this River at the time of its discovery by the whites had no knowledge even traditional of the making of these Fish Pots nor of the erection of the fortification."[7] Similarly, Hopkins was fascinated by the mystery of the ancient Indian mounds of the Ohio Valley; his journal includes several detailed sketches of those near Chillocothe.[8]

More recent material reminders of Native people also conveyed an image of a country emptied of its former inhabitants and rapidly refilling with Euro-American newcomers. "We have Observed hunting Camps erected by the Indians but no Indians in them," he wrote as the party reached the Great Miami River. The absent hunters had also left behind "many curious and to us uninteligeble Indian Hieroglyphics cut upon the trees . . . and painted in various colours upon the wood after Cutting away the Bark."[9] Perhaps because of his Quaker pacifism, Hopkins also remarked on physical reminders of fortifications and battles during the war between the United States and the Western Confederacy that had ended nine years earlier with the Treaty

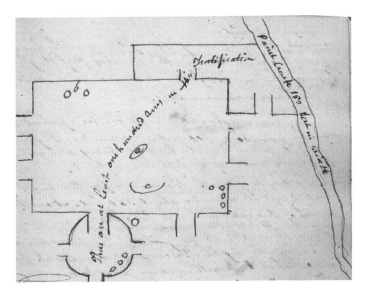

Sketch of Indian mounds near Chillicothe, Gerard Hopkins Journal (DAMS 8044), The Historical Society of Pennsylvania (HSP). Hopkins's lack of interest in living Native experiences is suggested by his inclusion of only five sketches in the polished version of his diary of travel to and from the Miami country. One was of Niagara Falls; the other four were, like this one, examples of what he called "Ancient fortification." As evidence of the antiquity of the mound labeled "a," he noted that it had "upon it trees of large size as well as the remains of decaying trees which after acquiring their full growth have fallen."

of Greenville. Most notably, where Fort Wayne now stood, fragments of the soldiers' skeletons could still be seen "scattered upon the surface of the Earth," as testimony to the great victory of Little Turtle's forces over General Josiah Harmar's army in 1790. Hopkins was "told that the route by which his army made their escape can be readily traced for the distance of 5 or 6 miles by the bones of those who were slain by the Indians." With his own eyes he saw "Skulls which had marks of the scalping knife and of the Tommahawk." But the battles were over, and an Indian town that had "contained upwards of One thousand Warriors" was gone, replaced by Fort Wayne and its sleepy contingent of "about 40 officers and Soldiers."[10]

For Hopkins, the Indian cemeteries the travelers frequently passed perhaps most fully evoked the end of an era for Native people—and the beginning of one for the White farmers who were replacing them. Near Fort Wayne he "viewed the remains of Old Indian houses also of the fields in which they cultivated corn" and "also observed large numbers of Indian Graves . . . discoverable at present only by the sunken Cavities in the surface of the earth." Reiterating that, elsewhere in their travels, the Friends had "seen many of the Graves of the Indians of more recent date," Hopkins was inspired by "the many circumstantial evidances which have fallen under our Observation of the former vast Population of this western world . . . to adopt the expression of a pious author," the poet Edward Young:

Where is the dust that hath not been alive?
The spade the plough disturb our Ancestors.
From human mould we reap our daily Bread.[11]

To describe the kind of transition that the plow represented, in their speech to the Miami council, Hopkins and his fellows evoked a fanciful vision of their own ethnic past. "The time was when the forefathers of your brothers the White people lived beyond the Great waters in the same manner that our red brethren now lived," the Quakers declared. "The Winters can yet be counted when they went almost naked when they procured their living by fishing and by the bow and arrow in hunting and when they lived in houses no better than yours." Fortunately, the ancient Britons "were encouraged by some who came from toward the sun-rising and lived amongst them to change their mode of living." After this beneficent conquest by the Roman Empire, Britons "cultivated the earth and we are sure the change was a happy one."[12] In this context, one wonders whether Hopkins contemplated some additional lines from Young's *Night Thoughts*, which appear in the stanza after the passage evoked by his visit to the Native graveyard:

Nor man alone; his breathing bust expires,
His tomb is mortal; empires die: where, now,
The *Roman? Greek?* they stalk, an empty name!
Yet few regard them in this useful light;
Tho' half our learning is *their* epitaph.[13]

In his linkage of ancient European history with the contemporary situation of North American Indians, Hopkins tapped a rich eighteenth-century vein of cultural images promulgated alike by the French *philosophes* and the Scottish Common Sense theorists whose influence was omnipresent in the intellectual life of the early republic. Enlightenment thinkers of various stripes disagreed on the details, but most postulated a lineal "conjectural history" of humanity composed of four developmental stages—"hunting," "pasturage," "agriculture," and "commerce"—each defined by its increasingly sophisticated mode of subsistence. The pursuit of game, and perhaps of fish, sustained the most primitive state of humankind, which many authors labeled "savagery"— a term they claimed to use with technical precision rather than as an insult. The presumed precariousness of this mode of subsistence led many popular writers to posit starvation as virtually its normal condition. The more advanced level of development often called "barbarism" rested on the more secure food supplies allowed by the nomadic herding of flocks. Finally, when people settled down to grow crops and to tend fully domesticated barnyard animals, they became "civilized"; this was the great gift Hopkins believed the Romans had brought to Albion. The final commercial stage, characterized by a complex division of labor and sophisticated mechanisms of exchange and finance, was clearly "civilized" too, and in the eighteenth century, it was certainly regarded as the wave of the future if not a description of the present.[14]

Whether that was a good thing was a matter of considerable controversy, however. Commerce either produced refined achievements that were the crowning glory of civilization or fostered the corrupted self-indulgence, the fall from manly virtue, that eighteenth-century thinkers called "luxury"; more likely, the result was a troubling mixture of both. As historians Drew McCoy and Joyce Chaplin point out, the effects of commercial development were nowhere more hotly debated than in the United States from the 1780s through the first decade of the 1800s.[15] The famous contrast between Alexander

Hamilton's Federalist insistence on "the necessity of enlarging the sphere of our domestic commerce" by encouraging the division of labor and Thomas Jefferson's Republican vision of an agricultural republic populated by "those who labour in the earth"—while too often overdrawn—nonetheless symbolizes the conflicting ways in which the age of commerce could be evaluated.[16]

However much they may have differed on whether the republic they were building was, or should be, agricultural or commercial, White Americans at the turn of the nineteenth century almost unanimously agreed on one thing: Indians still lived in the primitive hunter stage. As Roy Harvey Pearce concluded in his classic study of the ideology of savagery, Euro-Americans' "intellectual and cultural traditions, their idea of order, so informed their thoughts and their actions that they could see and conceive of nothing but the Indian who hunted."[17] Indeed, when Enlightenment figures wrote about "hunters" and the conjectural history of humankind, they almost always drew their main examples from American Indians—or rather from their fanciful library stereotypes about Native people—making the terms *hunter* and *Indian* virtually synonymous. "In the Beginning," John Locke famously said, "all the World was *America*."[18]

Almost all authors who explored conjectural history agreed that any society's progress from one stage to another rested on a simple ratio of population to resources. In the "age of hunters," Adam Smith postulated, "in process of time, as their numbers multiplied, they would find the chase too precarious for their support" and "be necessitated to contrive" a pastoral mode of subsistence that would suit them until renewed population growth made them "naturally turn themselves to the cultivation of land and the raising of such plants and trees as produced nourishment fit for them."[19] The problem was that, whether Indians were ready or not, the age of hunters was past in North America. For good or ill, the expansion of Euro-American agriculturalists would deprive Native people of the land resources necessary to support their hunting mode of subsistence. White public figures who professed any humanitarian concerns at all agreed that if Indians were to avoid extinction, they had to skip the pasturage stage and leap, almost overnight, to the agricultural level of development.[20]

In practical terms, therefore, few differences separated the Indian policies advocated by Federalists in the 1790s from those pursued by Republicans in the first decade of the 1800s. A "civilization" program, begun by Knox in the Washington administration and elaborated with yeoman-farmer themes under Jeffersonian leadership, sought to teach Indian men to farm, and to

farm lands held as private property. In their speeches to Native leaders, Federal officials wrapped the project in humanitarian rhetoric and promises of
concrete aid in the form of plows and tools. But in practice they engaged in
a relentless effort to deprive Indians of the "excess" land that made their ex-
travagant hunting lifestyle possible—an effort that was assuming new rigor at
the very moment Hopkins traveled west.[21]

Whatever Baltimore Quakers thought of the more coercive elements of
the Jeffersonian program, they saw themselves as great allies of the president
in bringing the plow to savage hunters. "We are . . . bound to acknowledge
those philanthropic exertions, which have been used to ameliorate the condition of the Indian natives, by introducing amongst them a knowledge of
agriculture, and some of the mechanic arts," Hopkins wrote to Jefferson on
behalf of the Yearly Meeting in 1807. The president in turn praised the Friends'
"judicious direction toward producing among those people habits of industry, comfortable subsistence, and civilized urges."[22] As English Quakers who
had contributed funds to support the Baltimore Friends efforts approvingly
stated, the lofty aim of all good people was to hasten along "the advancement
of our Indian brethren in the scale of civil life."[23]

*   *   *

However appealing the ideal of raising Indians from the hunter to the agricultural state may have seemed—and quite apart from any general logical
fallacies inherent in the four-stage theory of human development—the basic
assumptions of the Baltimore Friends, like those of nearly all White Americans, rested on four basic errors about the role of hunting in the eastern Indian cultures of their day. First and most obvious was the inconvenient fact
that the Miamis and their neighbors, like virtually all other Native peoples
east of the Mississippi, already *were* farmers, and their food supply traditionally rested far less on the chase than on the Indian horticultural trinity of
corn, beans, and squash. The stereotype of improvident hunters was particularly ill-suited to the Miamis, and when the Quakers proposed to teach them
how to grow crops, it must have required all of interpreter Wells's ingenuity to
phrase the offer in a way that did not provoke laughter. In the eighteenth century, as the Miamis' most comprehensive historian concludes, they enjoyed
a "stable and provident village life" and were renowned for a distinctive soft
white maize that was considered far superior to the run-of-the-mill flint corn
grown by their neighbors. Families typically stored a surplus of five bushels

of this crop to get through the winter.[24] In late March and early April, when
the Baltimore Quakers arrived at Fort Wayne, those supplies would have
been largely exhausted, but their impact on the health of the local population
should nonetheless have been clear. The sugaring camp Hopkins visited, for
example, apparently had no corn, but it was "well supplied with Jerk-Venison,
Dryed Racoon, Sturgeon etc." More importantly, the "very fat and healthy
looking children" he saw there hardly looked like they had eked their way
through the winter on meager hunter's fare.[25]

The second conceptual error about Indian hunting was an apparent failure to recognize—or rather to legitimize—the gendered division of labor in
Native societies. Everywhere in eastern North America, agriculture was primarily women's work. Men assisted in clearing new fields, and they cultivated
the ritually important tobacco plant. But women were in charge of corn,
beans, and squash, and so—no small matter—they controlled the staple food
supply. At least a few late eighteenth-century Euro-American social theorists
recognized that Indian women grew crops, but they invariably dismissed
the phenomenon to irrelevance. As no less influential an intellectual figure
than Smith put it, "their women plant a few stalks of Indian corn at the back
of their huts. But this can hardly be called agriculture" because "it does not
make any considerable part of their food" and "serves only as a seasoning or
something to give a relish to their common food; the flesh of those animalls
they have caught in the chase." Similarly, New England writer William Douglass asserted that Indians did "not cultivate the Earth by planting or grazing:
Excepting a very inconsiderable Quantity of *Mays* or *Indian Corn*, and of
Kidney-Beans . . . which some of their *Squaas* or Women plant."[26]

The pronouns are important: "Their women" may have sown a few trifling crops, but Indian men—the people who mattered—were by definition
hunters, and thus their societies by definition remained at the hunter stage.
When Whites said they wanted to teach Indians to farm, then, what they really meant was that they wanted to teach Indian *men* to become farmers, and
to reduce Indian women to their proper position indoors behind a spinning
wheel. "Your brothers the white people," the Quaker's prepared speech to the
Miamis explained, "in order to get their land cultivated find it necessary that
their young men should be employed in it and not their women. Women are
less than men. They are not as strong as men. They are not as able to endure
fatigue and toil as men."[27] These may seem strange words from a member of
an Anglo-American religious community that had long idealized courageous
women who traveled the world to preach and be persecuted for the faith, yet

turn-of-the-nineteenth-century Quaker men nonetheless embraced a model of domesticity in which the gendered division of labor remained very clear. Women inspired by the spirit might preach to reap a spiritual harvest, but the crops of this world were to be watered with the sweat of male brows.[28]

And so a third error related not just to gender roles but to Indian labor patterns more generally. Instead of the heavy plows and neat monoculture that made European agriculture so laborious, Native women used a few simple tools—a digging stick and perhaps a European-manufactured hoe— to plant fields where corn, beans, and squash jumbled together in the same hills so that the maize derived some natural fertilizer from the nitrogen-fixing roots of the legumes and both profited from the natural weed control of spreading squash vines. Once the process was well started and beans started curling around their symbiotic cornstalk poles, fields needed hardly any tending until the crops became ripe enough to attract hungry birds. In Euro-American eyes, these "few stalks of Indian corn at the back of their huts" (even if, as in the Miami country, they typically stretched a mile or more outside a village) simply didn't require enough hard work. The sight of Indian men who refused even the minimal requirements of such effortless horticulture only further reinforced their reputation for improvidence and laziness.[29] Thus in 1798 another Quaker missionary had condemned "the oppressive labour which the Senecas imposed upon their women, in getting and bringing home fire-wood, and similar employments, whilst the men and boys were amusing themselves with shooting arrows, and in other diversions." Instead, he "recommended" that they "take their boys out to hoe and work in the fields."[30]

Which points to the final, and perhaps most important, error embedded in the image of the Male Indian Hunter. Far from a matter of "amusing themselves with shooting arrows," hunting *was* serious labor to the region's Native men. In that, the gender and developmental stereotype was correct. The primary purpose of the work of hunting, however, was *not* to obtain food. Dietary benefits (meat more often provided the "relish" for corn soup than vice versa) were secondary to the need to acquire furs and hides to be traded for European manufactured goods. By 1804, Great Lakes Indians had relied on trade with Euro-Americans for well over a century. In exchange for furs, hides, and other commodities, they purchased cloth, tools, cooking and eating utensils, weapons, liquor, and countless other items not just enriching but crucial for everyday life. As Anthony F. C. Wallace observes, "professional huntsmen . . . were used to traveling hundreds of miles in search of the game needed in the trade." In this economy, "skins and furs were the traditional cash crop that procured hardware, cloth, and other necessaries for Indian families."[31]

Hopkins's journal contains multiple unanalyzed glimpses of the complex ways in which the region's Indian men—and women—participated in the market economy that was supposedly characteristic of only the most advanced stage of human development. A couple of days before they reached Fort Wayne, Hopkins's party crossed the St. Mary's River in a canoe operated by an English-speaking Delaware ferryman named Stephen, who gave the Quakers a 75 percent discount on the usual dollar fare. (Alas, his previous customers—White traders who evidently paid their toll with liquor—left Stephen so drunk he fell out of the canoe halfway across and had to be rescued by Dennis.)[32] At Fort Wayne, the Baltimoreans were shown the grave of Little Turtle's son, which, like that of most high-status eighteenth-century eastern Indians, contained not only the corpse but "his Rifle hunting Apparatus his best clothing all his Ornaments, Trinkets etc. etc. etc." The value of these trade goods, his market-oriented hosts told him, was "not less than 300 Dollars."[33] Fort Wayne itself was notable to Hopkins not only for its government factory—"a large store of goods Established by the United states for the purpose of supplying the Indians"—but also for the "Several Cannadian Traders" who "reside[d] here who exchange goods with the Indians for furs and skins." These men had "generally intermarried with the Indians and some of them have resided here for more than 30 Years." Native men were, Hopkins said, "daily arriving here with Peltry[;] some of them exchange it for goods and others require money." Women, meanwhile, traded maple sugar, which was "generally very completely Packed in a Square Box made of bark containing about 50 pound[s]."[34]

On the return trip to Baltimore as well, the travelers saw repeated evidence of how market-oriented the region's Native people were, and of how important resident Canadian traders were to their societies. On the Auglaize River at the site of what, in the Fallen Timbers campaign of 1794, had been General Anthony Wayne's Fort Defiance (and before that a settlement of British traders based at Fort Miami), at least one "Cannadian Trader" had gone back into business, in an area thickly settled with Shawnee and Ottawa towns, to which hunters were returning from their winter's work. As a result, houses in these villages were well "stocked with peltry, also Jerk venison Dryed Raccoon etc. etc." Meanwhile, women were "mostly employed in knitting bags belts etc. and making mockasins," some of which no doubt were intended for sale to Whites or Natives from other communities. "A considerable number of Indians" clogged "the River in bark canoes loaded with Peltry" on its way to market. Similarly, in the neighborhood of the former British post at Fort Miami, "many Indian Villages" lined "both shores of the [Maumee] River" with "many Cannadian Traders . . . residing amongst them." The Canadians—most of them ethnically French—had "generally intermarried with the Indians and . . . adopted their manners." That "some of the Indian Houses" were "built of small round logs" rather than the traditional poles and bark, however, might have suggested to Hopkins that the exchange of "manners" went both ways. Like nearly all Anglo-Americans of the period, though, he placed the Creole French and the métis culture they and their wives and children were creating in the same category of doomed nonagricultural hunters in which he classed the Miamis and Potawatomis.[35]

Yet the Indian communities Hopkins and his compatriots visited were populated by anything but the primitive subsistence hunters of Anglo-American imaginations. Indeed, it would make more sense to describe the region's Native people as producers and consumers in a global market economy. Quaker schemes to "advance" them to subsistence agriculture thus asked them not only to withdraw from the markets in which they had been enmeshed for generations but actually threatened to *lower* the standard of living they had enjoyed for most of the eighteenth century. In this context, the Friends' insistence that Indian women cease their agricultural labors and learn to spin yarn becomes even more ironic than their notion that the males' reliance on hunting threatened Native people with starvation. In precisely the same era when White women were beginning to banish their spinning wheels to the attic in favor of cheap store-bought cotton cloth—and in the process to liberate themselves from the mind-numbing work of turning raw flax into crude homemade cloth—Indian women were being urged to abandon purchased textiles in favor of homespun.[36]

*   *   *

Within the terms of the four-stage theory of human progress, then, the Miamis and their Native neighbors should have been considered to be on the cusp of the transition from agriculture to commerce—just as were the Whites who considered themselves destined to take the continent from them. The Baltimore Quakers' own unease with their role in this transition thus might help explain their curious blindness to the Indians' situation. For if the tendency of commerce to encourage vicious luxury was a general concern in the early republic, the dilemma was particularly acute for urban Friends. As one religious historian concludes, "perhaps the leading trait" of American Quakerism at the turn of the nineteenth century "was its increased devotion to simplicity." The ideal was to shun "the enjoyment of wealth as well as power in favor of a standard of living attainable by any industrious self-supporting man."[37] Yet many prominent Baltimore Quakers were prosperous merchants for whom such an ideal was fraught with personal tension—and no one more than Hopkins, who ran one of the city's most successful provision stores, and his traveling companion Ellicott, whose family ran its most prominent flour mill. Significantly, both dealt in foodstuffs, and thus found themselves at precisely the point where commerce intersected agricultural self-sufficiency. As the Baltimore Yearly Meeting's published book of *Discipline*—revised only two years after the journey to Fort Wayne—put it, "the inordinate love and pursuit of the things of this world, hath prevailed with too many amongst us, and produced the fruits of pride and ambition."[38]

To complicate matters further, tensions between simplicity and luxury joined broader contradictions among Quakers torn between an inward-turning impulse to maintain a separate identity in an increasingly complicated American religious landscape and an outward-focused emphasis on humanitarian reforms that set an example of Christian benevolence. All developed against the backdrop of the loss of political power—indeed the political ostracism—that the Quakers' pacifism had earned them during the generation between the Seven Years War and the American Revolution. To some degree, projects targeted at Native Americans—like those designed to aid African Americans, prisoners, and other social outcasts—can be understood as uneasy resolutions of these tensions, melding the self-sacrifice of distinctively Quaker unpopular causes with exemplary assaults on worldly problems that had material as well as spiritual dimensions. But this solution exposed additional fault lines in the realm of gender roles. In reclaiming their public influence through humanitarianism, Quaker men asserted themselves in areas that might otherwise have fallen within the female sphere of domesticity; women, pointedly, were not members of such bodies as committees on Indian affairs, although they participated creatively across a range of new humanitarian activities, including Indian missions sponsored by the Baltimoreans' Philadelphia counterparts.[39]

In light of their own varied problems in reconciling gender identity, economic behavior, political activism, and religious belief, it is no wonder that

the Baltimore Quakers saw little virtue in Indians' gender roles and commercial activity, even when they recognized them—or that they attempted
to impose an idealized model of virtuous simplicity upon the targets of their
benevolence. The *Discipline* admonished Baltimore Friends to "be careful not to venture upon business they do not understand; nor to launch in
trade beyond their abilities, and at the risk of others."[40] How much more
must that advice have applied to male Indians alleged to be in the hunter
state and who, unlike those in the more advanced agrarian and commercial
stages of human development, could not possibly fathom the dangers of the
marketplace?

Moreover, in the Baltimore Friends' eyes, the most visible impact of trade
on Indians had been "the baneful effects of spiritous liquors . . . , they being at
that time supplied with it in almost every village, by Canadian traders, residing amongst them."[41] The authors of the Baltimore *Discipline* would not have
been surprised. Drunkenness being a symptom of the more general spiritual
disease of "baneful excess," it became "incumbent on all, both by example
and affectionate entreaty, to caution and dissuade all our members, against
either the importation, distillation, or vending of" alcohol.[42] That Hopkins in
particular took this message to heart is suggested by the quarrel he had with
his nephew Johns Hopkins in 1819. The younger Hopkins, who saw nothing wrong with letting customers use whiskey to pay for their goods, left the
elder's firm to go into business with his brothers and begin the fortune that
funded his later philanthropies.[43]

On the moral and economic dangers of the commerce in liquor, Indian
leaders of the southern Great Lakes region agreed with Gerard T. Hopkins.
Its disastrous economic, social, and medical effects were, of course, nothing
new to them. But the issue assumed particular urgency after the Greenville
Treaty of 1795, as political demoralization among the defeated remnants of
the Western Indian confederacy combined with the movement of villages
and refugees to new homes and a wide-open trading environment.[44] In what
one Friend called "a very pathetic and impressive speech" delivered during his Baltimore visit in 1801, Little Turtle lamented that liquor had left
"more of us dead since the treaty of Greenville, than we lost by the six years
war before."[45] Partly in response to this oration—which Baltimore Friends
rushed into print in order to press its message on the Jefferson administration before the Indian delegation left Washington—under the terms of the
revised Indian Trade and Intercourse Act of 1802, the War Department established the Federal agency at Fort Wayne, to which Wells was appointed.

Soon thereafter, the trade factory opened there. One aim of both innovations was to suppress the commerce in liquor by licensing traders and putting much of the area's economy under government control. As the Baltimore Friends saw it, these reforms "in some measure provided a remedy for the evil" and removed "the principal obstruction to the introduction of agriculture amongst the Indians."[46] Little Turtle and Five Medals agreed that when Jefferson endorsed these measures, "it was the best thing he could do for his red children."[47]

*   *   *

If the Baltimore Quakers had very real reasons for stressing the horrors of the liquor trade—and thus found support for their ideological fears of the pernicious effects of market commerce on Native people—we might also suspect they had some empirical basis for concluding that Indians really did "suffer much for the want of food." Indeed, the first group of Indians described in Hopkins's journal actually were male hunters rather than female farmers, and they really were desperately short of basic supplies. Their story, although it came to Hopkins secondhand, apparently made a major impact on him, for it seemingly confirmed his assumption that the hunting mode of subsistence doomed Indians to starvation.

At Redstone in western Pennsylvania, the Baltimoreans attended the local Quarterly Meeting and discussed with some Ohio Friends two messages the latter had recently received from the Wyandot leader Tarhe, who, with perhaps a hundred of his people, had gotten trapped by a blizzard while hunting bear on Mahoning Creek. "My Dear Brothers Quakers listen to what I now say to You," his first letter began. "You always called us Indians your brothers and now dear white brothers I am in distress and all my young men who are with me[.] Brothers Will you Please to help me to fill my Kettles and my horses trough, for I am afraid my horses will not be able to carry me home again." Before the Monthly Meeting could respond, Quakers who lived nearer the stranded hunters contributed enough food to ease the crisis. Tarhe then sent the Friends a second letter. "Brothers Quakers," he began,

> I want you should all know what distress I am in.
> Brothers
> I want you to know I have got help from some of my near neighbour[s].

Brothers

> I would be glad to know what you will do for me if it is but a little.

Brothers

> If you cannot come soon it will do by and by for my belly is now full.

Brothers

> I hope you have not forgotten our great fathers when they first met it was in friendship we are of the same race.

In response, the Ohio Quakers sent "a considerable quantity of provisions . . . to these Indians for which they expres[sed] great tha[n]kfulness." Hopkins noted that "Tahhee himself divi'd the presents between man and man making no difference for distinction in rank."[48]

Surely if any "red people" were starving, they were these Wyandot hunters. Yet several things have to be considered before we can accept the story on the terms Hopkins apparently understood it. First, while of course the Wyandots, trapped as they were by "a fall of Snow 3 feet in depth," faced a dire predicament, it was a freak emergency that said nothing about the everyday ability of agricultural Great Lakes Indian economies to feed their populations. Second, Tarhe ("the Crane"), whom Hopkins's journal describes only as "a Wyandot of Great distinction," was not just any unfortunate Native American; he was one of the most important figures in Great Lakes politics and diplomacy at the turn of the nineteenth century. At the Greenville Treaty, he had mediated disputes among the Native participants and—particularly over the objections of Little Turtle—had helped to ensure that they would leave convinced that they genuinely negotiated, rather than simply acquiesced, to Wayne's terms. "Have done trifling: let us conclude this great Work," Tarhe had then proclaimed to his wartime Indian allies; "let us sign our names to the Treaty now proposed and finish our business."[49] Later, as headman of the Upper Sandusky (Cranetown) Wyandots, he was one of the most consistent pro-U.S. figures in the Great Lakes region. Throughout the period of the War of 1812, he—like Little Turtle and Five Medals—would consistently oppose the efforts of the Shawnees Tecumseh and Tenskwatawa ("the Prophet") to build a new religiously based anti-U.S. confederacy.[50]

Nor was Tarhe previously unknown to the Baltimore Quakers. When the Ohio Friends delivered their gifts to Tarhe, he complained "that Several years ago he had sent a Talk to the Indian committee at Baltimore accompanied by a Belt of Wampum worth fifty Dollars and that he had been long waiting for an Answer but had not received one."[51] As was often the case in intercultural diplomacy, however, things were not so simple as a costly message sent by a trusting Indian and rudely snubbed by insensitive Whites. The earliest contact between the Baltimore committee and Tarhe occurred less than two years after the group's founding. In the spring of 1797, three committee members journeyed to the country of the Wyandots and Delawares in present-day north-central Ohio "for the purpose of obtaining a more satisfactory knowledge respecting them." This voyage evidently had helped to fix the image of starving Natives in Baltimore Quaker minds. According to the published record of the committee, "Having passed by a number of their hunting camps, and several of their towns," the Baltimoreans "had large opportunity of discovering their situation, often exposed to the inclemency of the seasons, with a very precarious, and often a very scanty supply of food and cloathing." The Wyandots and Delawares, the Friends concluded, "suffered all the miseries of extreme poverty, in a country, which, from its great fertility, would, with but a little cultivation, abundantly supply them with all the necessaries of life."[52]

The published account does not tell us exactly where the Quakers went or how much time they spent trying to understand conditions in Indian country. If they merely "passed by" towns and hunting camps, their knowledge must have been superficial. Still, the Indians probably were in considerable distress. It was, after all, early spring, a time of year when stores of food would have been exhausted and when people would have appeared most heavily reliant on hunting and gathering, if only to escape the winter tedium of parched corn and dried beans. And it was not only early spring, but early spring of 1797, a little over a year after two diplomatic earthquakes had redrawn the map and economic relationships of their part of North America. The Greenville Treaty had deprived the Delawares of most of their lands on the Muskingum River in present-day eastern Ohio, and the majority of that nation were in the process of establishing new homes on the White River in present-day Indiana. Those who remained in the east clung to villages just north of the treaty line and were no doubt entertaining large numbers of refugees in search of new homes. Meanwhile, the Jay Treaty between the United States and Great Britain, which mandated the withdrawal of British posts from the area by June 1796, caused additional turmoil, even for the Wyandots, whose possessions on the Sandusky and upper Great Miami Rivers were somewhat more securely beyond the Greenville boundary. Fort Miami, on the Maumee River, ceased to exist, and the next-closest post, Detroit, became a U.S. garrison. Neither any longer supplied the subsidies of food, materials, and weapons available during the wars of the early 1790s, and trade routes and supply lines had not yet stabilized under the new regime. The disruption of vital commercial links, rather than any deficiency in the ability of Native people to feed themselves, was what really threatened impoverishment.[53]

Seemingly oblivious to these complexities, the 1797 Quaker delegation met "some of the chiefs and hunters of the *Wyandot* and *Delaware* nations." The Native leaders listened politely to a speech about "the advantages they would derive, from permitting to be introduced amongst their people, a knowledge of agriculture, and some of the most useful mechanic arts" and "promised to lay the matter before their grand council." More than a year passed before Tarhe responded on behalf of that council in a speech and wampum belt delivered at Detroit. Five more months elapsed before his message got to Baltimore in February 1799. It said nothing specific about the Friends' proposal to teach the agricultural Wyandots how to farm, but instead invited the Quakers to come to Tarhe's home at Sandusky. From thence he promised to escort them to a grand council of his nation's leaders to renew the old alliance between Friends and Indians—"a chain of silver, that would never get rusty" and "would bind us in brotherly affection forever." He looked forward to the chance to "talk of those things that were done between our GOOD GRAND-FATHERS, when they first met upon our lands—upon this great island!"[54]

Tarhe's rhetoric of a covenant chain, of grandfathers, of the legend of peaceful beneficence epitomized by the Quaker founder William Penn, were part of the ritualized vocabulary of eighteenth-century intercultural diplomacy. To one attuned to their meaning, such phrases conveyed a desire for something quite different than chasing women out of the fields so men could take up the plow. The language evoked the kinds of connections that, before the American Revolution, Indian leaders repeatedly articulated with European imperial governments. The Covenant Chain was a metaphor for the relationship Indians allied to the British had with their "brethren"; in the Great Lakes region a generation earlier, a more common usage would be to speak of filial obligations to the French "father." In both instances, the fundamental concept was that Natives—without diminishing their political autonomy—placed themselves under the protection of more powerful Europeans. In exchange for their allegiance, they expected their "father" or "brethren" to keep the peace among Indians in the alliance and to provide military protection and economic benefits, the latter in the form of both diplomatic gifts and a secure trading environment.[55] "Listen to your children, here assembled; be strong, now, and take care of all your little ones," Tarhe instructed Wayne at the Greenville Treaty. "Should any of your children come to you crying, and in distress, have pity on them, and relieve their wants."[56]

In the 1790s and 1800s, as Great Lakes Indians faced an aggressive, expansive U.S. government that acted like anything but a fatherly protector, Native leaders repeatedly requested that Quaker observers be present at treaty conferences to provide a moral check on government negotiators and in other ways to mediate between them and authorities in the Federal and state capitals. Tarhe, it seems likely, hoped that the Baltimore Quakers would go still farther to protect their interests and provide economic (not just narrowly agricultural) assistance and take up the Covenant Chain broken when the British withdrew from Indian country. Reflective of just how quaint these eighteenth-century concepts of diplomatic protection and economic alliance had become in the U.S.-dominated world after the Jay and Greenville Treaties, however, is the tragic comedy of errors that followed Tarhe's invitation. The translator at Detroit had gotten the date of the upcoming Wyandot grand council wrong, and so a delegation from Baltimore showed up at Tarhe's Sandusky village several weeks early. Rather than wait, the Friends held a hastily arranged conference with their host, who again promised to "communicate fully" to the council the Quakers' proposals and to send "a written speech of their conclusion thereon." That speech—probably the one accompanied by Tarhe's $50 wampum belt—never reached the shores of the Chesapeake. Having thus heard nothing, the Baltimoreans sent an inquiring letter to Sandusky, "but the person to whose care it was directed . . . not being at home, it was returned to the committee."[57] Meanwhile, the more promising invitation from Little Turtle and Five Medals had encouraged the Baltimore Friends to shift their humanitarian efforts away from the Wyandots toward the apparently more receptive Miamis and Potawatomis.

Hopkins's journal betrays not the slightest acknowledgment of the complicated history behind Tarhe's complaint or the eagerness with which he had earlier sought a protective alliance with the Baltimore Friends. Nor, for that matter, does it seem to make much of a distinction among Wyandots, Miamis, and other "red people." But the importance the Wyandot leader placed on establishing that alliance provides a final explanation for the pathetic rhetoric in which he phrased his temporarily snowbound condition—and his plea to Wayne at Greenville in 1795. As anthropologist Mary Black-Rogers points out, when Great Lakes Algonquian speakers said they were "starving," in "distress," or in other ways presented themselves as objects of pity, they were often using a coded social vocabulary that really was not about economic privation at all. Instead, it was about the etiquette of social and political alliance. Especially in relationships between parties of unequal status, it was important for everyone to behave in ways that did not imply a pride in his own power or, especially, an overt attempt to control other persons. (Such coercion was the definition of sorcery.) As a result, a host, in a position of superiority, must display generosity by lavishly feeding his guest, but he must not offer food unless asked, lest he betray too much pride in his own possessions and humiliate a person of lesser power. A visitor, by the same token, was supposed to ask for food in what Euro-Americans would consider an excessively self-deprecatory fashion, using language that translated into English as begging for pity on one's starving condition. "I'm poor, I'm poor in food—I'm starving," moans a traditional Ojibwa song. "Have pity," Tarhe said at Greenville. Such words were not to be taken literally. They encoded, explains Black-Rogers, "the approved way of behaving as a visitor, the host having avoided being coercive by politely allowing a guest to decide whether he wished to receive food" while allowing the guest to display an appropriate lack of pride in power and material possessions. Tarhe's rhetorical cries of distress, then—especially in his second message, when real starvation no longer threatened—spoke more about the nature of the relationship he perceived between his people and the Baltimore Quakers than about his hunting party's short-term woes.[58]

The Baltimore Quakers were not at all mistaken, then, when they believed that at least some Great Lakes Indian leaders were eager for their assistance. It was the complexities of the *kind* of assistance—and the diplomatic and political difficulties involved with gaining Native acceptance of their aid—that they failed to appreciate. At Fort Wayne, Five Medals lodged almost the same complaint on account of his Potawatomis that Tarhe had earlier made with regard to the Wyandots: the Quakers in their haste to leave were missing a vital opportunity to make a personal appearance before a council of his nation's chiefs and establish political support for a productive diplomatic relationship. "Our young men are out hunting and our women and children are now at work at their sugar Camps," he told Hopkins. "The time is far off when th[e]y will return to our towns and when it is usual for us to meet together," and he begged the Quakers' patience to "allow us time to Collect our people generally." When the Friends said they really could only stay a few days and asked the Potawatomi leader simply "to get together some of your people" to hear their presentation, Five Medals "Observ'd that in the time proposed they could easily convene a considerable number of their Indolent people who were too Lazy to hunt or make sugar but such they did not wish us to see."[59] Both activities, it should be stressed, produced marketable commodities.

Thus, just as the Baltimore Quakers misunderstood the political needs of their Indian hosts, so too they misinterpreted Native economic expectations. When Five Medals and Little Turtle visited Baltimore in 1801, Hopkins's colleague on the Indian committee, Evan Thomas, reported that the Miami leader "appeared to be much rejoiced at" the Friends' proposal to instruct his people in Euro-American methods of agriculture, "for although the game was not so scarce, but that they could get enough to eat, yet they were sensible it was daily diminishing, and that the time was not far distant, when they would be compelled to take hold of such tools as they saw in the hands of the white people.'" Despite his apparently genuine advocacy of a controversial policy that faced considerable opposition at home, however, Little Turtle had not brought the subject of agriculture up. Moreover, he emphatically did not propose to renounce commerce more generally in favor of the subsistence farming that Friends had in mind. "Brothers fetch us useful things—bring goods that will cloth us, our women and our children, and not this evil *liquor* that destroys our reason; that destroys our health; that destroys our lives," he said he had repeatedly told the traders who lived in his people's villages.[60]

Similar themes echo in most of the requests the Miamis, Potawatomis, Delawares, and Wyandots—and Senecas and Oneidas and others—sent to Quakers in the east at the turn of the nineteenth century. Indian leaders who expressed interest in the "civilization" program sought not help with agriculture per se but with the broader dilemma of how to ensure safe and secure trade and the survival of the productive resources necessary to obtain imported goods. Indeed, as anthropologist Diane Rothenberg has shown, Quakers' and other White reformers' only hope of succeeding in their efforts to introduce plow agriculture and domestic animals came when they also contributed such market-oriented improvements as water-powered grain and lumber mills that would provide cash income for Native communities. More typically, as Rothenberg concludes of the Philadelphia Friends who worked with Seneca Iroquois in this period, "the Quakers had no clear markets in mind for the sale of the products resulting from the more intensive farming methods that they advocated. Without such a system of distribution to supply the cash needed by the community to purchase items essential to them that they could not themselves manufacture, attempts to divert a male population from cash deriving activities to non-cash deriving activities were doomed to failure."[61]

*   *   *

"It must be a prospect truly gladdening to the enlightened christian mind, to survey the hastening of that day, when this part of the human family, weaned from savage habits, and allured by the superior advantages of civilized life, shall exchange the tomahawk and scalping knife for the *plough* and the *hoe*," the Baltimore Indian committee proclaimed in a published account of the work Dennis had begun in Indian country.[62] Yet the Miamis whom the Quakers hoped to save from starvation and extinction lived not in the hunter state of Euro-American imaginations, but in a complicated, multicultural, market-oriented economy. That economy—while rooted in ancient patterns—was superbly adapted to the eighteenth-century imperial world in which it evolved. Whether it would be equally suited to nineteenth-century conditions of U.S. domination and the relentless pressure of westward-migrating White settlers was very much in doubt—but not because the "red people" were somehow locked in ancient patterns of behavior, showed an inexplicable fondness for the wild, free ways of the hunting life, or were unable to adapt to changing circumstances. (No Native people who survived the demographic, military, and economic carnage of the seventeenth and eighteenth centuries could be accused of the latter flaw.) If starvation loomed, it would not literally be for lack of food. Instead it would be because the Jeffersonian design of systematically expropriating Indian hunting territories deprived them of the opportunity to produce marketable products to exchange for manufactured goods or cash.

In retrospect, the future of something else in the complex market economy of the southern Great Lakes was just as profoundly in doubt as that of hunting: the coexistence of Whites and Indians, the intermarriage of traders and Native women, the resulting métis population—the very blurring of ethnic and cultural lines that was so utterly incompatible with the ever-hardening racial categories of the nineteenth century. Even so well-meaning a folk as the Baltimore Quakers could only categorize the targets of their humanitarianism by the stereotypical labels of "red people" and "hunters," rather than as human participants in a complicated milieu in which people both hunted animals and produced sugar for market in neatly weighed bundles, carved "hieroglyphics" on trees and wrote letters on paper, charged cash for ferrying customers and buried costly items with their dead, dressed mostly in tattoos rather than clothes and lived in log cabins. There was no room in the emerging constructions of Whiteness and Redness for such complications.

"The passion of the red man for the hunter life has proved to be a principle too deeply inwrought, to be controlled by efforts of legislation," wrote anthropologist Lewis Henry Morgan a generation after Hopkins composed his journal. "The effect of this powerful principle has been to enchain the tribes of North America to their primitive state," and so, he concluded, "we have here the true reason why the red race has never risen, or can rise above its present level."[63] The "powerful principle" was indeed the key factor—not because it accurately described Native realities but because it utterly dominated White analyses of what they were coming to describe as the "Indian Problem." Morgan, like the Quakers before him, considered himself to be on the Indians' side. That even the defenders of Native American rights could not escape the overwhelming power of racial categories—could see Indians only as primitive hunters doomed to pitiable extinction—reveals just how bleak the future was for Indians in a White man's republic.

NOTES

Introduction

1. In the category of exceptions, I would include T. H. Breen's *Puritans and Adventurers: Change and Persistence in Early America* (New York: Oxford University Press, 1980); and three volumes by James Axtell: *The European and the Indian: Essays in the Ethnohistory of Colonial North America* (New York: Oxford University Press, 1981); *After Columbus: Essays in the Ethnohistory of Colonial North America* (New York: Oxford University Press, 1988); and *Beyond 1492: Encounters in Colonial North America* (New York: Oxford University Press, 1992). I will not otherwise name names.

2. Chapters 3, 5, and 7 appear in print here for the first time. Bibliographic information on the original publications from which other essays have been reprinted appears at the beginning of the notes for each relevant chapter. The texts of Chapters 1, 3–4, and 9–11 appear as first published, except for some slight alterations in titles, the deletion of subheadings, a few standardizations of spelling, the correction of an occasional typographical or other error, and the replacement of some maps and illustrations. I have resisted the urge to update references to secondary sources or to revise the substance of arguments in the light of more recent scholarship or my own subsequent rethinking; for better or worse, the words stand as originally written. The same is true for the bodies of Chapters 2 and 6, which appear here with opening and closing sections modified to suit the structure of this volume. Chapter 8 is a substantial reworking of material previously published in a quite different context. All notes have been reduced to a common style; apart from replacing references to a few unpublished studies with now-published equivalents and deleting descriptions of long-ago works as "recent," no effort has been made to update them bibliographically. Inevitably, with essays written over a period when broader projects were also in the works, ideas, examples, passages of prose, and occasionally whole paragraphs found their way into those broader projects, especially *The Ordeal of the Longhouse: The Peoples of the Iroquois League in the Era of European Colonization* (Chapel Hill: University of North Carolina Press, 1992); *Facing East from Indian Country: A Native History of Early America* (Cambridge, Mass.: Harvard University Press, 2001); and *Before the Revolution: America's Ancient Pasts* (Cambridge, Mass.: Harvard University Press, 2011). I thank the publishers of those books for their indulgence.

3. *Minutes of Conferences, Held with the Indians, at Easton, in the Months of July and November, 1756* (Philadelphia, 1757), 8. Throughout this volume, the following conventions for dealing with seventeenth- and eighteenth-century quotations are used. I have silently modernized punctuation and uses of the formerly interchangeable letters *i* and *j* and *u* and *v*, and instances of *ff* and *vv* (antique forms of *F* and *w*). The Old English letter *thorn* (often rendered as *y* and for centuries used as shorthand for *th*) has also been modernized. Superscripts in usages such as *yᵉ* were also a form of shorthand. These and other abbreviations have been expanded or replaced with modern equivalents (*the* for *yᵉ*, *that* for *yᵗ*, *Mr.* for *Mʳ*, *nation* for *nac̄on*, and *and* for *&*). In words taken from

French-language sources, the symbol often rendered as $ʒ$ (actually a u perched atop an o) has been replaced by ou or w to conform to modern usage. The Dutch ij has similarly been replaced with y.

4. *Minutes of Conferences, Held with the Indians*, 8 (quotation). At the July 1756 conference, Weiser said "he was a Stranger to Teedyuskung and his company and must have time to inform himself of his Temper and Expectations" ("Material Pertaining to Pennsylvania Indian Affairs," n.p., s.v. 27 July 1756, Manuscripts on Indian Affairs, 1755–1792, American Philosophical Society, Philadelphia). On go-betweens in general, and on Weiser in particular, see James H. Merrell, *Into the American Woods: Negotiators on the Pennsylvania Frontier* (New York: W. W. Norton, 1999). For the events surrounding Teedyuscung's 1756 speech, see "Material Pertaining to Indian Affairs," s.v. 26, 30 July 1756; Anthony F. C. Wallace, *King of the Delawares: Teedyuscung, 1700–1763* (Philadelphia: University of Pennsylvania Press, 1949), 87–115; and Chapter 8 below. As Merrell notes, Teedyuscung's speeches on this and other occasions were transcribed and edited by various Euro-American witnesses possessed of varied translating expertise, often with dramatic differences in content and tone (" 'I Desire All That I Have Said . . . May Be Taken down Aright': Revisiting Teedyuscung's 1756 Treaty Council Speeches," *William and Mary Quarterly*, 3d ser., 63 [2006], 777–826). Several versions gloss over this speech in a few words, but those that reproduce details are in substantial agreement; see Merrell, ed., "Easton Treaty Texts: July and November 1756," http://oieahc.wm.edu/wmq/Oct06/merrell_final.pdf, pp. 20–21, accessed 16 February 2012. The version in *Minutes of the Provincial Council of Pennsylvania, from the Organization to the Termination of the Proprietary Government*, 10 vols. (Harrisburg, Pa., 1851–1852), 7:209, contains at least one whopping typographical error: "put the means into our heads."

5. "Material Pertaining to Pennsylvania Indian Affairs," s.v. 28 July 1756 (1st quotation); John Heckewelder, *History Manners, and Customs of the Indian Nations Who Once Inhabited Pennsylvania and the Neighbouring States*, ed. William C. Reichel (Philadelphia: Historical Society of Pennsylvania, 1876), 439 (2nd and 3rd quotations); Daniel G. Brinton and Albert Seqaqkind Anthony, eds., *A Lenâpé-English Dictionary* (Philadelphia: Historical Society of Pennsylvania, 1888), 162 (4th quotation); Merrell, ed., "Easton Treaty Texts," 20, 92n. I am grateful to Ives Goddard for his guidance on these linguistic issues.

6. James Sullivan et al., eds., *The Papers of Sir William Johnson*, 14 vols. (Albany: University of the State of New York, 1921–1965), 3:515 (quotation); Wilbur R. Jacobs, *Diplomacy and Indian Gifts: Anglo-French Rivalry Along the Ohio and Northwest Frontiers, 1748–1763* (Stanford, Calif.: Stanford University Press, 1950). On Amherst's policies, see Chapter 9 below.

7. See Chapters 1–2 below.

8. Daniel Gookin, *Historical Collections of the Indians of New England: Of Their Several Nations, Numbers, Customs, Manners, Religion and Government, before the English Planted There* [1674] (Boston, 1792), 12.

9. "Material Pertaining to Pennsylvania Indian Affairs," s.v. 30 July 1756.

10. *Minutes of Conferences, Held with the Indians*, 10–11.

11. E. B. O'Callaghan and B. Fernow, eds., *Documents Relative to the Colonial History of the State of New-York*, 15 vols. (Albany, N.Y., 1853–1887), 7:301. See also the version in *Minutes of the Provincial Council of Pennsylvania*, 7:676–677.

12. On the probable translation of *Tsenacomoco* (also spelled *Tsenacommacah*), see Frederic W. Gleach, *Powhatan's World and Colonial Virginia: A Conflict of Cultures* (Lincoln: University of Nebraska Press, 1997), 25; but see also Helen C. Rountree, *The Powhatan Indians of Virginia: Their Traditional Culture* (Norman: University of Oklahoma Press, 1989), 191n, which says that "the meaning of the name is uncertain."

13. Frederick B. Tolles, *Quakers and the Atlantic Culture* (New York: Macmillan, 1960), 116.

14. *Minutes of the Provincial Council of Pennsylvania*, 7:213.

15. For varying perspectives on these processes of racial differentiation, see Alden T. Vaughan, "From White Man to Redskin: Changing Anglo-American Perceptions of the American Indian," *American Historical Review*, 87 (1982), 917–953; Nancy Shoemaker, *A Strange Likeness: Becoming Red and White in Eighteenth-Century North America* (New York: Oxford University Press, 2004); and Peter Silver, *Our Savage Neighbors: How Indian War Transformed Early America* (New York: W. W. Norton, 2008).

16. Theodore Roosevelt, *The Winning of the West* (Lincoln: University of Nebraska Press, 1995 [orig. publ. 1889–1896]), 2:373–374, 3:45.

17. Quoted in Andrew R. L. Cayton, "'Noble Actors' upon 'the Theatre of Honour': Power and Civility in the Treaty of Greenville," in Cayton and Fredrika J. Teute, eds., *Contact Points: American Frontiers from the Mohawk Valley to the Mississippi, 1750–1830* (Chapel Hill: University of North Carolina Press, 1998), 265.

18. Historian Richard White traces this process through the interviews that U.S. Indian Department official Charles Trowbridge conducted with the Shawnee prophet Tenskwatawa in 1824. Tenskwatawa tried to tell stories steeped in complicated metaphor, while Trowbridge stuck to a list of dry ethnographic questions. Thus a man who "once . . . had been a human being whom whites had spoken to, listened to, argued with, and feared" became "but an object of study" (*The Middle Ground: Indians, Empires, and Republics in the Great Lakes Region, 1650–1815* [New York: Cambridge University Press, 1991], 518–523 [quotation from p. 523]).

19. Vine Deloria, Jr., *Custer Died for Your Sins: An Indian Manifesto* (New York: Avon Books, 1969), 174, 57.

20. Francis Jennings, *The Invasion of America: Indians, Colonialism, and the Cant of Conquest* (Chapel Hill: University of North Carolina Press, 1975); Alden T. Vaughan, *New England Frontier: Puritans and Indians, 1620–1675*, 3rd ed. (Norman: University of Oklahoma Press, 1995 [orig. publ. 1965]), esp. ix–lxv; Deloria, *Custer Died for Your Sins*, 13 (quotation).

21. Which is to say, for example, that I present Chapter 4 here with less empirical confidence than I did when it was first published in 1983. The subsequent historiography on these issues for eastern North America has been enormous, and cannot be surveyed adequately here, but see, in particular, Paul Kelton, *Epidemics and Enslavement: Biological Catastrophe in the Native Southeast, 1492–1715* (Lincoln: University of Nebraska Press, 2007); Robbie Ethridge and Sheri M. Shuck-Hall, eds., *Mapping the Mississippian Shatter Zone: The Colonial Indian Slave Trade and Regional Instability in the American South* (Lincoln: University of Nebraska Press, 2009); and Christina Snyder, *Slavery in Indian Country: The Changing Face of Captivity in Early America* (Cambridge, Mass.: Harvard University Press, 2010). For other parts of the continent, see, for example, James F. Brooks, *Captives and Cousins: Slavery, Kinship, and Community in the Southwest Borderlands* (Chapel Hill: University of North Carolina Press, 2002); Ned Blackhawk, *Violence over the Land: Indians and Empires in the Early American West* (Cambridge, Mass.: Harvard University Press, 2006); and Brian DeLay, *War of a Thousand Deserts: Indian Raids and the U.S.-Mexican War* (New Haven, Conn.: Yale University Press, 2008).

Chapter 1. Tsenacomoco and the Atlantic World: Stories of Goods and Power

This chapter was originally published as "Tsenacommacah and the Atlantic World," in Peter
C. Mancall, ed., *The Atlantic World and Virginia, 1550–1624*, pp. 29–65. Copyright © 2007 by the
University of North Carolina Press. Used by permission of the publisher. www.uncpress.unc.edu.

1. William Strachey, *The Historie of Travell into Virginia Britania (1612)*, ed. Louis B. Wright
and Virginia Freund (London: The Hakluyt Society, 1953), 85–86. On Strachey's linguistic skills,
see Frank T. Siebert, Jr., "Resurrecting Virginia Algonquian from the Dead: The Reconstituted and
Historical Phonology of Powhatan," in James M. Crawford, ed., *Studies in Southeastern Languages*
(Athens: University of Georgia Press, 1975), 291–294.

2. Strachey's gloss, of course, also needs a gloss, thanks to the irregularities of seventeenth-
century punctuation and the ambiguity of the word *for*. While it is possible that Strachey meant
that the English had been killed *for* their weapons—to take possession of them—the references to
Newport and Savage and, especially, the combination of the word *all* with the singular sword and
hatchet makes "in spite of" a more likely reading, for all Prof. April Hatfield's much-appreciated
efforts to convince me otherwise.

3. Elman R. Service, *Primitive Social Organization: An Evolutionary Perspective* (New York:
Random House, 1962), 143–177 (quotations from pp. 144, 150).

4. Morton H. Fried, *The Evolution of Political Society: An Essay in Political Anthropology* (New
York: Random House, 1967), 52 (quotation), 185–226. Fried's four-stage evolutionary scheme of
"egalitarian," "ranked," and "stratified" "societies" and "the state" does not entirely coincide with
Service's "band," "tribe," "chiefdom," and "state" levels of "sociocultural integration," but clearly the
two scholars had similar views on the political-economic principles at work. The literature critiqu-
ing and elaborating evolutionary typologies is vast. For useful overviews, see Thomas E. Emerson,
Cahokia and the Archaeology of Power (Tuscaloosa: University of Alabama Press, 1997), 12–18; and
Timothy Earle, "Archaeology, Property, and Prehistory," *Annual Review of Anthropology*, 29 (2000),
39–60. For comments on the continued heuristic value of such an approach, see Robert D. Drennan, "Regional Demography in Chiefdoms," in Robert D. Drennan and Carlos A. Uribe, eds., *Chiefdoms in the Americas* (Lanham, Md.: University Press of America, 1987), 313–315; Patricia Galloway,
Choctaw Genesis, 1500–1700 (Lincoln: University of Nebraska Press, 1995), 38–40; and Timothy K.
Earle, *How Chiefs Come to Power: The Political Economy in Prehistory* (Stanford, Calif.: Stanford
University Press, 1997), 1–16. For an introduction to chiefdom forms in the southeast during the
period of European contact, see Charles Hudson, *The Southeastern Indians* (Knoxville: University
of Tennessee Press, 1976), 202–211.

5. Susan M. Frankenstein and Michael J. Rowlands, "The Internal Structure and Regional Context of Early Iron Age Society in South-Western Germany," *Institute of Archaeology Bulletin*, 15
(1978), 73–112 (quotation from p. 76).

6. Mary W. Helms, "Political Lords and Political Ideology in Southeastern Chiefdoms: Com-
ments and Observations," in Alex W. Barker and Timothy R. Pauketat, eds., *Lords of the Southeast:
Social Inequality and the Native Elites of Southeastern North America*, Archaeological Papers of the
American Anthropological Association, no. 3 (1992), 187–188 (quotations); Timothy R. Puketat,
"The Reign and Ruin of the Lords of Cahokia: A Dialectic of Dominance," ibid., 31–51. Impor-
tant theoretical statements on the political economy of gift-giving include Marcel Mauss, *The Gift:
The Form and Reason for Exchange in Archaic Societies*, trans. W. D. Halls (London: Routledge,
2002 [orig. publ. 1924]); Marshall Sahlins, *Stone Age Economics* (Chicago: Aldine-Atherton, 1972);

Mary Douglas and Baron Isherwood, *The World of Goods* (New York: Basic Books, 1979); Annette B. Weiner, *Inalienable Possessions: The Paradox of Keeping-While-Giving* (Berkeley: University of California Press, 1992); and Maurice Godelier, *The Enigma of the Gift*, trans. Nora Scott (Chicago: University of Chicago Press, 1999).

7. Timothy K. Earle, "Chiefdoms in Archaeological and Ethnohistorical Perspective," 281, 297; Galloway, *Choctaw Genesis*, 67–74; Emerson, *Cahokia and the Archaeology of Power*, 17–18; Frankenstein and Rowlands, "Internal Structure and Regional Context of Early Iron Age Society," 78–79.

8. Helen C. Rountree, *The Powhatan Indians of Virginia: Their Traditional Culture* (Norman: University of Oklahoma Press, 1989),103–125; John Smith, *A True Relation . . .* (1608), in Philip L. Barbour, ed., *The Complete Works of Captain John Smith (1580–1631)*, 3 vols. (Chapel Hill: University of North Carolina Press, 1986), 1:61 (quotation).

9. Kathleen M. Brown, *Good Wives, Nasty Wenches, and Anxious Patriarchs: Gender, Race, and Power in Colonial Virginia* (Chapel Hill: University of North Carolina Press, 1996), 45–53; Alex W. Barker, "Powhatan's Pursestrings: On the Meaning of Surplus in a Seventeenth Century Algonkian Chiefdom," in Barker and Pauketat, eds., *Lords of the Southeast*, 61–80; E. Randolph Turner III, "Native American Protohistoric Interactions in the Powhatan Core Area," in Helen C. Rountree, ed., *Powhatan Foreign Relations, 1500–1722* (Charlottesville: University Press of Virginia, 1993), 78–83; Stephen R. Potter, *Commoners, Tribute, and Chiefs: The Development of Algonquian Culture in the Potomac Valley* (Charlottesville: University Press of Virginia, 1993), 149–173 (quotation from p. 169); Martin D. Gallivan, *James River Chiefdoms: The Rise of Social Inequality in the Chesapeake* (Lincoln: University of Nebraska Press, 2003), esp. 1–8, 21–31; Margaret Holmes Williamson, *Powhatan Lords of Life and Death: Command and Consent in Seventeenth-Century Virginia* (Lincoln: University of Nebraska Press, 2003), esp. 129–172. On the droughts and crop failures of this period, see David W. Stahle et al., "The Lost Colony and Jamestown Droughts," *Science*, 280 (1998), 564–567.

10. Strachey, *Historie of Travell*, 114.

11. Brown, *Good Wives*, 66–67.

12. John Smith, *A Map of Virginia* (1612), in Barbour, ed., *Works of Smith*, 1:173–174.

13. Gallivan, *James River Chiefdoms*, 169.

14. Ibid. (quotation); Frederic W. Gleach, *Powhatan's World and Colonial Virginia: A Conflict of Cultures* (Lincoln: University of Nebraska Press, 1997), 28–34.

15. Williamson, *Powhatan Lords of Life and Death*, 152. See also Sahlins, *Stone Age Economics*, 185–191.

16. Smith, *A Map of Virginia*, 169 (quotation); Strachey, *Historie of Travell*, 94–95; Potter, *Commoners, Tribute, and Chiefs*, 210–220.

17. As Helen C. Rountree observes, "things is the operative word" in describing the Powhatans' agenda in dealing with Europeans ("The Powhatans and the English: A Case of Multiple Conflicting Agendas," in Rountree, ed., *Powhatan Foreign Relations*, 177–183 [quotation from p. 178]). See also Seth Mallios, *The Deadly Politics of Giving: Exchange and Violence at Ajacan, Roanoke, and Jamestown* (Tuscaloosa: University of Alabama Press, 2006)..

18. Clifford M. Lewis and Albert J. Loomie, *The Spanish Jesuit Mission in Virginia, 1570–1572* (Chapel Hill: University of North Carolina Press, 1953), 28–40, 58–62 (quotation from p. 58); Helen C. Rountree, *Pocahontas's People: The Powhatan Indians of Virginia Through Four Centuries* (Norman: University of Oklahoma Press, 1990), 15–20. None of the documents in Lewis and Loomie give Paquiquineo's Algonquian name, which, as far as I know, first appeared in English-language scholarship in Paul E. Hoffman, *A New Andalucia and a Way to the Orient: The American Southeast During the Sixteenth Century* (Baton Rouge: Louisiana State University Press, 1990), 184.

19. "Relation of Luis Gerónimo de Oré" (c. 1617), in Lewis and Loomie, *Spanish Jesuit Mission*, 179; "Relation of Juan de la Carrera . . . March 1, 1600," ibid., 131; "Relation of Juan Rogel Between 1607 and 1611," ibid., 118; "Relation of Bartolomé Martínez" (1617), ibid., 156; Francisco Sacchini, *Borgia, the Third Part of the History of the Society of Jesus* (1649), ibid., 221.

20. "Relation of Martínez," 156; Sacchini, *Borgia*, 221.

21. Lewis and Loomie, *Spanish Jesuit Mission*, 58–62; Carl Bridenbaugh, *Jamestown, 1544–1699* (New York: Oxford University Press, 1981), 10–17; Rountree, *Pocahontas's People*, 18–19. Ralph Hamor reported that the Chickahominies, who were not part of Powhatan's paramount chiefdom, considered the Spanish "odious," because "*Powhatan's* father was driven by them from the *west-Indies* into those parts" (Raphe Hamor, *A True Discourse of the Present Estate of Virginia, and the Success of the Affaires There till the 18 of June, 1614* [London, 1615], 13).

22. Entry 85, Contaduría 286 no. 1, Datas, fol. 171v, Archivo General de Indias, Seville. I thank Juan José Ponce-Vázquez for this reference.

23. Sacchini, *Borgia*, 221; "Relation of Gerónimo de Oré," 179; "Relation of Martínez," 156; Hoffman, *A New Andalucia*, 181–187.

24. Lewis and Loomie, *Spanish Jesuit Mission*, 13 (quoting Deposition of "John, An Englishman born in Bristol"), 16; William C. Sturtevant, "Spanish-Indian Relations in Southeastern North America," *Ethnohistory*, 9 (1962), 54–56; Potter, *Commoners, Tribute, and Chiefs*, 161–166; Turner, "Native American Protohistoric Interactions," 92.

25. Charlotte M. Gradie, "The Powhatans in the Context of the Spanish Empire," in Rountree, ed., *Powhatan Foreign Relations*, 154–172.

26. "Relation of Carrera," 133, 131; "Relation of Rogel," 118.

27. Gradie, "Powhatans in the Context of the Spanish Empire," 168–169.

28. "Relation of Rogel," 118.

29. "Relation of Gerónimo de Oré," 180; N. David Cook, "Beyond the Martyrs of Florida: The Versatile Career of Luis Gerónimo de Oré," *Florida Historical Quarterly*, 71 (1992), 169, 182 .

30. "Relation of Carrera," 131–133.

31. Luis de Quirós and Juan Baptista de Segura to Juan de Hinistrosa, 12 September 1570, in Lewis and Loomie, *Spanish Jesuit Mission*, 90, 89.

32. Ibid., 89–90.

33. James Axtell, *The Invasion Within: The Contest of Cultures in Colonial North America* (New York: Oxford University Press, 1985), 122–123.

34. Quirós and Segura to Hinistrosa, 12 Sept 1570, 92 (quotations); Maillos, "In the Hands of 'Indian Givers,' " 105–153.

35. "Relation of Carrera," 134.

36. An excellent summary of the standard narrative of Paquiquineo, on which an alternate perspective appears here, is James Horn, *A Land as God Made It: Jamestown and the Birth of America* (New York: Basic Books, 2005), 1–10.

37. Juan Rogel to Francis Borgia, 28 August 1572, in Lewis and Loomie, *Spanish Jesuit Mission*, 109–109 (1st, 2nd, and 5th quotations); "Relation of Juan Rogel," 120–121 (3rd and 4th quotations).

38. Lewis and Loomie, *Spanish Jesuit Mission*, 46–47; Hoffman, *New Andalucia*, 261–266; Gleach, *Powhatan's World*, 89–97.

39. J. Frederick Fausz, "An 'Abundance of Blood Shed on Both Sides': England's First Indian War, 1609–1614," *Virginia Magazine of History and Biography*, 98 (1990), 3–56; Rountree, *Pocahontas's People*, 29–55; Martin H. Quitt, "Trade and Acculturation at Jamestown, 1607–1609: The Limits of Understanding," *William and Mary Quarterly*, 3rd ser., 52 (1995), 227–258; Gleach, *Powhatan's*

World; James Axtell, *After Columbus: Essays in the Ethnohistory of Colonial North America* (New York: Oxford University Press, 1988), 182–221.

40. [Gabriel Archer], "A Relatyon of the Discovery of our River . . . ," 21 May–21 June 1607, in Philip L. Barbour, *The Jamestown Voyages Under the First Charter*, 2 vols. (Cambridge: Cambridge University Press, 1969), 1:83–84. It took the better part of a month for the colonists to figure out that the Parahunt was merely "a wyroaunce, and under this great Powaton" (Edward Maria Wingfield, "A Discourse of Virginia," 1608, ibid., 215).

41. Archer, "Relatyon," 84–86, 89.

42. In Archer's firsthand account, the next day Parahunt simply concluded that his guests' "hott Drynckes he thought caused his greefe, but that he was well agayne, and . . . [the English] were very wellcome" (ibid., 89). But if the comments of Sir Walter Cope a couple of months later are accurate, Newport may have used the occasion to further increase his reputation among the Powhatans: "One of ther kinges syck with drinkinge our aquavite, thought him selfe poysoned. Newport tolde him by signes that the nextday he showld be well and he was so: and tellinge hys cuntry men thereof they came apace olde men and old women upon Every belliach to him, to know when they showld be well" (Cope to Lord Salisbury, 12 August 1607, in Barbour, *Jamestown Voyages*, 1:110).

43. Archer, "Relatyon," 87.

44. Ibid., 87–89.

45. Ibid., 89–95 (quotations from p. 94).

46. Cope to Salisbury, 12 August 1607, 110 (quotation); Rountree, *Pocahontas's People*, 29–34; Horn, *A Land as God Made It*, 54–59.

47. Fausz, "An 'Abundance of Blood Shed,'" 17; Gleach, *Powhatan's World*, 106–122.

48. George Percy, "Observations gathered out of a Discourse of the Plantation of the Southerne Colonie in Virginia by the English, 1606," in Barbour, *Jamestown Voyages*, 1:143.

49. Smith, *True Relation*, 35–39 (quotation from p. 35); Smith, *The Generall History of Virginia, the Somer Iles, and New England . . .* (1624), in Barbour, ed., *Works of Smith*, 2:142–146; Quitt, "Trade and Acculturation," 247.

50. Smith, *True Relation*, 53–57.

51. Axtell, *Beyond 1492*, 187.

52. *The Proceedings of the English Colonie in Virginia since their first beginning from England in the yeare of our Lord 1606, till this present 1612 . . .* , in Barbour, ed., *Works of Smith*, 1:215 (1st and 2nd quotations); Smith, *True Relation*, 61–63 (remaining quotations).

53. Rountree, *Pocahontas's People*, 40–43.

54. Smith, *True Relation*, 63–65.

55. Ibid, 65–67.

56. Ibid., 69–71 (1st, 2nd, and 4th quotations); *Proceedings of the English Colonie*, 215–217 (3rd quotation from p. 217). The four great kettles of the *True Relation* are not mentioned in Smith's later versions of this story, which instead say only that "Newport [was] thinking to out brave this Salvage in ostentation of greatnes, and so to bewitch him with his bounty" and that the transaction "bred some unkindes betweene our two captaines" (*Proceedings of the English Colonie*, 217 [quotations]; *Generall Historie*, 156).

57. Francis Perkins "to a Friend in England," 28 March 1608, in Barbour, *Jamestown Voyages*, 1:160 (editor's bracketed words omitted).

58. *Proceedings of the English Colonie*, 216 (1st quotation); Smith, *True Relation*, 79 (2nd quotation).

59. On the dangers of overemphasizing the symbolic aspects of the underlying economic

relationships prestige goods represent, see Camilla Townsend, *Pocahontas and the Powhatan Dilemma* (New York: Hill and Wang, 2004), 62–63.

60. *Proceedings of the English Colonie*, 220–221.

61. Smith, *True Relation*, 79.

62. Don Pedro de Zúñiga to Philip III, 26 June 1608, in Barbour, *Jamestown Voyages*, 1:163; "Relation of What Francis Magnel, an Irishman, Learned in the Land of Virginia during the Eight Months He Was There," 1 July 1610, ibid., 154.

63. *Proceedings of the English Colonie*, 234.

64. Ibid., 235–236.

65. Ibid., 236–237.

66. See Francis Jennings, *The Invasion of America: Indians, Colonialism, and the Cant of Conquest* (Chapel Hill: University of North Carolina Press, 1975), 116–117; Alden T. Vaughan, *American Genesis: Captain John Smith and the Founding of Virginia* (Boston: Little, Brown, 1975), 41–46; James Axtell, *Beyond 1492: Encounters in Colonial North America* (New York: Oxford University Press, 1992), 187–188; Rountree, *Pocahontas's People*, 47–48; Gleach, *Powhatan's World*, 126–127; Williamson, *Powhatan Lords of Life and Death*, 35. Two exceptions to the general dismissal of the coronation ceremony are Gallivan, who concludes that, "upon receiving exotic symbols of authority, purportedly from King James, Powhatan had in many ways reached the pinnacle of his status as Mamanatowick" (*James River Chiefdoms*, 169); and April Lee Hatfield, who takes seriously Newport's "intention to overlay Powhatan territory with an English unit of governance" ("Spanish Colonization Literature, Powhatan Geographies, and English Perceptions of Tsenacommacah/Virginia," *Journal of Southern History*, 69 [2003], 245–282 [quotation from p. 265]).

67. *Proceedings of the English Colonie*, 237.

68. Strachey, *Historie of Travell*, 85–86; Alden T. Vaughan, "Powhatans Abroad: Virginia Indians in England," in Robert Appelbaum and John Wood Sweet, eds., *Envisioning an English Empire: Jamestown and the Making of the North Atlantic World* (Philadelphia: University of Pennsylvania Press, 2005), 51–55.

69. *Proceedings of the English Colonie*, 239–244 (quotations); Smith, *Generall Historie*, 185–193.

70. *Proceedings of the English Colonie*, 244–246.

71. Ibid., 246–250. The omission of what must be the word "my" from Powhatan's description of Smith as a weroance seems more than a slip. As Smith's modern editor notes, "Both the *Generall Historie* and Purchas's *Pilgrimes* omit 'of'" from the same sentence (Barbour, ed., *Works of Smith*, 1:248n). My suspicion is that this declaration of English subordination was hastily (and thus incompletely) edited out of *Proceedings of the English Colonie* and then further cleaned up in later versions. On any subordination implied by kinship, Smith was a little more ambiguous, but also seemed to declare his independence: "I call you father indeed, and as a father you shall see I will love you," he claimed to have told Wahunsonacock, "but the smal care you had of such a child, caused my men [to] perswade me to shift for my selfe." Significantly, the paragraph containing this exchange bears the marginal note "Captaine Smith's discourse to delay time, that hee might surprise Powhatan" (*Proceedings of the English Colonie*, 249).

72. Fausz, "An 'Abundance of Blood Shed,'" 19–47; Quitt, "Trade and Acculturation," 251–258.

73. Mark Nicholls, ed., "George Percy's 'Trew Relacyon,'" *Virginia Magazine of History and Biography*, 113 (2005), 244–245, 247.

74. Henry Spelman, "Relation of Virginea," in Edward Arber and A. G. Bradley, eds., *Travels and Works of Captain John Smith, President of Virginia and Admiral of New England, 1580–1631*, 3 vols. (Edinburgh: John Grant, 1910), 1: cv, cxii. Rountree and Williamson are among the few

scholars who seem to have recognized the significance of this account. Rountree minimizes the significance of "the paste-jewel crown," despite its clear prominence in Spelman's account (*Powhatan Indians of Virginia*, 110). Williamson, pointing out that "in the deep Southeast beads were structurally analogous to white body emissions," elaborates upon the fertility symbolism of Powhatan's acts: "Powhatan circled his newly planted field symbolically shooting semen all over his subjects, his workers, who faced him just as a woman might face a man during intercourse" (*Powhatan Lords of Life and Death*, 157). On beads as fertility symbols, see Townsend, *Pocahontas*, 86–87.

75. Fausz, "An 'Abundance of Blood Shed,'" 43–49.

76. Samuel Purchas, *Purchas his Pilgrimage, Or Relations of the World and the Religions Observed in Al Ages and Places Discovered, from the Creation unto this Present* (London, 1617), 954. On *uttama-*, see Townsend, *Pocahontas*, 149–150.

77. Hamor, *True Discourse*, 38. After Wahunsonacock's coronation, Namontack had left with Newport as his guide on the ill-conceived expedition against the Monacans (Smith, *Proceedings of the English Colonie*, 237) and exploration of "the head of the Falls which takes the name of Namantack the Fynder of yt" (Strachey, *Historie of Travell*, 131). It is possible the mamanatowick never saw him again.

78. Hamor, *True Discourse*, 38–43.

79. Ibid., 43–45. The "table book" was probably made up of paper treated to make it erasable. I thank Professor Peter Stallybrass for this insight.

80. Nicholls, ed., "Percy's 'Trew Relacyon,'" 261–262.

81. Samuel Argall to Council for Virginia?, 9 June 1617, in Susan Myra Kingsbury, ed., *The Records of the Virginia Company of London*, 4 vols. (Washington, D.C.: Government Printing Office, 1906–1935), 3:73.

82. Smith, *Generall Historie*, 261.

83. Ibid., 261 (1st and 5th quotations); Purchas, *Purchas his Pilgrimage*, 954–955 (2nd and 3rd quotations); Norman Egbert McClure, ed., *The Letters of John Chamberlain* (Philadelphia: American Philosophical Society, 1939), 2:12, 50 (4th quotation), 56–57, 66; Vaughan, "Powhatans Abroad," 58–65.

84. K. R. Andrews, "Christopher Newport of Limehouse, Mariner," *William and Mary Quarterly*, 3rd Ser., 11, (1954), 39–40; David R. Ransome. "Newport, Christopher," *American National Biography*, http://www.anb.org/articles/20/20-00718.html (accessed 2 February 2004).

85. Argall to Council for Virginia?, 9 June 1617, 73–74.

86. "Treasurer and Company to Governor and Council in Virginia, 25 July 1621, in Kingsbury, ed., *Records of the Virginia Company*, 3:488 (1st quotation); Council of Virginia Company to Governor and Council in Virginia, 26 November, 5 December 1621, ibid., 526–527 (2nd quotation), 530.

Chapter 2. Brothers, Scoundrels, Metal-Makers

This chapter was originally published in *de Halve-Maen*, 61, no. 3 (Fall 1998), 59–64. Reprinted with permission of The Holland Society of New York. The introductory and concluding sections have been revised for this volume.

1. Oliver A. Rink, *Holland on the Hudson: An Economic and Social History of Dutch New York* (Ithaca, N.Y.: Cornell University Press, 1986), 50–116; Andrew Charles Lipman, "The Saltwater Frontier: Indians, Dutch, and English on Seventeenth-Century Long Island Sound" (Ph.D. diss., University of Pennsylvania, 2010).

2. For an interesting discussion of recorded Euro-American descriptions of Indians "as constructions of indigenous lifeways rather than faithful *reconstructions*," see Elizabeth Vibert, *Traders' Tales: Narratives of Cultural Encounters in the Columbia Plateau, 1807–1846* (Norman: University of Oklahoma Press, 1997), xiii.

3. For examples, see J. Franklin Jameson, ed., *Narratives of New Netherland, 1609–1664* (New York: Charles Scribner's Sons, 1909), 1–133.

4. See, for instance, Charles T. Gehring, ed. and trans., *Fort Orange Court Minutes, 1652–1660* (Syracuse, N.Y.: Syracuse University Press, 1990).

5. Examples include A. J. F. van Laer, ed. and trans., *Van Rensselaer Bowier Manuscripts: Being the Letters of Kiliaen Van Rensselaer, 1630–1643, and Other Documents Relating to the Colony of Rensselaerwyck* (Albany: University of the State of New York, 1908); and van Laer, ed. and trans., *Correspondence of Jeremias van Rensselaer, 1651–1674* (Albany: University of the State of New York, 1932).

6. These works of these authors are familiar to most students of New Netherland, and the portions of each dealing with American Indians were republished in the 1990s: Harmen Meyndertsz van den Bogaert, "A Journey into Mohawk and Oneida Country, 1634–1635," in Dean R. Snow, Charles T. Gehring, and William A. Starna, *In Mohawk Country: Early Narratives About a Native People* (Syracuse, N.Y.: Syracuse University Press, 1996), 1–13; Johannes Megapolensis, Jr., "An Account of the Mohawk Indians, 1644," ibid., 38–46; Adriaen Cornelissen van der Donck, "Description of New Netherland, 1653," trans. Diederik Goedhuys, ibid., 104–130; Jasper Danckaerts, "Journal of a Voyage to New York and a Tour in Several of the American Colonies in 1679–1680," ibid., 193–220. For ease of reference, wherever possible the notes below are to the Snow, Gehring, and Starna editions.

7. Charles T. Gehring and William A. Starna, trans. and eds., *A Journey into Mohawk and Oneida Country, 1634–1635: The Journal of Harmen Meyndertsz van den Bogaert* (Syracuse, N.Y.: Syracuse University Press, 1988), xix–xxii. The Gehring and Starna edition (reprinted sans scholarly apparatus in Snow, Gehring, and Starna, *In Mohawk Country*) is a new translation that supersedes two earlier published versions. The first, which erroneously identified the author of the unsigned manuscript, is James Grant Wilson, "Arent van Curler and his Journal of 1634–35," *American Historical Association Annual Report for 1895* (Washington, D.C., 1896), 81–101. The second—which ruled out van Curler as author, tentatively attributed the text to van den Bogaert, and included revisions to Wilson's translation by S. G. Nissensen—appeared as "Narrative of a Journey into the Mohawk and Oneida Country, 1634–1635," in Jameson, ed., *Narratives of New Netherland*, 135–162.

8. Gerald Francis De Jong, "Dominie Johannes Megapolensis: Minister to New Netherland," *New-York Historical Society Quarterly*, 52 (1968), 7–47. The standard translation of Megapolensis's text (reprinted by Snow, Gehring, and Starna) is "A Short Account of the Mohawk Indians, by Reverend Johannes Megapolensis, Jr., 1644," in Jameson, ed., *Narratives of New Netherland*, 163–180.

9. Snow, Gehring, and Starna, eds., *In Mohawk Country*, 104–105. Goedhuys's new translation in Snow, Gehring, and Starna supersedes Adriean van der Donck, "Description of the New Netherlands," trans. Jeremiah Johnson, *New-York Historical Society, Collections*, 2nd ser., 2 (1841), 125–242.

10. Bartlett Burleigh James and J. Franklin Jameson, eds., *Journal of Jasper Danckaerts, 1679–1680* (New York: Charles Scribner's Sons, 1913), xi–xxvi; Charles T. Gehring and Robert S. Grumet, "Observations of the Indians from Jasper Danckaerts's Journal, 1679–1680," *William and Mary Quarterly*, 3rd ser., 44 (1987), 104–106 (quotations from p. 104). The excerpts reprinted by Snow, Gehring, and Starna combine material from the James and Jameson edition with a portion of Danckaerts's manuscript omitted from that translation first published by Gehring and Grumet.

11. Gordon M. Sayre, *Les Sauvages Américains: Representations of Native Americans in French and English Colonial Literature* (Chapel Hill: University of North Carolina Press, 1997), 24–25.

12. Ibid., 28–30.

13. Van den Bogaert, "Journey," 5, 11.

14. Ibid., 3–6.

15. Megapolensis, "Account," 41, 43.

16. Danckaerts, "Journal of a Voyage to New York," 195; van der Donck, "Description of New Netherland," 115.

17. Jaap Jacobs, personal communication, 4 October 1998.

18. Van den Bogaert, "Journey," 8–9.

19. Jacobs, personal communication, 4 October 1998.

20. Gehring and Starna, eds., *Journey into Mohawk and Oneida Country*, 60.

21. Van den Bogaert, "Journey," 2–3, 11.

22. Megapolensis, "Account," 45.

23. Gehring and Starna, eds., *Journey into Mohawk and Oneida Country*, 63, 64n.

24. Van den Bogaert, "Journey," 6. Van den Bogaert reported similar Indian requests for displays of marksmanship—or rather of an ability to make a lot of noise—on at least two other occasions (ibid., 7, 12). The Iroquois did not acquire significant numbers of firearms until the early 1640s; it is quite possible that there were no guns at all in the Mohawk and Oneida countries when van den Bogaert visited in 1634–1635. See Daniel K. Richter, *The Ordeal of the Longhouse: The Peoples of the Iroquois League in the Era of European Colonization* (Chapel Hill: University of North Carolina Press, 1992), 62–64.

25. Van den Bogaert, "Journey," 3, 5, 11.

26. Megapolensis, "Account," 46.

27. Ibid., 45.

28. Van der Donck, "Description," 126.

29. Danckaerts, "Journal," 218.

30. Ibid., 211.

31. Van der Donck, "Description," 115.

32. Ibid., 121.

33. Ibid., 122.

34. Megapolensis, "Account," 44.

35. Gehring and Starna, eds., *Journey into Mohawk and Oneida Country*, 60.

36. Megapolensis, "Account," 45.

37. Van der Donck, "Description," 129–130.

38. The classic discussion of North American racial constructions of Indianness is Robert F. Berkhofer, Jr., *The White Man's Indian: Images of the American Indian from Columbus to the Present* (New York: Knopf, 1978). See also Olive Patricia Dickason, *The Myth of the Savage and the Beginnings of French Colonialism in the Americas* (Edmonton: University of Alberta Press, 1984); Stephen Greenblatt, *Marvelous Possessions: The Wonder of the New World* (Chicago: University of Chicago Press, 1991); Anthony Pagden, *European Encounters with the New World, From Renaissance to Romanticism* (New Haven, Conn.: Yale University Press, 1992); and John F. Moffitt and Santiago Sebastián, *O Brave New People: The European Invention of the American Indian* (Albuquerque: University of New Mexico Press, 1996).

39. Hayden White, "The Noble Savage Theme as Fetish," in Fredi Chiapelli, ed., *First Images of America: The Impact of the New World on the Old*, 2 vols. (Berkeley: University of California Press,

1976), 1:121. See also David Murray, *Forked Tongues: Speech, Writing, and Representation in North American Indian Texts* (Bloomington: Indiana University Press, 1991), 35; and Sayre, *Les Sauvages*, 124.

40. Sayre, *Les Sauvages*, 123–143 (quotations from pp. 138, 139).

41. Gehring and Grumet, "Observations of the Indians," 106.

42. Megapolensis, "Account," 41–42.

43. Danckaerts, "Journal," 204.

44. Van der Donck, "Description," 106–107.

45. Anthony Grafton, *New Worlds, Ancient Texts: The Power of Tradition and the Shock of Discovery* (Cambridge, Mass.: Harvard University Press, 1992), 42.

Chapter 3. "That Europe Be not Proud, nor America Discouraged"

Evolving versions of this chapter were presented at the American Historical Association Annual Meeting, Seattle, Washington, 8 January 2005, the Symposium on Material Cultures in the Atlantic, University of Florida, Gainesville, 9 February 2007, and as the Crossroads Lecture, University of North Carolina, Chapel Hill, 25 March 2009. Versions of several paragraphs appeared in different context in Daniel K. Richter, "Stratification and Class in Eastern Native America," in Simon Middleton and Billy G. Smith, eds., *Class Matters: Early North America and the Atlantic World* (Philadelphia: University of Pennsylvania Press, 2008), 41–45.

1. Roger Williams, *A Key into the Language of America: Or, An Help to the Language of the Natives in That Part of America, Called New-England* (London, 1643), 158.

2. T. H. Breen, "An Empire of Goods: The Anglicization of Colonial America, 1690–1776," *Journal of British Studies*, 25 (1986), 467–499. Foundational works on Native involvement with the Atlantic economy include Harold A. Innis, *The Fur Trade in Canada: An Introduction to Canadian Economic History* (New Haven, Conn.: Yale University Press, 1930); and George I. Quimby, *Indian Culture and European Trade Goods: The Archaeology of the Historic Period in the Western Great Lakes Region* (Madison: University of Wisconsin Press, 1966).

3. James Axtell, *Beyond 1492: Encounters in Colonial North America* (New York: Oxford University Press, 1992), 125–151 (quotations from pp. 147–150); Francis Jennings, *The Invasion of America: Indians, Colonialism, and the Cant of Conquest* (Chapel Hill: University of North Carolina Press, 1975), 84–104 (quotations from pp. 89, 102). See also Arthur J. Ray, "Indians as Consumers in the Eighteenth Century," in Carol Judd and Arthur J. Ray, eds., *Old Trails and New Directions: Papers of the Third North American Fur Trade Conference* (Toronto: University of Toronto Press, 1980), 255–271; and Daniel K. Richter, *Facing East from Indian Country: A Native History of Early America* (Cambridge, Mass.: Harvard University Press, 2001), 174–179.

4. Richard White, *The Roots of Dependency: Subsistence, Environment, and Social Change Among the Choctaws, Pawnees, and Navajos* (Lincoln: University of Nebraska Press, 1983).

5. Axtell, *Beyond 1492*, 125. I have outlined this evolutionary process in *Facing East*, Chapter 2.

6. Quimby, *Indian Culture and European Trade Goods*, 63–80; Arthur J. Ray, "Indians as Consumers in the Eighteenth Century," in Carol Judd and Arthur J. Ray, eds., *Old Trails and New Directions: Papers of the Third North American Fur Trade Conference* (Toronto: University of Toronto Press, 1980), 255–271.

7. Williams, *Key*, 160.

8. Ibid., 155.

9. Patricia E. Rubertone, *Grave Undertakings: An Archaeology of Roger Williams and the Narragansett Indians* (Washington, D.C.: Smithsonian Institution Press, 2001), 114.

10. Williams, *Key*, A1.

11. Ibid., 144–145.

12. Ibid., 44–45.

13. Neal Salisbury, "Toward the Covenant Chain: Iroquois and Southern New England Algonquians, 1637–1684," in Daniel K. Richter and James H. Merrell, eds., *Beyond the Covenant Chain: The Iroquois and Their Neighbors in Indian North America, 1600–1800* (Syracuse, N.Y.: Syracuse University Press, 1987), 64–65.

14. For early articulations of these themes see George T. Hunt, *The Wars of the Iroquois: A Study in Intertribal Trade Relations* (Madison: University of Wisconsin Press, 1940); and E. E. Rich, "Trade Habits and Economic Motivation among the Indians of North America," *Canadian Journal of Economics and Political Science*, 26 (1960), 35–53.

15. Neal Salisbury, "The Indians' Old World: Native Americans and the Coming of Europeans," *William and Mary Quarterly*, 3rd ser., 53 (1996), 435–458 (quotations from pp. 457–458).

16. Christopher L. Miller and George R. Hamell, "A New Perspective on Indian-White Contact: Cultural Symbols and Colonial Trade," *Journal of American History*, 73 (1986), 311–328 (quotations from pp. 318, 326).

17. Richter, *Facing East*, 42–53; Laurier Turgeon, "French Beads in France and Northeastern North America During the Sixteenth Century," *Historical Archaeology*, 35 (2001), 58–82.

18. James W. Bradley, *Evolution of the Onondaga Iroquois: Accommodating Change, 1500–1655* (Syracuse, N.Y.: Syracuse University Press, 1987), 69–78.

19. Laurier Turgeon, "The Tale of the Kettle: Odyssey of an Intercultural Object," *Ethnohistory*, 44 (1997), 1–29 (quotations from pp. 10, 17, 2).

20. Ibid., 15.

21. Williams, *Key*, 132. On chiefdoms and prestige goods, see Chapter 1, above.

22. Karen Ordahl Kupperman, *Indians and English: Facing Off in Early America* (Ithaca, N.Y.: Cornell University Press, 2000), 92–93.

23. Reuben Gold Thwaites, ed. *The Jesuit Relations and Allied Documents: Travels and Explorations of the Jesuit Missionaries in New France, 1610–1791*, 73 vols. (Cleveland, Ohio: Burrows Brothers, 1896–1901), 63, 185–187; William N. Fenton, *The Great Law and the Longhouse: A Political History of the Iroquois Confederacy* (Norman: University of Oklahoma Press, 1998), 199; Joseph François Lafitau, *Customs of the American Indians Compared with the Customs of Primitive Times*, ed. William N. Fenton and Elizabeth L. Moore, 2 vols. (Toronto: The Champlain Society, 1977), 1:290. On the role of material goods in the political structures of the Haudenosaunee, see Daniel K. Richter, *The Ordeal of the Longhouse: The Peoples of the Iroquois League in the Era of European Colonization* (Chapel Hill: University of North Carolina Press, 1992), 30–49; and for a view at odds with the one presented here, see Bruce G. Trigger, "Maintaining Economic Equality in Opposition to Complexity: An Iroquoian Case Study," in Steadman Upham, ed., *The Evolution of Political Systems: Sociopolitics in Small-Scale Sedentary Societies* (Cambridge: Cambridge University Press, 1990), 127–130.

24. Charles Hudson, *The Southeastern Indians* (Knoxville: University of Tennessee Press, 1976), 202–211, 223–226.

25. Thwaites, ed. *Jesuit Relations*, 10:75.

26. See Chapter 1, above.

27. See James D. Drake, *King Philip's War: Civil War in New England, 1675–1676* (Amherst: University of Massachusetts Press, 1999), esp. 16–34.

28. For analyses of the evolution of southern New England polities in the eighteenth century, see David J. Silverman, "Deposing the Sachem to Defend the Sachemship: Indian Land Sales and Native Political Structure on Martha's Vineyard, 1680–1740," *Explorations in Early American Culture*, 5 (2001), 9–44; and John Wood Sweet, *Bodies Politic: Negotiating Race in the American North, 1730–1830* (Baltimore: Johns Hopkins University Press, 2003), 16–57.

29. John Smith, *The Generall Historie of Virginia, New-England, and the Summer Isles* (London, 1624), 38.

30. Neal Salisbury, *Manitou and Providence: Indians, Europeans, and the Making of New England, 1500–1643* (New York: Oxford University Press, 1982), 236.

31. Marvin T. Smith, "Aboriginal Population Movements in the Early Historic Period Interior Southeast," in Peter H. Wood, Gregory A. Waselkov, and M. Thomas Hatley, eds., *Powhatan's Mantle: Indians in the Colonial Southeast* (Lincoln: University of Nebraska Press, 1991), 21–34; Alan Gallay, *The Indian Slave Trade: The Rise of the English Empire in the American South, 1670–1717* (New Haven, Conn.: Yale University Press, 2002), 23–39; Steven C. Hahn, *The Invention of the Creek Nation, 1670–1763* (Lincoln: University of Nebraska Press, 2004), 13–26.

32. Raymond Fogelson, "Who Were the *Aní-Kutáni*? An Excursion into Cherokee Historical Thought," *Ethnohistory*, 31 (1984), 255–263.

33. Lawrence A. Clayton, Vernon James Knight, Jr., and Edward C. Moore, eds., *The De Soto Chronicles: The Expedition of Hernando De Soto to North America in 1539–1543*, 2 vols. (Tuscaloosa: University of Alabama Press, 1993), 1:83; Smith, *Generall Historie*, 37–38.

34. Lafitau, *Customs of the American Indians*, 1:290–293.

35. David Peterson De Vries, "Voyages from Holland to America, A.D. 1632 to 1644," *New-York Historical Society Collections*, 2nd ser., 3 (1857), 96–97.

36. Thwaites, ed., *Jesuit Relations*, 10:229–231.

37. Bruce G. Trigger, *Natives and Newcomers: Canada's "Heroic Age" Reconsidered* (Kingston, Ont.: McGill-Queen's University Press, 1985), 226–297; Richter, *Ordeal of the Longhouse:* 50–74.

38. Treaty minutes, 12 July 1697, New York Colonial Manuscripts, vol. 41, folio 93, New York State Archives, Albany.

39. Lafitau, *Customs of the American Indians*, 1:290–293.

40. Patricia E. Rubertone, "The Historical Archaeology of Native Americans," *Annual Review of Anthropology*, 29 (2000), 425–446 (quotation from p. 435).

41. Susan M. Frankenstein and Michael J. Rowlands, "The Internal Structure and Regional Context of Early Iron Age Society in South-Western Germany," *Institute of Archaeology Bulletin*, 15 (1978), 79, 83.

42. Dena F. Dincauze and Robert J. Hasenstab, "Explaining the Iroquois: Tribalization on a Prehistoric Periphery," in Timothy C. Champion, *Centre and Periphery: Comparative Studies in Archaeology* (London: Unwin Hyman, 1989), 67–87. On Moundville's trading networks, see Christopher S. Peebles, "Moundville from 1000 to 1500 AD as Seen from 1840 to 1985 AD," in Robert D. Drennan and Carlos A. Uribe, eds., *Chiefdoms in the Americas* (Lanham, Md.: University Press of America, 1987), 21–41.

43. For an exploration of some of these transformations, see Fenton, *Great Law and the Longhouse.*

44. David J. Silverman, *Faith and Boundaries: Colonists, Christianity, and Community among*

the Wampanoag Indians of Martha's Vineyard, 1600–1871 (Cambridge: Cambridge University Press, 2005), 123–124.

45. Richard White, *The Middle Ground: Indians, Empires, and Republics in the Great Lakes Region, 1650–1815* (Cambridge: Cambridge University Press, 1991), 94–119; Timothy J. Shannon, "Dressing for Success on the Mohawk Frontier: Hendrick, William Johnson, and the Indian Fashion," *William and Mary Quarterly,* 3rd ser., 53 (1996), 13–42.

46. For introductions to the culture of diplomacy in the eighteenth century, which radiated outward from the Hodenasaunee Iroquois, see Francis Jennings et al., eds., *The History and Culture of Iroquois Diplomacy: An Interdisciplinary Guide to the Treaties of the Six Nations and Their League* (Syracuse, N.Y.: Syracuse University Press, 1985); Mary Druke [Becker], "Linking Arms: The Structure of Iroquois Intertribal Diplomacy," in Richter and Merrell, eds., *Beyond the Covenant Chain;* and James H. Merrell, *Into the American Woods: Negotiators on the Pennsylvania Frontier* (New York: W. W. Norton, 1990), esp. 253–276.

47. Robert A. Williams, Jr., *Linking Arms Together; American Indian Treaty Visions of Law and Peace, 1600–1800* (New York: Oxford University Press, 1997), 79.

48. E. B. O'Callaghan and B. Fernow, eds., *Documents Relative to the Colonial History of the State of New-York,* 15 vols. (Albany, 1853–1887), 6:106.

49. Peter Wraxall, *An Abridgement of the Indian Affairs . . . Transacted in the Colony of New York, from the Year 1678 to the Year 1751,* ed. Charles Howard McIlwain (Cambridge, Mass., 1915), 195.

Chapter 4. War and Culture

This chapter was originally published in *William and Mary Quarterly,* 3rd ser., 40 (1983), 528–559. Reprinted by permission. For a survey of the voluminous literature on topics related to Iroquois warfare published after this article originally appeared, see Jon Parmenter, "Historiographical Note," *William and Mary Quarterly,* 3rd ser., 64 (2007), 77–82. Were I to rewrite this essay today, among the subsequent works that would force me to rethink some points are Matthew Dennis, *Cultivating a Landscape of Peace: Iroquois-European Encounters in Seventeenth-Century America* (Ithaca, N.Y. : Cornell University Press, 1993); José António Brandão and William A. Starna, "The Treaties of 1701: A Triumph of Iroquois Diplomacy," *Ethnohistory,* 43 (1996), 209–244; Brandão, *"Your Fyre Shall Burn No More": Iroquois Policy Towards New France and its Native Allies to 1701* (Lincoln: University of Nebraska Press, 1997); Gilles Havard, *The Great Peace of Montreal of 1701: French-Native Diplomacy in the Seventeenth Century,* trans. Phyllis Aronoff and Howard Scott (Montreal: McGill-Queen's University Press, 2001); Starna and Brandão, " From the Mohawk-Mahican War to the Beaver Wars: Questioning the Pattern," *Ethnohistory,* 51 (2004), 725–750; and Roger M. Carpenter, *The Renewed, the Destroyed, and the Remade: The Three Thought Worlds of the Huron and the Iroquois, 1609–1650* (East Lansing: Michigan State University Press, 2004).

1. Reuben Gold Thwaites, ed., *The Jesuit Relations and Allied Documents: Travels and Explorations of the Jesuit Missionaries in New France, 1610–1791,* 73 vols. (Cleveland, Ohio, 1896–1901), 43: 263.

2. See, for example, George T. Hunt, *The Wars of the Iroquois: A Study in Intertribal Trade Relations* (Madison: University of Wisconsin Press, 1940); W. W. Newcomb, Jr., "A Re- Examination of the Causes of Plains Warfare," *American Anthropologist,* n.s., 52 (1950), 317–330; and Francis

266 Notes to Pages 69–71

Jennings, *The Invasion of America: Indians, Colonialism, and the Cant of Conquest* (Chapel Hill: University of North Carolina Press, 1975), 146–170.

3. While anthropologists disagree about the precise distinctions between the wars of state-organized and non-state societies, they generally agree that battles for territorial conquest, economic monopoly, and subjugation or enslavement of conquered peoples are the product of the technological and organizational capacities of the state. For overviews of the literature, see C. R. Hallpike, "Functionalist Interpretations of Primitive Warfare," *Man*, n.s., 8 (1973), 451–470, and Andrew Vayda, "Warfare in Ecological Perspective," *Annual Review of Ecology and Systematics*, 5 (1974), 183–193.

4. My use of the term *mourning-war* differs from that of Marian W. Smith in "American Indian Warfare," New York Academy of Sciences, *Transactions*, 2nd ser., 13 (1951), 348–365, which stresses the psychological and emotional functions of the mourning-war. As the following paragraphs seek to show, the psychology of the mourning-war was deeply rooted in Iroquois demography and social structure; my use of the term accordingly reflects a more holistic view of the cultural role of the mourning-war than does Smith's. On the dangers of an excessively psychological explanation of Indian warfare, see Jennings, *Invasion of America*, 159; but see also the convincing defense of Smith in Richard Drinnon, "Ravished Land," *Indian Historian*, 9 (Fall 1976), 24–26.

5. Joseph François Lafitau, *Customs of the American Indians Compared with the Customs of Primitive Times*, ed. and trans. William N. Fenton and Elizabeth L. Moore, 2 vols. (Toronto: Champlain Society, 1974, 1977 [orig. publ. Paris, 1724]), 2:98–99.

6. Cadwallader Colden, *The History of the Five Indian Nations of Canada, Which Are Dependent on the Province of New-York in America, and Are the Barrier between the English and French in That Part of the World* (London, 1747), 4.

7. Gabriel Sagard, *The Long Journey to the Country of the Hurons*, ed. George M. Wrong and trans. H. H. Langton (Toronto: Champlain Society, 1939 [orig. publ. Paris, 1632]), 151–152; Thwaites, ed., *Jesuit Relations*, 42:139; William N. Fenton, ed., "The Hyde Manuscript: Captain William Hyde's Observations of the 5 Nations of Indians at New York, 1698," *American Scene Magazine*, 6 (1965), [9]; Bruce G. Trigger, *The Children of Aataentsic: A History of the Huron People to 1660*, 2 vols. (Montreal: McGill-Queen's University Press, 1976), 2:68–69, 145–147.

8. Louis Hennepin, *A New Discovery of a Vast Country in America . . .* , 1st English ed., 2 vols. (London, 1698), 2:88.

9. Newcomb, "Re-Examination of Plains Warfare," 320.

10. Andrew P. Vayda, "Expansion and Warfare Among Swidden Agriculturalists," *American Anthropologist*, n.s., 63 (1961), 346–358; Anthony Leeds, "The Functions of War," in Jules Masserman, ed., *Violence and War, with Clinical Studies* (New York: Grune and Stratton, 1963), 69–82; William Tulio Divale and Marvin Harris, "Population, Warfare, and the Male Supremacist Complex," *American Anthropologist*, n.s., 78 (1976), 521–538.

11. J. N. B. Hewitt, "Orenda and a Definition of Religion," *American Anthropologist*, n.s., 4 (1902), 33–46; Morris Wolf, *Iroquois Religion and Its Relation to Their Morals* (New York: Columbia University Press, 1919), 25–26; Alvin M. Josephy, Jr., *The Indian Heritage of America* (New York: Knopf, 1968), 94; Åke Hultkrantz, *The Religions of the American Indians*, trans. Monica Setterwall (Berkeley: University of California Press, 1979), 12.

12. Thwaites, ed., *Jesuit Relations*, 23:165–169; Lafitau, *Customs of American Indians*, 1:71; B. H. Quain, "The Iroquois," in Margaret Mead, ed., *Cooperation and Competition Among Primitive Peoples* (New York: McGraw-Hill, 1937), 276–277.

13. Fenton, ed., "Hyde Manuscript," [16].

14. Philip Mazzei, *Researches on the United States*, ed. and trans. Constance B. Sherman (Charlottesville: University of Virginia Press, 1976 [orig. publ. Paris, 1788]), 349. See also P[ierre] de Charlevoix, *Journal of a Voyage to North-America . . .* , 2 vols. (London, 1761 [orig. publ. Paris, 1744]), 1:370–373, 2:33–34, and George S. Snyderman, "Behind the Tree of Peace: A Sociological Analysis of Iroquois Warfare," *Pennsylvania Archaeologist*, 18, nos. 3–4 (1948), 13–15.

15. Lafitau, *Customs of American Indians*, 2:241–245 (quotation from p. 242).

16. Thwaites, ed., *Jesuit Relations*, 10:273–275, 19:91, 43:267–271, 60:35–41. On *wergild*, see Lewis H. Morgan, *League of the Ho-dé-no-sau-nee, or Iroquois* (Rochester, N.Y., 1851), 331–333, and Jennings, *Invasion of America*, 148–149. The parallel between Iroquois practice and the Germanic tradition of blood payments should not be stretched too far; Iroquois condolence presents were an integral part of the broader condolence process.

17. Smith, "American Indian Warfare," 352–354; Anthony F. C. Wallace, *The Death and Rebirth of the Seneca* (New York: Knopf, 1970), 101. It is within the context of the mourning-war that what are usually described as Indian wars for revenge or blood feuds should be understood. The revenge motive—no doubt strong in Iroquois warfare—was only part of the larger complex of behavior and belief comprehended in the mourning-war. It should also be noted that raids might be inspired by *any* death, not just those attributable to murder or warfare and for which revenge or other atonement, such as the giving of condolence presents, was necessary. Among Euro-American observers, only the perceptive Lafitau seems to have been aware of this possibility (*Customs of American Indians*, 2:98–102, 154). I have found no other explicit contemporary discussion of this phenomenon, but several accounts indicate the formation of war parties in response to deaths from disease or other nonviolent causes. See H. P. Biggar et al., eds. and trans., *The Works of Samuel de Champlain*, 6 vols. (Toronto: Champlain Society, 1922–1936), 2:206–208; Thwaites, ed., *Jesuit Relations*, 64:91; Jasper Dankers [Danckaerts] and Peter Sluyter, *Journal of a Voyage to New York and a Tour in Several of the American Colonies in 1679–80*, trans. and ed. Henry C. Murphy, Long Island Historical Society, Memoirs, 1 (Brooklyn, N.Y., 1867), 277; and William M. Beauchamp, ed., *Moravian Journals Relating to Central New York, 1745–66* (Syracuse, N.Y.: Onondaga Historical Association, 1916), 125–126, 183–186.

18. Thwaites, ed., *Jesuit Relations*, 10:225–227; E. B. O'Callaghan and B. Fernow, eds., *Documents Relative to the Colonial History of the State of New-York*, 15 vols. (Albany, N.Y., 1856–1887), 4:22; Lafitau, *Customs of American Indians*, 2:99–103; Snyderman, "Behind the Tree of Peace," 15–20.

19. The following composite account is based on numerous contemporary reports of Iroquois treatment of captives. Among the more complete are Thwaites, ed., *Jesuit Relations*, 22:251–267, 39:57–77, 50:59–63, 54:23–35; Gideon D. Scull, ed., *Voyages of Peter Esprit Radisson: Being an Account of His Travels and Experiences among the North American Indians, from 1652 to 1684* (Boston: Prince Society, 1885), 28–60; and James H. Coyne, ed. and trans., "Exploration of the Great Lakes, 1660–1670, by Dollier de Casson and de Brehant de Galinee," Ontario Historical Society, *Papers and Records*, 4 (1903), 31–35. See also the many other portrayals in Thwaites, ed., *Jesuit Relations*; and the discussions in Lafitau, *Customs of American Indians*, 2:148–172; Nathaniel Knowles, "The Torture of Captives by the Indians of Eastern North America," American Philosophical Society, *Proceedings*, 82 (1940), 181–190; and Wallace, *Death and Rebirth of the Seneca*, 103–107.

20. The gauntlet and the public humiliation and physical abuse of captives also served as initiation rites for prospective adoptees; see John Heckewelder, "An Account of the History, Manners, and Customs of the Indian Nations Who Once Inhabited Pennsylvania and the Neighbouring States," American Philosophical Society, *Transactions of the Historical and Literary Committee*, 1 (1819), 211–213. For a fuller discussion of Indian methods of indoctrinating adoptees, see James

Axtell, "The White Indians of Colonial America," *William and Mary Quarterly*, 3rd ser., 32 (1975), 55–88.

21. Usually only adult male captives were executed, and most women and children seem to have escaped physical abuse. Occasionally, however, the Iroquois did torture and execute women and children. See Scull, ed., *Voyages of Radisson*, 56, and Thwaites, ed., *Jesuit Relations*, 39:219–221, 42:97–99, 51:213, 231–233, 52:79, 157–159, 53:253, 62:59, 64:127–129, 65:33–39.

22. Several authors—from James Adair and Philip Mazzei in the eighteenth century to W. Arens in 1979—have denied that the Iroquois engaged in cannibalism (Adair, *The History of the American Indians . . .* [London, 1775], 209; Mazzei, *Researches*, 359; Arens, *The Man-Eating Myth: Anthropology and Anthropophagy* [New York: Oxford University Press, 1979], 127–129). Arens is simply wrong, as Thomas S. Abler has shown in "Iroquois Cannibalism: Fact Not Fiction," *Ethnohistory*, 27 (1980), 309–316. Adair and Mazzei, from the perspective of the late eighteenth century, were on firmer ground; by then the Five Nations apparently had abandoned anthropophagy. See Adolph B. Benson, ed., *Peter Kalm's Travels in North America* (New York: Wilson-Erickson, 1937), 694.

23. Robert L. Rands and Carroll L. Riley, "Diffusion and Discontinuous Distribution," *American Anthropologist*, n.s., 60 (1958), 284–289; Maurice R. Davie, *The Evolution of War: A Study of Its Role in Early Societies* (New Haven, Conn.: Yale University Press, 1929), 36–38; Hennepin, *New Discovery*, 2:92.

24. Thwaites, ed., *Jesuit Relations*, 62:85–87, 67:173; Knowles, "Torture of Captives," 210–211.

25. Thwaites, ed., *Jesuit Relations*, 19:81.

26. O'Callaghan and Fernow, eds., *Documents Relative to New-York*, 5:274.

27. Biggar et al., eds., *Works of Champlain*, 4:330; Charlevoix, *Voyage to North-America*, 1:316–333.

28. Thwaites, ed., *Jesuit Relations*, 39:221.

29. Biggar et al., eds., *Works of Champlain*, 3:73–74; Thwaites, ed., *Jesuit Relations*, 32:159.

30. Thwaites, ed., *Jesuit Relations*, 10:145, 39:29–31; J. N. B. Hewitt, "The Iroquoian Concept of the Soul," *Journal of American Folk-Lore*, 8 (1895), 107–116.

31. Sagard, *Long Journey*, 152–156; Thwaites, ed., *Jesuit Relations*, 22:309–311, 32:173–175, 34:197, 55:79, 56:273; Hennepin, *New Discovery*, 2:86–94; Patrick Mitchell Malone, "Indian and English Military Systems in New England in the Seventeenth Century" (Ph.D. diss., Brown University, 1971), 33–38.

32. Lafitau, *Customs of American Indians*, 2:98.

33. Paul A. W. Wallace, *The White Roots of Peace* (Philadelphia: University of Pennsylvania Press, 1946); A. F. C. Wallace, *Death and Rebirth of the Seneca*, 39–48, 93–98; William M. Beauchamp, *Civil, Religious and Mourning Councils and Ceremonies of Adoption of the New York Indians*, New York State Museum Bulletin 113 (Albany, N.Y., 1907). For a suggestive discussion of Indian definitions of peace, see John Phillip Reid, *A Better Kind of Hatchet: Law, Trade, and Diplomacy in the Cherokee Nation During the Early Years of European Contact* (University Park: Pennsylvania State University Press, 1976), 9–17.

34. On the devastating impact of European diseases—some Indian populations may have declined by a factor of 20 to 1 within a century or so of contact—see the works surveyed in Russell Thornton, "American Indian Historical Demography: A Review Essay with Suggestions for Future Research," *American Indian Culture and Research Journal*, 3, no. 1 (1979), 69–74.

35. Trigger, *Children of Aataentsic*, 2:602; Cornelius J. Jaenen, *Friend and Foe: Aspects of French Amerindian Cultural Contact in the Sixteenth and Seventeenth Centuries* (New York: Columbia

University Press, 1976), 100. Most of the early Iroquois epidemics went unrecorded by Europeans, but major smallpox epidemics are documented for the Mohawks in 1634 and the Senecas in 1640–1641; see [Harmen Meyndertsz van den Bogaert], "Narrative of a Journey into the Mohawk and Oneida Country, 1634–1635," in J. Franklin Jameson, ed., *Narratives of New Netherland, 1609–1664* (New York: Charles Scribner's Sons, 1909), 140–141; and Thwaites, ed., *Jesuit Relations*, 21:211.

36. Thwaites, ed., *Jesuit Relations*, 30:273, 44:43, 47:193, 205, 48:79–83, 50:63, 54:79–81, 57:81–83, 60:175.

37. Biggar et al., eds., *Works of Champlain*, 2:95–100; Malone, "Indian and English Military Systems," 179–200; Jennings, *Invasion of America*, 165–166. After the introduction of firearms the Iroquois continued to raise armies of several hundred to a thousand men, but they almost never engaged them in set battles. Large armies ensured safe travel to distant battlegrounds and occasionally intimidated outnumbered opponents, but when they neared their objective they usually broke into small raiding parties. See Daniel Gookin, "Historical Collections of the Indians in New England" (1674), Massachusetts Historical Society, *Collections*, 1 (1792), 162, and Cadwallader Colden, *The History of the Five Indian Nations Depending on the Province of New-York in America* (New York, 1727), 8–10.

38. O'Callaghan and Fernow, eds., *Documents Relative to New-York*, 150; "Journal of New Netherland, 1647," in Jameson, ed., *Narratives of New Netherland*, 274; Thwaites, ed., *Jesuit Relations*, 24:295; Carl P. Russell, *Guns on the Early Frontiers: A History of Firearms from Colonial Times Through the Years of the Western Fur Trade* (Berkeley: University of California Press, 1957), 11–15, 62–66.

39. Thwaites, ed., *Jesuit Relations*, 27:71, 45:205–207; Elisabeth Tooker, "The Iroquois Defeat of the Huron: A Review of Causes," *Pennsylvania Archaeologist*, 33 (1963), 115–123; Keith F. Otterbein, "Why the Iroquois Won: An Analysis of Iroquois Military Tactics," *Ethnohistory*, 11 (1964), 56–63; John K. Mahon, "Anglo-American Methods of Indian Warfare, 1676–1794," *Mississippi Valley Historical Review*, 45 (1958), 255.

40. Bruce G. Trigger, "The Mohawk-Mahican War (1624–28): The Establishment of a Pattern," *Canadian Historical Review*, 52 (1971), 276–286.

41. Harold A. Innis, *The Fur Trade in Canada: An Introduction to Canadian Economic History* (New Haven, Conn.: Yale University Press, 1930), 1–4, 32–33; Hunt, *Wars of the Iroquois*, 33–37; John Witthoft, "Ancestry of the Susquehannocks," in John Witthoft and W. Fred Kinsey III, eds., *Susquehannock Miscellany* (Harrisburg: Pennsylvania Historical and Museum Commission, 1959), 34–35; Thomas Elliot Norton, *The Fur Trade in Colonial New York, 1686–1776* (Madison: University of Wisconsin Press, 1974), 9–15.

42. The classic account of the beaver wars is Hunt, *Wars of the Iroquois*, but three decades of subsequent scholarship have overturned many of that work's interpretations. See Allen W. Trelease, "The Iroquois and the Western Fur Trade: A Problem in Interpretation," *Mississippi Valley Historical Review*, 49 (1962), 32–51; Raoul Naroll, "The Causes of the Fourth Iroquois War," *Ethnohistory*, 16 (1969), 51–81; Allan Forbes, Jr., "Two and a Half Centuries of Conflict: The Iroquois and the Laurentian Wars," *Pennsylvania Archaeologist*, 40, nos. 3–4 (1970), 1–20; William N. Fenton, "The Iroquois in History," in Eleanor Burke Leacock and Nancy Oestreich Lurie, eds., *North American Indians in Historical Perspective* (New York: Random House, 1971), 139–145; Karl H. Schlesier, "Epidemics and Indian Middlemen: Rethinking the Wars of the Iroquois, 1609–1653," *Ethnohistory*, 23 (1976), 129–145; and Trigger, *Children of Aataentsic*, esp. 2:617–664.

43. Biggar, ed., *Works of Champlain*, 2:31–32; see also 2:118–119, 186–191, 246–285, 3:207–228.

44. Ibid., 2:65–107, 120–138, 3: 48–81.

45. Thwaites, ed., *Jesuit Relations*, vols. 31–50, passim; Robert A. Goldstein, *French-Iroquois Diplomatic and Military Relations, 1609–1701* (The Hague: Mouton, 1969), 62–99. The actual Canadian death toll in wars with the Iroquois before 1666 has been shown to have been quite low. Only 153 French were killed in raids, while 143 were taken prisoner (perhaps 38 of those died in captivity); John A. Dickinson, "La guerre iroquoise et la mortalité en Nouvelle-France, 1608–1666," *Revue d'histoire de l'amérique française*, 36 (1982), 31–54. On seventeenth-century French captives of the Iroquois, see Daniel K. Richter, *The Ordeal of the Longhouse: The Peoples of the Iroquois League in the Era of European Colonization* (Chapel Hill: University of North Carolina Press, 1992), 64–69, 210.

46. Thwaites, ed., *Jesuit Relations*, 50:127–147, 239; O'Callaghan and Fernow, eds., *Documents Relative to New-York*, 3:121–127; A. J. F. van Laer, trans. and ed., *Correspondence of Jeremias van Rensselaer, 1651–1674* (Albany: University of the State of New York, 1932), 388.

47. Thwaites, ed., *Jesuit Relations*, 35:183–205, 36:177–191, 41:43–65, 43:115–125, 187–207, 44:69–77, 165–167, 187–191; A. J. F. van Laer, trans. and ed., *Minutes of the Court of Fort Orange and Beverwyck, 1657–1660*, 2 vols. (Albany: University of the State of New York, 1923), 2:45–48; Scull, ed., *Voyages of Radisson*, 93–119; Nicholas Perrot, "Memoir on the Manners, Customs, and Religion of the Savages of North America" (c. 1680–1718), in Emma Helen Blair, ed. and trans., *The Indian Tribes of the Upper Mississippi Valley and Region of the Great Lakes . . .* , 2 vols. (Cleveland, Ohio: Arthur H. Clark Co., 1911), 1:148–193.

48. Thwaites, ed., *Jesuit Relations*, 47:139–153.

49. Ibid., 43:265.

50. Ibid., 45:207, 51:123, 187.

51. O'Callaghan and Fernow, eds., *Documents Relative to New-York*, 9:80; Victor Konrad, "An Iroquois Frontier: The North Shore of Lake Ontario During the Late Seventeenth Century," *Journal of Historical Geography*, 7 (1981), 129–144.

52. Thwaites, ed., *Jesuit Relations*, 51:81–85, 167–257, 52:53–55.

53. Ibid., 55:61–63, 57:133–141, 58:211, 60:187–195.

54. Ibid., 53:281–283.

55. Ibid., 56:29, 58:247–253, 60:145–147, 61:195–199, 63:141–189.

56. Ibid., 55:33–37, 58:75–77.

57. E. B. O'Callaghan, ed., *The Documentary History of the State of New-York*, octavo ed., 4 vols. (Albany, N.Y., 1849–1851), 1:12–14; Thwaites, ed., *Jesuit Relations*, 24:295. Reflecting the purposes of most Euro-Americans who made estimates of Indian population, figures are usually given in terms of the number of available fighting men. The limited data available for direct comparisons of estimates of Iroquois fighting strength with estimates of total population indicate that the ratio of one warrior for every four people proposed in Sherburne F. Cook, "Interracial Warfare and Population Decline Among the New England Indians," *Ethnohistory*, 20 (1973), 13, applies to the Five Nations. Compare the estimates of a total Mohawk population of 560–580 in William Andrews to the Secretary of the Society for the Propagation of the Gospel in Foreign Parts, 7 September 1713, 17 October 1715, Records of the Society for the Propagation of the Gospel, Letterbooks, Ser. A, 8:186, 11:268–269, S.P.G. Archives, London (microfilm ed.), with the concurrent estimates of approximately 150 Mohawk warriors in Bernardus Freeman to the Secretary of S.P.G., 28 May 1712, ibid., 7:203; Peter Wraxall, *An Abridgement of the Indian Affairs . . . Transacted in the Colony of New York, from the Year 1678 to the Year 1751*, ed. Charles Howard McIlwain (Cambridge, Mass.: Harvard University Press, 1915), 69; O'Callaghan and Fernow, eds., *Documents Relative to New-York*, 5:272; and Lawrence H. Leder, ed., *The Livingston Indian Records, 1666–1723* (Gettysburg: Pennsylvania Historical Association, 1956), 220.

58. The estimate of 10,000 for the 1640s is from Trigger, *Children of Aataentsic*, 1:98; the figure of 8,600 for the 1670s is calculated from Wentworth Greenhalgh's 1677 estimate of 2,150 Iroquois warriors, in O'Callaghan, ed., *Documentary History of New-York*, 1:12–14. Compare the late 1670s estimate in Hennepin, *New Discovery*, 2:92–93, and see the tables of seventeenth- and eighteenth-century Iroquois warrior populations in Snyderman, "Behind the Tree of Peace," 42; Bruce G. Trigger, ed., *Northeast*, in William C. Sturtevant, ed., *Handbook of North American Indians*, 15 (Washington, D.C.: U.S. Government Printing Office, 1978), 421; and Gunther Michelson, "Iroquois Population Statistics," *Man in the Northeast*, no. 14 (1977), 3–17. William Starna has suggested that all previous estimates for 1635 and earlier of the Mohawk—and by implication Five Nations—population are drastically understated ("Mohawk Iroquois Populations: A Revision," *Ethnohistory*, 27 [1980], 371–382).

59. Thwaites, ed., *Jesuit Relations*, 62:71–95 (quotation from p. 83).

60. Leder, ed., *Livingston Indian Records*, 35–38; Allen W. Trelease, *Indian Affairs in Colonial New York: The Seventeenth Century* (Ithaca, N.Y.: Cornell University Press, 1960), 229–230; Francis Jennings, "Glory, Death, and Transfiguration: The Susquehannock Indians in the Seventeenth Century," *Proceedings of the American Philosophical Society*, 112 (1968), 15–53.

61. Thwaites, ed., *Jesuit Relations*, 56:43–45, 59:251, 60:211, 62:185; Hennepin, *New Discovery*, 1:100–295. Although the western nations had been included in the Franco-Iroquois peace of 1667, skirmishing in the west had never totally ceased; see Thwaites, ed., *Jesuit Relations*, 53:39–51, 54:219–227, and O'Callaghan and Fernow, eds., *Documents Relative to New-York*, 9:79–80.

62. Baron [de] Lahontan, *New Voyages to North-America . . .* , 2 vols. (London, 1703), 1:41.

63. Thwaites, ed., *Jesuit Relations*, 62:71.

64. For fuller accounts of the complex diplomacy, intrigue, trade wars, and military conflicts concerning the west between 1675 and 1689 touched on in the following paragraphs, see, from a Canadian perspective, W. J. Eccles, *Frontenac: The Courtier Governor* (Toronto: McClelland and Stewart, 1959), 99–229, and from a New York perspective, Trelease, *Indian Affairs in Colonial New York*, 204–301. A discussion of the Iroquois role is Richard Aquila, *The Iroquois Restoration: Iroquois Diplomacy on the Colonial Frontier, 1701–1754* (Detroit, Mich.: Wayne State University Press, 1983), 43–81.

65. O'Callaghan and Fernow, eds., *Documents Relative to New-York*, 3:254–259; Francis Paul Jennings, "Miquon's Passing: Indian-European Relations in Colonial Pennsylvania, 1674 to 1755" (Ph.D. diss., University of Pennsylvania, 1965), 10–50; Douglas Edward Leach, *Flintlock and Tomahawk: New England in King Philip's War* (New York: Macmillan, 1958), 59–60, 176–177.

66. O'Callaghan, ed., *Documentary History of New-York*, 1:391–420; Wraxall, *Abridgement of Indian Affairs*, 10; Helen Broshar, "The First Push Westward of the Albany Traders," *Mississippi Valley Historical Review*, 7 (1920), 228–241; Henry Allain St. Paul, "Governor Thomas Dongan's Expansion Policy," *Mid-America*, 17 (1935), 172–184, 236– 272; Gary B. Nash, "The Quest for the Susquehanna Valley: New York, Pennsylvania, and the Seventeenth-Century Fur Trade," *New York History*, 48 (1967), 3–27; Daniel K. Richter, "Rediscovered Links in the Covenant Chain: Previously Unpublished Transcripts of New York Indian Treaty Minutes, 1677–1691," *Proceedings of the American Antiquarian Society*, 92 (1982), 63–66.

67. Hennepin, *New Discovery*, 1:20–144; Lahontan, *New Voyages*, 1:269–274; Thwaites, ed., *Jesuit Relations*, 62:151–165; O'Callaghan and Fernow, eds., *Documents Relative to New-York*, 9:296–303.

68. O'Callaghan and Fernow, eds., *Documents Relative to New-York*, 3:417.

69. Ibid., 9:234–248, 358–369, 550–561, 639–656; Thwaites, ed., *Jesuit Relations*, 63:269–281,

64:239–259, 65:25–29; Lahontan, *New Voyages*, 1:29–45, 68–80; Francis Parkman, *Count Frontenac and New France under Louis XIV* (Boston: Little, Brown, 1877), 89–115, 139–157, 309–316, 410–417.

70. O'Callaghan and Fernow, eds., *Documents Relative to New-York*, 3:814–816.

71. Ibid., 4:38–39.

72. Ibid., 9:531–535 (quotation from p. 531).

73. Leder, ed., *Livingston Indian Records*, 172–174; O'Callaghan and Fernow, eds., *Documents Relative to New-York*, 9:599–632; Colden, *History of the Five Indian Nations of Canada*, 180–181.

74. Leder, ed., *Livingston Indian Records*, 136–137.

75. Ibid., 139–140; Thwaites, ed., *Jesuit Relations*, 63:279, 287–289, 64:249–259, 65:29; O'Callaghan and Fernow, eds., *Documents Relative to New-York*, 9:503–504, 538, 554–555.

76. Treaty Minutes, 17 June 1689, untitled notebook, Indians of North America, Miscellaneous Papers, 1620–1895, Manuscript Collections, American Antiquarian Society, Worcester, Massachusetts.

77. Richard A. Preston, trans., and Leopold Lamontagne, ed., *Royal Fort Frontenac* (Toronto: Champlain Society, 1958), 175–180; Lahontan, *New Voyages*, 1:98–102, 147–151; O'Callaghan and Fernow, eds., *Documents Relative to New-York*, 9:434–438; Eccles, *Frontenac*, 186–197. English sources claimed 200 French deaths and 120 captures at Lachine (Trelease, *Indian Affairs in Colonial New York*, 297–298).

78. Treaty Minutes, 2 August 1684, untitled notebook, Indians of North America.

79. O'Callaghan, ed., *Documentary History of New-York*, 1:284–319, 2:130–132; Leder, ed., *Livingston Indian Records*, 158–160.

80. O'Callaghan, ed., *Documentary History of New-York*, 2:164–290; O'Callaghan and Fernow, eds., *Documents Relative to New-York*, 3:800–805, 4:193–196, 9:513–515, 520–524.

81. O'Callaghan and Fernow, eds., *Documents Relative to New-York*, 3:836–844; Leder, ed., *Livingston Indian Records*, 165–166; O'Callaghan, ed., *Documentary History of New-York*, 1:323–325, 341–345; Herbert L. Osgood, *The American Colonies in the Eighteenth Century*, 4 vols. (New York, 1924), 1:228–265.

82. O'Callaghan and Fernow, eds., *Documents Relative to New-York*, 4:6–7, 14–24, 222; Colden, *History of the Five Indian Nations of Canada*, 142–150.

83. O'Callaghan, *Documents Relative to New-York*, 9:384–393, 515–517, 565–572, 596–599; Thwaites, ed., *Jesuit Relations*, 64:143–145.

84. O'Callaghan and Fernow, eds., *Documents Relative to New-York*, 3:841–844; see also 4:77–98, 279–282.

85. Thwaites, ed., *Jesuit Relations*, 64:259.

86. O'Callaghan and Fernow, eds., *Documents Relative to New-York*, 9:601–671.

87. Trelease, *Indian Affairs in Colonial New York*, 323–342; O'Callaghan and Fernow, eds., *Documents Relative to New-York*, 4:367–374, 402–409.

88. Leroy V. Eid, "The Ojibwa-Iroquois War: The War the Five Nations Did Not Win," *Ethnohistory*, 26 (1979), 297–324; Wraxall, *Abridgement of Indian Affairs*, 29–30; O'Callaghan, *Documents Relative to New-York*, 9:681–688, 708–709.

89. Aquila, *Iroquois Restoration*, 70–80.

90. A 1698 report on New York's suffering during the War of the League of Augsburg states that there were 2,550 Iroquois warriors in 1689 and only 1,230 in 1698. The report probably contains some polemical overstatement: the first figure seems too high and the second too low. By comparison, 2,050 Iroquois warriors were estimated by Denonville in 1685, 1,400 by Bellomont in 1691, 1,750

by Bernardus Freeman in 1700, and 1,200 by a French cabinet paper in 1701 (O'Callaghan, *Documents Relative to New-York*, 4:337, 768, 9:281, 725; Freeman to the Secretary, 28 May 1712, Records of S.P.G., Letterbooks, Ser. A, 7:203). If the figure of 1,750 warriors cited by Freeman—a minister who worked with the Mohawks—is correct, the total Iroquois population in 1700 was approximately 7,000, calculated by the ratio in note 57, above.

91. Thwaites, ed., *Jesuit Relations*, 44:59–61.

92. O'Callaghan and Fernow, eds., *Documents Relative to New-York*, 4:648–661, 689–690.

93. Trigger, *Children of Aataentsic*, 2:709–724. See also the discussions of Indian factionalism in Robert F. Berkhofer, Jr., "The Political Context of a New Indian History," *Pacific Historical Review*, 40 (1971), 373–380; and Edward H. Spicer, *Cycles of Conquest: The Impact of Spain, Mexico, and the United States on the Indians of the Southwest, 1533–1960* (Tucson: University of Arizona Press, 1962), 491–501.

94. Anthony F. C. Wallace, "Origins of Iroquois Neutrality: The Grand Settlement of 1701," *Pennsylvania History*, 24 (1957), 223–235. The best reconstruction of the Iroquois diplomacy that led to the Grand Settlement is Richard L. Haan, "The Covenant Chain: Iroquois Diplomacy on the Niagara Frontier, 1697–1730" (Ph.D. diss., University of California, Santa Barbara, 1976), 64–147.

95. Bacqueville de La Potherie, *Histoire de l'Amerique Septentrionale*, 4 (Paris, 1722), passim; O'Callaghan and Fernow, eds., *Documents Relative to New-York*, 9:715–725.

96. O'Callaghan and Fernow, eds., *Documents Relative to New-York*, 4:889–911; *Minutes of the Provincial Council of Pennsylvania, from the Organization to the Termination of the Proprietary Government*, 10 vols. (Harrisburg, Pa., 1851–1852), 2:142–143; William M. Beauchamp, *A History of the New York Iroquois, Now Commonly Called the Six Nations*, New York State Museum Bulletin 78 (Albany, N.Y., 1905), 256; Jennings, "Miquon's Passing," 118–121.

97. Eid, "Ojibwa-Iroquois War," 297–324.

98. Aquila, *Iroquois Restoration*, 85–204; Richard Haan, "The Problem of Iroquois Neutrality: Suggestions for Revision," *Ethnohistory*, 27 (1980), 317–330.

99. O'Callaghan and Fernow, eds., *Documents Relative to New-York*, 5:724–725.

100. Leder, ed., *Livingston Indian Records*, 192–200; O'Callaghan and Fernow, eds., *Documents Relative to New-York*, 9:759–765, 848–849, 876–878; Yves F. Zoltvany, "New France and the West, 1701–1713," *Canadian Historical Review*, 46 (1965), 315–321.

101. Wraxall, *Abridgement of Indian Affairs*, 44–67; Cadwallader Colden, "Continuation of Colden's History of the Five Indian Nations, for the Years 1707 through 1720," *Collections of the New-York Historical Society*, 68 (1935), 360–367; Haan, "Covenant Chain," 152–153.

102. Wraxall, *Abridgement of Indian Affairs*, 64–69; O'Callaghan and Fernow, eds., *Documents Relative to New-York*, 9:902; Leder, ed., *Livingston Indian Records*, 207–210; Colden, "Continuation of History," 370–380.

103. Colden, "Continuation of History," 398–409; O'Callaghan and Fernow, eds., *Documents Relative to New-York*, 5:242–249, 267–277; G. M. Waller, "New York's Role in Queen Anne's War, 1702–1713," *New York History*, 33 (1952), 40–53; Bruce T. McCully, "Catastrophe in the Wilderness: New Light on the Canada Expedition of 1709," *William and Mary Quarterly*, 3rd ser., 11 (1954), 441–456; Haan, "Covenant Chain," 148–198.

104. O'Callaghan and Fernow, eds., *Documents Relative to New-York*, 5:372–376, 382–388, 437, 484–487; Wraxall, *Abridgement of Indian Affairs*, 98–105.

105. O'Callaghan and Fernow, eds., *Documents Relative to New-York*, 5:445–446, 584; Colden, "Continuation of History," 414–432; Haan, "Problem of Iroquois Neutrality," 324.

106. O'Callaghan and Fernow, eds., *Documents Relative to New-York*, 5:545, 569, 632, 9:816;

Thomas Barclay to Robert Hunter, 26 January 1713 (extract), Records of S.P.G., Letterbooks, Ser. A, 8:251–252. For examples of Claeson's and Joncaire's activities, see Colden, "Continuation of History," 360–363, 432–434, and O'Callaghan and Fernow, eds., *Documents Relative to New-York*, 5:538, 562–569, 9:759–765, 814, 876–903.

107. O'Callaghan and Fernow, eds., *Documents Relative to New-York*, 5:217–227; Colden, "Continuation," 408–409; Wraxall, *Abridgement of Indian Affairs*, 79n–80n.

108. The evolution of Iroquois, French, and English policies concerning Niagara and Oswego may be followed in O'Callaghan and Fernow, eds., *Documents Relative to New-York*, vol. 5, passim, 9:897–1016; Jennings, "Miquon's Passing," 256–274; and Haan, "Covenant Chain," 199–237.

109. Andrews to the Secretary, 11 October 1716, Records of S.P.G., Letterbooks, Ser. A, 12:241; O'Callaghan and Fernow, eds., *Documents Relative to New-York*, 5:484–487, 9:878.

110. Thwaites, ed., *Jesuit Relations*, 66:203–207, 67:39–41; O'Callaghan and Fernow, eds., *Documents Relative to New-York*, 9:882– 884; George F. G. Stanley, "The Policy of 'Francisation' as Applied to the Indians during the Ancien Regime," *Revue d'histoire de l'amérique française*, 3 (1949–1950), 333–348; Cornelius J. Jaenen, "The Frenchification and Evangelization of the Amerindians in the Seventeenth Century New France" (sic), Canadian Catholic Historical Association, *Study Sessions*, 35 (1969), 57–71.

111. Thwaites, ed., *Jesuit Relations*, 67:27.

112. Andrews to the Secretary, 20 April 1716, 23 April 1717, Records of S.P.G., Letterbooks, Ser. A, 11:319–320, 12:310–312.

113. Henry R. Schoolcraft, *Notes on the Iroquois: Or, Contributions to the Statistics, Aboriginal History, Antiquities and General Ethnology of Western New York* (New York, 1846), 148–149; Fenton, "Iroquois in History," 147–148; Beauchamp, *History of New York Iroquois*, 139.

114. On Iroquois-"Flathead" conflicts before 1710, see Colden, *History of the Five Indian Nations Depending on New-York*, 30– 71; Colden, "Continuation of History," 361–363; and Wraxall, *Abridgement of Indian Affairs*, 50–61. References to raids after 1710 in O'Callaghan and Fernow, eds., *Documents Relative to New-York*, and other sources are too numerous to cite here; a useful discussion is Aquila, *Iroquois Restoration*, 205–232.

115. Wraxall, *Abridgement of Indian Affairs*, 94–96; O'Callaghan, *Documents Relative to New-York*, 5:372–376, 382–388, 484–493; Verner W. Crane, *The Southern Frontier, 1670–1732* (Durham, N.C.: Duke University Press, 1928), 158–161.

116. O'Callaghan and Fernow, eds., *Documents Relative to New-York*, 5:542–545, 562–569, 635–640.

117. Ibid., 9:876–878, 884–885, 1085, 1097–1098.

118. Colden, "Continuation of History," 382–383, brackets in original.

119. For examples of shifting New York policies regarding the Iroquois southern campaigns, see O'Callaghan and Fernow, eds., *Documents Relative to New-York*, 5:446–464, 542–545; and Wraxall, *Abridgement of Indian Affairs*, 123.

120. Andrews to the Secretary, 20 April 1716, Records of S.P.G., Letterbooks, Ser. A., 11:320.

Chapter 5. Dutch Dominos

An early version of this chapter was presented at a conference on "'Transformations: The Atlantic World in the Late Seventeenth Century," Harvard University, 31 March 2006.

1. Reuben Gold Thwaites, ed., *The Jesuit Relations and Allied Documents: Travels and*

Explorations of the Jesuit Missionaries in New France, 1610–1791 (Cleveland: Burrows Brothers, 1896–1901), 21:117, 22:305.

2. Jaap Jacobs, *New Netherland: A Dutch Colony in Seventeenth-Century America* (Leiden: Brill, 2005), 475; Alan Taylor, *American Colonies* (New York: Viking, 2001), 248; C. R. Boxer, *The Dutch Seaborne Empire: 1600–1800* (New York: Knopf, 1965), 321, 325.

3. Oliver A. Rink, *Holland on the Hudson: An Economic and Social History of Dutch New York* (Ithaca, N.Y.: Cornell University Press, 1986), 50–68, 94–116, 172–213 (quotations from pp. 62, 61); Jacobs, *New Netherland*, 261.

4. Rink, *Holland on the Hudson*, 160–164; Ira Berlin, *Many Thousands Gone: The First Two Centuries of Slavery in North America* (Cambridge, Mass.: Harvard University Press, 1998), 18–22, 29, 50–51.

5. John R. Pagden, "Dutch Maritime and Commercial Activity in Mid-Seventeenth-Century Virginia," *Virginia Magazine of History and Biography*, 90 (1982), 485–501; Cathy Matson, *Merchants and Empire: Trading in Colonial New York* (Baltimore: Johns Hopkins University Press, 1998), 17–25; April Lee Hatfield, *Atlantic Virginia: Intercolonial Relations in the Seventeenth Century* (Philadelphia: University of Pennsylvania Press, 2004), 48–51, 99–102; Christian J. Koot, *Empire at the Periphery: British Colonists, Anglo-Dutch Trade, and the Development of the British Atlantic, 1621–1713* (New York: New York University Press, 2011), 17–83; Jacobs, *New Netherland*, 228–233, 261; Warren M. Billings, *Sir William Berkeley and the Forging of Colonial Virginia* (Baton Rouge: Louisiana State University Press, 2004), 77, 126–127 (quotation), 140.

6. Lawrence Averell Harper, *The English Navigation Laws: A Seventeenth-Century Experiment in Social Engineering* (New York: Columbia University Press, 1939), 34–39 (quotation from p. 49); John J. McCusker and Russell R. Menard, *The Economy of British America, 1607–1789* (Chapel Hill: University of North Carolina Press, 1985), 46–50; Carla Gardina Pestana, *The English Atlantic in an Age of Revolution, 1640–1664* (Cambridge, Mass.: Harvard University Press, 2004), 99–100, 170–177.

7. Kenneth J. Banks, *Chasing Empire Across the Sea* (Montreal: McGill-Queen's University Press, 2002), 22–27; Billings, *Sir William Berkeley*, 101, 114–115, 132–133, 160–161.

8. Lynn Ceci, "The First Fiscal Crisis of New York," *Economic Development and Cultural Change*, 28 (1980), 839–847; Ceci, "Native Wampum as a Peripheral Resource in the Seventeenth-Century World-System," in Laurence M. Hauptman and James D. Wherry, eds., *The Pequots in Southern New England: The Fall and Rise of an American Indian Nation* (Norman: University of Oklahoma Press, 1990), 48–63; Neal Salisbury, "Toward the Covenant Chain: Iroquois and Southern New England Algonquians, 1637–1684," in Daniel K. Richter and James H. Merrell, eds., *Beyond the Covenant Chain: The Iroquois and Their Neighbors in Indian North America, 1600–1800* (Syracuse, N.Y., 1987), 61–65.

9. Thwaites, ed. *Jesuit Relations*, 28:111 (1st quotation), 21:117 (2nd quotation), 22:305; Daniel K. Richter, *The Ordeal of the Longhouse: The Peoples of the Iroquois League in the Era of European Colonization* (Chapel Hill: University of North Carolina Press, 1992), 60–65, 75–98.

10. Thwaites, ed., *Jesuit Relations*, 28:107 (1st quotation); Francis Jennings, "Glory, Death, and Transfiguration: The Susquehannock Indians in the Seventeenth Century," *Proceedings of the American Philosophical Society*, 112 (1968), 17–23 (2nd quotation from p. 21); Karen Ordahl Kupperman, "Scandinavian Colonists Confront the New World," in Carol E. Hoffecker et al., eds., *New Sweden in America* (Newark: University of Delaware Press, 1995), 94–105.

11. E. B. O'Callaghan and B. Fernow, eds., *Documents Relative to the Colonial History of the State of New-York*, 15 vols. (Albany, N.Y., 1853–1887), 12:40.

12. Albert Cook Myers, ed., *Narratives of Early Pennsylvania, West New Jersey, and*

Delaware, 1630–1707 (New York: Charles Scribner's Sons, 1912), 104–105 (1st quotation), 124–127 (2nd quotation).

13. Myers, ed., *Narratives of Early Pennsylvania*, 97–101, 120, 133.

14. Ibid., 98, 144–145, 145n, 158–159, 162 (quotation); Stellan Dahlgren and Hans Norman, *The Rise and Fall of New Sweden: Governor Johan Risingh's Journal, 1654–1655, in Its Historical Context* (Uppsala: Almqvist and Wisell International, 1988), 207–209, 231–235; Amandus Johnson, *The Swedish Settlements on the Delaware: Their History and Relation to the Indians, Dutch and English* (Philadelphia: Swedish Colonial Society, 1911), 309–318, 380–449, 572–580.

15. Myers, ed., *Narratives of Early Pennsylvania*, 96–97 (quotation), 120; 157n; Dahlgren and Norman, *Rise and Fall of New Sweden*, 185–187; Johnson, *Swedish Settlements*, 317–318, 332, 516.

16. Jennings, "Glory, Death, and Transfiguration," 23.

17. O'Callaghan and Fernow, eds., *Documents Relative to New-York*, 12:98–99; Johnson, *Swedish Settlements*, 571; Allen W. Trelease, *Indian Affairs in Colonial New York: The Seventeenth Century* (Ithaca, N.Y.: Cornell University Press, 1960), 138–174; Kupperman, "Scandinavian Colonists," 105–106.

18. John J. McCusker, *Money and Exchange in Europe and America, 1600–1775* (Chapel Hill: University of North Carolina Press, 1978), 157, 157n; Ceci, "First Fiscal Crisis," 846–847; Thomas J. Burke, "The New Netherland Fur Trade, 1657–1661: Response to Crisis," *de Halve Maen*, 59 (March 1986), 1–4, 21; Jacobs, *New Netherland*, 191–197; O'Callaghan and Fernow, eds., *Documents Relative to New-York*, 14:448–453 (quotation from p. 450).

19. Richter, *Ordeal of the Longhouse*, 98–102, 134–135; Thwaites, ed., *Jesuit Relations*, 57:25 (quotation).

20. See Chapter 4 in this volume, and Richter, *Ordeal of the Longhouse*, 133–166.

21. Richard White, *The Middle Ground: Indians, Empires, and Republics in the Great Lakes Region, 1650–1815* (Cambridge: Cambridge University Press, 1991), 1–33.

22. James D. Drake, *King Philip's War: Civil War in New England, 1675–1676* (Amherst: University of Massachusetts Press, 1999), esp. 35–56; Neal Salisbury, "Introduction: Mary Rowlandson and Her Removes," in Mary Rowlandson, *The Sovereignty and Goodness of God, Together with the Faithfulness of His Promises Displayed*, ed. Salisbury (Boston: Bedford Books, 1997), 2 (2nd quotation).

23. Neal Salisbury, "Social Relationships on a Moving Frontier: Natives and Settlers in Southern New England, 1638–1675," *Man in the Northeast*, no. 33 (1987), 89–99; Jenny Hale Pulsipher, *Subjects unto the Same King: Indians, English, and the Contest for Authority in Colonial New England* (Philadelphia: University of Pennsylvania Press, 2005), 70–82, 94–100.

24. Russell Bourne, *The Red King's Rebellion: Racial Politics in New England, 1675–1678* (New York: Oxford University Press, 1991), 89.

25. Francis Jennings, *The Invasion of America: Indians, Colonialism, and the Cant of Conquest* (Chapel Hill: University of North Carolina Press, 1975), 254–326; Jill Lepore, *The Name of War: King Philip's War and the Origins of American Identity* (New York: Knopf, 1998), 21–26; Drake, *King Philip's War*, 16–74.

26. Charles H. Lincoln, ed., *Narratives of the Indian Wars, 1675–1699* (New York: Charles Scribner's Sons, 1913), 9–11.

27. Edmund S. Morgan, *American Slavery, American Freedom: The Ordeal of Colonial Virginia* (New York: W. W. Norton, 1975), 196–204, 269 (quotation); James Horn, *Adapting to a New World: English Society in the Seventeenth-Century Chesapeake* (Chapel Hill: University of North Carolina Press, 1994), 143, 155–159.

28. Quoted in Horn, *Adapting to a New World*, 156. McCusker and Menard warn against

attributing too much influence to the Navigation Acts in the fall of tobacco prices (*Economy of British America*, 123), but nonetheless it seems clear that many people at the time made just that attribution.

29. Charles M. Andrews, ed., *Narratives of the Insurrections, 1675–1690* (New York: Charles Scribner's Sons, 1915), 113.

30. Anthony S. Parent, Jr., *Foul Means: The Formation of a Slave Society in Virginia, 1660–1740* (Chapel Hill: University of North Carolina Press, 2003), 21–23; Elisabeth Tooker, "The Demise of the Susquehannocks: A 17th Century Mystery," *Pennsylvania Archaeologist*, 54, nos. 3–4 (Sept.–Dec. 1984), 2–3; Francis Jennings, *The Ambiguous Iroquois Empire: The Covenant Chain Confederation of Indian Tribes with English Colonies from its Beginnings to the Lancaster Treaty of 1744* (New York: W. W. Norton, 1984), 120–121; J. Frederick Fausz, "Merging and Emerging Worlds: Anglo-Indian Interest Groups and the Development of the Seventeenth-Century Chesapeake," in Lois Green Carr, Philip D. Morgan, and Jean B. Russo, eds., *Colonial Chesapeake Society* (Chapel Hill: University of North Carolina Press, 1988), 83–85.

31. Jacobs, *New Netherland*, 125–132.

32. Quoted in Jennings, *Ambiguous Iroquois Empire*, 123.

33. Jennings, "Glory, Death, and Transfiguration," 26–27 (quotation from p. 27); O'Callaghan and Fernow, eds., *Documents Relative to New-York*, 12:347, 431, 439.

34. Matson, *Merchants and Empire*, 52–53; Jacobs, *New Netherland*, 178–187.

35. O'Callaghan and Fernow, eds., *Documents Relative to New-York*, 12:477, 484–489, 493–494 (quotations), 505–506, 518–520.

36. Ibid., 465–472; Evan Haefeli, "The Revolt of the Long Swede: Transatlantic Hopes and Fears on the Delaware, 1669," *Pennsylvania Magazine of History and Biography*, 130 (2006), 137–180.

37. O'Callaghan and Fernow, eds., *Documents Relative to New-York*, 12:543; Andrews, ed., *Narratives of the Insurrections*, 18 (1st quotation); Thwaites, ed., *Jesuit Relations*, 59:251 (2nd quotation).

38. Victor Hugo Paltsits, ed., *Minutes of the Executive Council of the Province of New York: Administration of Francis Lovelace, 1668–1673* (Albany: State of New York, 1910), 2:502.

39. Andrews, ed., *Narratives of the Insurrections*, 109.

40. Jennings, "Glory, Death, and Transfiguration," 34–35 (quotation); Tooker, "Demise of the Susquehannocks," 4–9. These two sources agree on almost nothing but the fact that the Susquehannocks relocated to Maryland in February 1675. For brief accounts of the origins of the war between Virginians and Indians, see Morgan, *American Slavery, American Freedom*, 250–270; and Hatfield, *Atlantic Virginia*, 197–202.

Chapter 6. Brokers and Politics

This essay first appeared as "Cultural Brokers and Intercultural Politics: New York-Iroquois Relations, 1664–1701," *Journal of American History*, 75 (1988), 40–67. Reprinted by permission. To frame the argument more suitably for this volume and to avoid repetition of material in other chapters, the first four paragraphs and the closing paragraph as they appear here have been rewritten, and a few brief passages have been omitted or slightly modified. Alert readers will also notice that the term "cultural brokers" no longer appears in the title or text. Shortly after the *Journal of American History* article appeared, I realized that I had allowed the euphony of the phrase "Cultural Brokers and Intercultural Politics" to crowd out the analytical rigor embedded in the question of how something as abstract, malleable, and endlessly incorporative as "culture" could be "brokered."

Political and economic relationships, however, certainly are subject to that process and to the activities of the intermediaries called "brokers," and those realms, far more than the cultural, were and still are the subject of this essay. In all this, my thinking has been clarified by conversations with James H. Merrell, Nancy L. Hagedorn, and many other colleagues.

1. Patricia U. Bonomi, *A Factious People: Politics and Society in Colonial New York* (New York: Columbia University Press, 1971), 17–55; Michael Kammen, *Colonial New York: A History* (New York: Scribner, 1975), 1–160; William N. Fenton, "Locality as a Basic Factor in the Development of Iroquois Social Structure," in *Symposium on Local Diversity in Iroquois Culture*, ed. William N. Fenton, Bureau of American Ethnology Bulletin 149 (Washington, D.C., 1951), 35–54; Jack Campisi, "The Iroquois and the Euro-American Concept of Tribe," *New York History*, 63 (1982), 165–182; Daniel K. Richter, "Ordeals of the Longhouse: The Five Nations in Early American History," in Daniel K. Richter and James H. Merrell, eds., *Beyond the Covenant Chain: The Iroquois and Their Neighbors in Indian North America, 1600–1800* (Syracuse, N.Y.: Syracuse University Press, 1987), 11–27.

2. Eric R. Wolf, "Aspects of Group Relations in a Complex Society: Mexico," *American Anthropologist*, 58 (1956), 1065–1078 (quotation from p. 1075); Adrian C. Mayer, "The Significance of Quasi-Groups in the Study of Complex Societies," in *The Social Anthropology of Complex Societies*, ed. Michael Banton (New York: F. A. Praeger, 1966), 113–115; Anthony Leeds, "Locality Power in Relation to Supralocal Power Institutions," in Aidan Southall, ed., *Urban Anthropology: Cross-Cultural Studies of Urbanization* (New York: Oxford University Press, 1973), 15–41; Jeremy Boissevain, *Friends of Friends: Networks, Manipulators and Coalitions* (Oxford: Blackwell, 1974); Billie R. DeWalt and Pertti J. Pelto, eds., *Micro and Macro Levels of Analysis in Anthropology: Issues in Theory and Research* (Boulder, Colo.: Westview Press, 1985); Michael D. Olien, "Micro/Macro-Level Linkages: Regional Political Structures on the Mosquito Coast, 1845–1864," *Ethnohistory*, 34 (1987), 256–287.

3. A. J. F. van Laer, trans. and ed., *Van Rensselaer Bowier Manuscripts: Being the Letters of Kiliaen van Rensselaer, 1630–1643, and Other Documents Relating to the Colony of Rensselaerswyck* (Albany: University of the State of New York, 1908), 390–690; A. J. F. van Laer, "Arent van Curler and His Historic Letter to the Patroon," *Dutch Settlers Society of Albany Yearbook*, 3 (1927–1928), 11–29; Oliver A. Rink, *Holland on the Hudson: An Economic and Social History of Dutch New York* (Ithaca, N.Y.: Cornell University Press, 1986).

4. E. B. O'Callaghan and B. Fernow, eds., *Documents Relative to the Colonial History of the State of New York*, 15 vols. (Albany, 1856–1887), 3:121–127, 14:444, 450–451; A. J. F. van Laer, ed. and trans., *Minutes of the Court of Fort Orange and Beverwyck, 1652–1656*, 2 vols. (Albany: University of the State of New York, 1920–1923), 2:222–223, 255–298, 325–326; A. J. F. van Laer, ed. and trans., *Correspondence of Jeremias van Rensselaer, 1651–1674* (Albany: University of the State of New York, 1932), 325–332, 345–346, 358–371, 412–413, 440–449; Reuben Gold Thwaites, ed., *The Jesuit Relations and Allied Documents: Travels and Explorations of the Jesuit Missionaries in New France, 1610–1791*, 73 vols. (Cleveland, 1896–1901), 50:127–147; Allen W. Trelease, *Indian Affairs in Colonial New York: The Seventeenth Century* (Ithaca, N.Y.: Cornell University Press, 1960), 112–74; Lynn Ceci, "The First Fiscal Crisis in New York," *Economic Development and Cultural Change*, 28 (1980), 839–847; Thomas E. Burke, "The New Netherland Fur Trade, 1657–1661: Response to Crisis," *de Halve Maen*, 59 (1986), 1–4, 21. For an argument that the Anglo-Dutch wars had little impact on trade at Albany, see Jan Kupp, "Aspects of New York-Dutch Trade Under the English, 1670–1674," *New-York Historical Society Quarterly*, 58 (1974), 139–147.

5. John Baker to John Winthrop, Jr., 9 August 1666, in *Iroquois Indians: A Documentary History*

of the *Diplomacy of the Six Nations and Their League*, microfilm, 50 reels (Woodbridge, Conn., 1985), reel 2 (quotation); Lawrence H. Leder, ed., *The Livingston Indian Records, 1666–1723* (Gettysburg: Pennsylvania Historical Association, 1956), 29–33; O'Callaghan and Fernow, eds., *Documents Relative to New-York*, 3:118–119, 127–135, 146–154; Cadwallader Colden, *The History of the Five Indian Nations Depending on the Province of New-York in America* (New York, 1727), 22–24; Nicholas Perrot, "Memoir on the Manners, Customs, and Religion of the Savages of North America," in *The Indian Tribes of the Upper Mississippi Valley and Region of the Great Lakes . . .* , trans. and ed. Emma Helen Blair, 2 vols. (Cleveland, Ohio: Arthur H. Clark Co., 1911), 1:199–203.

6. Daniel K. Richter, "Iroquois Versus Iroquois: Jesuit Missions and Christianity in Village Politics, 1642–1686," *Ethnohistory*, 32 (1985), 1–16.

7. O'Callaghan and Fernow, eds., *Documents Relative to New-York*, 3:254–257; Thwaites, ed., *Jesuit Relations*, 60:133-135; Treaty minutes, 9–10 November 1680, Massachusetts Archives Collection, 30:254–254a, Massachusetts Archives, Boston; Francis Jennings, "The Constitutional Evolution of the Covenant Chain," *Proceedings of the American Philosophical Society*, 115 (1971), 88–96; Stephen Saunders Webb, *The Governors-General: The English Army and the Definition of the Empire, 1569–1681* (Chapel Hill: University of North Carolina Press, 1979), 39–49, 498.

8. Thwaites, ed., *Jesuit Relations*, 57:81; A. J. F. van Laer, trans. and ed., *Minutes of the Court of Albany, Rensselaerswyck, and Schenectady, 1668–1673*, 3 vols. (Albany: State University of New York, 1926–1932), 2: 91, 105–108, 137–141, 159, 173, 187, 193, 241–278, 336–354; Trelease, *Indian Affairs*, 204–227; Thomas Elliot Norton, *The Fur Trade in Colonial New York, 1686–1776* (Madison: University of Wisconsin Press, 1974), 43–50; Donna Merwick, "Becoming English: Anglo-Dutch Conflict in the 1670s in Albany, New York," *New York History*, 62 (1981), 411–413.

9. Alice P. Kenney, "Dutch Patricians in Colonial Albany," *New York History*, 49 (1968), 249–283; Donna Merwick, "Dutch Townsmen and Land Use: A Spatial Perspective on Seventeenth-Century Albany, New York," *William and Mary Quarterly*, 3rd ser., 37 (1980), 53–78; Merwick, "Becoming English," 389–414. The term *anglicizer* is borrowed from John M. Murrin, "English Rights as Ethnic Aggression: The English Conquest, the Charter of Liberties of 1683 and Leisler's Rebellion in New York," in William Pencak and Conrad Wright, eds., *Authority and Resistance in Early New York* (New York: New York Historical Society, 1988), 56–94.

10. Joel Munsell, comp., *The Annals of Albany*, 10 vols. (Albany, N.Y., 1850–1853), 2:61–87; Arthur H. Buffinton, "The Policy of Albany and English Westward Expansion," *Mississippi Valley Historical Review*, 8 (1922), 327–135; Lawrence H. Leder, *Robert Livingston, 1654–1728, and the Politics of Colonial New York* (Chapel Hill: University of North Carolina Press, 1961), 36–53; Kammen, *Colonial New York*, 100–111.

11. Leder, ed., *Livingston Indian Records*, 75–81; Francis Jennings et al., eds., *The History and Culture of Iroquois Diplomacy: An Interdisciplinary Guide to the Treaties of the Six Nations and Their League* (Syracuse, N.Y.: Syracuse University Press, 1985), 250.

12. Treaty minutes, 5 April 1687, *Iroquois Indians*, reel 3 (quotation); A. J. F. van Laer, trans. and ed., *Correspondence of Maria van Rensselaer, 1669–1689* (Albany: University of the State of New York, 1935), 69–82, 151–152; Randall H. Balmer, "The Social Roots of Dutch Pietism in the Middle Colonies," *Church History*, 53 (1984), 187–199.

13. O'Callaghan and Fernow, eds., *Documents Relative to New-York*, 3:799, 4:77–78, 125; [Edward T. Corwin, ed.], *Ecclesiastical Records of the State of New York*, 7 vols. (Albany: State of New York, 1901–1916), 2:885, 1002–1004; Munsell, comp., *Annals of Albany*, 2:163–165; Treaty minutes, 4 January 1690, Untitled Notebook, Indians of North America, Miscellaneous Papers, 1620–1895, Manuscript Collections, American Antiquarian Society, Worcester, Massachusetts; Charles E.

Corwin, "Efforts of the Dutch-American Colonial Pastors for the Conversion of the Indians," *Journal of the Presbyterian Historical Society*, 12 (1925), 238–241; Lois M. Feister, "Indian-Dutch Relations in the Upper Hudson Valley: A Study of Baptism Records in the Dutch Reformed Church, Albany, New York," *Man in the Northeast*, no. 24 (1982), 89–113.

14. Jasper Dankers [Danckaerts] and Peter Sluyter, *Journal of a Voyage to New York and a Tour in Several of the American Colonies in 1679–80*, trans. and ed. Henry C. Murphy, *Memoirs of the Long Island Historical Society*, 1 (Brooklyn, N.Y., 1867), 301–314; Jonathan Pearson, *Contributions for the Genealogies of the Descendants of the First Settlers of the Patent and City of Schenectady, from 1622 to 1800* (Albany, N.Y.: J. Munsell, 1873), 239; Trelease, *Indian Affairs*, 212. On the significance of interpreters as brokers, see Nancy L. Hagedorn, "'A Friend to Go Between Them': The Interpreter as Cultural Broker During Anglo-Iroquois Councils, 1740–70," *Ethnohistory*, 35 (1988), 60–80.

15. O'Callaghan and Fernow, eds., *Documents Relative to New-York*, 3:250–257, 13: 483 (quotation); van Laer, ed., *Minutes of Albany, Rensselaerswyck, and Schenectady*, 2:211–212; W. Noel Sainsbury et al., eds., *Calendar of State Papers, Colonial Series, America and the West Indies*, 44 vols. (London: Public Record Office, 1860–1969), *1681–1685*, no. 874.

16. Leder, ed., *Livingston Indian Records*, 47 (quotation); Treaty minutes, 22 August 1677, *Iroquois Indians*, reel 2.

17. O'Callaghan and Fernow, eds., *Documents Relative to New-York*, 3:559; Daniel K. Richter, "Rediscovered Links in the Covenant Chain: Previously Unpublished Transcripts of New York Indian Treaty Minutes, 1677–1691," *Proceedings of the American Antiquarian Society*, 92 (1982), 48–49; William N. Fenton, "Structure, Continuity, and Change in the Process of Iroquois Treaty Making," in Jennings et al., eds., *History of Iroquois Diplomacy*, 3–36; Mary A. Druke, "Iroquois Treaties: Common Forms, Varying Interpretations," ibid., 85–98.

18. Thwaites, ed., *Jesuit Relations*, 60:177–179, 61:19–33; Treaty minutes, 31 July–6 August 1684, Colonial Papers, folder 4, item 2a (Virginia State Library, Richmond) (quotation from minutes of August 2, 1684); O'Callaghan and Fernow, eds., *Documents Relative to New-York*, 9:228–236, 14:771–774; Richter, "Iroquois Versus Iroquois," 10–12.

19. Leder, ed., *Livingston Indian Records*, 99–147; O'Callaghan and Fernow, eds., *Documents Relative to New-York*, 9:236–248, 324–369, 681–685; Sainsbury et al., eds., *Calendar of State Papers, 1685–1688*, nos. 2072, 2091, 2151; [Louis-Armand,] Baron [de] Lahontan, *New Voyages to North-America* (London, 1703), I, 34–43; Helen Broshar, "The First Push Westward of the Albany Traders," *Mississippi Valley Historical Review*, 7 (1920), 228–241; W. J. Eccles, *Frontenac: The Courtier Governor* (Toronto: McClelland and Stewart, 1959), 173–197.

20. Leder, ed., *Livingston Indian Records*, 154–158.

21. Van Laer, ed., *Minutes of Albany, Rensselaerswyck, and Schenectady*, 1:255–257; Sentence of William Loveridge, 7 October 1676, New York Colonial Manuscripts, 25:184, New York State Archives, Albany; Increase Mather, *A Brief History of the Warr with the Indians in New England . . .* (Boston, 1696), 38–42; Mary Maples Dunn and Richard S. Dunn, eds., *The Papers of William Penn*, 5 vols. (Philadelphia: University of Pennsylvania Press, 1981–1987), 2:423, 469–471, 479–482, 487–489; E. B. O'Callaghan, ed., *The Documentary History of the State of New-York*, octavo ed., 4 vols. (Albany, 1842–1851), 1:393–297; O'Callaghan and Fernow, eds., *Documents Relative to New-York*, 9:226–228 (quotation).

22. O'Callaghan, ed., *Documentary History of New-York*, 2:112–132; Robert C. Ritchie, *The Duke's Province: A Study of New York Politics and Society, 1664–1691* (Chapel Hill: University of North Carolina Press, 1977), 198–211.

23. O'Callaghan, ed., *Documentary History of New-York*, 2:137–139 (quotations); Treaty minutes, 27 December 1689, 4 January 1690, Notebook, Indians of North America Papers.

24. O'Callaghan, ed., *Documentary History of New-York*, 2:141–142, 246, 268; Corwin, ed., *Ecclesiastical Records*, 2:1132, 1412–1415.

25. O'Callaghan, ed., *Documentary History of New-York*, 2:137–144; Treaty minutes, 4, 6, 18 January, 3 February 1690, Notebook, Indians of North America Papers; David Arthur Armour, "The Merchants of Albany, New York: 1686–1760" (Ph.D. diss., Northwestern University, 1965), 45–46. On Sanders, see O'Callaghan and Fernow, eds., *Documents Relative to New-York*, 3:469; and Charles T. Gehring and Robert S. Grumet, "Observations of the Indians from Jasper Danckaerts' Journal, 1679–1680," *William and Mary Quarterly*, 3rd ser., 44 (1987), 105–106, 108n.

26. Dirck Wesselse to Henry Sloughter, 2 July 1691, New York Colonial Manuscripts, 27:176 (quotation); O'Callaghan, ed., *Documentary History of New-York*, 2:171–290; O'Callaghan and Fernow, eds., *Documents Relative to New-York*, 3:751–754, 771–791, 800–809, 4:193–196, 9:513–515.

27. Examination of two Frenchmen, 1 August 1692, New York Colonial Manuscripts, 38:158; *Propositions made by the Five Nations of Indians . . . to his Excellency Richard Earl of Bellomont . . . the 20th of July, Anno Dom. 1698* (New York, 1698), 4 (quotation); O'Callaghan and Fernow, eds., *Documents Relative to New-York*, 3:814–818, 840–844, 9:520–527, 539–543; Leder, ed., *Livingston Indian Records*, 162–168; Thwaites, ed., *Jesuit Relations*, 64:109–113; Leroy V. Eid, "The Ojibwa-Iroquois War: The War the Five Nations Did Not Win," *Ethnohistory*, 26 (1979), 297–324.

28. O'Callaghan and Fernow, eds., *Documents Relative to New-York*, 4:14–24; Deposition of John Baptist van Eps, 1 July 1693, New York Colonial Manuscripts, 39:73; John Pynchon to Benjamin Fletcher, 4, 13, 20 July 1693, Massachusetts Archives, 30:330a, 331–332, 335a; *Propositions made by Five Nations*, 11; Richard Irwin Melvoin, "New England Outpost: War and Society in Colonial Frontier Deerfield, Massachusetts" (Ph.D. diss., University of Michigan, 1983), 396–405. The Mohawks escaped from jail before orders for their release reached Deerfield.

29. O'Callaghan, ed., *Documentary History of New-York*, 2:246–269; O'Callaghan and Fernow, eds., *Documents Relative to New-York*, 4:59–63, 369–374, 716; Schuyler, Account of expenses, [ca. 1688], *Iroquois Indians*, reel 3. On "treating," see Rhys Isaac, *The Transformation of Virginia, 1740–1790* (Chapel Hill: University of North Carolina Press, 1982), 104–114.

30. Henry Sloughter to William Stoughton, n.d., New York Colonial Manuscripts, 37:fol. 160a; Relation concerning Canada, 28 April 1691, ibid., 56; Examination of Jurian, 25 July 1693, ibid., 39:82; Treaty minutes, 25 November, 22 December 1696, 9–12 March 1697, ibid., 41:16, 38; Godfridius Dellius to Benjamin Fletcher, 6, 17 May, 2 June 1697, Massachusetts Archives, 30:417–418, 423–424, 427–428; O'Callaghan and Fernow, eds., *Documents Relative to New-York*, 3:771–772, 4:92–97; Leder, ed., *Livingston Indian Records*, 179–180; Feister, "Indian-Dutch Relations," 96.

31. See Chapter 4, above.

32. Buffinton, "Policy of Albany and Westward Expansion," 348–349.

33. Broshar, "First Push Westward," 238–241; Norton, *Fur Trade in New York*, 121–123; Jean Lunn, "The Illegal Fur Trade Out of New France, 1713–60," Canadian Historical Association *Report* (1939), 61–76.

34. O'Callaghan and Fernow, eds., *Documents Relative to New-York*, 4:362–367; Treaty minutes, 25 July 1698, *Iroquois Indians*, reel 6; Bellomont, Reports on Dellius case, 9 July 9, 2 August 1698, ibid.; Corwin, ed., *Ecclesiastical Records*, 2:1313–1320, 1394–1436; John D. Runcie, "The Problem of Anglo-American Politics in Bellomont's New York," *William and Mary Quarterly*, 3rd ser., 26 (1969), 191–217.

35. O'Callaghan and Fernow, eds., *Documents Relative to New-York*, 4:329–330 (quotations).

36. *Propositions made by Five Nations*, 18–19; Stephen van Cortlandt to William Blathwayt, 18 July 1698, Blathwayt Papers, 9, folder 4, Research Library, Colonial Williamsburg Foundation, Williamsburg, Virginia; Nicholas Bayard to John Povey, ibid., 7, folder 1.

37. O'Callaghan and Fernow, eds., *Documents Relative to New-York*, 4:647–661, 689, 716, 694.

38. Leder, ed., *Livingston Indian Records*, 176–180; O'Callaghan and Fernow, eds., *Documents Relative to New-York*, 4:690–696; [Claude-Charles Le Roy de] Bacqueville de La Potherie, *Histoire de l'amérique Septentrionale*, 4 vols. (Paris, 1722), 4:135–148, 193–266; Daniel Karl Richter, "The Ordeal of the Longhouse: Change and Persistence on the Iroquois Frontier, 1609–1720" (Ph.D. diss., Columbia University, 1984), 381–437.

39. O'Callaghan and Fernow, eds., *Documents Relative to New-York*, 4:888–911 (quotations from pp. 888, 904–905).

40. Munsell, comp., *Annals of Albany*, 5:116–120, 135–138, 154–158, 162–164, 186, 194; O'Callaghan and Fernow, eds., *Documents Relative to New-York*, 4:972–978, 5:64–65; Leder, *Robert Livingston*, 129–199; Norton, *Fur Trade in New York*, 60–82.

41. James Sullivan et al., eds., *The Papers of Sir William Johnson*, 14 vols. (Albany: University of the State of New York, 1921–1965), 9:177 (quotation); Francis Jennings, "Iroquois Alliances in American History," in Jennings et al., eds., *History of Iroquois Diplomacy*, 37–65.

42. Cadwallader Colden, *The History of the Five Indian Nations of Canada, Which Are Dependent On the Province of New-York in America, and Are the Barrier between the English and French in that Part of the World* (London, 1747); Francis Jennings, *The Ambiguous Iroquois Empire: The Covenant Chain Confederation of Indian Tribes with English Colonies from Its Beginnings to the Lancaster Treaty of 1744* (New York: W. W. Norton, 1984), 10–24; Richard L. Haan, "Covenant and Consensus: Iroquois and English, 1676–1760," in Richter and Merrell, eds., *Beyond the Covenant Chain*, 41–57.

Chapter 7. Land and Words

Earlier versions of this chapter were presented at the Annual General Meeting of the American Philosophical Society, Philadelphia, 27 April 2007; as the Charles R. and Elizabeth C. Wilson Endowed Lecture in History, Miami University, Oxford, Ohio, 10 March 2008; as a Dean's Distinguished Lecture, Rowan University, Glassboro, New Jersey, 23 February 2011; and as the Bosworth Lecture, Yale University, New Haven, Connecticut, 2 November 2011. I thank Richard Dunn and Mary Maples Dunn for the inspiration and the invitation to tackle the topic.

1. *Minutes of the Provincial Council of Pennsylvania, from the Organization to the Termination of the Proprietary Government*, 10 vols. (Harrisburg, 1851–1853), 3:363.

2. The original draft discussed below is William Penn to the Kings of the Indians, 18 October 1681, Penn Family Papers, Box 7, folder 48, Historical Society of Pennsylvania, Philadelphia. This is the text printed in Mary Maples Dunn and Richard S. Dunn, eds., *The Papers of William Penn*, 5 vols. (Philadelphia: University of Pennsylvania Press, 1981–1987), 2:128–129. The contemporary signed copy, which contains a few minor variations, is in the Ferdinand J. Dreer Collection, 1492–1925, Collection 175, series CLXXVI: Letters and Papers of William Penn, box 320, folder 9, Historical Society of Pennsylvania.

3. Francis Jennings, *The Ambiguous Iroquois Empire: The Covenant Chain Confederation of Indian Tribes with English Colonies from Its Beginnings to the Lancaster Treaty of 1744* (New York: W. W. Norton, 1984), 242. See also Jennings, "Miquon's Passing: Indian-European Relations in Colonial Pennsylvania, 1674–1755" (Ph.D. diss., University of Pennsylvania, 1965), 56–60.

4. Penn to the Kings of the Indians, 18 October 1681, Penn Family Papers, Box 7, folder 48.

5. Jennings, *Ambiguous Iroquois Empire*, 243.

6. David Beers Quinn, *Set Fair for Roanoke: Voyages and Colonies, 1584–1606* (Chapel Hill: University of North Carolina Press, 1985), 241–272; John Smith, *A True Relation of Such Occurences and Accidents of Noate as hath Hapned in Virginia . . .* (London, 1608), C2v. See Chapter 1, above.

7. R[obert] C[ushman], "Reasons and Considerations Touching the Lawfulnesse of Removing out of England into the Parts of America," in [William Bradford], *A Relation or Journall of the Beginning and Proceedings of the English Plantation Setled at Plimoth in New England* (London, 1622), 68–69.

8. Robert Gray, *A Good Speed to Virginia* (London, 1609), C3v–[C4r]; W[illiam] Crashaw, *A Sermon Preached in London before the Right Honorable the Lord Lawarre, Lord Governour and Captaine Generall of Virginea . . .* (London, 1610), D3r–[D3v].

9. [Stewart Mitchell, ed.,] *Winthrop Papers*, vol. 2 ([Boston]: Massachusetts Historical Society, 1931), 106–145 (quotation from p. 141).

10. Charles Gibson, *The Spanish Tradition in America* (Columbia: University of South Carolina Press, 1968), 58–60.

11. The mixed Indian-English juries that Penn envisioned seem never to have gone into operation in Pennsylvania, not least because they would have required Native people to acknowledge the legitimacy of English courts and legal procedures. See John Smolenski, *Friends and Strangers: The Making of a Creole Culture in Colonial Pennsylvania* (Philadelphia: University of Pennsylvania Press, 2010), 96–102, 274–275.

12. *Minutes of the Provincial Council of Pennsylvania*, 3:363 (1st quotation), 93 (2nd quotation). Delawares spoke in almost identical terms; see, for example, Sassoonan's proclamation in 1738 "that it was formerly said that the English and Indians should be as one Body or one People, half the one and half the other; but they were now to be all as one heart, not divided into haves, but intirely the same without any Distinction" (ibid., 4:308).

13. Smolenski, *Friends and Strangers*, 27–53 (quotation from pp. 42–43). I am grateful to Steve Pincus for pointing me to the importance of Quaker epistolary culture for understanding Penn's letter.

14. Robert C. Ritchie, *The Duke's Province: A Study of New York Politics and Society, 1664–1691* (Chapel Hill: University of North Carolina Press, 1977), 17.

15. Richard S. Dunn, "Penny Wise and Pound Foolish: Penn as a Businessman," in Richard S. Dunn and Mary Maples Dunn, eds., *The World of William Penn* (Philadelphia: University of Pennsylvania Press, 1986), 41, 48; Mary Maples Dunn, *William Penn: Politics and Conscience* (Princeton, N.J.: Princeton University Press, 1967), 76–78.

16. *The Fundamental Constitutions of Carolina* ([London, 1670]); *The Colonial Laws of New York, from the Year 1664 to the Revolution . . .* , 5 vols. (Albany, N.Y.: J. B. Lyon, 1894–1896), 1:24–26, 40–42 (quotations); Daniel K. Richter, *Before the Revolution: America's Ancient Pasts* (Cambridge, Mass.: Harvard University Press, 2011), 236–237, 252–254.

17. Stuart Banner, *How the Indians Lost Their Land: Law and Power on the Frontier* (Cambridge, Mass.: Harvard University Press, 2005), 10–48. I have explored these matters further in "The Strange Colonial North American Career of Terra Nullius," in Tom Griffiths and Bain Attwood, eds., *Frontier, Race, Nation: Henry Reynolds and Australian History* (Melbourne: Australian Scholarly Publishing, 2009), 159–184.

18. Francis Jennings, *The Invasion of America: Indians, Colonialism, and the Cant of Conquest* (Chapel Hill: University of North Carolina Press, 1975), 128–145 (1st quotation reproduced on p. 132, 2nd quotation from p. 128).

19. Quoted in Banner, *How the Indians Lost Their Land*, 21.

20. Roger Williams, *Mr. Cottons Letter Lately Printed, Examined and Answered* (London, 1644), 4.

21. Jennings, *Invasion of America*, 132.

22. William A. Whitehead, ed., *Documents Relating to the Colonial History of the State of New Jersey*, 1st series, 33 vols. (Newark, N.J., 1880–1928), 1: 241–270

23. Banner, *How the Indians Lost Their Land*, 25. The official vocabulary of European international law, however, continued to assert that only a title from a crown was strictly necessary to make a land title valid. An opinion drafted by lawyers for Penn and the other West New Jersey proprietors in 1677 concluded that "Tho' it hath bene and still is the Usual Practice of all Proprietors to give their Indians some Recompence for their Lands and so seems to Purchase it of them it is not done for want of sufficient title from the King or Prince who hath the Right of Discovery" (Whitehead, ed., *Documents Relating to New Jersey*, 1:272–274). Penn's charter for Pennsylvania made no reference to Indian land titles or purchases (Dunn and Dunn, eds., *Papers of William Penn*, 2:40–49, 57–78).

24. See, for example, [Benjamin Tompson], *New-England's Tears for Her Present Miseries . . .* (London, 1676); [Anon.], *A New and Further Narrative of the State of New-England* (London, 1676); and William Hubbard, *The Present State of New-England . . .* (London, 1677).

25. [Anon.], *Strange News from Virginia . . .* (London, 1677); *Articles of Peace between the Most Serene and Mighty Prince Charles II . . . and Several Indian Kings and Queens, and Concluded the 29th Day of May, 1677* (London, 1677). King Charles's Privy Council ordered the printing of the treaty so that it could be sent back to Virginia to educate English colonists about their obligations (Order in council, 19 October 1677, CO 1/41, no. 82, The National Archives, Kew).

26. E. B. O'Callaghan and B. Fernow, eds., *Documents Relative to the Colonial History of the State of New-York*, 15 vols. (Albany, N.Y., 1853–1887), 3:271.

27. Dunn and Dunn, eds., *Papers of William Penn*, 2:59, 59n, 71.

28. Ibid., 109.

29. Charles II to Inhabitants of Pennsylvania, 2 April 1681, Penn Papers Microfilm, Reel 3, Historical Society of Pennsylvania; Dunn and Dunn, eds., *Papers of William Penn*, 2:84 (quotations).

30. Dunn and Dunn, eds., *Papers of William Penn*, 2:84, 129.

31. Ibid., 84.

32. Ibid., 129. Two additional items joined the apparently hastily compiled list: "That all Evidence or Engagements be without Oaths, thus I. A.B. does Promise in the Sight of God and them that heare me to speake the Truth, the whole Truth and nothing but the whole Truth," and that "the Citty to be layd out" was to be called "by the Name of Philadelphia."

33. John Werden to William Blathwayt, 20 November 1680, Penn Papers Microfilm, reel 3.

34. "Mr. Penn's Boundaries Settled by my Lord C. J. North" [December 1680], CO1/46, no. 60; William A. Russ, Jr., *How Pennsylvania Acquired Its Present Boundaries*, Pennsylvania History Studies no. 8 (University Park: Pennsylvania State University, 1966), 4, 47–48.

35. "Mr. Penn's Boundaries Settled."

36. Dunn, "Penny Wise and Pound Foolish," 43–45.

37. [William Penn,] *Some Account of the Province of Pennsilvania in America . . .* (London: Benjamin Clark, 1681), 4–5.

38. Quoted in Ritchie, *Duke's Province*, 13.

39. Joseph E. Illick, *William Penn the Politician: His Relations with the English Government* (Ithaca, N.Y.: Cornell University Press, 1965), 58; John A. Munroe, *Colonial Delaware: A History*

(Millwood, N.Y.: KTO Press, 1978), 60–66; Ritchie, *Duke's Province*, 9–24; Mary K. Geiter, *William Penn* (London: Longman, 2000), 38–41. A further complication involved whether the Dutch ever really asserted a claim to anything beyond the water route of the Delaware and the small areas for their settlements purchased from local Indians. On Dutch concepts of possession, see Donna Merwick, *Possessing Albany, 1630–1710: The Dutch and English Experiences* (Cambridge: Cambridge University Press, 1990); and Patricia Seed, *Ceremonies of Possession in Europe's Conquest of the New World, 1492–1640* (Cambridge: Cambridge University Press, 1995).

40. Munroe, *Colonial Delaware*, 66–78; Jennings, *Ambiguous Iroquois Empire*, 136–139.

41. Penn to Lords of Trade, 6 August 1683, CO 1/52, no. 49 (1st quotation); Deeds and leases, 24 August 1682, Penn Papers Microfilm, reel 3; "John Moll's Account [of the] Surrender of the Three Lower Counties," n.d. 1682, ibid. (2d quotation); Monroe, *Colonial Delaware*, 79–85.

42. Dunn and Dunn, eds., *Papers of William Penn*, 2:472–473.

43. Ibid., 473. See also the version of many of these arguments rehearsed in William Penn to Earl of Rochester, 2 February 1684, Penn Family Papers, Collection 485A, Box NB-012, folder 13, Historical Society of Pennsylvania. In a draft heavy with cross-outs and revisions, Penn complained that Baltimore's failure to contest Swedish and Dutch possession or even, supposedly, to bother to mark out the boundaries of his colony should have voided Maryland's claims, "for as there is no Transgression, where no Law so where there is no bounds sett, noe possession found." Moreover, "what he seeks, never was as well as it's not in his possession, consequently never cost him any thing, to improve, nor has he lost any income by its being mine to this I add, that . . . he hath 200 miles (for three Degrees) upon both sides of the bravest bay in the world, cheseapeack, while I have but one side of an inferior one, and none at all it seems if he would have his will." Penn's tone then turned increasingly petulant: "I have but two Creeks that ships of 200 tun can enter out of, the River for Harbourage, he has fourty, (and to spare) that ships of 1500 tun can enter and ride in. And tho this argument ought not to prevaile against absolute right, yet in a case circumstanced, as this of mine is; I hope that prudence and proportion, together with my arguments of Contrary Right, will more then even the Scale." As noted above, Penn exaggerated, to say the least, when he claimed "that the Kings of England have alwaies commanded the English to purchase the Land of the Natives."

44. Dunn and Dunn, eds., *Papers of William Penn*, 2:126.

45. J. W. Fortescue, ed., *Calendar of State Papers, Colonial Series, America and West Indies*, 44 vols. (London: Her Majesty's Stationery Office, 1860–1969), *1681–1685*, 208; Illick, *William Penn the Politician*, 59–72.

46. William Penn to the Indians, 21 April 1682, Penn Papers Microfilm, reel 3.

47. Dunn and Dunn, *Papers of William Penn*, 2:261–269 (quotation from p. 264, citing an unlocated original document reprinted in Albert Cook Myers, *William Penn: His Own Account of the Lenni Lenape or Delaware Indians, 1683* [Moylan, Pa.: A. C. Myers, 1937], 79–81).

48. Dunn and Dunn, eds., *Papers of William Penn*, 2:492. A third surviving letter from Penn to Native people, addressed "to the Emperor of Canada," 12 June 1682 (Dunn and Dunn, *Papers of William Penn*, 2:261), was a salvo in his controversy with Governor Thomas Dongan of New York over rights to the upper Susquehanna River Valley. See ibid., 466–468, and Gary B. Nash, "The Quest for the Susquehanna Valley: New York, Pennsylvania, and the Seventeenth-Century Fur Trade," *New York History*, 53 (1967), 3–17.

49. Penn to Lords of Trade, 6 August 1683, CO 1/52, no. 49.

50. *Minutes of the Provincial Council of Pennsylvania*, 3:273.

51. Francis Jennings et al., eds., *The History and Culture of Iroquois Diplomacy: An*

Interdisciplinary Guide to the Treaties of the Six Nations and Their League (Syracuse, N.Y.: Syracuse University Press, 1985), 246.

Chapter 8: "No Savage Should Inherit"

This chapter is adapted and expanded from Daniel K. Richter, *Native Americans' Pennsylvania* (University Park: Pennsylvania Historical Association, 2005), 42–65. Several paragraphs also appeared in slightly different form in Daniel K. Richter, *Before the Revolution: America's Ancient Pasts* (Cambridge, Mass.: Harvard University Press, 2011), 370–376, 392. My debt to the scholarship of the late Francis Jennings will be apparent to all who know the literature.

1. E. B. O'Callaghan and B. Fernow, eds., *Documents Relative to the Colonial History of the State of New-York* (Albany, N.Y., 1853–1857), 7:301.

2. Beverly W. Bond, Jr., ed., "The Captivity of Charles Stuart, 1755–57," *Mississippi Valley Historical Review,* 13 (1926), 63.

3. Francis Jennings, *The Ambiguous Iroquois Empire: The Covenant Chain Confederation of Indian Tribes and English Colonies from its Beginnings to the Lancaster Treaty of 1744* (New York: W. W. Norton, 1984), 248–320. On the origins of the Penn family's financial problems, see Richard S. Dunn, "Penny Wise and Pound Foolish: Penn as a Businessman," in Richard S. Dunn and Mary Maples Dunn, eds., *The World of William Penn* (Philadelphia: University of Pennsylvania Press, 1986), 37–54.

4. Francis Jennings, "Brother Miquon: Good Lord!" in Dunn and Dunn, eds., *World of William Penn,* 200–202; Stuart Banner, *How the Indians Lost Their Land: Law and Power on the Frontier* (Cambridge, Mass.: Harvard University Press, 2005), 49–84.

5. See the Introduction, above.

6. See Richard White, *The Middle Ground: Indians, Empires, and Republics in the Great Lakes Region, 1650–1815* (Cambridge: Cambridge University Press, 1991), 52–53.

7. Mary Maples Dunn and Richard S. Dunn, eds., *The Papers of William Penn,* 5 vols. (Philadelphia: University of Pennsylvania Press, 1981–1987), 2:84.

8. *Minutes of Conferences, Held with the Indians, at Easton, in the Months of July and November, 1756* (Philadelphia, 1757), 23 (quotation).

9. John Heckewelder, *History, Manners, and Customs of the Indian Nations Who Once Inhabited Pennsylvania and the Neighbouring States,* ed. William C. Reichel (Philadelphia, 1876), 75 (quotation); Andrew Newman, *On Records: Delaware Indians, Colonists, and the Media of History and Memory* (Lincoln: University of Nebraska Press, 2012).

10. Peter C. Mancall, *Valley of Opportunity: Economic Culture Along the Upper Susquehanna, 1700–1800* (Ithaca, N.Y.: Cornell University Press, 1991), 27–94; Michael N. McConnell, *A Country Between: The Upper Ohio Valley and Its Peoples, 1724–1774* (Lincoln: University of Nebraska Press, 1992), 5–20; Jane T. Merritt, *At the Crossroads: Indians and Empires on a Mid-Atlantic Frontier, 1700–1763* (Chapel Hill: University of North Carolina Press, 2003), 19–86; Laura Keenan Spero, " 'Stout, Bold, Cunning and the Greatest Travellers in America': The Colonial Shawnee Diaspora" (Ph.D. diss., University of Pennsylvania, 2010), 44–57, 204–261.

11. Joseph E. Illick, *Colonial Pennsylvania: A History* (New York: Charles Scribner's Sons, 1976), 164–178; Patrick Griffin, *The People with No Name: Ireland's Ulster Scots, America's Scots Irish, and the Creation of a British Atlantic World, 1689–1764* (Princeton, N.J.: Princeton University Press, 2001), 65–124; Aaron Spencer Fogleman, *Hopeful Journeys: German Immigration, Settlement, and*

Political Culture in Colonial America, 1717–1775 (Philadelphia: University of Pennsylvania Press, 1996); *Minutes of the Provincial Council of Pennsylvania, from the Organization to the Termination of the Proprietary Government*, 10 vols. (Harrisburg, 1851–1853), 3:319 (quotation).

12. James Logan to John Penn, Penn Papers, Official Correspondence, 2:21, Historical Society of Pennsylvania, Philadelphia (quotation); Jennings, *Ambiguous Iroquois Empire*, 265–274.

13. James Logan to John Penn, 11 February 1725, and 14 May 1729, Logan Letter Books, 2:11, 261, 3:294–299, Logan Papers, Historical Society of Pennsylvania, Philadelphia; Patrick Kehoe Spero, "Creating Pennsylvania: The Politics of the Frontier and the State, 1682–1800" (Ph.D. diss., University of Pennsylvania, 2009), 116–164; Francis Jennings, *The Invasion of America: Indians, Colonialism, and the Cant of Conquest* (Chapel Hill: University of North Carolina Press, 1975), 128–145. See also Chapter 7, above.

14. McConnell, *A Country Between*, 21–60; Eric Hinderaker, *Elusive Empires: Constructing Colonialism in the Ohio Valley, 1673–1800* (Cambridge: Cambridge University Press, 1997), 3–77; James H. Merrell, *Into the American Woods: Negotiators on the Pennsylvania Frontier* (New York: W. W. Norton, 1999).

15. Daniel K. Richter, *The Ordeal of the Longhouse: The Peoples of the Iroquois League in the Era of European Colonization* (Chapel Hill: University of North Carolina Press, 1992), 243–244, 273–276; *Minutes of the Provincial Council of Pennsylvania*, 3:331 (quotation).

16. *Minutes of the Provincial Council of Pennsylvania*, 3:334 (1st quotation); Samuel Hazard, ed., *Pennsylvania Archives*, ser. 1, vol. 1 (Philadelphia, 1852), 329 (2nd quotation).

17. Gunlög Fur, *A Nation of Women: Gender and Colonial Encounters Among the Delaware Indians* (Philadelphia: University of Pennsylvania Press, 2009), 160–198 (quotation from p. 161).

18. Logan to John Penn, 2 August 1731, Logan Letter Books, 2:7.

19. Hazard, ed., *Pennsylvania Archives*, ser. 1, 1:494–499 (quotation from p. 498); Jennings, *Ambiguous Iroquois Empire*, 320–324; Francis Jennings, "'Pennsylvania Indians' and the Iroquois," in Daniel K. Richter and James H. Merrell, eds., *Beyond the Covenant Chain: The Iroquois and Their Neighbors in Indian North America, 1600–1800* (Syracuse, N.Y.: Syracuse University Press, 1987), 88–90.

20. Anthony F. C. Wallace, *King of the Delawares: Teedyuscung* (Philadelphia: University of Pennsylvania Press, 1949), 4–6, 18–30.

21. C. Hale Sipe, *The Indian Chiefs of Pennsylvania* (Butler, Pa.: Ziegler Printing Co., 1927), 165–176; Jennings, *Ambiguous Iroquois Empire*, 320–336.

22. Jennings, *Ambiguous Iroquois Empire*, 336–346.

23. Wallace, *King of the Delawares*, 25–30 (1st quotation reproduced on p. 25); Hazard, ed., *Pennsylvania Archives*, ser. 1, 1:539–540 (2nd quotation).

24. Wallace, *King of the Delawares*, 31–39.

25. *Minutes of the Provincial Council of Pennsylvania*, 4:575–580 (quotation from p. 579).

26. Jay Miller, "The Delaware as Women: A Symbolic Solution," *American Ethnologist* 1 (1974), 507–514; Daniel K. Richter, "Rediscovered Links in the Covenant Chain: Previously Unpublished Transcripts of New York Indian Treaty Minutes, 1677–1691," *Proceedings of the American Antiquarian Society*, 92 (1982), 64; William A. Starna, "The Diplomatic Career of Canasatego," in William A. Pencak and Daniel K. Richter, eds., *Friends and Enemies in Penn's Woods: Indians, Colonists, and the Racial Construction of Pennsylvania* (University Park: Pennsylvania State University Press, 2004), 144–163; Fur, *Nation of Women*, 162–167.

27. Francis Jennings, *Empire of Fortune: Crowns, Colonies, and Tribes in the Seven Years War in America* (New York: W. W. Norton, 1988), 8–108; Steven C. Harper, "Delawares and Pennsylvanians

after the Walking Purchase," in Pencak and Richter, eds., *Friends and Enemies in Penn's Woods*, 167–179; Amy C. Schutt, *Peoples of the River Valleys: The Odyssey of the Delaware Indians* (Philadelphia: University of Pennsylvania Press, 2007), 62–123.

28. The best summary of these events is Fred Anderson, *Crucible of War: The Seven Years' War and the Fate of Empire in British North America, 1754–1766* (New York: Knopf, 2000), 5–107.

29. On the arrival at Easton of news of the European declaration of war, see "Material Pertaining to Pennsylvania Indian Affairs," n.p., s.v. 30 July 1756, Manuscripts on Indian Affairs, 1755–1792, American Philosophical Society, Philadelphia.

30. Ibid. In place of a series of dashes in the manuscript version, the word in brackets is supplied (with reasonable confidence) from *Minutes of the Provincial Council of Pennsylvania*, 7:218, which otherwise contains some major transcription errors. Benjamin Franklin's printed text substitutes "Power" for the p-word (*Minutes of Conferences, Held with the Indians*, 14).

31. *Minutes of Conferences, Held with the Indians*, 10–11. See Introduction, above.

32. "Material Pertaining to Pennsylvania Indian Affairs," s.v. 26 July 1756.

33. O'Callaghan and Fernow, eds., *Documents Relative to New-York*, 10:269.

34. David L. Preston, *The Texture of Contact: European and Indian Settler Communities on the Frontiers of Iroquoia, 1667–1783* (Lincoln: University of Nebraska Press, 2009), 116–146; Merritt, *At the Crossroads*, 178 (quotation).

35. Merritt, *At the Crossroads*, 169–197 (quotations from p. 179).

36. *Minutes of the Provincial Council of Pennsylvania*, 7:88–90 (quotations from p. 89).

37. Peter Silver, *Our Savage Neighbors: How Indian War Transformed Early America* (New York: W. W. Norton, 2008).

38. On these complex developments, see Anderson, *Crucible of War*, 108–293.

39. Thomas Brainerd, *The Life of John Brainerd, The Brother of David Brainerd, and His Successor as Missionary to the Indians of New Jersey* (Philadelphia, 1865), 234–235.

40. [Robert Navarre?], *Journal of Pontiac's Conspiracy*, ed. M. Agnes Burton, trans. R. C. Ford (Detroit: Speaker-Hines Printing Company, 1912), 30; Gregory Evans Dowd, *A Spirited Resistance: The North American Indian Struggle for Unity, 1745–1815* (Baltimore: Johns Hopkins University Press, 1992), 23–36; Daniel K. Richter, *Facing East from Indian Country: A Native History of Early America* (Cambridge, Mass.: Harvard University Press, 2001), 199–201.

41. *Minutes of the Provincial Council of Pennsylvania*, 8:269.

42. James Sullivan et al., eds., *The Papers of Sir William Johnson*, 14 vols. (Albany: University of the State of New York, 1921–1965), 3:315 (quotation); Wilbur R. Jacobs, *Diplomacy and Indian Gifts: Anglo-French Rivalry Along the Ohio and Northwest Frontiers, 1748–1763* (Stanford, Calif.: Stanford University Press, 1950), 160–185; Jennings, *Empire of Fortune*, 438–447 (quotation from p. 438). Pontiac—an Ottawa war chief who was one of Neolin's adherents—had little direct influence outside his own region near Detroit, to which he laid siege for several months.

43. Wallace, *King of the Delawares*, 258–266; Jennings, *Empire of Fortune*, 438–453 (quotation from p. 438); Ian K. Steele, *Warpaths: Invasions of North America* (New York: Oxford University Press, 1994), 234–242; Woody Holton, *Forced Founders: Indians, Debtors, Slaves, and the Making of the American Revolution in Virginia* (Chapel Hill: University of North Carolina Press, 1999), 138–139; Howard H. Peckham, *Pontiac and the Indian Uprising* (Princeton, N.J.: Princeton University Press, 1947), 130–220; Gregory Evans Dowd, *War Under Heaven: Pontiac, the Indian Nations, and the British Empire* (Baltimore: Johns Hopkins University Press, 2002); Richter, *Facing East from Indian Country*, 199–200.

44. Colin G. Calloway, *The American Revolution in Indian Country: Crisis and Diversity in*

Native American Communities (New York: Cambridge University Press, 1995); Gregory T. Knouff, *The Soldiers' Revolution: Pennsylvanians in Arms and the Forging of Early American Identity* (University Park: Pennsylvania State University Press, 2003), 155–193.

45. Theodore Roosevelt, *The Winning of the West* (Lincoln: University of Nebraska Press, 1995 [orig. publ. 1889–1896]), 2:373–374.

46. Carl Lotus Becker, *The History of the Political Parties in the Province of New York, 1760–1776* (Madison: University of Wisconsin Press, 1968 [orig. publ. 1909]), 5, 22.

Chapter 9: The Plan of 1764

This chapter was originally published as "Native Americans, the Plan of 1764, and a British Empire That Never Was," in Alan Tully and Robert Olwell, eds., *Cultures and Identities in Colonial British America*, pp. 269–292. © 2006 The Johns Hopkins University Press. Reprinted with permission of The Johns Hopkins University Press. Several passages have been omitted to avoid repetition with previous chapters.

1. The text is of the Plan of 1764 is printed in E. B. O'Callaghan and B. Fernow, eds., *Documents Relative to the Colonial History of the State of New-York* (Albany, N.Y., 1853–1887), 7:637–641.

2. Ibid., 8:84.

3. E. B. O'Callaghan, ed., *The Documentary History of the State of New-York*, octavo ed., 4 vols. (Albany, N.Y., 1849–1851), 2:783.

4. William L. McDowell, Jr., ed., *Documents Relating to Indian Affairs*, 2 vols. (Columbia: South Carolina Archives Department, 1958–1970), 2:354 (quotation); Kathryn E. Holland Braund, *Deerskins and Duffels: Creek Indian Trade with Anglo-America, 1685–1815* (Lincoln: University of Nebraska Press, 1993), 103–108; J. Russell Snapp, *John Stuart and the Struggle for Empire on the Southern Frontier* (Baton Rouge: Louisiana State University Press, 1996), 54–67.

5. O'Callaghan, ed., *Documentary History of New-York*, 2:784.

6. Gregory Evans Dowd, *War Under Heaven: Pontiac, the Indian Nations, and the British Empire* (Baltimore: Johns Hopkins University Press, 2002), while taking a more critical perspective on British policy than that offered here, agrees that basic structural questions concerning the British empire were at the heart of this conflict. The quotation is from Francis Jennings, *Empire of Fortune: Crowns, Colonies, and Tribes in the Seven Years War in America* (New York: W. W. Norton, 1988), 438.

7. [Robert Navarre?], *Journal of Pontiac's Conspiracy*, ed. M. Agnes Burton, trans. R. C. Ford (Detroit: Speaker-Hines Printing Company, 1912), 28–30; Gregory Evans Dowd, *A Spirited Resistance: The North American Indian Struggle for Unity, 1745–1815* (Baltimore: Johns Hopkins University Press, 1992), 23–46.

8. Samuel Hazard, ed., *Minutes of the Provincial Council of Pennsylvania, from the Organization to the Termination of the Proprietary Government*, 10 vols. (Harrisburg, Pa., 1851–1852), 7:269, 766–767; John W. Jordan, ed., "Journal of James Kenny, 1761–1763," *Pennsylvania Magazine of History and Biography*, 37 (1913): 12–13; James Sullivan et al., eds., *The Papers of Sir William Johnson*, 14 vols. (Albany: University of the State of New York, 1921–1965), 4:95 (quotation).

9. *Journal of Pontiac's Conspiracy*, 38.

10. Sullivan et al., eds., *Papers of William Johnson*, 3:529–535.

11. Ibid., 515 (quotation), 597–598.

12. Michael N. McConnell, *A Country Between: The Upper Ohio Valley and Its Peoples, 1724–1774*

(Lincoln: University of Nebraska Press, 1992), 161–163; Richard White, *The Middle Ground: Indians, Empires, and Republics in the Great Lakes Region, 1650–1815* (Cambridge: Cambridge University Press, 1991), 256–268.

13. Sullivan et al., eds., *Papers of William Johnson*, 3:515, 10:634 (quotation), 648–649; McConnell, *Country Between*, 159–181; White, *Middle Ground*, 142–185; Fred Anderson, *Crucible of War: The Seven Years' War and the Fate of Empire in British North America, 1754–1766* (New York: Knopf, 2000), 534; Jane T. Merritt, *At the Crossroads: Indians and Empires on a Mid-Atlantic Frontier, 1700–1763* (Chapel Hill: University of North Carolina Press, 2003), 176–180.

14. Sullivan et al., eds., *Papers of William Johnson*, 4:62.

15. Ibid., 3:721–722.

16. Ibid., 4:134.

17. O'Callaghan, ed., *Documentary History of New-York*, 2:771–772.

18. For examples, see ibid., 842; Sullivan et al., eds., *Papers of William Johnson*, 5:490–491; and O'Callaghan and Fernow, eds., *Documents Relative to New-York*, 7:868–870.

19. Sullivan et al., eds., *Papers of William Johnson*, 5:762.

20. John Shy, *Toward Lexington: The Role of the British Army in the Coming of the American Revolution* (Princeton, N.J.: Princeton University Press, 1965), 122–135, 192–204 (quotations from p. 122).

21. See, for just one example, the plan outlined to Johnson by John Christopher Hartwick in January 1756, in O'Callaghan and Fernow, eds., *Documents Relative to New-York*, 4:294–295.

22. On 1 July 1763, Johnson wrote to the Board of Trade about the attacks on British posts in the Great Lakes and Ohio countries. His message was evidently received in mid- to late September and acknowledged in a return letter of 29 September (O'Callaghan and Fernow, eds., *Documents Relative to New-York*, 7:567). The Proclamation, issued on 7 October, arrived in New York City on 30 November (Sullivan et al., eds., *Papers of William Johnson*, 4:255–266).

23. Sullivan et al., eds., *Papers of William Johnson*, 10:977–984 (quotation from p. 977).

24. Ibid., 982–983 (quotations); R. A. Humphreys, "Lord Shelburne and the Proclamation of 1763," *English Historical Review*, 49 (1934), 246–247, 259–260.

25. Sullivan et al., eds., *Papers of William Johnson*, 5:547–548, 737; O'Callaghan, ed., *Documentary History of New-York*, 2:892.

26. Woody Holton, *Forced Founders: Indians, Debtors, Slaves, and the Making of the American Revolution in Virginia* (Chapel Hill: University of North Carolina Press, 1999), 3–38.

27. O'Callaghan and Fernow, eds., *Documents Relative to New-York*, 7:881.

28. Ibid., 836; Sullivan et al., eds., *Papers of William Johnson*, 5:375, 737; William A. Russ, Jr., *How Pennsylvania Acquired Its Present Boundaries*, Pennsylvania Historical Studies no. 8 (University Park: Pennsylvania Historical Association, 1966), 12–26; David L. Preston, "Squatters, Indians, Proprietary Government, and Land in the Susquehanna Valley," in William A. Pencak and Daniel K. Richter, eds., *Friends and Enemies in Penn's Woods: Indians, Colonists, and the Racial Construction of Pennsylvania* (University Park: Pennsylvania State University Press, 2004), 199.

29. Jennings, *Empire of Fortune*, 101–108.

30. O'Callaghan and Fernow, eds., *Documents Relative to New-York*, 7:849–850, 891–892; Sung Bok Kim, *Landlord and Tenant in Colonial New York: Manorial Society, 1664–1775* (Chapel Hill: University of North Carolina Press, 1978), 281–415.

31. O'Callaghan and Fernow, eds., *Documents Relative to New-York*, 7:930–941.

32. Ibid., 671–674; Georgianna C. Nammack, *Fraud, Politics, and the Dispossession of the*

Indians: The Iroquois Land Frontier in the Colonial Period (Norman: University of Oklahoma Press, 1969).

33. O'Callaghan and Fernow, eds., *Documents Relative to New-York,* 7:873–874.

34. Marjoleine Kars, *Breaking Loose Together: The Regulator Rebellion in Pre-Revolutionary North Carolina* (Chapel Hill: University of North Carolina Press, 2002), 27–54; Merritt, *At the Crossroads,* 19–49, 171–172; Preston, "Squatters, Indians, Proprietary Government, and Land," 180–200.

35. Daniel K. Richter, *The Ordeal of the Longhouse: The Peoples of the Iroquois League in the Era of European Colonization* (Chapel Hill: University of North Carolina Press, 1992), 137–138, 250–254, 263–265.

36. Verner W. Crane, *The Southern Frontier, 1670–1732* (Durham, N.C.: Duke University Press, 1928), 120–154; Braund, *Deerskins and Duffels,* 81–100.

37. For examples see McDowell, ed., *Documents Relating to Indian Affairs,* 2:566–569, 576–579.

38. W. J. Eccles, *France in America* (New York: Harper and Row, 1972), 119–120; Eccles, "The Fur Trade and Western Imperialism," *William and Mary Quarterly,* 3rd ser., 40 (1983), 341–362; White, *Middle Ground,* 108–119.

39. Sullivan et al., eds., *Papers of William Johnson,* 4:443–444.

40. Ibid., 10:983–984; Braund, *Deerskins and Duffles,* 100–102.

41. McConnell, *Country Between,* 43–45, 148–150, 161–163. Particularly under legislation passed in 1722, Pennsylvania attempted to license traders in a way similar to South Carolina's system. But a lack of enforcement mechanisms, along with an explicit exemption that allowed any Euro-American to trade with Indians from his own house, made the effort a virtual dead letter. See Albright G. Zimmerman, "The Indian Trade of Colonial Pennsylvania" (Ph.D. diss., University of Delaware, 1966), 179–204.

42. O'Callaghan and Fernow, eds., *Documents Relative to New-York,* 7:560–561, 674.

43. McDowell, ed., *Documents Relating to Indian Affairs,* 2:481; John Smolenski, "The Death of Sawantaeny and the Problem of Justice on the Frontier," and Louis Waddell, "Justice, Retribution and the Case of John Toby," in Pencak and Richter, eds., *Friends and Enemies,* 104–143.

44. G. S. Rowe, "The Frederick Stump Affair, 1768, and Its Challenge to Legal Historians of Early Pennsylvania," *Pennsylvania History,* 49 (1982), 259–288; Alden T. Vaughan, "Frontier Banditti and the Indians: The Paxton Boys' Legacy, 1763–1775," *Pennsylvania History,* 51 (1984), 19–22; Linda A. Ries, "'The Rage of Opposing Government': The Stump Affair of 1768," *Cumberland County History,* vol. 1, no. 1 (1984), 21–45.

45. Sullivan et al., eds., *Papers of William Johnson,* 5:201.

46. O'Callaghan and Fernow, eds., *Documents Relative to New-York,* 7:877.

47. Ibid., 842.

48. Sullivan et al., eds., *Papers of William Johnson,* 4:79; O'Callaghan and Fernow, eds., *Documents Relative to New-York,* 7:661–666, 976.

49. O'Callaghan and Fernow, eds., *Documents Relative to New-York,* 7:968.

50. Ibid., 668.

51. Sullivan et al., eds., *Papers of William Johnson,* 5:319–320, 336; O'Callaghan and Fernow, eds., *Documents Relative to New-York,* 8:30.

52. O'Callaghan and Fernow, eds., *Documents Relative to New-York,* 7:634–635.

53. Ibid., 637–638.

54. Ibid., 638–639.

55. To my knowledge, no systematic comparison of British policies in South Asia and North America in the 1760s has ever been undertaken, but for an introduction to the issues involved on

the subcontinent, see Rajat Kanta Ray, "Indian Society and the Establishment of British Supremacy, 1765–1818," *The Oxford History of the British Empire*, vol. 2: *The Eighteenth Century*, ed. P. J. Marshall (Oxford: Oxford University Press, 1998), 508–529.

56. O'Callaghan and Fernow, eds., *Documents Relative to New-York*, 7:640–641.

57. Ibid., 637, 639–641.

58. Ibid., 638, 641.

59. Ibid., 661–666 (quotation from p. 663).

60. Clarence E. Carter, ed., "Observations of Superintendent John Stuart and Governor James Grant of East Florida on the Proposed Plan of 1764 for the Future Management of Indian Affairs," *American Historical Review*, 20 (1915), 817–827 (quotations from pp. 817, 820).

61. Snapp, *John Stuart and the Struggle for Empire*, 68–107.

62. Dorothy V. Jones, *License for Empire: Colonialism by Treaty in Early America* (Chicago: University of Chicago Press, 1982), 42–52.

63. Sullivan et al., eds., *Papers of William Johnson*, 4:466–481, 485–488, 503–508, 526–533, 547–549, 579–583; O'Callaghan and Fernow, eds., *Documents Relative to New-York*, 7:652–653, 750–758; McConnell, *A Country Between*, 196–206; Anderson, *Crucible of War*, 617–637.

64. O'Callaghan and Fernow, eds., *Documents Relative to New-York*, 7:746–747.

65. Ibid., 838.

66. Sullivan et al., eds., *Papers of William Johnson*, 4:339, 396.

67. O'Callaghan and Fernow, eds., *Documents Relative to New-York*, 7:747–748, 842 (1st quotation); Sullivan et al., eds., *Papers of William Johnson*, 5:1–5, 566–567 (2nd quotation); Jack M. Sosin, *Whitehall and the Wilderness: The Middle West in British Colonial Policy, 1760–1775* (Lincoln: University of Nebraska Press, 1961), 73–98, 128–169.

68. O'Callaghan and Fernow, eds., *Documents Relative to New-York*, 7:880–882.

69. Ibid., 877–878, 915 (quotation).

70. Edmund S. and Helen M. Morgan, *The Stamp Act Crisis: Prologue to Revolution*, rev. paperback ed. (New York: Collier Books, 1963), 217–230; Kars, *Breaking Loose Together*, 46.

71. O'Callaghan and Fernow, eds., *Documents Relative to New-York*, 7:914.

72. Ibid., 881.

73. Sullivan et al., eds., *Papers of William Johnson*, 6:61.

74. O'Callaghan and Fernow, eds., *Documents Relative to New-York*, 7:981–983 (quotation from p. 981); 8:7.

75. Ibid., 8:19–31, 57–58 (quotations from pp. 22–23).

76. Ibid., 24–25, 31.

77. Ibid., 7:637. If it had been passed, this provision of the Plan of 1764 would have been a major constitutional innovation, in overturning laws that had long since been approved by the Crown and in its assertion of a Parliamentary, rather than Crown, veto power. The Currency Act of 1764, by comparison, only banned *future* provincial emissions of paper money, and did nothing to call into question legislation that had previously passed without veto (Danby Pickering, ed., *Statutes at Large*, 109 vols. [Cambridge, 1762–1869], 26:103–105).

78. Moncure Daniel Conway, ed., *The Writings of Thomas Paine*, 4 vols. (New York: G. P. Putnam's Sons, 1894–1896), 1:100 (quotation); Edward Countryman, "Indians, The Colonial Order, and the Social Significance of the American Revolution," *William and Mary Quarterly*, 3rd ser., 53 (1996), 342–362; Holton, *Forced Founders*, 35–38.

Chapter 10. Onas, the Long Knife

This chapter was originally published as "Onas, the Long Knife: Pennsylvanians and Indians, 1783–1794," in Frederick Hoxie, Ronald Hoffman, and Peter Albert, eds., *Native Americans and the Early Republic*, pp. 125–161. © 1999 by the Rector and Visitors of the University of Virginia. Reprinted by permission of the University of Virginia Press. The opening paragraph has been slightly modified for this volume.

　1. Samuel Hazard et al., eds., *Pennsylvania Archives*, 9 ser., 138 vols. (Philadelphia and Harrisburg, 1852–1935), 9th ser., vol. 1, pt. 1, 345–346.

　2. John Parrish, "Trip to Lower Sandusky, 1793," 1882 ms. copy by Richard Eddy, pp. 118–121, Historical Society of Pennsylvania, Philadelphia.

　3. William Hartshorne, "Journal of a Journey to Detroit, 1793" (typescript copy), s.v. 14 June 1793, Friends Historical Library, Swarthmore College, Swarthmore, Pennsylvania. The Ojibwas' simultaneous use of *Shemockteman* (Virginian) and *Boston* may not have been unusual and perhaps epitomizes the degree to which they conflated all residents of the United States. In the mid-1780s Native diplomats in the Great Lakes region and Ohio country often applied phrases interpreters translated as "Bostonians" to the United States as a whole; for examples, see Speech of Joseph Brant, 21 May 1783, John Deserundyon to Daniel Claus, 7 July 1783, Haldimand Papers, Add. Mss. 21,756, folio 140v, 21,774, folio 322r, British Library, London; and Richard Butler to William Butler, 11 September 1786, *Iroquois Indians: A Documentary History of the Diplomacy of the Six Nations and Their League*, microfilm, 50 reels (Woodbridge, Conn., 1985), reel 38. For similar uses of "Big Knives" or "Virginians" as names for people and leaders of the United States during the same period, see Treaty minutes, 30 June, 8 September, 6 October 1783, Haldimand Papers, Add. Mss. 21,799, folios 113r, 138v, 144v–145r. On the origin of the term in the colonial period (its Iroquoian version, *Assaryquoa*, had been used at least since Virginia Governor Lord Howard of Effingham presented a cutlass to headmen of the Five Nations Iroquois at a treaty council in 1684), see Francis Jennings et al., eds., *The History and Culture of Iroquois Diplomacy: An Interdisciplinary Guide to the Treaties of the Six Nations and Their League* (Syracuse, N.Y.: Syracuse University Press, 1985), 230. Today, Great Lakes Native peoples still sometimes refer to Euro-Americans as *Chomokomon* (R. David Edmunds, personal communication, 4 March 1992).

　4. *Minutes of the Supreme Executive Council of Pennsylvania, from Its Organization to the Termination of the Revolution*, 6 vols. numbered 11–16 (Harrisburg, 1852–1853), 16:404.

　5. Hazard et al., eds., *Pennsylvania Archives*, 1st ser., 11:148 (quotation); Thomas P. Slaughter, *The Whiskey Rebellion: Frontier Epilogue to the American Revolution* (New York: Oxford University Press, 1986), 75–77.

　6. Parrish, "Trip to Lower Sandusky," 57–59. Moravian minister John Heckewelder confirmed that the Wyandots, too, called "all the People of the United States . . . Brothers the big Knifes," and as early as 1786 a Seneca headman had addressed a land surveyor from Pennsylvania in similar terms (Heckewelder, "Journey with the Commissioners to the Indian Treaty," 8 April–25 September 1793, folio 24v [2nd pagination], Ferdinand Julius Dreer Collection, Historical Society of Pennsylvania; Hazard et al., eds., *Pennsylvania Archives*, 1st ser., 10:740–741).

　7. "Names by which the different Indian Nations address each other in public conferences," n.d., *Iroquois Indians*, reel 1; William N. Fenton, "Structure, Continuity, and Change in the Process of Iroquois Treaty Making," in Jennings et al., eds., *History and Culture*, 10–14, 21–22; Richard

White, *The Middle Ground: Indians, Empires, and Republics in the Great Lakes Region, 1650–1815* (Cambridge: Cambridge University Press, 1991), 84–85.

8. Two prominent examples are the council titles for the governors of New France and New York, used widely in the intercultural diplomacy of the northeastern quarter of the continent. *Onontio* ("Great Mountain") was an Iroquoian translation of the surname of an early governor of New France, Charles Huault de Montmagny. *Corlaer*, an alternate spelling of the name of Arent van Curler (a prominent figure in early relations between Dutch colonists and Native peoples of the Hudson and Mohawk River Valleys), was applied to English governors of New York beginning in the late 1670s (Jennings et al., eds., *History and Culture*, 235, 240, 247; Daniel K. Richter, *The Ordeal of the Longhouse: The Peoples of the Iroquois League in the Era of European Colonization* [Chapel Hill: University of North Carolina Press, 1992], 93–95, 131–132, 140–141).

9. Francis Jennings, *The Ambiguous Iroquois Empire: The Covenant Chain Confederation of Indian Tribes with English Colonies from Its Beginnings to the Lancaster Treaty of 1744* (New York: W. W. Norton, 1984), 309–346.

10. White, *Middle Ground*, 52–53.

11. Hazard et al., eds., *Pennsylvania Archives*, 9th ser., vol. 1, pt. 1, 346.

12. Peter C. Mancall, "The Revolutionary War and the Indians of the Upper Susquehanna Valley," *American Indian Culture and Research Journal*, 12 (1988), 39–57; Solon J. Buck and Elizabeth Hawthorn Buck, *The Planting of Civilization in Western Pennsylvania* (Pittsburgh: University of Pittsburgh Press, 1939), 135–203. The violent struggle between Connecticut and Pennsylvania claimants for control of the Wyoming Valley may be followed in *Minutes of Executive Council*, vols. 12–15; and Hazard et al., eds., *Pennsylvania Archives*, 1st ser., vol. 10. For brief overviews of Pennsylvania's boundary disputes, see Buck and Buck, *Planting of Civilization*, 156–174; and Peter S. Onuf, *The Origins of the Federal Republic: Jurisdictional Controversies in the United States, 1775–1787* (Philadelphia: University of Pennsylvania Press, 1983), 49–73. Among the state governments involved, the border with Virginia was finally resolved in 1785 and that with New York in 1787; Pennsylvania's western boundary line was surveyed and marked in 1786 (*Minutes of Executive Council*, 14:360, 15:116–118, 340).

13. George P. Donehoo, *A History of the Indian Villages and Place Names in Pennsylvania, with Numerous Historical Notes and References* (Harrisburg, Pa.: Telegraph Press, 1928), 39–40; Anthony F. C. Wallace, *The Death and Rebirth of the Seneca* (New York: Knopf, 1969), 168–169; Donald H. Kent, *Iroquois Indians I: History of Pennsylvania Purchases from the Indians* (New York: Garland, 1974), 224–228.

14. Charles F. Wray and Harry L. Schoff, "A Preliminary Report on the Seneca Sequence in Western New York, 1550–1687," *Pennsylvania Archaeologist*, 23, no. 2 (1953), 53–63; Richter, *Ordeal of the Longhouse*, 256.

15. Guy Johnson to Frederick Haldimand, 23 April, 19 May 1781, 11 January 1783, Haldimand Papers, Add. Mss. 21,767, folios 175–176, 181–184, 21,768, folios 129–132; Barbara Graymont, *The Iroquois in the American Revolution* (Syracuse, N.Y.: Syracuse University Press, 1972), 192–222.

16. Allan Maclean to Ephraim Douglass, 16 July 1783, Haldimand Papers, Add. Mss. 21,763, folio 192; Wallace, *Death and Rebirth*, 163–172, 195.

17. *Minutes of Executive Council*, 14, 40. See also ibid., 45–46; and Hazard et al., eds., *Pennsylvania Archives*, 1st ser., 11:507–509.

18. William Bradford to Elias Boudinot, 24 July [1794], Wallace Papers, vol. 2, folio 95, John William Wallace Collection, Historical Society of Pennsylvania (quotation); Carl B. Lechner, "The Erie Triangle: The Final Link Between Philadelphia and the Great Lakes," *Pennsylvania Magazine*

of History and Biography, 116 (1992), 59–85. Lechner discounts the role of land speculation, but Norman Wilkinson, "Land Policy and Speculation in Pennsylvania, 1779–1800: A Test of the New Democracy" (Ph.D. diss., University of Pennsylvania, 1958), esp. 61–63, makes a strong case for its role in the state's actions.

19. Buck and Buck, *Planting of Civilization*, 203–207; Wilkinson, "Land Policy," 19–44. Statistics calculated from *Minutes of Executive Council*, vols. 13–14, passim, and 16:264–266. The exact recorded total of payments authorized in 1783–1785 for interest due as of April 1782 and April 1784 was £37,486:10:9. That this was only a fraction of the total actually due (claimants apparently had to apply for payment) is indicated by a comparison of the $1,500,000 total principal cited for 1790 and the amounts of principal due listed with the interest payments: £147,704 ($459,359) in 1783; £235,642 ($732,847) in 1784; and (inferring from the interest rate of 6%) £241,317 ($750,496) in 1785 (figures rounded to the nearest pound or dollar). Thanks to JoAnna McDonald for her assistance in compiling these figures.

20. *Minutes of Executive Council*, 14:271–274 (quotations); Hazard et al., eds., *Pennsylvania Archives*, 1st ser., 10:379–384; Wilkinson, "Land Policy," 19 (quotation).

21. *Minutes of Executive Council*, 14:477, 596; Hazard et al., eds., *Pennsylvania Archives*, 1st ser., 10:53–54. On patents for Philadelphia city lots, see *Minutes of Executive Council*, vols. 13–15, passim. The Donation Lands were formally set aside in March 1785; surveys began the following summer, and distributions in late 1786 (*Minutes of Executive Council*, 14:386, 15:71; Hazard et al., eds., *Pennsylvania Archives*, 1st ser., 11:513–520).

22. Daniel Brodhead to Joseph Reed, 2 November 1780, Daniel Brodhead Letterbook, 1780–1781, Historical Society of Pennsylvania; *Minutes of Executive Council*, 13:425–426, 617, 644–645, 14:16; Treaty minutes, 31 August 1783, Alexander McKee to John Johnson, 9 September 1783, Haldimand Papers, Add. Mss. 21,779, folios 132, 141; Frederick Muhlenberg to Pennsylvania Delegates, 12 September 1783, *Iroquois Indians*, reel 37; Hazard et al., eds., *Pennsylvania Archives*, 1st ser., 10:448; Robert L. Brunhouse, *The Counter-Revolution in Pennsylvania, 1776–1790* (Harrisburg: Pennsylvania Historical Commission, 1942), 135–140. Most of the depreciation certificates and rights to Donation Lands were gobbled up at heavy discount by speculators who sat on them in hopes of nice profits. As a result, not only were dreams of a republic of happy, debt-free yeoman thwarted, the patenting of the Donation and Depreciation Lands—like all western Pennsylvania acreage—moved very slowly until early in the nineteenth century. The state liquidated its debt instead through sales of lands farther east, through taxation, through statutes of limitation, and, finally, through the Federal Funding and Assumption Plan of 1790 (Thomas Henry, "Depreciation Lands—Pennsylvania Population Company," in Joseph H. Bausman, *History of Beaver County, Pennsylvania and Its Centennial Celebration* [New York, 1904], 2:1227–1233; Buck and Buck, *Planting of Civilization*, 206–214; Wilkinson, "Land Policy," 27–44, 126–136). Yet it matters little that the scheme for erasing the state's debt through creative real estate marketing came to naught. The important point is that, as state officials approached their earliest postwar Indian treaties, the scheme stood foremost in their minds.

23. Hazard et al., eds., *Pennsylvania Archives*, 1st ser., 10:25.

24. *Journals of the Continental Congress*, 34 vols. (Washington, D.C.: U.S. Government Printing Office, 1904–1937), 23:516–517; Hazard et al., eds., *Pennsylvania Archives*, 1st ser., 10:45 (quotation); Treaty minutes, 2 July 1783, Haldimand Papers, Add. Mss. 21,779, folios 115–116; Reginald Horsman, "American Indian Policy in the Old Northwest, 1783–1812," *William and Mary Quarterly*, 3rd ser., 18 (1961), 35–40; Dorothy V. Jones, *Licence for Empire: Colonialism by Treaty in Early America* (Chicago: University of Chicago Press, 1982), 139–156.

25. Maclean to Haldimand, 18 May 1783, Haldimand Papers, Add. Mss. 21,763, folio 118.

26. Hazard et al., eds., *Pennsylvania Archives*, 1st ser., 10:54. The same rhetorical juxtaposition that occurs in this Dickinson letter of June 1783 appears in his 19 April 1783 letter to the state's congressional delegation, in which the phrase "extirpate them from the Land where they were born and now live" is followed immediately by "But, that if they behave as they ought to do, they shall be treated not only justly, but friendly" (ibid., 45).

27. Ibid., 46, 119–125 (quotation), 320–321; *Minutes of Executive Council*, 14:40.

28. Muhlenberg to Delegates, 12 September 1783, *Iroquois Indians*, reel 37 (1st quotation); Hazard et al., eds., *Pennsylvania Archives*, 1st ser., 10:111 (2nd quotation), 316–317 (3rd quotation), 318–319; *Minutes of Executive Council*, 14:186–187. An additional £1,000 ($3,110) was allocated for the commissioners' expenses. The 1784–1785 exchange rate of £1 = $3.11 (conversely, $1.00 = £0.32) is based on "State of the Accounts of the Pennsylvania Indian Commissioners . . . ," Hazard et al., eds., *Pennsylvania Archives*, 3rd ser., 7:483.

29. "List of Indians at Fort Stanwix (dated) October 22d 1784," *Iroquois Indians*, reel 38; Hazard et al., eds., *Pennsylvania Archives*, 1st ser., 10:346 (1st quotation); Arthur Lee and Richard Butler to George Clinton, 19 August 1784, in "Proceedings of the Commissioners appointed to hold Treaties with the Indians in the State of New York . . . ," *Iroquois Indians*, reel 37 (2nd quotation); U.S. Commissioners minutes, 12 October 1784, in Neville B. Craig, *The Olden Time*, 2 vols., reprint ed. (Cincinnati, 1876 [1848]), 2:415; Hallock F. Raup, ed., "Journal of Griffith Evans, 1784–1785," *Pennsylvania Magazine of History and Biography*, 65 (1941), 208–209. On Pennsylvania's plans to proceed alone, see Hazard et al., eds., *Pennsylvania Archives*, 1st ser., 10:111, 124–125, 152, 317; and *Minutes of Executive Council*, 14:45–46. Only the fact that "a separate treaty must be attended with a very great expence" prevented the Pennsylvanians from following the example of their New York neighbors, who did conduct independent negotiations (*Minutes of Executive Council*, 14:46).

30. "Extracts from the Journal of The Commissioners of Indian Affairs, for the Northern and Middle departments—Commencing in 1784; and Ending 8th February 1786," Indian Treaties, 27r–31r, Wayne Papers, Historical Society of Pennsylvania (quotation from p. 30r).

31. "Captain Brants Account of . . . the Treaty in October 1784," *Iroquois Indians*, reel 38. See also David Hill to his brother-in-law [Daniel Claus?], 6 November 1784, ibid.

32. [Butler], Notes on meeting of Commissioners, 18–20 October 1784, *Iroquois Indians*, reel 38; Raup, ed., "Journal of Evans," 212, 214 (1st and 3rd quotations, brackets in original); "Extracts from Journal of Commissioners," Indian Treaties, 31r–42v, Wayne Papers (remaining quotations from p. 37v); Commissioners minutes, in Craig, ed., *Olden Time*, 2:422–423; Randolph C. Downes, *Council Fires on the Upper Ohio: A Narrative of Indian Affairs in the Upper Ohio Valley Until 1795* (Pittsburgh: University of Pittsburgh Press, 1968 [1940]), 277–292; Graymont, *Iroquois in American Revolution*, 266–283; Kent, *Iroquois Indians I*, 40–71. Because of confusion over Indian place names, the commissioners may not have understood the extent of Cornplanter's offer to revise the 1768 treaty line. Even so, Cornplanter seemed to be overstepping his authority. When the Iroquois leaders agreed to attend the Fort Stanwix council, they stated explicitly that they were "not impowered to conclude a final Peace with the United States" and were only "to settle some Points necessary to be arranged previous to a more general Meeting which is intended to be held, to establish an everlasting Peace and Friendship between all the Nations and the United States" (Joseph Brant to Henry Glen, 11 August 1784, *Iroquois Indians*, reel 37).

33. "Extracts from Journal of Commissioners," Indian Treaties, 44r–55v, 63v–64v, 72r–94r, Wayne Papers; "Articles of a treaty concluded at Fort McIntosh . . . ," 21 January 1785, "Articles of a Treaty concluded at the mouth of the Great Miami . . . ," 31 January 1786, Wayne Papers, vol. 19,

folios 47, 50; *Minutes of Executive Council*, 14:143; Hazard et al., eds., *Pennsylvania Archives*, 1st ser., 10:332, 508–509, 11:510.

34. Benjamin Smith Barton, Journal (Pa.—Indian Visits), n.d. [1785], s.v. "Fort McIntosh, Indian Treaty," Historical Society of Pennsylvania (quotation); Hazard et al., eds., *Pennsylvania Archives*, 1st ser., 10:279; "Extracts from Journal of Commissioners," Indian Treaties, pp. 42v–44r, 64v–66r, 90r–91v, Wayne Papers; "Speech of the United Indian Nations, at their Confederate Council, held near the mouth of the Detroit river, the 28th November and 18th December, 1786," *New American State Papers: Indian Affairs*, 13 vols. (Wilmington, Del: Scholarly Resources, 1972), 4:17–18; Wallace, *Death and Rebirth*, 150–154; Wiley Sword, *President Washington's Indian War: The Struggle for the Old Northwest, 1790–1795* (Norman: University of Oklahoma Press, 1985), 23–30. Griffith Evans, secretary to the Pennsylvania commissioners, belittled the charges against liquor traders as politically motivated, but his journal recounts plenty of drinking and, on one occasion, notes with some surprise that the Native participants were "sober for want of an opportunity to get intoxicated" (Raup, ed., "Journal of Evans," 208–214 [quotation from p. 214]).

35. Hazard et al., eds., *Pennsylvania Archives*, 1st ser., 10:357, 360 (quotation).

36. Copy of ms. deed from Six Nations to Pennsylvania, 23 October 1784 (brackets supplied from accompanying typescript), *Iroquois Indians*, reel 38.

37. *Minutes of Executive Council*, 16:501. According to the Pennsylvania commissioners' fiscal accounts, goods worth a total of £2,104:5:7 (slightly over $6,544) were delivered to the Indian participants at Fort Stanwix and Fort McIntosh. The Fort McIntosh Treaty stipulates a payment to the Wyandots and Delawares of "two thousand dollars, consisting of an excellent assortment of goods of the first quality, calculated in the best manner to supply your wants, which is a greater proportion than what we have given to your uncles, the Six Nations, and is certainly a very generous consideration" (Treaty minutes, 9–25 January 1785, in Bausman, *History of Beaver County*, 2:1203–1210 [quotation from p. 1204]). If the Wyandots and Delawares indeed received $2,000 in goods, $4,544 would remain for the Iroquois at Fort Stanwix. The commissioners had purchased an additional £732:13:1 ($2,280) worth of goods, which they did not see fit to distribute and resold after completing their work (Hazard et al., eds., *Pennsylvania Archives*, 3rd ser., 7:477–480; Raup, ed., "Journal of Evans," 232).

38. Hazard et al., eds., *Pennsylvania Archives*, 1st ser., X, 360.

39. "The speech of the Cornplanter, Half-Town, and the Great Tree . . ." 1 December 1790, *New American State Papers*, 4:24 (2nd and last quotations); *Minutes of Executive Council*, 16:501–502 (remaining quotations); *Minutes of the First [through Third] Session[s] of the Ninth General Assembly of the Commonwealth of Pennsylvania . . .* (Philadelphia, 1784[–1785]), 314–320.

40. Raup, ed., "Journal of Evans," 214.

41. *Minutes of Executive Council*, 16:501–502 (quotations); Hazard et al., eds., *Pennsylvania Archives*, 1st ser., 10:507; Thomas S. Abler, ed., *Chainbreaker: The Revolutionary War Memoirs of Governor Blacksnake as Told to Benjamin Williams* (Lincoln: University of Nebraska Press, 1989), 163–168.

42. *Minutes of Ninth General Assembly*, 317–318 (2nd quotation); Hazard et al., eds., *Pennsylvania Archives*, 1st ser., 10:508–509 (1st and 3rd quotations); Brant to Peter Schuyler, 23 March 1785, *Iroquois Indians*, reel 37; Kent, *Iroquois Indians I*, 59–69.

43. "Extracts from Journal of Commissioners," Indian Treaties, folio 35v, Wayne Papers.

44. Memorial from Cornplanter, 20 May 1785, *Iroquois Indians*, reel 38. Although his language seemed to include all of the Six Nations, Cornplanter set the Allegany communities apart from other Iroquois—even other Senecas—who protested the treaties. "We count Ourselves a people

Capable of Speaking and Acting for Ourselves, and the Lands granted were Ours and not theirs," the Allegany leader said in answer to his Indian critics.

45. Treaty minutes, 12 July 1785 (enclosed in Harmar to Knox, 16 July 1785), Treaty minutes, 27 March 1786, *Iroquois Indians*, reel 38 (quotations from 12 July 1785).

46. Hazard et al., eds., *Pennsylvania Archives*, 1st ser., 10:412–413, 418 (1st quotation), 11:178, 12:322 (2nd quotation); *Minutes of Ninth General Assembly*, 320–322. On the activities of the surveyors, see *Minutes of Executive Council*, 14:364, 399, 454, 539–540, 15:12, 16, 19, 38–39, 180, 190–191, 202, 204, 212, 220, 340. On the Seneca Tiowanies' observation of the survey from Conewango Creek to Lake Erie, see Merle H. Deardorff and Donald H. Kent, "John Adlum on the Allegheny: Memoirs for the Year 1794," *Pennsylvania Magazine of History and Biography*, 84 (1960), 318n–319n; and Kent, *Iroquois Indians I*, 104–105. Kent's evaluation of Seneca reactions to survey parties in general (*Iroquois Indians I*, 85–128) sharply disagrees with the interpretation offered here.

47. Hazard et al., eds., *Pennsylvania Archives*, 3rd ser., 7:478–485 (1st quotation from p. 485), 1st ser., 10:489–490 (2nd quotation), 496; *Minutes of Executive Council*, 14:400, 507–508, 528. Surviving records indicate even less of an effort to comply with the terms of the deed extracted from the Wyandots and Delawares at Fort McIntosh in January 1785, which pledged rifles for two of the chiefs who signed it. See Hazard et al., eds., *Pennsylvania Archives*, 1st ser., 11:510, 10:395–396, 9th ser., vol. 2, pt. 1, 820; *Minutes of Executive Council*, 14:365–367, 379.

48. Hazard et al., eds., *Pennsylvania Archives*, 1st ser., 10:510 (1st quotation; emphasis added); *Minutes of Executive Council*, 14:531, 536–537, 644 (2nd quotation).

49. Hazard et al., eds., *Pennsylvania Archives*, 1st ser., 10:740–741.

50. Butler to President of Congress, 25 April 1786, Speech of Cornplanter to Congress, 2 May 1786, Speeches of Butler and Cornplanter, 1 June 1786, *Iroquois Indians*, reel 38; *Journals of Continental Congress*, 30:234–236.

51. Hazard et al., eds., *Pennsylvania Archives*, 1st ser., 12:300–302.

52. Ibid., 1st ser., 10:763.

53. Samuel H. Parsons to President of Continental Congress, 27 October 1785, "Speech of the United Indian Nations, at their confederate Council held . . . Between the 28th November and 18th December 1786," *Iroquois Indians*, reel 38; White, *Middle Ground*, 413–468.

54. Butler to Knox, 13 December 1786 (extract), Treaty minutes, 31 January, 10, 19, 22–24 February 1787, *Iroquois Indians*, reels 38 (1st quotation), 39; *Minutes of Executive Council*, 16:504–505 (2nd quotation).

55. Jonathan Heart to Knox, 18, 23 October 1787, *Iroquois Indians*, reel 39; Thomas Hughes to Wayne, 22 November 1792, 24 February 1793, Wayne Papers, vol. 23, folio 41 (quotation), vol. 25, folio 50(2). On the establishment of Fort Franklin, see Hazard et al., eds., *Pennsylvania Archives*, 1st ser., 11:271, 12:361–362. Great Tree was evidently living on the Genesee in 1789 (Sharongyowanew et al. to Clinton, 30 July 1789, Great Tree and Sagoyadyastha to same, 10 December 1789, *Iroquois Indians*, reel 39).

56. *Minutes of Executive Council*, 15:116, 121, 382; Hazard et al., eds., *Pennsylvania Archives*, 1st ser., 11:211, 237, 241–243; William A. Russ, Jr., *How Pennsylvania Acquired Its Present Boundaries* (University Park: Pennsylvania Historical Association, 1966), 61–65; Lechner, "Erie Triangle," 59–68.

57. Hazard et al., eds., *Pennsylvania Archives*, 1st ser., 11:245, 395–396, 9th ser., vol.1, pt. 1, 276; *Minutes of Executive Council*, 15:530–532, 553–555. The 1788 exchange rate of $1.00 = £.375 (£1 = $2.67) comes from Hazard et al., eds., *Pennsylvania Archives*, 1st ser., 11:390; the figure agrees with Wilkinson's equation of £5393:16:7 with $14,350 in a discussion of a settling of the treaty commissioners'

accounts that occurred in 1791 ("Land Policy," 25–27). The purchase agreement with the Federal government calculated the area of the Triangle at 202,187 acres.

58. Hazard et al., eds., *Pennsylvania Archives*, 1st ser., 11:395–396 (quotations), 405.

59. "Minutes of the Treaty of Fort Harmar, Commencing 13th December 1788, And Ending 11th January 1789," "Return of Indians of the Six Nations, present at the Treaty at Fort Harmar," n.d., "Appendix to the Minutes of the Treaty of Fort Harmar, 1789 . . . ," "Minutes of a treaty . . . begun at Greene Ville on the 16th day of June, and ended on the 10th day of August 1795," Indian Treaties, 99r–v, 105r–v, 111(a)r–115r, 129v–130r, 132r, 140v–141r, 271r (quotation), Wayne Papers; Sword, *President Washington's Indian War*, 73–75; Isabel Thompson Kelsay, *Joseph Brant: Man of Two Worlds* (Syracuse, N.Y.: Syracuse University Press, 1984), 424–426.

60. Hazard et al., eds., *Pennsylvania Archives*, 1st ser., 11:529–533; Deed, Gyatwache, alias the Cornplanter, et al. to the State of Pennsylvania, Jan. [ ] 1789, RG 26, no. 47, Pennsylvania State Archives, Harrisburg; *Minutes of Executive Council*, 16:502–503.

61. "Minutes of Fort Harmer," 11 January 1789, Indian Treaties, 129v–130r, Wayne Papers.

62. Hazard et al., eds., *Pennsylvania Archives*, 1st ser., 11:529–533, 593–594, 9th ser., vol. 1, pt. 2, 555, 559–560, 731–733, 740, 743, 747, 749–750; *Minutes of Executive Council*, 16:161–162, 169, 375, 547; Kent, *Iroquois Indians I*, 173.

63. Hazard et al., eds., *Pennsylvania Archives*, 1st ser., 11:245; *Minutes of Executive Council*, 15:553–555, 605, 607, 609, 616 (quotation), 629.

64. *Minutes of Executive Council*, 16:503–504 (quotations); Hazard et al., eds., *Pennsylvania Archives*, 1st ser., 11:732–733.

65. *Minutes of Executive Council*, 16:353, 357–358 (quotation), 396–399, 437–440, 442, 456–457, 508; Hazard et al., eds., *Pennsylvania Archives*, 1st ser., 11:719–720, 12:319–321.

66. Hazard et al., eds., *Pennsylvania Archives*, 1st ser., 11:732–733, 741, 12:86–87, 321; *Minutes of Executive Council*, 16:497, 502 (quotation).

67. "Speech of Guayshuta, [n.d.] 1790," Ayer Manuscripts, N.A. 317, Newberry Library, Chicago.

68. *Minutes of Executive Council*, 16:36–37, 505, 507–508, 510, –511; Hazard et al., eds., *Pennsylvania Archives*, 1st ser., 11:562–563, 741.

69. Hazard et al., eds., *Pennsylvania Archives*, 1st ser., 12:322; Hazard et al., eds., *Pennsylvania Archives*, 9th ser., vol. 1, pt. 1, 25–26 (quotation).

70. Hazard et al., eds., *Pennsylvania Archives*, 1st ser., 12:83–86; 9th ser., vol. 1, pt. 1, 23–24, 26, 120–121; Merle H. Deardorff, "The Cornplanter Grant in Warren County," *Western Pennsylvania Historical Magazine*, 24 (1941), 1–22.

71. Instructions to Arthur St. Clair, 26 October 1787, 2 July 1788, Henry Knox to George Washington, 23 May 1789, *New American State Papers*, 4:16–18; "Articles of Treaty at Fort McIntosh," "Articles of a Treaty made at Fort Harmar . . . ," 9 January 1789, Wayne Papers, XIX, folios 47 (1st quotation), 73 (remaining quotations).

72. Instructions to Rufus Putnam, 3–4 April 1792, "Extracts from Journal of Commissioners of United States," "Minutes of a treaty . . . at Greene Ville," Indian Treaties, 211r–215v, 254r–261r, 262r–313r, Wayne Papers; Knox to Wayne, 5 January 1792 [sic: 1793], Timothy Pickering to same, 8 April 1795, Wayne Papers, vol. 24, folio 38½, XL, folio 35.

73. Speeches of Cornplanter, Half-Town, and Great Tree, 1 December 1790, 10 January, 7 February 1791, with replies of Washington, 29 December 1790, 19 January 1791, and of Knox, 8 February 1791, *New American State Papers*, 4:24–29 (quotations from pp. 28, 27; Hazard et al., eds., *Pennsylvania Archives*, 1st ser., XII, 32.

74. Hazard et al., eds., *Pennsylvania Archives*, 9th ser., vol. 1, pt. 1, 28, 89, 98, 160–161, 325, 328;

Speech of Cornplanter, 9 April 1791, Procter, Diary, s.v. 27 April 1791, *New American State Papers*, 4:52, 43–44; *Minutes of Executive Council*, 16:547.

75. John O'Bail (Cornplanter) to John Polhemus, 8 May 1794, Knox to Wayne, 7 June 1794, Wayne Papers, vol. 34, folio 103, vol. 35, folio 88; Ebenezer Denny to Commissioners for survey of Presque Isle, 25 April 1794, Same to Mifflin, 2, 30 May 1794, Deposition of Daniel Ransom, 11 June 1794 (quotation), Polhemus to John Gibson, 12 June 1794, Treaty minutes, 26 June 1794, Correspondence of Ebenezer Denny, Denny and O'Hara Papers, Ser. III, Box 11, folder 2, Historical Society of Western Pennsylvania, Pittsburgh; Wilkinson, "Land Policy," 107–125A.

76. Hazard et al., eds., *Pennsylvania Archives*, 9th ser., vol. 1, pt. 2, 731–814. The intercultural controversy over the Erie Triangle would only be put to rest in the fall of 1794 at the Treaty of Canandaigua, where Iroquois leaders received from the United States an additional payment of $10,000 and pledges of a $4,500 annual annuity. Significantly, Governor Mifflin refused an invitation for state commissioners to participate in the federal negotiations. See Harry M. Tinkcom, "Presque Isle and Pennsylvania Politics, 1797," *Pennsylvania History*, 16 (1949), 96–121; Kent, *Iroquois Indians I*, 173–181; and Jack Campisi, "From Stanwix to Canandaigua: National Policy, States' Rights, and Indian Land," in Christopher Vecsey and William A. Starna, eds., *Iroquois Land Claims* (Syracuse, N.Y.: Syracuse University Press, 1988), 60–64.

77. Deardorff and Kent, eds., "John Adlum on Allegheny," 287–324 (quotations from pp. 304, 306).

78. Wallace, *Death and Rebirth*, 179–183; Henry Rowe Schoolcraft, *Information Respecting the History, Condition, and Prospects of the Indian Tribes of the United States*, 6 vols. (Philadelphia: Lippincott, Grambo and Co., 1851–1857), 3:439–524, 583–586, 590–598.

79. Bernard W. Sheehan, *Seeds of Extinction: Jeffersonian Philanthropy and the American Indian* (Chapel Hill: University of North Carolina Press, 1973); Jones, *Licence for Empire*, 165–186.

Chapter 11. "Believing That Many of the Red People Suffer Much for the Want of Food"

This chapter was originally published as " 'Believing That Many of the Red People Suffer Much for the Want of Food': Hunting, Agriculture, and a Quaker Construction of Indianness in the Early Republic," *Journal of the Early Republic*, 19 (1999), 601–628. Reprinted by permission.

1. Gerard T. Hopkins, Journal, 1804–1805 (unpaginated), Historical Society of Pennsylvania, Philadelphia (quotations from introductory paragraph, extract from Baltimore Indian committee minutes, 6 February 1804, and entry for 10 April 1804). According to a late nineteenth-century New York local historian, Hopkins's journal "was published as a pamphlet" shortly after it was completed (Frank H. Severance, "Visit of Gerard T. Hopkins, A Quaker Ambassador to the Indians who Visited Buffalo in 1804," *Publications of the Buffalo Historical Society*, 6 [1903], 217–222). No such work, however, is listed in Ralph R. Shaw and Richard H. Shoemaker, *American Bibliography, a Preliminary Checklist, 1801 to 1819* (New York, 1958–1966). A version was printed by Ellicott's daughter Martha Tyson in 1862, with an appendix based on her own recollections and on papers of the Baltimore Yearly Meeting (Gerard T. Hopkins, *A Mission to the Indians, from the Indian Committee of Baltimore Yearly Meeting, to Fort Wayne, in 1804* [Philadelphia, 1862]). Tyson's text— much abridged and with a number of inaccuracies in transcription—forms the bulk of William H. Love, "A Quaker Pilgrimage: A Mission to the Indians from the Indian Committee of the Baltimore Yearly Meeting, to Fort Wayne, 1804," *Maryland Historical Magazine*, 4 (1909), 1–24; a portion of the Tyson version dealing with Hopkins's visit to Niagara on his return trip is printed in Severance,

"Visit of Hopkins," 217–222. An accurate modern edition of major portions of the document appears in Joseph E. Walker, ed., "Plowshares and Pruning Hooks for the Miami and Potawatomi: The Journal of Gerard T. Hopkins, 1804," *Ohio History*, 88 (1979), 361–407.

2. Hopkins, Journal, s.v. 2, 15 April.

3. Love, "A Quaker Pilgrimage," 19–24; Bliss Forbush, *A History of Baltimore Yearly Meeting of Friends: Three Hundred Years of Quakerism in Maryland, Virginia, the District of Columbia, and Central Pennsylvania* (Sandy Spring, Md.: Baltimore Yearly Meeting of Friends, 1972), 60; Sydney V. James, *A People Among Peoples: Quaker Benevolence in Eighteenth-Century America* (Cambridge, Mass.: Harvard University Press, 1963), 298–311; Diane Brodatz Rothenberg, "Friends Like These: An Ethnohistorical Analysis of the Interaction Between Allegany Senecas and Quakers, 1798–1823" (Ph.D. diss., City University of New York, 1976), 124–141.

4. *A Brief Account of the Proceedings of the Committee, Appointed by the Yearly Meeting of Friends, Held in Baltimore, for Promoting the Improvement and Civilization of the Indian Natives* (Baltimore, Md., 1805), 15–20 (quotation from p. 20).

5. Little Turtle and Five Medals to Evan Thomas et al., 18 September 1803, in Hopkins, Journal; Indian committee minutes, 6 February 1804, ibid.

6. *Brief Account of the Proceedings*, 39–45, 45n–46n (quotations from p. 40); *The Report of a Sub-Committee to the General Committees on Indian Concerns, Appointed by the Yearly Meetings of Baltimore and Ohio* (Mount Pleasant, [Ohio,] 1816); Harvey Lewis Carter, *The Life and Times of Little Turtle: First Sagamore of the Wabash* (Urbana: University of Illinois Press, 1987), 197–208.

7. Hopkins, Journal, s.v. 9 March 1804.

8. Ibid., s.v. 10–19 March 1804.

9. Ibid., s.v. 27 March 1804.

10. Ibid., s.v. 31 March, 5 April 1804; see also s.v. 26 March, 7 April 1804. On Harmar's defeat, see Wiley Sword, *President Washington's Indian War: The Struggle for the Old Northwest, 1790–1795* (Norman: University of Oklahoma Press, 1985), 96–122.

11. Ibid., s.v. 4 April 1804. Hopkins quotes here one of the mostly widely read poems of his era, Edward Young's *The Complaint: Or, Night-thoughts on Life, Death, and Immortality* (Edinburgh, 1774 [orig. publ. 1742]), 272. The passage from "Night the Ninth and Last: Consolation"—which Hopkins, omitting the poet's name, attributes only to "Nights Thoughts"—continues as follows: "Where is the dust that has not been alive? / The spade, the plough, disturb our ancestors;/ From human mould we reap our daily bread. / The globe around earth's hollow surface shakes, / And is the ceiling of her sleeping sons./ O'er devastation we blind revels keep:/ Whole buried towns support the dancer's heel/ The *moist* of human frame the Sun exhales, / Winds scatter, thro' the mighty void, the *dry*; / Each repossesses part of what she gave;/ And the freed spirit mounts on wings of fire; / Each element partakes our scatter'd spoils;/ As nature, wide, our ruins spread: man's *death* / Inhabits all things, but the thought of man." For other remarks on Indian cemeteries, see Hopkins, Journal, s.v. 10, 14, and 31 March 1804.

12. Hopkins, Journal, s.v. 10 April 1804. The parallel between the Roman conquest of Britain and the English conquest of peoples they considered culturally less developed was a commonplace drawn at least since the sixteenth century. See Nicholas P. Canny, "The Ideology of English Colonization: From Ireland to America," *William and Mary Quarterly*, 3rd ser., 30 (1973), 585–593.

13. Young, *The Complaint*, 272.

14. Roy Harvey Pearce, *Savagism and Civilization: A Study of the Indian and the American Mind* (Berkeley: University of California Press, 1988 [orig. publ. 1953]), 82–91; Ronald L. Meek, *Social Science and the Ignoble Savage* (Cambridge: Cambridge University Press, 1976), passim; Theda

Notes to Pages 233–237

Perdue, *Cherokee Women: Gender and Culture Change, 1700–1835* (Lincoln: University of Nebraska Press, 1998), 110; Elizabeth Vibert, *Traders' Tales: Narratives of Cultural Encounters in the Columbia Plateau, 1807–1846* (Norman: University of Oklahoma Press, 1997), esp. 162–204.

15. Drew R. McCoy, *The Elusive Republic: Political Economy in Jeffersonian Virginia* (Chapel Hill: University of North Carolina Press, 1980), 13–47; Joyce E. Chaplin, *An Anxious Pursuit: Agricultural Innovation and Modernity in the Lower South, 1730–1815* (Chapel Hill: University of North Carolina Press, 1993), 23–65.

16. Thomas Jefferson, *Notes on the State of Virginia* (New York: Harper and Row, 1964), 157; Harold C. Syrett, ed., *The Papers of Alexander Hamilton*, 27 vols. (New York: Columbia University Press, 1961–1987), 230; Joyce Appleby, "Commercial Farming and the 'Agrarian Myth' in the Early Republic," *Journal of American History*, 68 (1982), 833–849; Charles Sellers, *The Market Revolution: Jacksonian America, 1815–1846* (New York: Oxford University Press, 1991), 3–40; James Henretta, "The 'Market' in the Early Republic," *Journal of the Early Republic*, 18 (1998), 289–304.

17. Pearce, *Savagism and Civilization*, 66.

18. Meek, *Social Science and the Ignoble Savage*, 37–67.

19. Quoted ibid., 117–118.

20. Robert F. Berkhofer, Jr., *The White Man's Indian: Images of the American Indian from Columbus to the Present* (New York: Knopf, 1978), 134–153.

21. Bernard W. Sheehan, *Seeds of Extinction: Jeffersonian Philanthropy and the American Indian* (Chapel Hill: University of North Carolina Press, 1973), 148–181; James P. Ronda, "'We Have a Country': Race, Geography, and the Invention of Indian Territory," *Journal of the Early Republic*, 19 (1999), 739–755.

22. Society of Friends, Baltimore Yearly Meeting, *An Address of the Yearly Meeting of Friends . . . , to Thomas Jefferson, President of the United States, and His Reply* ([Baltimore,] 1807).

23. *The Epistle from the Yearly Meeting, Held in London, by Adjournment, from the 20th to the 29th of the Fifth Month, 1807, Inclusive, to the Quarterly and Monthly Meetings of Friends in Great Britain, Ireland, and Elsewhere* (Baltimore, Md., [1807]), 2.

24. Bert Anson, *The Miami Indians* (Norman: University of Oklahoma Press, 1970), 20–22 (quotation from p. 22); Carter, *Life and Times of Little Turtle*, 15–16.

25. Hopkins, Journal, s.v. 15 April 1804. Hopkins was not completely ignorant of Native agricultural traditions and settled living arrangements, although he seemed to place them in the past rather than the present. "Their corn hills," he noted, were "still discernable" near the cemetery that inspired his poetic lament on the triumph of the plow (ibid., s.v. 4 April 1804).

26. Quoted in Meek, *Social Science and the Ignoble Savage*, 117–118, 137.

27. Hopkins, Journal, s.v. 10 April 1804.

28. J. William Frost, *The Quaker Family in Colonial America: A Portrait of the Society of Friends* (New York: St. Martin's Press, 1973), 183; Barry Levy, *Quakers and the American Family: British Settlement in the Delaware Valley* (New York: Oxford University Press, 1988), 193–230; Rebecca Larson, *Daughters of Light: Quaker Women Preaching and Prophesying in the Colonies and Abroad, 1700–1775* (New York: Knopf, 1999), 133–171.

29. Richard White, *The Middle Ground: Indians, Empires, and Republics in the Great Lakes Region, 1650–1815* (Cambridge: Cambridge University Press, 1991), 41–43; James Axtell, *The European and the Indian: Essays in the Ethnohistory of Colonial North America* (New York: Oxford University Press, 1981), 46–53. For a brief introduction to traditional Eastern Native American agricultural practices, see Carolyn Merchant, *Ecological Revolutions: Nature, Gender, and Science in New England* (Chapel Hill: University of North Carolina Press, 1989), 74–81.

30. [Religious Society of Friends, London Yearly Meeting,] Aborigines Committee of the Meeting for Sufferings, *Some Account of the Conduct of the Religious Society of Friends towards the Indian Tribes in the Settlement of the Colonies of East and West Jersey and Pennsylvania: With a Brief Narrative of their Labours for the Civilization and Christian Instruction of the Indians, from the Time of their Settlement in America, to the Year 1843* (London, 1844), 122.

31. Charles Callendar, "Miami," in William C. Sturtevant, gen. ed., *Handbook of North American Indians*, XV: *Northeast*, ed. Bruce G. Trigger (Washington, D.C.: Smithsonian Institution, 1978), 682; James Axtell, *Beyond 1492: Encounters in Colonial North America* (New York: Oxford University Press, 1992), 125–151; Anthony F. C. Wallace, *Jefferson and the Indians: The Tragic Fate of the First Americans* (Cambridge, Mass.: Harvard University Press, 1999), 297–298 (quotation).

32. Hopkins, Journal, s.v. 29 March 1804.

33. Ibid., s.v. 31 March 1804.

34. Ibid., s.v. 3 April 1804. See also s.v. 7, 15 April 1804.

35. Ibid., s.v. 17, 19 April 1804 (quotations); Helen Hornbeck Tanner, ed., *Atlas of Great Lakes Indian History* (Norman: University of Oklahoma Press, 1987), 90; R. David Edmunds, "'Unacquainted with the Laws of the Civilized World': American Attitudes Toward the Métis in the Old Northwest," in Jacqueline Peterson and Jennifer S. H. Brown, eds., *The New Peoples: Being and Becoming Métis in North America* (Lincoln: University of Nebraska Press, 1985), 185–193. On the Canadian traders and the origins of métis communities south of the Great Lakes, see Jacqueline Peterson, "Many Roads to Red River: Métis Genesis in the Great Lakes Region, 1680–1815," ibid., 37–71; and Susan Sleeper-Smith, "Silent Tongues, Black Robes: Potawatomi, Europeans, and Settlers in the Southern Great Lakes, 1640–1850" (Ph.D. diss., University of Michigan, 1994).

36. For an evocative description of the impact of machine-made cloth on White women's domestic work in the early nineteenth century, see Jack Larkin, *The Reshaping of Everyday Life, 1790–1840* (New York: Harper and Row, 1988), 25–27, 50, 187–191.

37. James, *People Among Peoples*, 271–272.

38. Forbush, *History of Baltimore Yearly Meeting*, 48–49, 57; Society of Friends, Baltimore Yearly Meeting, *Discipline of the Yearly Meeting of Friends, Held in Baltimore, Printed by Direction of the Meeting, Held in the Year 1806* (Baltimore, Md., [1807]), 71–72 (quotation). On the tensions within Quakerism in the late eighteenth and early nineteenth centuries, see also Jean R. Soderlund, *Quakers and Slavery: A Divided Spirit* (Princeton, N.J.: Princeton University Press, 1985); Jack Marietta, *The Reformation of American Quakerism, 1748–1783* (Philadelphia: University of Pennsylvania Press, 1984); Thomas D. Hamm, *The Transformation of American Quakerism: Orthodox Friends, 1800–1907* (Bloomington: Indiana University Press, 1988); and H. Larry Ingle, *Quakers in Conflict: The Hicksite Reformation* (Knoxville: University of Tennessee Press, 1986).

39. Mary Maples Dunn, "Women of Light," in Carol Ruth Berkin and Mary Beth Norton, eds., *Women of America: A History* (Boston: Houghton Mifflin, 1979), 131–132; Margaret Hope Bacon, *Mothers of Feminism: The Story of Quaker Women in America* (San Francisco: Harper and Row, 1986), 80–81; Margaret Morris Haviland, "Beyond Women's Sphere: Young Quaker Women and the Veil of Charity in Philadelphia, 1790–1810," *William and Mary Quarterly*, 3rd ser., 51 (1994), 418–446; Bruce Dorsey, "Friends Becoming Enemies: Philadelphia Benevolence and the Neglected Era of American Quaker History," *Journal of the Early Republic*, 18 (1998), 395–428.

40. Baltimore Yearly Meeting, *Discipline*, 107. One of the "Nine Queries" to be answered annually in every Preparative or Monthly Meeting was whether members were "careful to live within the bounds of their circumstances, and to avoid involving themselves in business beyond their ability to manage" (ibid., 95).

41. *Brief Account of the Proceedings*, 12–14.

42. Baltimore Yearly Meeting, *Discipline*, 72–73.

43. Dumas Malone, ed., *Dictionary of American Biography* (New York: Scribner, 1932), s.v. "Hopkins, Johns."

44. *Brief Account of the Proceedings*, 16. For a carefully researched overview of this sensitive subject, see Peter C. Mancall, *Deadly Medicine: Indians and Alcohol in Early America* (Ithaca, N.Y.: Cornell University Press, 1995).

45. *Memorial of Evan Thomas, and Others, A Committee Appointed for Indian Affairs, By the Yearly Meeting of the People Called Friends, Held in Baltimore, 7th January, 1802* (n.p., 1802), 6–8.

46. Anson, *Miami Indians*, 144; Carter, *Life and Times of Little Turtle*, 161–163; Wallace, *Jefferson and the Indians*, 211–212; *Brief Account of the Proceedings*, 19–20 (quotations). From 1797 until the establishment of Indiana Territory in 1800, Wells had been deputy agent at Fort Wayne, which lacked full agency status during the period of his appointment and had no official Indian Department presence from 1800 to 1802.

47. Little Turtle and Five Medals to Evan Thomas et al., 18 September 1803, in Hopkins, Journal.

48. Hopkins, Journal, s.v. 1–8 March 1804.

49. "Minutes of a treaty with the tribes of Indians called the Wyandots, Delawares, Shawanoes, Ottawas, Chipewas, Putawatimes, Miamis, Eel River, Kickapoos, Piankashaws, and Kaskaskias; begun at Greene Ville on the 16th day of June, and ended on the 10th day of August 1795," Indian Treaties, 1778–1795, fol. 293r, Wayne Papers, 1765–1890, Historical Society of Pennsylvania (quotation); Anson, *Miami Indians*, 135–136; Andrew R. L. Cayton, "'Noble Actors' upon 'the Theatre of Honour': Power and Civility in the Treaty of Greenville," in Cayton and Fredrika J. Teute, eds., *Contact Points: American Frontiers from the Mohawk Valley to the Mississippi, 1750–1830* (Chapel Hill: University of North Carolina Press, 1998), 252–267.

50. Sword, *President Washington's Indian War*, 328–336; R. David Edmunds, *Tecumseh and the Quest for Indian Leadership* (Boston: Little, Brown, 1984), 118–119; Tanner, ed., *Atlas*, 117; Gregory Evans Dowd, *A Spirited Resistance: The North American Indian Struggle for Unity, 1745–1815* (Baltimore: Johns Hopkins University Press, 1992), 123–147.

51. Hopkins, Journal, s.v. 1–8 March 1804.

52. *Brief Account of the Proceedings*, 6–8.

53. Tanner, *Atlas*, 98–102.

54. *Brief Account of the Proceedings*, 7–12.

55. William N. Fenton, "Structure, Continuity, and Change in the Process of Iroquois Treaty Making," in Francis Jennings et al., eds., *The History and Culture of Iroquois Diplomacy: An Interdisciplinary Guide to the Treaties of the Six Nations and Their League* (Syracuse, N.Y.: Syracuse University Press, 1985), 10–14, 21–22; White, *Middle Ground*, 84–85. See also Chapter 10, above.

56. Quoted in Cayton, "'Noble Actors' upon 'The Theatre of Honour,'" 265.

57. *Brief Account of the Proceedings*, 12–15.

58. Mary Black-Rogers, "Varieties of 'Starving': Semantics and Survival in the Subarctic Fur Trade, 1750–1850," *Ethnohistory*, 33 (1986), 353–383 (quotations from p. 370); Bruce White, "'Give Us a Little Milk': The Social and Cultural Meaning of Gift-Giving in the Lake Superior Fur Trade," *Minnesota History*, 48 (1982), 60–71.

59. Hopkins, Journal, s.v. 2 April 1804.

60. *Memorial of Evan Thomas*, 6. On Little Turtle's and Wells's attitudes toward the Jeffersonian "civilization" program, see Carter, *Life and Times of Little Turtle*, 197–208. On Miami opposition to

Little Turtle, see Rob Mann, "The Silenced Miami: Archaeological and Ethnohistorical Evidence for Miami-British Relations, 1795–1812," *Ethnohistory*, 46 (1999), 399–427.

61. Rothenberg, "Friends Like These," 144–148.

62. *Brief Account of the Proceedings*, 47.

63. Lewis H. Morgan, *League of the Ho-dé-no-sau-nee, Iroquois* (New York: Corinth Books, 1962 [orig. publ. 1851]), 57.

INDEX

Abler, Thomas S., 268n22
Adair, James, 268n22
Adlum, John, 225
Adondarechaa, 120, 123
African Americans, 51, 173, 201, 240; slave
   trade and, 99–100, 142
Ajacán, 19–22. *See also* Chesapeake Bay
Albany, 42, 45, 101, 106, 109, 114–32; fur trade
   at, 44, 48, 101; Indian wars and, 82, 83, 85–87;
   map of, *70*; Native trading at, 77, 78, 83, 102,
   105, 187–88
Albany Congress, *161,* 168, 173, 186
alcohol, 26, 38, 213; Indian trade and, 55, 178,
   180, 182, 187, 195, 228, 237, 238; Quakers and,
   241, 242
Algonquians, 14, 64–65, 159; kinship terms of,
   16, 19; wars of, 78–80, 106–7, 116. *See also
   individual nations*
Algonquins, 75
Allerton, Isaac, 111
Amherst, Jeffrey, 3, 174, 180–83, 188, 196; por-
   trait of, *181*
Andrews, William, 94, 96
Andros, Edmund, 82–83, 106, 116, 120, 123,
   131, 146
Appomattoc, Queen of, 29
Aquendero, 88–89, 126–30
Aradgi, 129–30
Archer, Gabriel, 25–26, 257n42
Arendaronons, 79
Argall, Samuel, 40
Arrohateck, 25, 27
Atkin, Edmund, 183
Atlee, Samuel J., 211, 213–14
Attignawantans, 79
Augusta, Treaty of, 196
Austenaco, 66
Axtell, James, 28, 54–55, 251n1

Bacon's Rebellion, 99, 106–8, 111, 116, 145, 146

Bancker, Evert, 117, 128
Banner, Stuart, 144
Bartoli, F., *215*
Bartram, John, 93
beads, 16, 259n74; glass, 36–37, *37,* 40–41, 55–58,
   61, 65; shell, 3, 50, 100–105, *103,* 107, 112. *See
   also* prestige goods
beaver wars, 78–83, 90
Becker, Carl Lotus, 175–76
Bellomont, Earl of, 87–89, 128–29, 272n90
Berkeley, William, 99–100, 108, 111
Beverwyck. *See* Albany
Birch, William, *203*
Black-Rogers, Mary, 246–47
Blome, Richard, 110
Boxer, C. R., 97
Braddock, Edward, 155–57, 169–70, 173, 176
Bradford, William, 137–40
Bragdon, Kathleen, 64
Brainerd, John, 173
Brant, Joseph, 212, 218, 220, 296n32
Brébeuf, Jean de, 63
Breen, T. H., 53, 251n1
Bridenbaugh, Carl, 19
Brodhead, Daniel, 207
Bruyas, Jacques, 105–6
burial practices, 36, 59, 72, 75–76, 81, 232, 238
Burnet, William, 92
Butler, Richard, 211–12, 216, 218–21, 223

Cahokia, 64
Callière, Louis-Hector de, 87, 89, 90
Canandaigua, Treaty of, 300n76
Canasatego, 167–68
cannibalism, 74, 75, 81, 268n22
captives, 6, 19, 72–75, *73,* 79–81, 85–86, 96;
   adoption of, *73,* 77, 80; torture of, 73–74, 81
Carleton, Guy, 187, 198
Carolinas, 21–22, 95, 188; constitution of, 143;
   Creeks of, 178; justice system in, 192, 196

Carrera, Juan de la, 22
Catawbas, 95, 196
Cattaraugus, 207, 218, 219
Cayugas, 130; territory of, *70*; wars of, 82, 88, 91. *See also* Iroquois
Céloron de Blainville, Pierre-Joseph, *156*, 169
Champlain, Samuel de, 77
Chaplin, Joyce, 233
Charles I, 151
Charles II, 121, 142–46, 150, 284n24
Charles Town, S.C., 56, 188
Cherokees, 196; leaders of, 62, *66*; after Revolutionary War, 218; wars of, 174–75, 188
Chesapeake Bay, 6, *110*; Jamestown and, 27–41, 61, 62, 137; Penn on, 285n43; Spanish exploration of, 14, 19–22. *See also* Tsenacomoco
Chickahominies, 256n21
Chickasaws, 196
Chippewas, 182, 212
Choctaws, 196
Christianity, 48–52, 69; Native conversions to, 21, 80, 88–89, 94, 171; pietist, 44, 46. *See also* Jesuit missionaries; Moravians; Quakers
"civilizing mission," 233–35, 239–40, 248–50
Claeson, Jacob, 109
Claeson, Lawrence, 92
Claiborne, William, 108
Clarke, George, 67
Clinton, James, 207
Colden, Cadwallader, 71, 131, 192
Conestoga Indians, 133, 141; massacre of, 175, 191
Connecticut land claims, *161*, 162, 186, 206
Connecticut River, 42, *43*, *70*, 100–101
Conojocular War, 161–62, 165
Conoy Indians, 159
conquest theory, 8, 210–14
Cooper, Anthony Ashley, 143
Cope, Walter, 257n42
copper goods, 28, 30–35, *31*, 40–41, 58–59, 61, 65. *See also* prestige goods
Corlaer, Arent, 120, 294n8. *See also* van Curler, Arent
Cornbury, Lord, 131
Cornplanter, 207, 212–25, 296n32, 297n44; portrait of, *215*
council titles, 205–6, 294n8
Covenant Chain, 67–68, 113–16, 121–23, 131, 141, 162–63, 199, 245–46

Crashaw, William, 140
Creek Indians, 178, 191, 196, 204
Cresap's War, 161–62, 165
Croghan, George, 182, 197
Cromwell, Oliver, 143
Cushman, Robert, 140, 144
Cuyler, Johannes, 117

Dale, Thomas, 38–40
Danckaerts, Jasper, 44–46, 49, 51–52
Declaration of Independence, 156. *See also* Revolutionary War
De La Noy, Peter, 86
Delaware (colony), land claims of, 145, 150–53, *154*
Delaware Indians. *See* Lenapes
Delaware River, 41, 42, 104; maps of, *43*, *70*, *110*, *149*, *156*, *161*; Penn's land claims and, 148–51; Susquehanocks on, 102, 109
Dellius, Godfridius, 118, 120, 124–25, 127–29
Deloria, Vine, Jr., 9
Dennis, Phillip, 227–30, 238, 249
Denonville, Jacques-René de, 83–85, 272n90
depreciation certificates, 208–14, *209*, 295n22
Detroit, 89, *156*, 169, 174, 180, 188, 192, 202–7, 245–46
Dickinson, John, 210–11, 214, 217
Donation Lands, 208–14, *209*, 217, 295n22
Dongan, Thomas, 83, 85, 117, 121, 131
Douglass, William, 236
Dowd, Gregory Evans, 289n6
Downshire, Marquess of. *See* Hillsborough, Earl of
Dunn, Mary Maples, 135
Dunn, Richard S., 135
Duquesne, Fort, *156*, 169, 174. *See also* Pitt, Fort
Dutch East India Company, 112
Dutch West India Company, 44, 97, 99–105, 107; New Sweden and, 101–5, 109, 150

Easton, John, 107
Easton, Treaty of, 1–2, 173
Ellicott, George, 227, 230, 240, 300n1
epidemic diseases, 6, 62, 68, 268n34; among Iroquois, 63, 76–77, 94, 269n35; among Lenapes, 158; mourning-wars and, 70
Erie Indians, *70*, 79
Erie Triangle, *209*, 219, 220, 224, 299n57, 300n76
Evans, Griffith, 297n34

Fallen Timbers, Battle of, 224, 238
Fausz, J. Frederick, 25, 27, 36
firearms, 68, 76–79; British suppliers of, 31; Dutch suppliers of, 47, 97, 101, 261n24; Swedish suppliers of, 102
Five Medals, 229–30, 242, 246–48
Five Nations. *See* Iroquois
"Flatheads," 95–96
Fletcher, Benjamin, 86, 87, 128
Florida, 19–22, 142, 184, 185
Frankenstein, Susan, 15, 64
Franklin, Fort, 219, 222, 225
Freeman, Bernardus, 272n90
French and Indian War. *See* Seven Years War
French West India Company, 100
Fried, Morton, 15, 16, 254n4
Frisby, James, 153
Frontenac, Fort, 83–85, 92, *156*, 188
Frontenac, Louis de, 83, 84, 87, 124–25
funeral rites, 36, 59, 72, 75, 76, 81, 232, 238
Fur, Gunlög, 163
fur trade, 55–57, 68, 188–89, 237; British, 56, 111, 195–96; Dutch, 41, 44, 47–48, 97–99, 101; French, 82–87; Swedish, 102; wars over, 78–83, 90

Gage, Thomas, 191
Garakontié, 80, 106
gauntlet ritual, 73, 81, 267n20
gender roles: division of labor and, 236–41; Native rhetoric and, 163, 167–68, 170
George II, 170–71
German immigrants, 155, 160, 167, 168, 171
Gibson, Thomas, 218–22
gift exchange, 15–19, 56–58, 62–65, 267n17; British aversion to, 3, 27, 31–32, 35–40, 174, 180–82; Dutch aversion to, 47–48, 50; among Lenapes, 3–6, 158; among Oneidas, 47. *See also* prestige goods
Gleach, Frederic, 25
Glorious Revolution, 85, 121–24
Gookin, Daniel, 3
Gordon, Patrick, 163
Grafton, Anthony, 52
Grand Settlement, 89–94, 127–28, 130
Gray, Robert, 140, 144
Great Cross. *See* Guyasuta
Great Lakes region, 56, 99, 208, 219; British influence in, 174, 178–80, 188–89, 196; French influence in, 106

Great League of Peace, 76. *See also* Iroquois
Great Tree (Keandochgowa), 207, 219, 220, 222, 223
Greenville, Treaty of, 224, 231–32, 241, 243–47
Guyasuta, 207, 216, 220, 222

Half-Town (Hachuwoot), 207, 218–20, 222, 223, 225
Hamell, George, 57–59
Hamilton, Alexander, 233–34
Hamor, Ralph, 37–39, 256n21
Hard Labor, Treaty of, 199, 210
Hariot, Thomas, *17*
Harmar, Fort, 219–21, 223
Harmar, Josiah, 216, 223–24, 232
Hartshorne, William, 202–3
Haudenosaunee. *See* Iroquois
Heckewelder, John, 2, 159
Helms, Mary, 15
Hennepin, Louis, 71
Hicks, Edward, 154
Hill, Aaron, 214
Hillsborough, Earl of, *193*, 194, 199
Hockushakwego, 216–18
Hole, William, *17*
Holme, Thomas, 153
home rule, 175–76
Hopkins, Gerard T., 227–40, *231*, 242–43, 247
Hopkins, Johns, 241
Hudson River, 41, 42, 105, 186; maps of, *43, 70*
Huguenots, 21
Hunter, Robert, 74
Hurons, 61, 63; Christianity among, 89; wars of, 77–80, 82

Illinois Indians, 82, 87
Independence, War of. *See* Revolutionary War
India, 194, 291n55
Indian Trade and Intercourse Act, 223, 241–42
Ingoldsby, Richard, 86, 87
Irish immigrants, 155, 160, 168, 171
Iroquois, *70*, 101–5; beaver wars of, 78–83, 90; British relations with, 82–83, 105–7, 113–32, 205; captives of, 72–75, *73*, 79–81, 85–86, 96; Covenant Chain of, 67–68, 113–16, 121, 123, 130, 141, 162–63, 199; demographics of, 81, 84, 88, 94, 270n57, 271n58, 272n90; epidemics among, 63, 76–77, 94, 269n35; "Flathead" wars of, 95–96; French relations with, 78–80, 82–92, 124–31, 205; Jesuit missionaries

Iroquois (*cont.*)
  and, 80, 94, 101, 105–6, 111, 115, 118, 121; land
    treaties with, 154, *161*, 162–68, 187, 211–25,
    297n37; Lenape conflicts with, 163, 167–68,
    170; member nations of, 42, 69–70, 94, 159–
    60, 205; Ohio country and, 168–69; Ojibwa
    conflict with, 87; Pontiac's War and, 174–75;
    Susquehannock conflicts with, 109, 111–12,
    116; torture among, 69, 73–74, 81. *See also
    individual nations*

Jacobs, Jaap, 47
James I, 14, 26, 40, 41
James II, 121. *See also* York, Duke of
Jamestown, 26–41, 60, 137; attacks on, 27, 36–
    37, 41, 62
Jay's Treaty, 244–46
Jefferson, Thomas, 234–35, 242, 249
Jennings, Francis, 9, 55, 102, 104; on Covenant
    Chain, 163; on land deeds, 145; on Penn's
    letter to Indian Kings, 136–38
Jesuit missionaries, 21–24, 44; on Indian war-
    fare, 69–76; Iroquois and, 80, 94, 101, 105–6,
    111, 115, 118, 121
Jogues, Isaac, 44, 75, 101
Johnson, William, 131, 177–83, 189–92, 196–99;
    portrait of, *179*
Johnston, Francis, 211, 214, 217
Joncaire, Louis-Thomas de, 92
justice system, 177–201, 283n11

Kayaderosseras Patent, 187
Keandochgowa (or Karontowanen), 207, 219,
    220, 222, 223
Kentucky, 218
Khionontateronons, *70*, 77–79
Kieft, Willem, 102–4
King Philip's War, 99, 106–7, 116, 123, 145, 146
King William's War. *See* League of Augsburg,
    War of
kinship terms, 16, 19, 205
Kirk, William, 230
Knox, Henry, 224, 225, 234–35
Kupperman, Karen, 59–60, 102

La Barre, Joseph-Antoine de, 83, 121, *122*
Lafitau, Joseph-François, 60, 62, 63, 70, 267n17
Lalemant, Jerome, 74
Lamberville, Jean de, 81, 87, 123
La Salle, René-Robert de, 83

League of Augsburg, War of, 82, 113, 121–24,
    272n90
Lee, Arthur, 211–12
Leisler, Jacob, 85, 124–25, 128, 129
Le Jeune, Paul, 69, 74, 80, 101
Lenapes, *70*, 109–10, 159; Iroquois conflicts
    with, 163, 167–68, 170; land treaties of, 157–
    74, 205, 212–13, 297n37; massacre of, 204; in
    Ohio, 238, 244, 245, 248; Penn's treaties with,
    6–8, *7*, *141*, *154*, 158, 205; Pontiac's War and,
    174–75; during Seven Years War, 155–58, 171
Lewis, Clifford M., 19, 255n18
Little Turtle, 220, 227–32, 238, 241–43, 246, 248
Livingston, Robert, 117, 118, 120, 124, 127, 129, 130
Lock, Lars Carlsson, 152
Locke, John, 143, 234
Logan, James, 160–66, 205; portrait of, *164*
Loomie, Albert J., 19, 255n18
Lord, Richard, 104
Louis XV, 169
Lovelace, John, 110

Maclay, William, 211, 214, 217
Mahicans, 42, 44, 45, 52, 159; Mohawk conflicts
    with, 78, 82, 116; territory of, *70*
mamanatowick, 16, 18, 19
Manacam, 29
Manhattan, 86, 109, 114–18, 124
maple sugar, 228, 236, 238, 247–49
Markham, William, 147, 153
Martínez, Bartolomé, 20
Maryland, 150–53; maps of, *110*, *149*, *154*; Penn-
    sylvania boundary with, *161*, 161–62, 165, 186,
    285n43
Mason and Dixon Line, 161
Mazzei, Philip, 268n22
McCoy, Drew, 233
McIntosh, Fort, 212–13, 216, 218–20, 223,
    297n37
Mechkilikishi, 165, 166
Megapolensis, Johannes, Jr., 44–51
Menéndez, Pedro, 20–22, 24
Mexico City, 21
Miamis, 82, 106, 220, 229, 246, 248; agriculture
    among, 227–30, 235–39, 242; hunting among,
    231, 234, 236–39, 249
Miami, Fort, 238–39, 244–45
Michaelson, Gunther, 47
Michilimackinac, 65, 106, 174, 180, 189
Mifflin, Thomas, 202, 204, 206, 225

Milborne, Jacob, 124, 125
Miller, Christopher, 57–59
Millet, Pierre, 124, 125
Minuit, Peter, 101
Mohawks, 42, 52, 56, 115–32, 183; wars of, 78–83, 90; captives of, 79–81; Christianity among, 80; demographics of, 81, 84; Dutch accounts of, 44, 45; epidemics among, 76–77; French relations with, 78–80, 84–92, 115, 130; Mahican conflicts with, 78, 82, 116; population of, 271n58; in War of the Spanish Succession, 91; religious leaders of, 173–74; after Revolutionary War, 212–14, 218; rulers of, 60, 63; territories of, 43, 46, 70, 187; wampum trade of, 101. See also Iroquois
Mohegans, 107
Monacans, 33, 34, 259n77
Montanus, Arnoldus, 98
Montour, Alexander, 91
Montreal, Treaty of. See Grand Settlement
Moore, Henry, 187, 191, 198
Moravians, 2, 167, 171–73, 204
Morgan, Edmund, 107
Morgan, Lewis Henry, 250
Morris, Robert, 5, 224
mourning-wars, 70–73, 76–82, 88, 94–96, 113, 266n4
Muhlenberg, Frederick, 211
Munsees, 70, 159, 162, 163, 207
Murray, James, 198

Namontack, 25, 33, 259n77; death of, 34, 38, 41; trip to England of, 14, 30–32
Nanfan, John, 89, 130
Nanticokes, 159
Narragansetts, 55–61, 67, 101, 107, 183
Navigation Acts, 100, 104, 107–9, 200
Necessity, Fort, 156, 186
Neolin ("The Delaware Prophet"), 173–74, 178–80, 288n42
Neutrals, 70, 77–79
New Amsterdam, 42–52, 43, 70, 109, 144–45; fall of, 97–112; New Sweden and, 101–4; slaves of, 99
Newcastle (Seneca leader), 170
New Castle (New Amstel), Del., 109, 150, 154
New Hampshire, 186
New Jersey, 110, 145, 154
Newport, Christopher, 13–14, 25–36, 38–41
New Sweden, 101–5, 108, 109, 112

New York, 45, 186–90; Duke's Laws of, 143–44; New Hampshire boundary and, 186; Pennsylvania boundary with, 162, 186, 209, 211, 217, 219, 223
Niagara, Fort, 156, 180, 182, 188
Niantics, 107
Nicholson, Francis, 91, 222
Nicholson, Joseph, 224
Ninnimissinouks, 70
noble savage motif, 51, 52, 301n14
North, Francis, 148
Nutimus, 165–68

O'Bail, John. See Cornplanter
Ohio country, 159, 168–71, 180–86; Indian mounds in, 231; map of, 156; Pontiac's War in, 174–75, 178–80, 184; after Revolutionary War, 206–26; trade restrictions in, 174, 189–90
Ojibwas, 87, 130, 202–3, 247
Oneidas, 44–47, 52, 248; Christianity among, 80; French relations with, 84, 91, 124–25, 130; territory of, 70, 94; wars of, 82, 91, 96. See also Iroquois
Onnucheranorum, 130
Onondagas, 67, 88–89; captives of, 79, 81, 96; Christianity among, 80; French relations with, 84, 91, 106, 121, 122, 124, 130; Lenapes and, 167; territory of, 70, 94; wars of, 74–75, 82, 87, 91. See also Iroquois
Opechancanough, 19, 37, 40, 53
Opitchapam, 19
Orange, Fort. See Albany
Oré, Luis Gerónimo de, 20, 21
Oswego, Fort, 92, 93, 156, 187–88, 197
Otreouti, 82, 121, 122
Ottawa Indians, 70, 82–83, 87, 106, 212

Paine, Thomas, 201
Paquiquineo (Don Luis), 14, 19–25, 27, 30–33, 255n18, 256n36
Parahunt, 25–27, 257n42
Paris, Treaty of, 206, 207, 210, 212
Parrish, John, 202–4
Partridge, Nehemiah, 119
Paxton Boys, 191
Peach War, 105
Pearce, Roy Harvey, 234
Pemberton, Israel, 172–73
Penn, John, 157, 160–62, 165
Penn, Richard, 157, 160–62, 165

Penn, Thomas, 157, 160–62, 165–67, 199, 205,
     207–8
Penn, William, 123; family of, 157; father of, 143;
     Indian treaties with, 6–8, 7, 141, 154, 158, 165,
     202–6, 284n23; legacy of, 155, 157, 160, 245;
     letter to Indian kings, 133–54, 138, 139, 282n2
Pennsylvania: Indian treaties with, 161, 162–68,
     183, 202–26, 209; maps of, 110, 149, 154, 156,
     161; Maryland boundary with, 161, 161–62,
     165, 186, 285n43; militias of, 172; New York
     boundary with, 162, 186, 209, 211, 217, 219,
     223; Va. boundary with, 161, 162, 186, 206
Pequot War, 56, 100, 106
Percy, George, 27
Perkins, Francis, 30
Petuns. See Khionontateronons
Philip II, 20
Pisquetomen, 173
Pitt, Fort, 156, 174, 180, 182, 197. See also
     Duquesne, Fort
Pittsburgh, 216–22, 224
"Plan for the future Management of Indian
     Affairs," 177, 192–201
Pocahontas, 27, 31; death of, 41; marriage of, 37;
     trip to England of, 14, 37, 39
Pocoughtaonack, 29
Pontiac's War, 3, 174–75, 178–84, 189–90, 197,
     288n42
Post Frederick, 173
Potawatomis, 70, 212, 229, 239, 246–48
Potter, Stephen R., 16
Powhatan (Wahunsonacock), 17, 54, 61, 62;
     coronation of, 32–34, 259n74; death of, 41,
     62; enemies of, 29, 33; Newport and, 27–36,
     38, 39; Smith and, 27–37, 137; wives of, 16
Powhatan Indians, 13–14, 19, 25, 60. See also
     Tsenacomoco
prestige goods, 54, 64; beads as, 36–37, 37, 40–41,
     57–58, 61, 65; copper as, 28, 30–35, 31, 40–41,
     58–59, 61, 65; exchange of, 3–6, 15–19, 23–24,
     27, 62–65; symbolism of, 57–59, 61, 259n74
Printz, Johan, 102
Proclamation of 1763, 184–86, 189–91, 197, 199,
     201
Pueblo Revolt, 145
Purchas, Samuel, 37, 40

Quakers, 142–46, 172, 239–41; on alcohol, 241,
     242; missions to Indians, 227–29, 235–39,
     242–50

Quebec Act, 201
Queen Anne's War. See Spanish Succession,
     War of
Quirós, Luis de, 22–23
quitrents, 157, 160, 184, 187
Quitt, Martin, 25, 27

race, 51, 173–74; categories of, 7, 230, 238–40,
     249–50, 253n15; ethnic conflict and, 174–75,
     191; justice system and, 191–92, 201, 283n11;
     slave trade and, 99–100, 142
Ralegh, Walter, 32, 137
Red Jacket, 202, 204–7
Rensselaerswyck, 42, 44, 97, 101
requerimiento, 140–42
requickening ceremonies, 71, 72
Revolutionary War, 7–8, 156, 176, 177, 240;
     Pennsylvania land treaties after, 202–26, 209
Rhode Island, 53, 55–59, 61, 67
Rogel, Juan, 21, 24
Rolfe, John, 37
Roosevelt, Theodore, 8, 175–76
Rothenberg, Diane, 248
Roundtree, Helen C., 255n17, 259n74
Rowlands, Michael, 15, 64
Rubertone, Patricia, 56, 63
Ryswick, Peace of, 87, 128

Sacchini, Francisco, 19–20
Sadekanaktie, 88–89, 126–30
Salisbury, Neal, 56–57, 62, 107
Salisbury, Sylvester, 117
Sanders, Robert, 45, 125
Santa Elena, 21–22
Sassamon, John, 107
Sassoonan, 160, 163, 283n12
Savage, Thomas, 13–14, 25, 30, 38
Sayre, Gordon M., 45, 51
scalps, 73, 74, 172
Schuyler, Johannes, 126
Schuyler, Peter, 86, 117–20, 123–30; portrait
     of, 119
Scottish Enlightenment, 233, 234
Segura, Juan Baptista de, 22–24
Senecas, 83–84, 91, 121, 130, 205, 248; British
     relations with, 207; captives of, 79; Cov-
     enant Chain of, 120, 121, 123; division of
     labor among, 237; epidemics among, 76–77;
     Lenapes and, 170; after Revolutionary War,
     205–26; Susquehannock conflict with, 111;

territory of, *70*; wars of, 82, 87, 91. *See also* Iroquois

Service, Elman R., 15, 16, 254n4

Seven Years War, 1–2, 7, 155–58, 169–74, 240; Indian treaties after, 174–75, 177–78, 183, 184; origins of, 156, 169, 186

Shackamaxon, Treaty of, 154

Shawnees, 128, 159, 162, 163, 168, 169; Pontiac's War and, 174–75; Quakers and, 230; after Revolutionary War, 128; during Seven Years War, 171

Shingas, 156–57

Silverman, David, 64–65

Sioux Indians, 80

Six Nations. *See* Iroquois

slave trade, 99–100, 142

Sloughter, Henry, 125–28

Sluyter, Peter, 44

smallpox, 76–77, 94. *See also* epidemic diseases

Smith, Adam, 234, 236

Smith, John, 16–18, 25–36, 39–40, 53, 137, 258n71; *A Map of Virginia, 17; True Relation, 27*–28

Smith, William, *4*

Smolenski, John, 142

Soto, Hernando de, 62

Spangenberg, August Gottlieb, 3

Spanish conquistadors, 14, 19–22, 62, 140–42, 145

Spanish Succession, War of, 91

Spelman, Henry, 36, 259n74

Stamp Act, 197, 198

Stanwix, Fort, 199, 206, 211–18, 220, 297n37

Starna, William, 271n58

St. Clair, Arthur, 220–21, 223–24

Sterne, Laurence, 177

Stockbridge Indians, 186

Strachey, William, 13–14, 16

Stuart, John, 179, 183, 196–99

Stuyvesant, Petrus, 44

Sullivan, John, 207

Susquehanna Company, 186

Susquehanna River, 148–51, 159, 165, 206; European squatters on, 155; land treaties and, 168–69, 173, 175; maps of, *70, 110, 149, 156, 161*

Susquehannocks: Bacon's Rebellion and, 145; Iroquois conflicts with, 109, 111–12, 116; New Sweden and, 101–2, 105; territories of, *70*; trade with, 105–6, 108–9, 109–11; wars of, 77, 79, 82

Tacitus, 51

Tahiadoris, 118, 123, 126, 127

Tarhe, 242–47

Tawenna, 133, 141

Taylor, Alan, 97

Tecumseh, 243

Teedyuscung, 163, 165, 168, 173; Christianity of, 167; murder of, 174, 176; treaties of, 1–10, 155, 158, 169–71, 183, 252n4

Teganissorens, 74, 89, 129, 130

Tenskwatawa, 243, 253n18

Thomas, Evan, 248

Thomas, George, 167

tobacco, 48, 55, 56; exports of, 99, 100, 104, 107–8, 111; ritual use of, 25, 236

Tobacco Nation. *See* Khionontateronons

Tomakin (Tomocomo), 14, 37, 39–40

Tomassen, Willem, 47

torture, 69, 73–74, 81, 172

Townshend Duties, 197, 199, 200

Tsenacomoco, 6, 13–14, 19, 23, 28–41, 54; land treaties of, 137, 145; Newport's exploration of, 25–27. *See also* Chesapeake Bay

Turgeon, Laurier, 58–61

Tuscaroras, 94–96, 159, 213. *See also* Iroquois

Utrecht, Treaty of, 91

Uttamatomakkin, 14, 37, 39–40

van Curler, Arent van, 115, 120, 294n8

van den Bogaert, Harmen Meyndertsz, 44–48, 53, 261n24

van der Donck, Adriaen Cornelissen, 44–46, 49–52

van Eps, Jan Baptist, 127

van Olinda, Hilletie, 118–20, 127, 129

Vaudreuil, Philippe de, 84, 91

Vaughan, Alden, 9

Velasco, Luis de. *See* Paquiquineo

Velázquez, Antonio, 19

Verrazano, Giovanni da, 20

Vetch, Samuel, 91

Vielé, Arnout Cornelisz, 117, 120, 123, 125, 128, 129

Virginia, 80, 95, *110*, 204–5, 218; Jamestown colony of, 26–41, 61, 62, 137; Pennsylvania boundary with, *161*, 162, 186, 206

Virginia Company, 13, 41, 62, 137, 145

Wabanakis, *70*

Wahunsonacock. *See* Powhatan

Walking Purchase, *161*, 166–67, 171, 213

Wallace, Anthony F. C., 237–38
Wampanoags, 61, 83, 107
wampum, 38, 50, 58; belts of, 3–6, *4, 66*, 95,
    141, 170, 221, 244, 245; colonists' trade in, 56,
    100–105, 112; inflation of, 105, 107; strings
    of, *103*
Wappingers, 183
warfare, 69–82, *73*, 269n37; functions of, 70,
    78, 81, 88
War of 1812, 230, 243
Washington, George, 169, 186, 224–25, 234–35
Watson, James, *181*
Wayne, Anthony, 224, 238, 243, 246
Wayne, Fort, 227–29, 232, 235, 238, 240–42
Weiser, Conrad, 2, 5, 163–65, 252n4
Wells, William, 227, 230, 241, 304n46
Wendell, Johannes, 117
weroances, 16, 18–19, 25, 258n71
Wesselse Ten Broeck, Dirck, 117, 123, 126–28
West, Benjamin, *7,* 202
Westminster, Treaty of, 99, 150
Whish-shicksy, 2–3, 6, 8, 113, 158

Whiskey Rebellion, 224
White, Hayden, 51
White, John, *17*
White, Richard, 55, 106, 206, 253n18
William and Mary (British monarchs), 121–24
Williams, Isaac, 204
Williams, Roger, 53, 55–59, 61, 67, 145
Williamson, Margaret Holmes, 18
Wilson, James, 225
Winthrop, John, 140, 144
Wolcott, Oliver, 211–12
Wollaston, John, Jr., *179*
Wyandots, 82, 83, 106, 168; Pennsylvania trea-
    ties with, 212, 213, 297n37; Quakers and,
    242–48

York, Duke of, 85, 99, 106, 115, 142; exile of, 150;
    laws of, 143–44
Young, Edward, 232, 233, 301n11

Zeisberger, David, 2
Zúñiga, Pedro de, 32

ACKNOWLEDGMENTS

For a collection like this, with debts accumulating over a very long time, it is impossible to thank everyone who contributed intellectually, practically, and personally to the work. So I must here leave most of my expressions of gratitude implicit but nonetheless heartfelt, while singling out a few people who have been constant through it all or who have particularly aided in the production of this volume. In the first category are those who got me going—my departed parents, my first mentor Frank Bremer, my graduate adviser Alden Vaughan, my early guides Thad Tate and Mike McGiffert, and my prodding elder the late Francis Jennings—along with those who sustained and challenged me, including my colleagues and students at Dickinson College, the University of Pennsylvania, and the McNeil Center for Early American Studies. In the second category are Roy Ritchie, who facilitated a wonderful year of work at the Huntington Library; Gregory Dowd and Nancy Shoemaker, who provided thoughtful suggestions on the volume as a whole; Noreen O'Connor-Abel, who shepherded the manuscript to completion; Laura Keenan Spero, Amy Baxter-Bellamy, and Barbara Natello, who kept the McNeil Center and its director functioning; John Pollack and Nick Okrent, who kept the books and images flowing from Van Pelt Library; Mary and Richard Dunn and Michelle and Roderick McDonald, who kept the wine and good ideas pouring on Rittenhouse Square; and Bob Lockhart, who remained a prince among editors and collaborators, even if we seldom saw each other except when we were both on the road. Uniting both categories and countless others is my indomitable wife, Sharon, still with me after all these years.